D1462431

MUSIC
OF THE
MIDDLE AGES
Style and Structure

MUSIC OF THE MIDDLE AGES

Style and Structure

DAVID FENWICK WILSON

SCHIRMER BOOKS
A Division of Macmillan, Inc.
New York
Collier Macmillan Canada
Toronto
Maxwell Macmillan International
New York   Oxford   Singapore   Sydney

Schirmer Books
A Division of Macmillan, Inc.
866 Third Avenue, New York, N. Y. 10022

Collier Macmillan Canada, Inc.
1200 Eglinton Avenue East, Suite 200
Don Mills, Ontario M3C 3N1

Library of Congress Catalog Card Number: 90–38155

Printed in the United States of America

printing number
1 2 3 4 5 6 7 8 9 10

Library of Congress Cataloging-in-Publication Data
Wilson, David Fenwick.
  Music of the Middle Ages : style and structure / David Fenwick
Wilson.
     p. cm.
  Includes bibliographical references and index.
  ISBN 0-02-872951-X :
  1. Music—500–1400—History and criticism.   2. Style, Musical.
3. Music—Theory—500–1400.   I. Title.
ML 172.W6   1990
780'.9'02—dc20   90–38155
                                                         CIP
                                                         MN

To Barbara

Contents

PART I
The Carolingian Era
800–1150

PART II
The Flowering of Style
1050–1250

PART III
The Era of the Motet
1200–1400

PART IV
The Polyphonic Song
1330–1400

Preface

This book is dedicated to the belief that the historical study of music begins with music itself, and that music history is revealed in the changing styles that appear in the preserved artifacts of music. Growth and development in music is of course strongly influenced by outside events—its political, social, and cultural milieu. Nevertheless, music also exists apart from—at times, in seeming defiance of—these outward events. Take, for example, the strong musical production of France during the deprivations of the Hundred Years' War and the Black Death, or Italy's loss of musical vitality during the High Renaissance of its other arts, and its return after those arts had passed their zenith.

Although the seeds of each epoch may be found in the immediate past, growth and change in art and culture is best viewed not as a continuous upward spiral of good, better, best, but as a process of continual change on a level ground. While it can be argued that the technical processes of music have become more and more refined, the same cannot safely be said about its aesthetic effect. It must be accepted that the music of an era satisfies the needs and cultural aspirations of that time. While we may listen to tenth-century music with twentieth-century ears and consider it primitive, tenth-century listeners would undoubtedly consider our music unsettling and cacophonous, lacking the peace and simplicity of their own idiom.

The study of the music itself as viewed through the theoretical thought of the age and within the relevant political and cultural context of the time is the important focus of this text. To this end, the accompanying *Music of the Middle Ages: An Anthology for Performance and Study* and *Recording to Accompany Music of the Middle Ages* are valuable, almost indispensable adjuncts, for a full comprehension of style can only come about through listening and analysis.

To further the understanding of stylistic change, a series of Practicum units, graded studies in composition and analysis, appear at the end of many chapters. There can be little doubt that a hands-on approach to the use of material is far superior to mere conceptual learning. A student who has experimented with the rules of actual composition in a genre, or who has grappled with the analysis of an unfamiliar piece of early music, has made those concepts a part of his experience. No amount of intellectual conceptualization can match the understanding and length of retention of this combination of study and practice.

For pedagogical reasons Practicum units are not spread evenly through the text, but form two series of different complexity and intent. Units in Chapters 1 to 4 concern the establishment of basic skills: reading and transcribing modern plainchant notation (which simultaneously serves as an introduction into the complexities of medieval notation per se), principles of chant analysis, the practical use of hexachords, and the application of those hexachords in improvising early organum.

A subsequent series focuses on composition in each of the primary historical styles, with exercises in free organum, Aquitanian florid style, midthirteenth-century three-voice discant, and fourteenth-century song style, intermixed with occasional analytic studies. Unlike the introductory exercises, these more involved excursions into medieval techniques do not occur in each chapter, but are spread among the later chapters to allow time for practice and assimilation.

This text also incorporates a more comprehensive approach to polyphonic development, to the sacred and secular monophony of the later Middle Ages, and to word-tone relationships.

Much attention is given to early forms of polyphony because it is precisely then, in the eleventh and twelfth centuries, that the basic techniques of all later medieval polyphony were established. Only with a thorough comprehension of these seminal styles is it possible to understand and fully appreciate the more complex application of these techniques in the thirteenth and fourteenth centuries.

In considering later medieval monophony and its interrelation with polyphony, attention is given not only to secular music, but also to the often neglected sacred repertoires. Study begins with the Aquitanian monophonic versus, proceeds to the contemporaneous secular repertories in the vernacular, continues with the Notre Dame monophonic conductus and rondellus, and ends with a brief consideration of the monophony of Machaut. This more inclusive approach makes possible a greater awareness of the interaction between the various repertoires, sacred and secular, and the equally important interrelationships between later monophony and polyphony.

Finally, there is a stress on the importance of word-tone relationships and particularly of the interaction between the rhymed, rhythmic poetry of the late Middle Ages and its musical settings. In this all-vocal repertoire, the relationship of word and music is fundamental. Without a consideration of this, medieval music must remain one-dimensional.

Music of the Middle Ages is designed for an upper-level semester course in medieval music or a combined one covering the Middle Ages and Renaissance. It will also serve well as a graduate-level text. In addition, the early music performer and the interested musical amateur will find intellectual stimulation and a new repertoire of medieval masterworks. A fundamental prerequisite is merely a knowledge of musical rudiments and an intellectual curiosity: the music of the Middle Ages is pretonal, and needs only be met on those grounds.

Many people have assisted in the development of this book and the anthology. First of all, my many students who have tested the earlier and later formulations of the concepts expressed here. Among friends and colleagues, I must single out Christopher Allworth for many hours of talk about things medieval; my collaborating translators for the anthology texts, Drs. Robert Crouse and Hans T. Runte; and especially Paul Hillier, the Hilliard Ensemble and the Western Wind for their artistry in the production of the anthology recordings. Appreciation is expressed to the Research Development Fund of Dalhousie University for financial assistance in the form of grants, to the interlibrary loan department of the Killam Library for their persistence in tracking down hard-to-find volumes, and to my editors at Schirmer Books, Maribeth Anderson Payne and Robert J. Axelrod, whose careful supportive guidance has been invaluable. Most of all, I wish to thank my wife, Barbara, whose years of encouragement helped bring this book to fruition and whose comments and questions have helped sharpen the concepts expressed here.

Abbreviations

PERIODICALS

AM	*Acta Musicologica*
EM	*Early Music*
EMH	*Early Music History*
JAMS	*Journal of the American Musicological Association*
JoM	*Journal of Musicology*
JPMMS	*Journal of the Plainsong and Mediaeval Music Society*
MD	*Musica Disciplina*
Mf	*Musikforschung*
ML	*Music and Letters*
MM	*Miscellanae Musicologica: Adelaide Studies in Musicology*
MQ	*Musical Quarterly*
PRMA	*Proceedings of the Royal Musical Association*
RBM	*Revue Belge de Musicologie*
RMA-RC	*Royal Musical Association—Research Chronical*

OTHER

AIM	American Institute of Musicology (Stuttgart: Hänssler)
AMM	*Anthology of Medieval Music*, Richard Hoppin, ed. (New York: Norton, 1978)
CMM	Corpus mensurabilis musicae (American Institute of Musicology, 1948–)
COUSSE-MAKER	Edmund de Coussemaker, *Scriptorium de medii aevi nova series*, 4 vols. (Paris, 1864–76; rpt. Hildesheim: Georg Olms Verlag, 1963, 1987)
CSM	Corpus scriptorum de musica (American Institute of Musicology, 1950–)
GR	*Graduale Romanum*, 1974 edition (Tournai: Desclée and Co., 1974)
HAM	*Historical Anthology of Music*, Willi Apel and Archibald T. Davison, eds., 2nd ed. (Cambridge: Harvard University Press, 1949)
LU	*The Liber Usualis with Introduction and Rubrics in English* (Tournai and New York: Desclée, 1952)

MSD	Musicological Studies and Documents (American Institute of Musicology, 1951–)
NGD	*New Grove Dictionary of Music and Musicians*, Stanley Sadie, ed. (London: Macmillan, 1980)
OAMM	*Oxford Anthology: Medieval Music*, W. Thomas Marrocco and Nicholas Sandon, eds. (London: Oxford University Press, 1977)
NOHM	*New Oxford History of Music*. Vol. II, Dom Anselm Hughes, ed., *Early Medieval Music Up to 1300* (London: Oxford University Press, 1954); Vol. III, Dom Anselm Hughes and Gerald Abraham, eds., *Ars Nova and the Renaissance 1300–1540* (London: Oxford University Press, 1960)
PMFC	Polyphonic Music of the Fourteenth Century (Monaco: Editions de l'Oiseau-lyre, 1956–)
PMMM	Publications of Mediaeval Musical Manuscripts (Ottawa: Institute of Mediaeval Music, 1957–)
SSMS	*Study Scores of Musical Styles*, Edward R. Lerner, ed. (New York: McGraw-Hill, 1968)
Strunk	Oliver Strunk, *Source Readings in Music History* (New York: Norton, 1950); also published in paperback, of which Vol. 1, *Antiquity and the Middle Ages*, contains all the medieval readings
UMI	University Microfilms International, Ann Arbor, Mich.

STANDARD REFERENCES ON NOTATION

Willi Apel, *The Notation of Polyphonic Music*, 5th ed., rev. (Cambridge: The Medieval Academy of America, 1953).

Carl Parrish, *The Notation of Medieval Music* (New York: Norton, 1957).

GENERAL BIBLIOGRAPHIES

Andrew Hughes, *Medieval Music: The Sixth Liberal Art*, rev. ed. (Toronto: University of Toronto Press, 1980). An extensive bibliography of writings about medieval music.

Gilbert Reaney and Kurt von Fischer, eds., *Repertoire International des Sources Musicales*, Vol. B IV$_1$: Manuscripts of Polyphonic Music, 11th–Early 14th Century; Vol. B IV$_2$: Manuscripts of Polyphonic Music (c. 1320–1400); Vol. B IV$_3$: Handschriften mit Mehrstimmigen Musik des 14., 15., und 16. Jahrhunderts I; Vol. B IV$_4$: Handschriften mit Mehrstimmigen Musik des

14., 15., und 16. Jahrhunderts II (Munich: Henle, 1966, 1969, 1972, 1972). A listing by country, city, and library of all manuscripts containing medieval polyphony.

MEDIEVAL SYSTEM OF PITCH IDENTIFICATION AS ADAPTED FOR MUSIC OF THE MIDDLE AGES

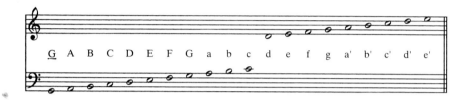

<u>G</u> A B C D E F G a b c d e f g a' b' c' d' e'

MUSIC
OF THE
MIDDLE AGES
Style and Structure

Part I

THE CAROLINGIAN ERA
800–1150

Introduction

The challenge of historical study is the re-creation of the past through the judicious and thoughtful reintegration of a plethora of minute details—books, manuscripts, artifacts that have withstood the vicissitudes of time—particles of evidence that must be carefully weighed and balanced against one another. In a sense, it is like assembling an extensive three-dimensional jigsaw puzzle in which some of the pieces are missing, for the farther one goes back in time, the greater the number of pieces that are lost: manuscripts and art are destroyed by carelessness, catastrophe, maliciousness; buildings and artifacts decay and disappear.

Music is no stranger to these problems of historical reconstruction, for it is an ephemeral art: the pop song of today is discarded tomorrow; of the over four hundred operas produced in seventeenth-century Venice, scores for less than one hundred remain, and these are often in woefully incomplete form. Manuscript evidence for earlier music is proportionally even more scarce.

A further difficulty in this quest for historical knowledge is that music is the art of sound: when the player finishes, the music is over. Musical notation can convey the general sense of a live performance, it cannot substitute for it.

A modern score, with precise details of pitch, harmony, rhythm, meter, tempo, dynamics, and instrumentation, endeavors to supply as fully as possible the complete information needed for a stylistic and correct performance, yet it in no way matches a recorded performance supervised by the composer as true musical evidence. The scores of past centuries are even less explicit in conveying on paper the sound of the work.

A seventeenth-century score may possibly include tempo indications, but, of course, no metronome marks. Dynamic markings will be sparse or nonexistent and confined to an occasional forte or piano. Instrumentation will be indicated, but with allowable substitutions within a permissible range. Some parts (for example, timpani if trumpets are present, bassoon if oboes are used) may be left for the performer to provide, and one essential to the performance, the realization of the figured bass, is to be completed in extemporaneous performance.

In the sixteenth century and earlier, we find dynamic and tempo markings missing entirely, nor is there any indication of the performing group. Texted music may well imply vocal performance, but we know that this was not always the case, since texted music could be performed instrumentally and nontexted music sung. In addition, when sung, it could be performed a capella, with instruments *colla parte*, or with some substituting for voices. Each of these alternatives was possible, but none was ever indicated.

Moving back to the Middle Ages, we find that rhythmic notation did not begin until after 1200, and precise indication of pitch only after 1000. Before 800, there is total obscurity. No pertinent document or musical manuscript exists from the crucial formative years of European music. This may be partly due to the vicissitudes of time, but it is also, and perhaps largely, due to the fact that medieval music existed in a predominantly oral, nonliterate society. Then, a capacious memory served in place of a later time's reliance on writing, and a musician's excellent recollection of music replaced his need for musical notation.

This is a fact so foreign to our modern conception that it warrants a moment of consideration, as does *musica,* the medieval concept of music. The learning that belonged to ancient Greece and Rome dissipated at the close of the Roman Empire, as Europe succumbed to wave after wave of barbarian invaders and, out of seeming chaos, formed a new society. Learning remained alive, however, particularly in the oasis of the monastery, where monks, banding together for mutual support, study, and prayer, became important preservers of the knowledge of the ancients. The expansion of education and learning that began with the eighth-century Carolingian renaissance set the stage for later medieval culture.

Musical training in the later Middle Ages was of two sorts, the practical training of the performer and the intellectual preparation that was a part of higher education. We will begin with the latter, which gives insight into the intellectual concepts of the age.

The basic format of higher education, including that of the future universities of the thirteenth century, was the study of the seven liberal arts—the *trivium* (grammar, rhetoric, and dialectic) and the *quadrivium* (arithmetic, geometry, music, and astronomy). Derived from Greek and Roman principles, the study of the trivium and quadrivium encompasses an attempt to see the various phenomena of the world not as separate entities, but as part of one interrelated world order. Thus, the various subjects of the quadrivium are not separate disciplines, but a series of phenomena interrelated by their reliance on the concept of measurement and proportion.

The concept of *musica* within this framework derives from the thoughts of several Greek philosophers, especially Plato, Pythagoras, and Aristotle, transmitted through a series of intermediaries to the *De musica* of Boethius (ca. 470–525), which is constantly cited by later medieval writers.

Musica, as one of the mathematical arts, is based on the proportional measuring of sound according to pitch and duration. The first of these considerations encompasses the relationship of intervals (2:1 for the octave, 3:2 for the fifth, etc.) and relates to what we might call elementary acoustics. The second consideration, the proportionality of sound duration, encompasses not only music but also Latin quantitative poetry, which serves very conveniently to illustrate durational measurement because it is based on the use of long and short syllables. This may be seen in the following example, where, as a long syllable equals two short ones, each *foot* or "measure" is equal:

Ā̆r - m̆a v̆i |r̄om - q̆ue c̆a -|n̄o Tr̄o -|īae q̄ui |pr̄i - m̆us ăb |ō - r̄is
2   1   1   2   1   1   2   2   2   2   2   1   1   2   2

A typical late medieval treatise on *musica* would include chapters on mathematical relationships and harmonic proportions, illustrations of harmonic relations as demonstrated on the monochord, and illustrations of duration through an exposition of the classic poetic meters.

Another major concept in the study of *musica* is the application of the principles of proportion to a unified conception of the universe. In this regard, music is divided into three categories: *musica mundana, musica humana,* and *musica instrumentalis. Musica mundana* may be called the "music of the spheres" because it relates to the proportionality and balance between the stars and the planets, whose movements through the heavens create an unheard music. *Musica humana* concerns the balance and harmony of the organs within the human body and the harmonious relationship of body and soul. It is only *musica instrumentalis* that concerns the proportionality of *heard* sounds, such as vocal and instrumental music.

The study of *musica* is thus abstract and concerned with relationships beyond the realm of mere practical music. To Boethius, music is divine number made audible. Since all things harmonious are similarly controlled by number and proportion, music reflects in microcosm a universe controlled by a unified God-given law and design.

What was it like to study in an age before printed textbooks were available, and before even manuscript texts were plentiful? The development of a capacious memory was fundamental. This is true of both the musical performer, the mere *cantore,* who knew only the "how to," rather than the "why," and the *musicus,* who knew the "why" and its relationship to the universe. A clerical singer had to have the ability to sing a year's worth of chant—several thousand melodies and texts—from memory! The singer-entertainer might proceed for hours in the presentation, in poetic form, of one story. Our visually oriented society gives little hint of this capacity of the mind. Yet we need think no farther than the blind organist Helmut Walcha, recording the complete organ works of Bach, to begin to grasp the potentialities of human memory.

Medieval musical instruction of a practical kind was by apprenticeship, whether individual, to a secular musician, or collective, in a monastic or cathedral school. The student learned through years of study and listening, and trial and error. Training would begin in childhood, and a youth attending a clerical school would listen over and over to the singing of various types of chant, absorbing the melodic patterns appropriate to each type and style. Then, having over a period of years absorbed the total idiom of a given type of melody, the singer would be able to re-create that idiom in performance to any appropriate text.

In such an oral culture, what might be called "mode" may vary from, on the one hand, a body of characteristic melodic formulas and procedures appropriate to a given idiom and genre to, on the other, an assumption of characteristic scale types or octave species.

In the early, oral culture of the Middle Ages, it was the former definition that seems most widely applied, and one needs to picture the medieval singer remembering the melody type and then applying it to the text of the moment. Memory supplies the concept of style and possibly some more precise melodic shapes or formulas; creative ability spontaneously welds those elements together during the performance in ways that are particularly appropriate for the occasion. The performance is neither pure memorization nor pure extemporization, but a flexible idiom in between.

This performance practice suggests a fluid melodic tradition, in which details could vary from performance to performance, gradually leading to permanent changes over generations of time. Indeed, change is characteristic of medieval oral culture. It is only the advent of notation that gives fixity to the tradition.

1

Roman-Gallican Chant

The history of European music begins around the year 800, long after the expanding Christian church had replaced the pagan religions of Rome and, upon the collapse of the Roman Empire, had become the sole unifying force in an otherwise disunited Europe. We know little of the music of the important formative years of the early Middle Ages beyond the bare fact that both secular and religious music existed and that music was of fundamental importance in the daily round of Christian worship. We know many of the types of music used within the service, but we have no record of the melodies sung in this age before notation. Some, and possibly many, of the melodies later written down may derive from these earlier times, but of precisely which ones, and whether they passed unchanged through the centuries, we can have no sure knowledge.

It is necessary therefore to begin with the earliest notated European music, that of the Christian church at the time of the Carolingian Empire. We will have to wait another two hundred years and more before we begin to find traces of the more ephemeral secular music of the Middle Ages—the music of court and countryside, of village dance and court banquet.

HISTORICAL BACKGROUND

The three great centers of power in eighth-century Europe were the Byzantine Empire (which was centered in Constantinople and controlled portions of Italy, the Balkans, the Near East, and Egypt); the papacy in Rome; and the kingdom of the Franks, which comprised Western Germany and France.

The Byzantine Empire

The Byzantine Empire remained the only unconquered remnant of the original Roman Empire. The western portion of the Empire, centered in Rome, had succumbed to invading barbaric hordes, while the Byzantine Empire remained relatively untouched. When the emperor Constantine moved the seat of his government from Rome to the ancient city of Byzantium in 330, renaming it Constantinople (now modern Istanbul), it became the actual imperial city, while Rome was ruled by a coemperor. When Romulus Augustus, the last of these Western emperors, was deposed in 476, the Byzantine Empire became the sole successor to Imperial Rome.

The emperor, as heir to a Roman Empire that once had ruled the civilized world, held a ceremonial position above that of all other leaders: he dealt with kings, but only he was emperor. His position was reflected and reinforced by the capital city of Constantinople, which became the wealthiest, most cultured city of seventh-century Europe. Moreover, the emperor's position surpassed the mere secular power of other monarchs because he also wielded power over the church. Under the title of *Basilius,* he summoned liturgical councils and controlled the appointment of the nominal head of the church, the patriarch of Constantinople.

Although the onslaught of the rising Islamic Empire and of European barbarian tribes considerably reduced the territory of the empire within the seventh century, this did not directly effect the emperor's control over his Italian territories or his liturgical position within the church. The geographical territory of the Byzantine Empire in the late eighth century and its relationship to other Christian and non-Christian lands is shown in Map 1-1.

The Papacy

The papacy in Rome had a multilayered relationship with the Byzantine Empire. As a temporal ruler of Rome and surrounding territories and of vast papal estates spread throughout Italy, the pope was nominally subject to the emperor, since the territory of the empire still included Venice, Ravenna, Rome, southern Italy, and Sicily. In the religious sphere, as the bishop of Rome, the pope's relationship with the Eastern church was even more uneasy. The postulated founding of the Roman church by Saint Peter meant that the papacy held primacy among Western bishops. However, there were four patriarchs of similar historical veneration in the East, those of Antioch (where the Christian Church had first been organized), Jerusalem, Alexandria, and Constantinople.

For a papacy with aspirations toward supreme leadership, the situation was uncomfortable, and further complicated by sometimes severe doctrinal disputes within the Eastern church, in which the emperor often exerted religious pressure on the pope. Not surprisingly, by the eighth century the papacy began looking for a counterweight to Byzantium. The clear choice, although surprising in terms of historical relationships, was the formerly barbaric Germanic people of northern Europe, now more or less united in the Frankish kingdom.

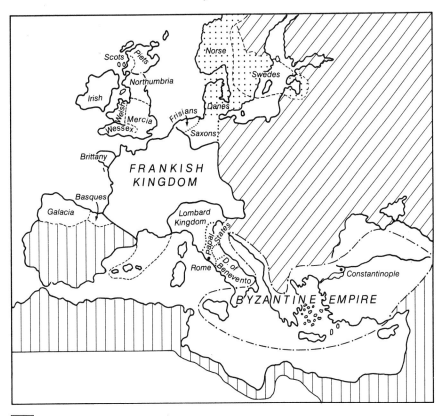

Christian areas

Norse tribes

Mohammedan territory

Barbarian tribes

Map 1.1   Europe in 771.

The Frankish Kingdom

The Frankish kingdom had been a political entity since the days of Clovis, who by 511 had united much of the old Roman province of Gaul with areas around the Rhine. Although his successors varied greatly in ability, the Frankish kingdom remained a power throughout the sixth and seventh centuries. By the early eighth century, however, the weakness of a succession of kings had permitted the real executive powers of the kingdom to be held by the mayor of the palace. In 732 one of these mayors, Charles Martel, defeated the Muslims near

Tours and stemmed the Islamic invasion of Europe through Spain only fourteen years after the Byzantine emperor Leo III had saved the eastern approaches of Europe from the same danger.

The Frankish-Papal Alliance

The rapprochement between the Franks and the pope, Saint Zacharias, began with the ascendancy of Charles Martel's son Pepin to the leadership of the Franks in 741. The new alliance grew rapidly. Between 741 and 747, Saint Boniface, sent by the pope and encouraged by Pepin, held a series of councils to wipe out corruption within the Gallican or Frankish church and to bring that church closer to Rome. In 751 the pope reciprocated by agreeing that Pepin, then still mayor of the palace, should replace the actual king.

Almost immediately, King Pepin was asked to repay the debt. Zacharias's successor, Pope Stephen II, was in imminent danger of subjection to the Lombard king, who controlled much of Italy (see Map 1-1). The pope's nominal sovereign, the emperor, was powerless to help, and Stephen turned to the Franks, requesting a meeting with them on Frankish soil. This meeting, which occurred in 754, had the desired results: Pepin pledged to aid the pope against the Lombards, beginning a Frankish-Papal alliance that would last, in various permutations, for centuries.

In terms of its influence on music, the meeting was equally momentous. Pepin, hearing papal Masses performed as they would have been in Rome, requested liturgical books and trained singers from Stephen, with the object of spreading this Roman chant throughout the Frankish territory. The suppression of the native Gallican liturgy and chant and their replacement with that of Rome thus began as a deliberate element of national policy. This was further reinforced during the reign of Pepin's son Charlemagne.

Charlemagne

Charlemagne himself was perhaps the greatest political mind of the Middle Ages. He expanded Frankish territory to include what would become present-day Germany, the Netherlands, France, and northern Italy, welding it into a single political unit. He did not neglect to support the arts, and the system of education he established paved the way for the future intellectual vigor of the West. Most importantly, he continued Pepin's policy of establishing a unified church allied to Rome as an instrument of political unification throughout the Frankish kingdom.

Conversion of newly conquered peoples was compulsory upon pain of death. New liturgical books were requested of Pope Hadrian I and received between 784 and 791. Found to be incomplete (the pope did not officiate at Mass throughout the year), first the monk Alcuin and then others, most importantly Benedict of Aniane, were entrusted to complete the yearly cycle so that proper liturgy and chant could be disseminated throughout the kingdom.

At the same time, Charlemagne maintained good relations with the Byzantine Empire, including interchange of music and musicians (Charlemagne himself requested the translation of several Byzantine chants). Most important was the impression made on the Carolingians by the *Oktoechos,* the Byzantine system of modal organization. Carolingian musicians would take this concept and develop for the first time in the West a method of "codifying" religious chant, a system that would form the theoretical basis of liturgical music for the next nine hundred years.

MUSIC IN THE WESTERN CHURCH

It is only through an understanding of the place of music in the medieval church that the real import of this early musical style can be understood. The Christian Church, in the largest sense, consists of all consecrated believers. In the Middle Ages, however, the specific task of offering unceasing praise to God was assumed by those especially dedicated to the task: monks and nuns, living in the relative seclusion of monastery and convent, and the so-called secular clergy—priests and clerics serving parish and cathedral churches. Their offering of praise took the form of both a series of eight daily services, spaced around the clock and known as the *Divine Offices* or *Canonical Hours,* and a more public service, the *Mass,* which has as its focus the celebration of the Lord's Supper (the Eucharist or Communion).

Central to the Offices, and prominent also in the Mass, is the singing of Psalms—all 150 were sung within a week's round of Offices—intermixed with other biblical and other nonbiblical texts. The singers were the clerics and monks of the church or monastery, regardless of ability, for in the praise of God talent counted for less than intent of heart. It is only within Carolingian times that the trained choir (always of monks or clerics) assumed greater responsibility within the services, but never to the exclusion of the total body of worshipers.

Plainchant, the music of the medieval church, is thus in an absolute sense music for worship. Shorn of its liturgical ambience it loses much of its inner meaning. Performed in isolation it may have great beauty, as an isolated opera aria may have great beauty, but neither, in isolation, can adequately convey the larger totality from which it was removed. It is this central fact that must be borne in mind as we proceed through an initial discussion of the specifically musical properties of plainchant, postponing the detailed discussion of the liturgy of the Mass and Office, and the structure of their chants, until Chapter 2. It was the intimacy of plainchant to the lives of the Carolingian clergy in fact that made them so concerned with its development and preservation.

Roman and Gallican Chant

Although there is no notated music from this period, it appears that there were considerable differences between the Gallican chant in common use throughout the Frankish territories of northern Europe and the newly imported chant from Rome. As might be expected, in a time when all chant was performed from memory the imposition of a new body of chant throughout the kingdom must have caused considerable disruption, involving the replacement of thousands of memorized chants. How pure did the Roman chant remain as it spread through the land? Was it correctly learned and passed on by the Frankish singers, or did melodic changes occur, either inadvertently or deliberately, as the new music was spread from monastery to monastery and city to city?

Our nearest witnesses, writing a century later, indicate that there were considerable problems in the dissemination of the "true" chant. One of these, John the Deacon, writing about 875, reports repeated difficulties:

> Again and again the Germans and Gauls were given the opportunity to learn this [Roman] chant. But they were unable to preserve it uncorrupted since they mixed elements of their own with the Gregorian melodies, and their barbarian savageness was coupled with vocal crudeness and inability to execute the technicalities.
>
> Charlemagne too was struck, when in Rome, by the discordance between Roman and Gallican singing, when the Franks in their precocity argued that their chant was corrupted by our [Roman] chanters with some poor melodies; ours probably showed the authentic antiphonal. . . . Hence he left two of his assiduous clerics with [Pope] Hadrian. After good instruction they restored for him the early chant at Metz and, by way of Metz, all over Gaul.
>
> But after a long time, when those educated in Rome had died, Charlemagne discovered that the chant of the other churches differed from that of Metz. "We must return again to the source," he said. And at his request—as present-day trustworthy information states—Hadrian sent two chanters, who convinced the King that all had corrupted the Roman chant through carelessness but that at Metz the differences were due to that natural savageness.[1]

It appears that for many years the melodies and the liturgy were in a state of flux. Amalarus of Metz, writing between 831 and 844, and speaking of his own time, says:

> Concerning these [chants], I asked the masters of the Roman church whether they sang them, and they said, not at all. Our chant masters, however, claim that they learned them from the Romans through the first chant teachers whom the Romans instructed in the melodies of Roman chant within Frankish territory. God knows if the Romans are in error, or [if] the Franks themselves, who glory in having learned those antiphons from the masters of the Roman church, have erred; or if the Romans have forgotten them out of carelessness and neglect, or, alternatively, never sang them in the first place. . . .
>
> After I had suffered a long time from weariness on account of the antiphoners of our province disagreeing among themselves . . . I compared the aforementioned

---

[1]As summarized by S. J. P. van Dijk, "Papal Schola *versus* Charlemagne," in *Organicae Voces: Festschrift Joseph van Waesberghe* (Amsterdam: Institut voor Middeleeuwse Muziekwetenschap, 1963), 23–24.

volumes [Roman antiphoners presumably revised by Pope Hadrian before 795 and received in Corbie in 825] with our antiphoners and found them to differ not only from ours in their order, but also in their words and in the multitude or responsories and antiphons that we do not sing. . . . I marveled how it could be that mother and daughter should disagree with each other so greatly.[2]

Roman-Gallican Chant

Given these discrepancies, a definitive understanding of the interaction between Roman and Gallican chant traditions is impossible. Logic suggests, however, that the new chant was a mixture of northern and southern idioms, a kind of composite Roman-Gallican chant (known today by that name or as Gregorian, Gregorian-Roman, or Carolingian-Roman chant).

The basic adjustment period must have been the late eighth century, for most chants of the Mass Proper and the Offices were modally classified by about 800, indicating the establishment of their form in at least broad terms by that time. Notated versions of these chants, appearing around 900, establish what is clearly a stable transmission of those melodies. Nonetheless, melodic adjustments continued even into the twelfth and thirteenth centuries, although these later changes generally occurred as "corrections" to fit errant melodies more precisely into later modal theory.

It is this chant, a composite of Roman and Gallican traditions, that was disseminated throughout the realm as the official chant. It was given a stamp of authority when, in the ninth century, the whole body of chant was attributed to the divine inspiration of Saint Gregory the Great, pope from 590 to 604 (from which comes the long-held myth that all chant derives from him). Although this was not the first pious deception of the Middle Ages (nor, indeed, the last), it was from this false attribution that the familiar name *Gregorian* became attached to this body of chant.

MELODIC AND RHYTHMIC CHARACTERISTICS

Melody

All chant melody moves through a relatively narrow range in a largely stepwise motion. Skips of a third are common, those of a fourth or a fifth, less so. Larger melodic intervals are not found, except between phrases. Phrasing is largely determined by the text, and in this sense there is a very close relationship between melodic and textual considerations; only in long textless passages do musical considerations take precedence.

Three general types of word-tone relationships can be isolated: *syllabic,* in which there is one note per syllable; *neumatic,* in which there are from two to

---

[2]In Edward Nowacki, "The Gregorian Office Antiphons and the Comparative Method," *JoM* 4 (1985–86), 263–64.

four notes per syllable; and *melismatic,* in which more lengthy ornamental passages are set over a single syllable. These three basic types are shown in Example 1-1.

EXAMPLE 1-1.   Syllabic, Neumatic, and Melismatic Styles of Chant.

While chants tend toward an identifiable style, few use a single style exclusively. More characteristic is a mixture within one predominant style.

Rhythm

There can be little doubt from the evidence of theoretical discussion and musical notation that early chant was sung in a rhythmic manner, at least until the mid-eleventh century. Regrettably, the meaning of the early rhythmic signs became lost as notation became increasingly pitch-oriented. Despite a century of investigation and experimentation, the rhythmic style of early chant remains an enigma.

Several of these early rhythmic signs, such as *t* for *trahere* or *tenere* ("draw out," "hold") and *c* for *cito* or *celeriter* ("fast," "quick"), may be seen in Facsimile 1-1 (see the section on notation below). Both a *c* and a *t* are clearly visible above (and almost attached to) the second line of neumes and elsewhere.

THE TONAL SYSTEM AND THE MODES

> We have said that there are eight modes in music through which all melody appears to hold together as if with a type of glue. . . . And in the manner that speech arises and is governed by letters, and the multiplication of numbers is governed by units, so all melody is regulated by the boundary of its sounds and its modes. (Aurelian of Reóme, *Musica disciplina*)

The first record we have of the application of the Byzantine modal system to Western chant is in a tonary (a book that arranges chants by mode and type) from around 800. It is Aurelian of Reóme who tells us, in his treatise *Musica disciplina* from around 843, that the modes were imported from the Byzantines.

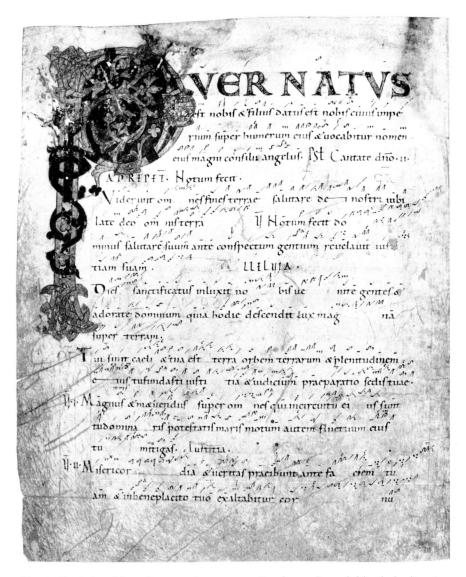

Facsimile 1-1. Non diastematic neumes. Bamberg, Staatsbibliothek, lit. 6, fol. 6', ca. 950–975.

The Oktoechos

We know little of the Byzantine *Oktoechos* or system of eight modes. It is first mentioned by one John of Damascus (ca. 675–ca. 749). From his remarks and later evidence, the Oktoechos appear to have represented not scales but melody types, presumably basic melody types from which a large body of chant could be re-created or improvised.

No notated Byzantine music exists from this period, and there is no definite evidence of a notation in the Eastern church prior to the tenth century. The Oktoechos were conveyed orally and were cued to a series of eight apparently meaningless words: *Annaneane, Nannaneagies, Aianeagies,* and so on. Each of these presumably would have brought to the mind of the singer the proper melody type.

The process of organization facing the Carolingian musician was complex. Roman chant, still in a state of amalgamation with the native Gallican idiom, was to be reduced to a theoretical system borrowed from an alien culture, that of Byzantium. To this was added an apparent need to reconcile in some way this codification with the revered knowledge of an even less related music, that of ancient Greece.

The accommodation to Byzantine theory was immediate and was probably largely complete by around 800. Accommodation to the musical system of ancient Greece took another one hundred years and longer. Given these circumstances, it is not surprising that the nature of modality changed as the Middle Ages changed, that medieval modality is different from Renaissance modality, and that both are different from twentieth-century formulations. To reach an understanding of medieval modality, it is wise to discard all modern concepts and to view it afresh, as it was seen in its time.

Western Modality

In imitation of the East, the Western modal system was based on eight modes arranged into four pairs given the Greek names *Protos* (first), *Deuterus* (second), *Tritus* (third), and *Tetrardus* (fourth). These modes were thought of as having *finals* (final tones) on the four tones D, E, F, and G. The melodies within each pair were divided by range, the *authentic* mode ranging from the final upwards, the *plagal* a fourth or a fifth above and below it (although a given melody might exceed these ranges by a few notes either way):

			THEORETICAL RANGE	FINAL
Protus		Authentic	D-d	
		Plagal	A-a	D
Deuterus		Authentic	E-e	
		Plagal	B-b	E
Tritus		Authentic	F-f	
		Plagal	C-c	F
Tetrardus		Authentic	G-g	
		Plagal	D-d	G

Subsequently two other systems of nomenclature were developed. One involves a simple numbering of the modes, in the order (1) Protus authentic, (2) Protus plagal, and so on. The other system applies, in a partially misunderstood manner, ancient Greek theoretical terms. The three systems of nomenclature may be seen below:

Protus		Authentic	Mode one	Dorian
		Plagal	Mode two	Hypodorian
Deuterus		Authentic	Mode three	Phrygian
		Plagal	Mode four	Hypophrygian
Tritus		Authentic	Mode five	Lydian
		Plagal	Mode six	Hypolydian
Tetrardus		Authentic	Mode seven	Mixolydian
		Plagal	Mode eight	Hypomixolydian

A secondary attribute of each mode, not derived from the Byzantine system yet found in some of the earliest chants, is the presence of a *reciting tone* or *tenor*, a secondary tonal center within the mode. A direct attribute of the *psalm tones* (where it is the main reciting note—see Chapter 2), this secondary center is also important in many other chants. In the authentic modes, the reciting tone lies a fifth above the final except in the case of Deuterus, where the b that appears in some ninth-century manuscripts is subsequently shifted to c in most manuscripts:

MODE	FINAL	RECITING TONE
Protus authentic	D	a
Deuterus authentic	E	c
Tritus authentic	F	c
Tetrardus authentic	G	d

Plagal modes alternate between a third and a fourth:

Protus plagal	D	F
Deuterus plagal	E	a
Tritus plagal	F	a
Tetrardus plagal	G	c

The choice of reciting tones may have been in part inherited custom, in part due to the underlying tonal structure of the chant. Particularly apparent is the distinct avoidance of the tone b. The resulting choice causes the sharing of some reciting tones by more than one mode:

F	Protus plagal
a	Protus authentic, Deuterus plagal, Tritus plagal
c	Deuterus authentic, Tetrardus plagal
d	Tetrardus authentic

It is clear that at this early stage, although ranges for each mode are given by all writers, they are meant largely as a rule of thumb in separating authentic and plagal melodies. The main attention in early theory is on melody types, the character of the notes immediately around the final, and practical matters of performance. The concept of modes as scale systems is a subsequent development.

Melody Types

The concept of melody types played a key role in the initial Carolingian modal classifications, although it lost ground to other considerations later. In essence, a melody type may be likened to a melodic skeleton that may be fleshed out in a variety of ways. It can result in various seemingly different melodies that are nevertheless related to the same basic structural outline.

This concept is foreign to our modern experience, and needs explanation. We may begin by considering the Carolingian "modal formulas," a group of short melodic passages that were thought to encapsule the essence of each mode. There are three different sets of these formulas; those for Protus authentic are illustrated in Example 1-2.

The first of these sets, the *Enechema* or *Noanoeane* syllables, is derived in imitation of the Byzantine modal words of the *Oktoechos*. It gives a simple phrase outlining the essential modal quality, that is, the basic tone-semitone arrangement above the final. There is some suggestion that such short passages were sung quietly by a singer to orient himself in the mode before beginning a chant.

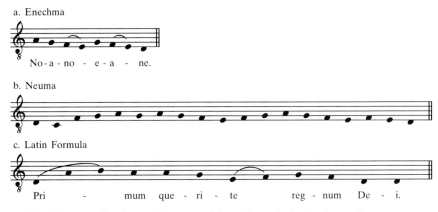

EXAMPLE 1-2. *Enechema,* Neuma, and Latin Formula for Authentic Protus.

The second, the *Neuma,* is usually written as a continuation of the *Enechema* and includes melodic turns characteristic of the mode. The third type, the *Latin formula,* begins to appear around 900, that is, about a hundred years later than the first two. It, like the *neuma,* incorporates characteristic melodic idioms of the mode. To see how these formulas apply in practice, we need to consider some actual chants.

Melodic types in practice.   We may start with the modal classifications given by Regino of Preum (ca. 900) as our guide, interpreted by François Gevaert in his *Mélopée Antique.* In his important study, Gevaert, following Regino's lead, reduces the 1,235 Office antiphon chants mentioned by Regino to forty-seven basic formulas. Since many of these forty-seven are still closely related, an even further reduction in the number of melodic formulas could be made.

Example 1-3 gives formulas 2, 3, and 4 from Gevaert ("themes" in his terminology), all from Regino's first category of Protus authentic melodies. Except for the Germanic preference for c as the tone above a, this melody type is similar to the Protus authentic Latin formula of Example 1-2, the three variants differing only in the use of introductory tones before the characteristic motive D-a. (Medieval melodic variants often take the form of the addition of anticipatory notes before a motive.)

Gevaert (pp. 234–39) lists forty different Office antiphons based on this formula, while Example 1-4 gives the beginnings of seven Introit antiphons also built on the same formula.

As these Introit antiphons are taken from a West Frankish (French) manuscript, the typical West Frankish b flat appears above a. The basic movement is the rise to b flat or c and a stepwise descent to F, variously ornamented, realized in simpler or more complex ways. The preliminary C-D of four of the Introits is a characteristic of version 2 of Example 1-3, while the F-C beginning of *Exclamaverunt* is a common substitution for the G-C of version 3. In early medieval chant idioms, contour was more important than exactness of intervals, and regional melodic dialects could alter details without effecting the identity of the melody. Similarity of text often, but not always, resulted in a similarity of

EXAMPLE 1-3.   A Protus Authentic Melodic Formula, with Alternate Beginnings. (From "Themes" 2, 3 and 4, Gevaert, *Mélopée*)

EXAMPLE 1-4. Introit Beginnings Illustrating the Same Protus Authentic Melody Type, from *Mo* H 159. For complete Introits, see G.R. pp. 281, 508, 591, 559, 326, 300, 336 or L.U. pp. 961, 1047, 1556, 1465A, 1040, 1361 and 1056.

melodic outline: compare the identity of Introits 1 and 2 with the different settings of the word *domine* in 5 and 7.

The continuation of the Introits also follows the outline of the basic melody type in its descent to D, sometimes directly (as in *Da pacem*), sometimes after lengthy expansion (as in *Factus est, Justus es*). This may be seen by viewing the complete chants in the modern editions of the *Graduale Romanum* or the *Liber Usualis*.

System of classification. The medieval modal system is above all a system of classification. As suggested by Aurelian in the quotation that began this section, "Every melody is governed by the boundary line both of its sounds and of its modes." Although only certain categories of chant specifically needed modal classification as a practical means of combining separate segments of chant, modal classification was applied to all chant. The frequent conflict between melody type and final was solved by the simple expedient of accepting the final as definitive in modal classification, regardless of melody type.

The modes came to be a simple means of classifying an immense body of chant by final. They serve our present analytical requirements only imperfectly, although they must remain a point of departure.

The Tonal System

In analyzing the tonal organization of Roman-Gallican chant, it is important that preconceived notions be laid aside. The first and most important fact to be grasped is that there need not be any equivalency between the concepts of final and tonic, even in the enlarged sense of "the tone around which the melody revolves." The final *may* on occasion function as tonic, but more often is merely another and often less important structural tone, or sometimes even a seeming afterthought, playing no important part in the melody until it forms the tone of conclusion.

It must be accepted that none of the medieval theories satisfy our modern musicological desire to "know how the music works—what makes it function and hang together." Other concerns were more pressing to the medieval mind. To arrive at even tentative analytical conclusions, we must theorize backward from our present vantage point, through analysis of the music itself. Although there is no consensus among modern scholars concerning the problem, two approaches have been put forward that, used judiciously, can aid our understanding of the structure of medieval melody.

Pentatonicism. One point of view suggests that Roman-Gallican chant operates in a loosely pentatonic environment, possibly a sign of a more strictly pentatonic past. In this system, the octave is divided into five primary pitches, most often represented by the notes C, D, F, G, a, and c: two groups of whole tones separated from each other by minor thirds. These five pitches form the melody's stable structure, but, in addition, the two minor thirds may be subdivided by a less stable intermediate pitch, one capable of chromatic or even microtonal inflection.

However, many chants cannot be reduced to a purely pentatonic skeleton, and the pentatonic base itself often appears divided into various intervallic chains that govern the particular structure of the piece involved.

Intervallic chains. In this second modern approach to the understanding of medieval melody, the most important structural tones are seen to be located in a chain of similar intervals. In Roman-Gallican chant, the most common of these is a chain of fourths, D-G-c (a *quartal* chain) or ones of thirds (*tertial* chains), D-F-a, D-F-a-c, F-a-c, F-a-c-e. Octave identification plays little part in this type of melodic construction, and the seventh is often more important than the octave. The chain may also be subdivided, with certain segments controlling portions of a chant.

This may be seen in simple form in the Gradual *Viderunt omnes* (Anthology Example 1). The melody outlines the tertial chain F-a-c-e throughout the first half-phrase (*Viderunt omnes fines terre*), with d and b as neighboring tones. F and e mark the outside of the chain, although the a-c third controls most of the phrase. In the second half-phrase, this basic chain begins to be mixed with a contrasting one on G-b-d-f. Although it is difficult to reduce the subtlety of this melody to a diagram, an analysis such as that of Example 1-5 can convey in a general way the structural control of the two chains. It is the superimposition of intervallic chains on top of a pentatonic foundation that colors the chant idiom and, possibly as much as the resulting scale structure, forms the awareness of mode.

Microintervals.   Before leaving this initial assessment of the underlying structure of Roman-Gallican melody, passing reference should be made to the apparent presence of microintervals within the idiom. Evidence for this is found both in the remarks of theorists and in the notation of such manuscripts as Mo H159 (ca. 1000; see the section on sources below), which uses a letter notation not only to distinguish between b and b flat, but other symbols to indicate a microtone placed "in the crack" between E and F and b and c. This interval appears most often as part of the lower-neighbor figure c-b+-c and F-E+-F (the + indicating the microinterval), possibly as a type of small semitone, but can even be seen in the configuration E-E+-F. It is of some support to the theory of the underlying pentatonic structure of the chant that these microintervals, as well as the variability between b and b flat, occur within the minor third of the pentatonic system, where pentatonic theory suggests the frequent presence of a variable ornamental pitch or *piene* tone.

These microintervals were suppressed in the subsequent move toward the diatonic staff notation that came into being after 1000. In later manuscripts a passage such as the earlier F-E+-F will be found reduced to either F-E-F or F-F-F.

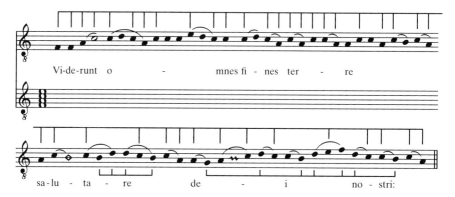

EXAMPLE 1-5.   Third Chain Structure of *Viderunt omnes*, first phrase. (Anthology Example 7)

Modality in Practice

Although the theory of modality would seem to suggest a relatively uniform set of melodic procedures, this is far from the case. The modal system in fact embraces a wide range of procedures. This may be amply illustrated by comparing two chants of differing construction.

A chant on F. An example of a clear, distinct modality may be seen in *Viderunt omnes* (Anthology Example 1). This chant ends on F and has a range of E to f. It is accordingly classified as authentic Tritus. As already noted, the melodic structure is based on an F-a-c-e tertial chain. This is immediately evident in the first section (the respond), which begins with a characteristic F-a-c figure, touches the e, and continues with an almost unadorned alternation between c and a. Of the thirty-two notes in this first half-phrase (*Viderunt omnes fines terrae*), c appears seventeen times, a eight times, d three times, F twice, and b and e once each. The primacy of c and a is made clear through reiteration, and through the placement of those tones at places of structural importance: the beginning and ending of words and the points of arrival and departure in melodic leaps.

The second half-phrase still pivots around a and c, but disguises that movement through the introduction of ornamental neighboring or passing tones. In the next phrase, the word *jubilate* emphasizes c through reiteration while *Deo* returns the melody to F and to the opening F-a-c figure, which appears again at the beginning and prominently near the end of the concluding phrase.

The verse continues to emphasize c and a, while the increased use of d (over *Dominus* and *conspectum*) gives that pitch a place of secondary importance. Although the counting of pitches is only a crude measure, at this elementary level of analysis it may be useful in calling attention to certain salient points:

PITCH	NUMBER OF APPEARANCES		
	Respond	*Verse*	*Composite*
f	1	2	3
e	3	2	5
d	9	15	24
c	41	47	88
b	6	4	10
b♭	3	5	8
a	27	40	67
G	11	13	24
F	11	14	25
E	0	1	1

In assessing this tabulation, we see that c, which is the normal recitation tone of the authentic Tritus, is by far the most prominent tone, followed by a.

The note d becomes a tone of secondary importance, particularly in the verse. What is most surprising in this enumeration is the relative infrequency of the F final. It begins and ends the respond and the verse, but is little emphasized in between. Instead the real structural tones are c and a, around which the melody revolves, only occasionally dropping down to the final. Indeed the secondary tone d appears exactly as often as the F final, although the latter's placement as cadential tone gives it added weight. The tone e, which marks the top of two third-chain ascents in the respond, loses its importance to f in the verse.

In analysis, it could be said that *Viderunt omnes* is based overall on the chain F-a-c-e plus the secondary tone d. The final is the lowest note of the chain but is of only secondary structural importance in the construct of the melody. It is a concluding tone, but not a true tonic. Also worthy of notice in passing is the alternation of b and b flat, passing inflections that are not deemed to change the basic modality of the piece.

A chant on E. *Viderunt omnes* displays a clear, unambiguous modality. A second chant example, the first section or antiphon of the Introit *Resurrexi* (Anthology Example 2) shows a quite different melodic structure.

The *Resurrexi* antiphon concludes on E and has a range of C to a. It is accordingly classed as plagal Deuterus. It begins on D, however, and throughout concentrates on F, not E. The F in fact makes up fully one half (61 of 131) of all the notes in the antiphon, and occurs constantly in positions of importance (beginnings of words, repeated recitation pitches, beginnings and conclusions of leaps). The alternate pole is D, which occurs much less often (seventeen times), but almost always in relationship to the F, usually by leap. G (twenty-six times), although more frequent than D, almost always appears at points of less structural importance: within a word and generally as an upper neighbor to F.

The tonal ambiguity becomes complete when we consider the role of the final E, which appears episodically and only in two positions of structural importance, the first and last *alleluia*. Although it appears twenty-seven times, it never seems the center of the tonal scheme. Its ambiguity is further reinforced through its appearing twice in Mo H159 as the microtonal inflection E+, an ornament further emphasizing F.

Tonally, *Resurrexi* operates around the third chain D-F-a (a being the focus of the Psalm verse), tones that particularly demarcate plagal Protus, yet this is a common tonal structure for plagal Deuterus chants, which, according to modal theory, should instead emphasize E and either G or a.

In the Deuterus modes, modal theory conflicts with a received tonal structure and forms a compromise that in itself becomes characteristic of the mode. Protus, Tritus, and Tetrardus, based on stable notes of the scale (that is, parts of the hypothetical pentatonic skeleton), tend to have stable tonal structures; Deuterus, based on the unstable tone E, borrows elements of Protus and is the most ambiguous of the modes (and the first to go out of frequent use).

Viderunt omnes and *Resurrexi* give some insight into the conflicts and compromises inherent in accommodating an adopted Byzantine modal system to an inherited European tonal system. Yet both of these chants are tonally consistent within themselves and adhere to a normative scale suitable to the modes.

The vast majority of the inherited Roman-Gallican chant melodies were able to be accommodated within the modal system. We shall return in Chapter 3 to the small number that could not.

NOTATION

Greek letter notation had been in use throughout the time of the Roman Empire, but went out of use during the early years of the Christian era, even though its principles were transmitted to the Middle Ages through such intermediaries as Boethius and Cassiodoris. They seem to have played no part in the recording of early Christian chant which, from all indications, developed in an entirely oral environment. The only known fragment of a Christian song in Greek notation, the Oxyrhynchos fragment from third-century Egypt, bears little resemblance to the idiom that became the liturgical music of the church.

Medieval notation started from a radically different premise from that of the ancient Greek: the notation not of specific individual pitches but of a generalized contour, the directionality of the melody, coupled with indications of nuances of performance.

This accords well with the medieval concept of melodic transmission. To the medieval mind, melodic identity meant identity of contour, not a literal identity of notes. An ascent of a fifth and a descent of a third in one performance could be matched by the ascent of a fourth and the descent of a second in another. This identity of generalized contour rather than exact pitch content continues throughout the medieval era, and later precisely pitched manuscripts seldom match each other exactly and may display a bewildering variety of incidental and unimportant variants. (Seldom, however, do these variants affect the essential melodic framework, the underlying intervallic chain or pentatonic structure.)

This early directional notation indicates melodic movement through the use of a series of symbols, called *neumes*, which were placed above the words of the text. These neumes could indicate individual notes or incorporate two or three separate notes into one shape, known as a *compound neume*. Although the exact shapes varied from region to region, their meaning and intent remained the same throughout Europe. The following table gives a selection of the St. Gall form of the neumes, similar to those found in Facsimile 1-1.

Neumes:	Name	Shape	Equivalent meaning
	Virga		A single note of higher pitch
	Punctum		A single note of lower pitch
	Pes		
	Clivis		
	Torculus		
	Porrectus		
	Scandicus		
	Climacus		
Neumes implying special performance procedures			
	Quilisma		
	Liquescent		
	Oriscus		

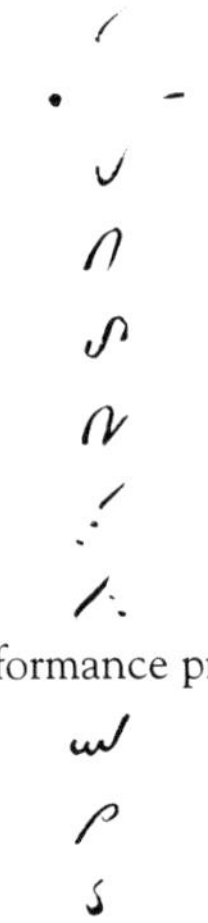

In this directional notation, using *nondiastematic* or unheightened neumes, the neume shapes indicate melodic direction but not interval size or any reference to tone-semitone arrangement. To fully understand this, the notation of *Viderunt omnes* in Facsimile 1-1, beginning on the sixth line of text, should be compared with that melody as given in Anthology Example 1.

This type of notation is known to exist by around 850 and may possibly date back to the time of Charlemagne. It seems an entirely Carolingian development and a part of that era's desire for codification and preservation. Notation would play a major role in the standardization and subsequent dissemination of Roman-Gallican chant.

The function of this early type of notation is to operate as a memory aid for melodies already known. One cannot use it to decipher an unknown melody. It is, nonetheless, not a primitive notation, but one that served its age well, as is proved by its continued use into the thirteenth century, long after the development of staff notation. It is particularly rich in the ability to indicate performance nuance, for, while imperfectly understood today, many of the neumes and accompanying letter symbols indicated elements of rhythm and vocal nuance.

Hucbald, writing around 900, although aware of the superiority of a precise pitch notation for teaching purposes, nevertheless defends directional notation:

> Yet the customary notes [the neumes] are not considered wholly unnecessary, since they are deemed quite serviceable in showing the slowness or speed of the melody, and where the sound demands a tremulous voice, or how the sounds are grouped together, or separated from each other, also where a cadence is made upon them,

lower or higher, according to the sense of certain letters—things of which these more scientific signs can show nothing whatsoever.[3]

The subsequent move to a precise notation of pitch was accordingly both a gain and a loss.

THE SOURCES

Although directional notation begins to appear occasionally by around 850, with completely notated chant manuscripts known by around 900, their non-diastematic notation makes them of little use in music analysis, except as they can be related to later, precisely pitched sources. Of these, *Mo H159*, a manuscript originally from Dijon but with the present location and shelf number of Montpellier, Faculté de Medicin, H 159, is of signal importance. Copied around 1000, it is notated in both nondiastematic neumes and letter notation, thus providing precise pitch notation as well as the performance directions of the neumatic notation. It is further useful in giving precise indications of b and b flat (not always carefully notated in medieval manuscripts) and also microtonal inflections above E and b.

Other eleventh-century sources quoted in the Anthology are from southern France (Aquitaine) and are now located in the Bibliothèque Nationale in Paris: latin 1118, 1121, 1338, and 1871. (Another important group of early manuscripts stems from in and around the monastery of St. Gall in modern-day Switzerland.)

Of equal or greater importance in understanding the early chant repertoire are a series of treatises written during the ninth and tenth centuries to explain aspects of chant theory. Several of these give examples in either a letter notation or in what is known as Dasien notation, which uses variants of Greek letters to indicate scale steps, including whole and half tones. These afford pitch-precise examples, while other treatises use directional neumes or merely refer to specified words from chants, which the reader is expected to reconstruct from memory.

The most important of these treatises are:

Aurelian of Reóme, *Musica disciplina* (ca. 843), directional neumes (possibly added later)

Anonymous, *Musica enchiriadis* and *Scholia enchiriadis* (late ninth century), Dasien notation

---

[3]Warren Babb, trans., *Hucbald, Guido, and John on Music*, ed. Claude V. Palisca (New Haven: Yale University Press, 1978), 37.

Hucbald, *De harmonica institutione* (ca. 900), Greek letter notation and neumes

Regino of Preum, *De harmonica institutione* (ca. 900), examples suggested by word citation

Anonymous, *Commemoratio brevis* (early tenth century), Dasien notation

Anonymous, *Alia musica* (early tenth century), examples suggested by word citation

Pseudo-Odo, *Enchiridion musices* (early eleventh century), letter notation

The primary modern editions of plainchant are the 1974 edition of the *Graduale Romanum* and the earlier *Antiphonale Monasticum* (see Bibliography). The first contains the music for the Mass, and the latter the music for the daytime monastic Offices. Earlier in the century, prior to Vatican II, the common source of plainchant was the *Liber Usualis*, a compilation of all the normal service music then needed in a parish. Although long out of print, it can be found in most libraries and is referred to frequently in musicological literature.[4]

Of even greater use to the serious student of early chant is the *Graduale Triplex*, a version of the *Graduale Romanum* of 1974 in which the square notation of the modern version is accompanied by the directional neumes of two different tenth- or eleventh-century versions, permitting direct comparison of early and late notational systems.

OTHER CHANT REPERTOIRES

Although the beginning of liturgical chant is lost in the dim, unrecorded past of the early Christian centuries, it is apparent that by around 600 several regional dialects of chant were in existence. We have already referred to two of these: the Gallican chant, which was suppressed by Charlemagne, and the Roman, which replaced it, although probably not without alteration. Let us look briefly at several other repertoires.

Ambrosian

Ambrosian is the chant idiom and liturgy of Milan and environs. It presumably was in existence before the Roman-Gallican merge, and remained

---

[4]Although these modern liturgical books are useful as an overview of the plainchant repertory and as an easy reference, they must be used with caution in historical study as they represent conflations of many medieval manuscripts and generally end up being true to no one of them. For this reason, while a variety of *Graduale Romanum* and *Antiphonale Monasticum* versions are used in the Anthology and the Practicum sections of the textbook, both in order to acquaint the student with the square notation and four-line staff of modern chant notation (which in itself affords an introduction to medieval notation) and to make comparison with other similar chants possible, the remaining plainsong repertory is taken from early medieval sources.

largely unaffected by it. It never adopted nor was modified by the system of the church modes and uses a very conjunct melodic idiom with a greater use of sequential passages than is found in Roman-Gallican. The underlying tonal structure is one that prefers leaps of fourths to those of a third or fifth.

Ambrosian continued as an oral idiom during Carolingian times and was committed to notation only in the twelfth century. It continued to resist suppression throughout the Middle Ages and Renaissance and still can be heard in Milan.

Mozarabic

Mozarabic (or *Old Spanish*) was the chant and liturgical idiom of Spain, which was officially suppressed in 1085, although it was revived in the fifteenth century and is still performed in a few areas, primarily Toledo. The early repertoire has come down to us in a number of manuscripts, but all in nondiastematic neumes, making re-creation of the repertoire impossible, especially as there is no provable connection between the earlier melodies and those of the fifteenth century.

Old Beneventan

Old Beneventan is the native chant of the Duchy of Benevento in south-central Italy. Although it began to be replaced by Roman-Gallican chant in the ninth century, part of the repertoire survived to appear as exceptional items in the earliest manuscripts from that area, two eleventh-century Graduals and a few other scattered manuscripts carrying a basically Roman-Gallican repertory.

Old Roman

Most interesting is the repertoire generally known as Old Roman, widely thought at one time to represent the idiom of the city churches of Rome, as distinct from the papal repertoire. Recent study, however, suggests instead that it may be an example of a continuing, oral tradition.

No trace of notated Old Roman chant exists from before the eleventh century, almost at the moment when it was being replaced by the Roman-Gallican and medieval chant from the North. The term "old" may be a misnomer because the repertoire is, at least in its notated form, about three centuries younger than the Roman-Gallican.

The most plausible explanation of the repertoire may be that what we call Old Roman and Roman-Gallican had a common ancestor in Roman chant of around 750. While this repertoire underwent modification when it was conveyed to the Franks, resulting in Roman-Gallican chant, it continued to be used in Rome, where it did not come into contact with Frankish influence. Instead, it remained an oral, unwritten performing tradition that was probably gradually modified according to changing taste and practice in Rome until its notation in the eleventh century, by which time it differed markedly from Roman-Gallican and, very possibly, from its eighth-century original.

Old Roman chant accordingly may give insight into a continuing oral tradition. Roman-Gallican melody often appears built on a pentatonic base and intervallic chains (whether so altered by the Franks or as part of its eighth-century Roman idiom); Old Roman melody is strongly conjunct and ornate, with even skips of thirds being decidedly rare.

Practicum

MODERN PLAINCHANT NOTATION

In order for the reader to gain access to the large repertory of plainchant that is contained in such modern chant books as the *Graduale Romanum* or the *Liber Usualis*, it is necessary to gain familiarity with the style of modern plainchant notation used there. This will also, incidentally, prove an easy introduction into the basic principles of medieval notation in general.

Modern plainchant notation is derived from thirteenth-century square notation, which uses square-shaped notes and neume shapes on a four-line staff. There are two moveable clefs: ⊧ , which designates middle c, and ⋕ , which designates the F below. (These would in time develop into our C and F clefs.) Note forms have no innate rhythmic value, with the result that ¶ , ■ , and ♦ all have the same meaning. Vertical lines through one or more lines of the staff indicate phrase divisions of varying importance, although most of these are modern interpolations. Lines above or below notes (for example, ⊤▪) and dots after notes indicate a lengthening of the duration, but again are modern additions attempting, imperfectly, to convey various lengthening signs found in the early manuscripts.

Compound neumes are shapes encompassing two or more notes sung to the same syllable and are read from left to right, except where one note occurs above another, in which case, the lower one is sung first. Typical neumes are given in Example 1-6.

Special Neume Shapes

Diagonal lines indicate only two notes, the ones at either end of the diagonal (for example, ◥ equals ▪ .).

Diamond-shaped notes have no special meaning, but form, in conjunction with the preceding square neume, a special neume shape that always appears in a downward pattern. Thus the configurations ¶♦♦ and ▌♦♦ are understood as composite neume shapes and would be transcribed ◜. and ◜◝. .

NAME	SHAPE	TRANSCRIPTION
Punctum		
Virga		
Podatus		
Clivus		
Scandicus		
Torculus		
Porrectus		
Climacus		
More complex forms:		

EXAMPLE 1-6. Neume Shapes in Square Notation and Their Transcription.

Liquescent neumes use a smaller note to indicate the liquescent (,). When interpreting these neumes, the liquescent is always performed last, the liquescent consonant it represents (such as l, m, or n) being pronounced on the way to the next syllable: would be sung . In the system of transcription used in the text and Anthology, an empty or void note-head is used to show the liquescent note. An alternate notation system is to use a tiny black notehead: .

The quilisma is a tremulous note that is almost always the middle note of an ascending third. It is indicated by a somewhat jagged note shape ( ). It may be transcribed with the sign .

Several repeated notes on the same pitch and syllable may have been sung tremolo (for example,).

A tiny note appearing at the end of a staff is a *custos*, which serves only to indicate the pitch of the first note on the following staff.

Chromatic Alterations

In plainchant, the only allowable chromatic alteration is the flatted b, indicted with the sign . It may appear somewhat ahead of the note it affects and sometimes seems a cue for a change of hexachord (see Chapter 3). The intended duration of the flat is not always clear. It may remain in force only until (1) a new word appears in the text, (2) a phrase mark appears, (3) a change of staff occurs in the original manuscript, or (4) it is cancelled by a natural sign.

Transcription

Example 1-7 will illustrate a method of transcription. The most useful modern clef is the transposing treble clef (ϕ) with middle c on the third space. Stemless noteheads are useful for transcription, with slurs indicating the original neumes.

Abbreviations

Other signs and abbreviations will occasionally be seen that have a peripheral musical meaning:

ij	means to repeat the previous phrase
*	indicates a change in performance from soloist to choir or from one side of the choir to the other in antiphonal chants
Ps or ℣	psalm verse (in distinction to the surrounding antiphon, respond, etc.)
℟	respond
E u o u a e	an abbreviation for the Latin words *Saeculorum Amen,* the end of the Doxology (the *Gloria patri*), the concluding formula to a psalm setting

Assignments

Transcribe the chants in Examples 1-8 and 1-9 into modern notation, or choose from Example 2-7 of the following chapter or Anthology Examples 11a, 12, or 13. Be careful to observe the placement of the clef sign. Neumes should be indicated through the use of slurs.

BIBLIOGRAPHY

Music

The primary modern chant books are mentioned above in the section on sources: the 1974 edition of the *Graduale Romanum* (Tournai: Desclée, 1974) and the *Antiphonale Monasticum* (Tournai: Desclée, 1934 and later years). The pre-Vatican II *Liber Usualis* was most widely disseminated in North America in the English language edition *The Liber Usualis with Introduction and Rubrics in English* (Tournai and New York: Desclée, 1952).

Unique among modern editions is the *Graduale Triplex* (Sablé-sur-Sarthe: Solesmes, 1979), a version of the *Graduale Romanum* of 1974 in which the square notation of the modern chant version is accompanied by the neumes of two tenth- or eleventh-century versions—those of Laon, Bibl. mun. 239, and of

EXAMPLE 1-7. Plainchant Transcripton. a. *Agnus Dei, Graduale Romanum*, p. 718. b. *Gloria, Graduale Romanum*, p. 716. © Abbaye Saint Pierre de Solesnes, France, 1974, reprinted by permission.

a representative member of the St. Gall family of manuscripts—making easy comparison possible.

Three medieval chant books are available in transcription into standard modern notation or modern chant notation: *H 159 Montpellier: Tonary of St. Bénigne of Dijon,* transcribed and annotated by Finn Egeland Hansen (Copenhagen, 1979), a unique tonary from around 1000 with complete chants in both letter and nondiastematic notation; Nancy van Deusen, *Music at Nevers Cathedral: Principal Sources of Medieval Chant,* Musicological Studies, Vol. 30 (Henryville, Pa.: Institute of Mediaeval Music, 1980), a twelfth-century West Frankish manuscript; and the *Graduale Sarisburiense* (London, 1894; rpt. Farnborough: Gregg Press, 1966) and *Antiphonale Sarisburiense* (London, 1901–26; rpt. Farnborough: Gregg Press, 1966), both edited by Walter H. Frere and containing the Mass and Office chants according to the rite of Sarum (Salisbury Cathedral), which had wide use throughout England and elsewhere.

Facsimiles of important medieval chant manuscripts are included in the series *Paléographie musicale: les principaux manuscrits de chant, grégorian, ambrosien, mozarabe, gallican,* 1st series, 20 vols. (Solesmes or Tournai, 1889–1958; rpt. Berne: Herbert Lang, 1968–74), 2nd series, 2 vol. (Tournai, 1900–1924; rpt. Berne: Herbert Lang, 1968–70).

The complete Sarum Procession and Mass for Easter is included in OAMM, while a reconstructed eleventh-century Matins service may be found in Donat R. Lamothe and Cyprian G. Constantine, *Matins at Cluny for the Feast of Saint Peter's Chains* (London: The Plainsong and Medieval Music Society, 1986).

Theory

Most of the relevant theory treatises are available in translation: Calvin M. Bower, "Boethius' 'The Principles of Music': An Introduction, Translation, and Commentary" (Ph.D. diss., UMI No. 67-15005); Joseph Ponte, trans., *Aurelian of Reóme (ca. 843): The Discipline of Music (Musica Disciplina),* Colorado College Translations No. 3 (Colorado Springs: Colorado College Music Press, 1968); Richard L. Holladay, "The 'Musica Enchiriadis' and the 'Scholia Enchiriadis': A Translation and Commentary" (Ph.D. diss., UMI No. 78-5855); Warren Babb, trans., *Hucbald, Guido, and John on Music,* ed. Claude V. Palisca (New Haven: Yale University Press, 1978); *Commemoratio brevis de tonis et psalmis modulandis,* trans. Terence Bailey (Ottawa: University of Ottawa Press, 1979); Edmund B. Heard, " 'Alia Musica': A Chapter in the History of Medieval Music Theory" (Ph.D. diss., UMI No. 66-13798); Pseudo-Odo, "Enchiridion musices," in Strunk, 103–16.

Modal theory from Aurelian to around 1500 is summarized in detail in Frederick Sturges Andrews, "Medieval Modal Theory" (Ph.D. diss., Cornell University, 1935).

Readings

Most modern research stems from Peter Wagner's *Einführung in die gregorianischen Melodien* (Leipzig, 1895–1921), of which only the first volume has been

Ps. 32, 11. 19 et 1

COGITA - TI - ONES * Cor- dis e- ius

in ge- ne- ra- ti- ó- ne et ge- ne- ra-

ti- ó- nem : ut é- ru- at a mor- te á- nimas e-

ó- rum et a- lat e- os in fa- me.

T. P. Alle- lú- ia, al- le- lú- ia.

EXAMPLE 1-8. Introit Antiphon, G.R., p. 384. © Abbaye Saint Pierre de Solesmes, France, 1974, reprinted by permission.

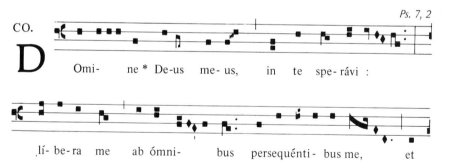

Ps. 7, 2

CO.

DOmi- ne * De- us me- us, in te spe- rávi :

lí- be- ra me ab ómni- bus persequénti- bus me, et

EXAMPLE 1-9. Communion Antiphon, G.R., p. 87. © Abbaye Saint Pierre de Solesmes, France, 1974, reprinted by permission.

translated into English: *Introduction to the Gregorian Melodies: Origin and Development of the Forms of the Liturgical Chant up to the End of the Middle Ages* (London, 1901; rpt. New York: Da Capo Press, 1986). The most complete treatment in English is Willi Apel, *Gregorian Chant* (Bloomington, Ind.: Indiana University Press, 1958), although it is based on modern versions of the chants and is now somewhat dated.

An excellent exposition of the changing nature of mode is that of Harold S. Powers, in the article "Mode" in *NGD*, vol. 12.

Two recent studies of the underlying tonal structure of plainchant are Finn Egeland Hansen, *The Grammar of Gregorian Tonality: An Investigation Based on the Repertory in Codex H 159, Montpellier* (Copenhagen: Dann Fog, 1979), which stresses pentatonicism, and Hendrik van der Werf, *The Emergence of Gregorian Chant*, Vol. 1 (Rochester: the author, 1983), which investigates intervallic chains.

François Gevaért's early study of melody types, *La mélopée antique dans le chant de l'église latine* (Gand: Librairie Générale de Ad. Hoste, 1895), although confused in his search for ancient Greek relationships, is still a basic starting point for the study of melody types.

Two current theories concerning the early history of the chant are summarized in Helmut Hucke, "Toward a New Historical View of Gregorian Chant" *JAMS* 33 (1980): 437–67, and David G. Hughes, "Evidence for the Traditional View of the Transmission of Gregorian Chant," *JAMS* 40 (1987): 377–404.

The problem of musical transmission in an oral culture has been extensively pursued by Leo Treitler in a series of articles: "Homer and Gregory: The Transmission of Epic Poetry and Plainchant," *MQ* 60 (1974): 368–72; "Oral, Written, and Literate Process in the Transmission of Medieval Music," *Speculum* 56 (1981): 471–91; "The Early History of Music Writing in the West," *JAMS* 35 (1982): 237–79; "Reading and Singing: On the Genesis of Occidental Music-Writing," *EMH* 4 (1984): 135–208; and, with Ritva Jonsson, "Medieval Music and Language: a Reconsideration of the Relationship," in *Studies in the History of Music*, Vol. 1, *Music and Language* (New York: Broude Bros., 1983).

For a comprehensive study of early neume forms, see Dom Cardine, *Gregorian Semiology*, trans. Robert M. Fowels (Solesmes: Abbaye Saint-Pierre de Solesmes, 1982). Speculation on the origin of notation is included in Kenneth Levy's "Charlemagne's Archetype of Gregorian Chant," *JAMS* 40 (1987): 1–30; and "On the Origin of Neumes," *EMH* 7 (1987): 59–90.

Introductions to the other chant dialects include: for Ambrosian, Terence Bailey, *The Ambrosian Alleluias* (Englefield Green: Plainsong and Medieval Music Society, 1983); for Mozarabic, Don Randel, *The Responsorial Psalm Tones of the Mozarabic Office* (Princeton, N.J.: Princeton University Press, 1963); for Beneventan, Thomas Forest Kelly, "Montecassino and the Old Beneventan Chant," *EMH* 5 (1985): 53–84; and for Old Roman, Paul F. Cutter, "Oral Transmission of the Old-Roman Responsories?" *MQ* 62 (1976): 182–94, and Edward Nowacki, "The Gregorian Office Antiphons and the Comparative Method," *JoM* 4 (1985–86): 243–75.

For Eastern chant, see Egon Wellesz, *A History of Byzantine Music and Hymnography*, 2nd ed. (London: Oxford University Press, 1961).

2

Liturgy and Chant

The history of music through much of the Middle Ages must necessarily focus on the music of the church. The secular music of the day is unknown to us, long lost in oblivion. In addition, and even more importantly, it was the church and its singers who carefully created not only voluminous quantities of music but also a theoretical system to explain it and a notational system to preserve it. It was this that was to color the music of Europe for centuries to come.

Plainchant, beautiful as its sinuous lines may be, is fundamentally functional music. Its duty is to beautify and adorn the worship of God in the context of the liturgy, and we must turn our attention to that context if we are to comprehend fully the music of these early centuries.

The Western church, as all ancient Christian churches, guided its yearly worship through a cyclical celebration of the most important events of the life of Christ. In the West this *liturgical year* begins four Sundays before Christmas with Advent, leading to the celebration of the birth of Christ, the Christ-Mass or Christmas. This first cycle of the liturgical year then continues with the Feast of the Circumcision of Our Lord on January 1 and Epiphany (the manifestation of Christ to the Wise Men) on January 6, and it concludes with the Feast of the Presentation of Jesus (later shifted in emphasis to the Purification of Mary) on February 2.

A second, longer cycle marks the closing events of Christ's life, including the Crucifixion and Resurrection: the three Sundays before Lent, the forty days of Lent culminating in Palm Sunday, Holy Week, and Easter, followed at a distance of another forty days by the Feast of the Ascension and, ten days later, Pentecost (to which were later added Trinity Sunday and Corpus Christi).

The first of these cycles is anchored on a firm date, December 25, as Christmas. The second, centered on an Easter celebration that changes according to the phases of the moon, may begin as early as January 18 or as late as February 21. As a result there is a variable number of Sundays (from one to six) between Epiphany and Septuagesima, the first of the prescribed Sundays before Lent. Also variable is the length of the long period during the summer and fall between Pentecost and Advent (twenty-four to twenty-nine Sundays).

Many additional feasts, commemorating various saints, are spread throughout the year and interact with the larger, Christ-oriented cycles. This complete liturgical year determines the chants of the individual Sundays and feasts of the year.

THE DIVINE OFFICES

Worship in the medieval church took two primary forms: the *Mass*, the most public of the services, and the *Divine Offices* or *Liturgical Hours*, a series of eight daily services beginning shortly after midnight and ending at the time of retiring to bed. The eight Offices are:

Matins	After midnight, often between two and three A.M.
Lauds	At daybreak
Prime	Shortly after
Terce	Third hour of daylight
Sext	Sixth hour of daylight
None	Ninth hour of daylight
Vespers	Sunset
Compline	Before retiring

This round of worship and prayer continues throughout the year as a relatively continuous offering of praise. The individual services consist largely of the singing of psalms; all 150 psalms of the Bible are included in each weekly cycle, joined with other biblical and nonbiblical texts.

The medieval day was measured from sunrise to sunset, and Compline would occur between six and eight o'clock, depending on the season of the year. Matins would begin some seven hours later, while the sky was still dark, as a lengthy nocturnal vigil.

Daybreak was celebrated with Lauds, while the four Day Offices—Prime, Terce, Sext and None, occurring as brief pauses within the regular activities of the day—were relatively short and simple. Vespers at twilight, however, afforded a more extended opportunity for pause and reflection, a solemn service of thanksgiving and praise at the end of day, followed shortly by Compline and sleep. Of these eight Offices, the most important from the musical point of view are Vespers and Matins, the longest and most complex of the Offices and the ones that subsequently came to be embellished with polyphony.

Vespers, taking the form used in nonmonastic churches as an example, has as its main section the singing of five psalms, each preceded and concluded with a refrain called an *antiphon*. This is then followed by a short reading, a hymn, prayers, and the *Benedicamus Domino*. (The monastic Office differs in reducing the number of psalms to four, but adding a Great Responsory and the *Magnificat*.)

Matins begins with an introductory section, followed by one to three *nocturns*, their number and specific content depending on the day (Sunday, feast, or weekday) and location (monastic or nonmonastic). Each nocturn comprises a series of psalms with antiphons that leads into the reading of one to four lessons, each followed by the singing of a Great Responsory. The entire Office ends, if a Sunday or designated feast, with the singing of the hymn *Te Deum*. A complete Matins service can be expected to include, depending on the occasion, the singing of fourteen to twenty-two psalms and three to twelve Great Responsories and lessons. The texts used in the readings and responsories are wide-ranging, including the prophetic and historical books of the Bible, the lives of saints, and writings of the church fathers. Matins provides a lengthy time of meditation before the day's activities.

Celebration of the Offices began in the monasteries but had spread long before Carolingian times to the nonmonastic clergy as well. It formed an intimate part of the life of monk and priest alike.

Rhymed Offices

In the later Middle Ages the composition of special Offices, each commemorating a particular saint, became commonplace as new canonizations increased the number of saint's days in the church calendar. These Offices most often consist of (1) prose lessons relating the life of the saint and (2) antiphons and responds in the form of rhymed poetry set either to new music or to revisions of older chants. Indicative of a late medieval desire for order, many of these new *rhymed Offices* arrange the antiphons and responds in modal order: authentic Protus, plagal Protus, authentic Deuterus, plagal Deuterus, and so on.

THE MASS

In contrast to the Offices, the Mass was intended from its earliest development to include all believers, laity and clergy alike. As such it was a combination of two early Christian practices, a service of scripture and prayer and the observation of the Eucharist. This gradually became more formalized as the church grew more powerful and independent, and was established in general form by around 600, although agreement on matters of detail has never been totally achieved.

The first section of the Mass, the Fore-Mass or Mass of the Catechumens (because it is open to those not yet baptized), is an expansion of the early Christian service of prayer and teaching, to which has been added a prominent use of psalms. The concluding portion, the Eucharist (Holy Communion), is the celebration of the Lord's Supper.

In addition to this bipartite structure, the Mass consists also of an inter-weaving of set texts used at every celebration (the *Ordinary*) and others that change from day to day and are thus "proper" to the particular service (the *Proper*). While composers of the Renaissance paid most attention to ornate settings of the Ordinary, the Middle Ages paid more attention to the Proper, both in settings in plainchant and as a basis for polyphony.

The following codification of the Mass is that of around 1000. The musically important chants are given in italics.

THE MASS

Proper	Ordinary

THE FORE-MASS

Proper	Ordinary
Introit	
	Kyrie
	Gloria
Collect	
Epistle	
Gradual	
Alleluia or *Tract*	
(*Sequence*)	
Gospel	
Sermon (optional)	
	Credo

THE EUCHARIST

Proper	Ordinary
Offertory	
	Offertory Prayers
Secret	
Preface	
	Sanctus
	Canon
	Pater noster
	Agnus Dei
Communion	
	Prayers
Postcommunion	
	Ite, missa est
	or *Benedicamus domino*

The Mass is a combination of standard and variable chants and recited texts. Aurelian of Reóme, writing around 843, discusses these Mass chants, giving some idea of the emotional context of each.

The Mass . . . consists of antiphons that are called *Introits*, so named because they are sung as the people enter the basilica. The singing of the Introit is prolonged until, in undisturbed order, both the bishop and the other clerical ranks, each according to his dignity, have entered the church and taken their respective positions. And thus, finally, after the litany has been finished in which God and Christ are called upon to have mercy on His people [the *Kyrie*], the priest, imitating the angel who announced glory to God in the heavens and peace on earth to men, intones the same chant with the voice of salvation [the *Gloria*].

There is also sung a response that is called the *Gradual*, a name applied to it from *gradus* (step), since it was customary for the ancients to stand upon steps when either singing or speaking [it]. . . .

The *Alleluia*, however, we took from the Jews, whose language, in fact, it is; it is said to mean praise to God, which, in accordance with its dignity, has not been translated into any other language. It is fittingly sung before the Gospel, so that by this chant the minds of the faithful may in some way begin to be purified for hearing the word of salvation.

The songs that the church sings over the sacrifices offered to the Lord are called *Offertories*; this it does in imitation of the ancient fathers, who were admonished: *if ever you should have a feast and festival days, blow upon the trumpets over your sacrifices, and the memory of you will be before God* (Numbers 10:10).

For the communicants, the first chant that is sung is: *Agnus Dei, qui tollis peccata mundi, miserere nobis* [Lamb of God, Who takest away the sins of the world, have mercy upon us], so that all the faithful communicating on the body and blood of the Lord, Whom they receive by mouth, may drink with the melody of the singing, and within themselves may contemplate crucified, dead, and buried, Him Whom they taste, in some way transformed into physical food, and may entreat to take away their sins Him Whom the whole church avows to have come for that purpose.

There is also sung, joined to that preceding, another song, which is called the *Communion*; so that, as long as the faithful people receive heavenly benediction, their minds may be drawn by the sweet melody and suspended in sublime contemplation.[1]

Missing from his account are two chants of the Ordinary, the *Sanctus* and the *Credo*. In the case of the first of these—the cry of the angels, "Holy, holy, holy, Lord God of Hosts"—the omission was probably unintentional, for the *Sanctus* had been widely accepted from at least the sixth century. The *Credo*—

---

[1]Joseph Ponte, trans., *Aurelian of Reóme (ca. 843): The Discipline of Music (Musica Disciplina)*, Colorado College Translations No. 3 (Colorado Springs: Colorado College Music Press, 1968), 54–55.

the Nicean Creed, the Christian statement of belief—was not accepted in the Mass until later, finally being incorporated into the Roman Mass only in the eleventh century.

THE CHANTS OF THE MASS PROPER AND OF THE OFFICES

The diverse meanings and purposes behind the different parts of the Mass and Office called forth a variety of musical forms. These are grouped here not in liturgical order but according to similarities of musical structure.

Liturgical Recitative and Psalmody

Liturgical recitative. The recitation of prayers and scripture readings proceeds in a very simple style consisting of a single recitation tone with one or two nearby tones used to mark the phrase structure of the text. Example 2-1 illustrates a setting of a text from the Gospel as it is sung in Mass. This type of recitation is almost devoid of modal character.

Psalm tones. Most ubiquitous of the musical idioms are the tones for the psalms, a prominent feature not only of the Offices but also of the Introit, Communion, and possibly at one time the Offertory of the Mass. The typical psalm verse falls into two halves: a first phrase, which makes a statement, and a concluding phrase, which parallels the first: "Blessed is the man that feareth the Lord: that delighteth greatly in His commandments." The body of each phrase is chanted on a designated reciting tone, while phrase punctuation is shown through melodic inflections.

An example of Introit psalmody may be seen in Anthology Example 2a— the Easter Introit *Resurrexi*, beginning at the designation *Ps* and the words *Domine, probasti me*. The first phrase begins with an intonation on the word *Domine*, continues with the *reciting tone* on the words *probasti me*, and concludes with the *mediant*, an internal, nonconclusive cadence, on the words *et cognovisti me*. The second phrase uses similar components: intonation (*tu co-*), reciting tone (*-gnovisti sessionem meam, et resurrecti-*), and closing *termination* (*onem meam*).

An Introit or Communion psalm tone thus consists of six parts: intonation, reciting tone, mediant; intonation, reciting tone, and termination (see Example 2-2).

Most psalm settings conclude with an added Doxology: *Gloria Patri et Filio, et Spiritui Sancto. Sicut erat in principio, et nunc et semper, et in saecula seculorum, Amen.* (Glory to the Father and the Son and the Holy Spirit. As it was in the beginning, is now and ever shall be, world without end, amen.) In the Introit,

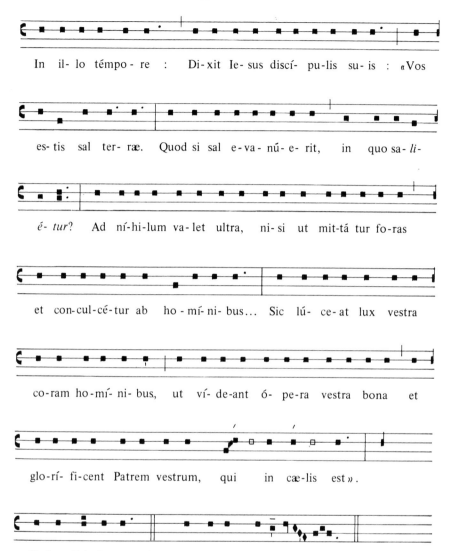

In il-lo témpo-re : Di-xit Ie-sus discí-pu-lis su-is : «Vos

es-tis sal ter-ræ. Quod si sal e-va-nú-e-rit, in quo sa-*li-*

é-tur? Ad ní-hi-lum va-let ultra, ni-si ut mit-tá tur fo-ras

et con-cul-cé-tur ab ho-mí-ni-bus... Sic lú-ce-at lux vestra

co-ram ho-mí-ni-bus, ut ví-de-ant ó-pe-ra vestra bona et

glo-rí-fi-cent Patrem vestrum, qui in cæ-lis est».

Verbum Dómi- ni. R̟. Laus ti-bi, Christe.

At that time Jesus said to his disciples: "Ye are the salt of the earth. But if the salt has lost its savour, how shall it be salted? It is good for nothing, but to be cast out and trodden under foot by men. . . . Let your light so shine before men, that they may see your good works and glorify your Father, who is in heaven." This is the word of the Lord.
Praise be to thee, O Christ.

EXAMPLE 2-1. Liturgical Recitative, *Graduale Romanum*, pp. 805–806. © Abbaye Saint Pierre de Solesmes, France, 1974, reprinted with permission.

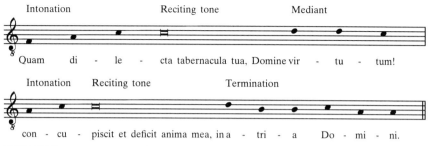

EXAMPLE 2-2.   Introit Psalm Tone (Authentic Tritus).

this is set as three phrases through the technique of concluding the second phrase with the psalm tone mediant and beginning the third phrase the same way as the second (see Example 2-3).

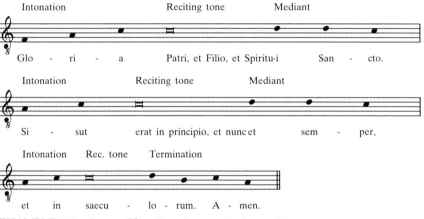

EXAMPLE 2-3.   Introit *Gloria Patri* Setting (Authentic Tritus).

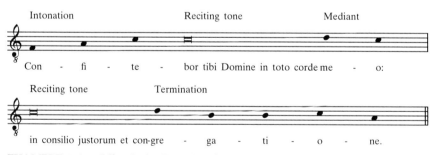

EXAMPLE 2-4.   Office Psalm Tone (Authentic Tritus).

Office psalm tones are simpler, omitting the second intonation and beginning the second half of the psalm verse directly on the reciting tone (see Example 2-4).

An additional element, the *flex,* may be added as an internal punctuation when a long first phrase is divided into two subphrases, as in the verse "He hath made a memorial of his wondrous works, the Lord is merciful and gracious: he hath given food to them that fear him" (see Example 2-5).

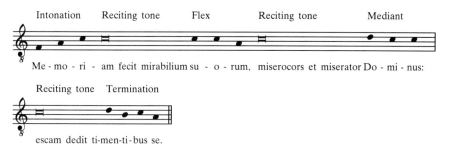

EXAMPLE 2-5. Office Psalm Tone with Flex (Authentic Tritus).

The use of the modal reciting tone is the most conspicuous feature of the psalm tones. It is, however, only one of the identifying features of psalmody. Another characteristic is the opening intonation, which varies according to mode. The intonation for each mode is given below:

Protus authentic	F G a	
Protus plagal	C D F	
Deuterus authentic	G a c	(G a b in some early sources)
Deuterus plagal	a G a	(E G a in some medieval sources)
Tritus authentic	F a c	
Tritus plagal	F G a	
Tetrardus authentic	c b c d	
Tetrardus plagal	G a c	

The termination of the psalm tone shows the greatest variance. This is due to the need to make a smooth connection with the antiphon which follows. Inasmuch as many antiphons do not begin on the modal final, various *differentiae* or alternate cadential motives are supplied for each psalm tone. The differentiae for the Introits are given in the *Graduale Romanum* (pages 822–24) and the *Liber Usualis* (pages 14–16), while Office psalm differentiae are notated in the *Antiphonale Monasticum* (pp. 1210–18) and the *Liber Usualis* (pp. 112–17).

Antiphonal Chants

Psalm tones are normally sung with the choir divided into two halves, singing verses or half-verses in alternation. The psalm is preceded and concluded with a free melodic refrain called the *antiphon,* which in early times was often repeated between each verse. In diagram, the resulting form would be:

$$A \ V1 \ A \ V2 \ A \ V3 \ A \ldots D \ A$$

where A refers to the antiphon; V1, V2, and so on to the various psalm verses; and D to the Doxology, the *Gloria patri.* In the later Middle Ages the antiphon simply frames the entire psalm:

$$A \ V1 \ V2 \ V3 \ldots D \ A$$

The term *antiphonal* refers, then, to two things: the alternation between antiphon and psalm verses, and the alternating performance between the two sides of the choir. Two important antiphonal chants in the Mass are the *Introit* and the *Communion.*

Introit.   As Aurelian explains, the Introit, the introductory chant of the Mass, initially functioned as a processional sung while the priests and higher clergy entered the church, continuing during the sometimes elaborate preparations for the celebration of the Mass at the altar. At first it consisted of the singing of an entire psalm with alternation of antiphon and psalm tone. Later, as many of the preparations for Mass came to be done before the Introit, it lost the need for great length and was shortened first by omitting the repetitions of the antiphon between the verses, and then by reducing the number of verses sung.

By the later Middle Ages it had lost its processional character and was reduced to a single verse: A V A D A or A V D A (see Anthology Example 2).

Communion.   The Communion in Carolingian times was identical in construction to the Introit: an antiphon framing the singing of a psalm to an appropriate psalm tone. Aurelian describes the Communion at the time in liturgical history when it still fulfilled its original purpose: to be sung while the people took communion. By the eleventh and twelfth centuries, however, the opportunities for the public taking of communion had become extremely restricted, Easter being the only required observance in the thirteenth century. With this change, the position of the chant was shifted to follow rather than accompany the Eucharist, and its form shortened, being reduced from an entire psalm to only the antiphon, without verse (see Anthology Example 3).

Office antiphons.   In the Offices, antiphons are used throughout to frame the numerous psalms. Because the antiphons change as the year progresses, while the cycle of psalms is repeated week by week, the relationship of antiphon to psalm changes continuously. Emotionally and theologically the effect is to emphasize, through the particular text of the antiphon, one or another specific aspect of the psalm. Musically, the connection between antiphon and psalm tone is made by letting the mode of the antiphon determine that of the psalm. A smooth return to the antiphon is made by choosing an appropriate differentiae. It was precisely the need to ensure a close musical and tonal connection between the psalm tones and their constantly changing antiphons that lay behind much of the early impetus for modal classification.

Responsorial Chants

Responsorial psalmody is based on the concept of a congregational or choral response to a solo performance of a psalm. In the early church it might take the simple form of a one- or two-word congregational response between verses of a psalm or litany: *alleluia*; *kyrie eleison*. By the ninth century it had become exclusively a choral response to a soloist who sang the psalm verses. In the Mass, it governs the form of the *Gradual* and the *Alleluia*, while in the Offices there are the *Great* and *Short Responsories*.

Gradual. The Gradual initially appeared between the reading of the Old Testament lesson and the Epistle. After the dropping of the Old Testament lesson, it joined the Alleluia as the first of two elaborate musical commentaries on the lessons, appearing between the readings of the Epistle and the Gospel.

Although consisting of refrain and verse, the Gradual is different from the Introit in several important aspects.

One is in the verse, which is not choral but sung by a soloist, and which does not follow a psalm tone but is an elaborate, free setting of the psalm verse. Another is the nature of the choral *respond*, the name given to the refrain in responsorial chant. It is the most elaborate and melismatic of all the chant forms, with melismas of sometimes twenty or thirty notes. As the Gradual uses only a single psalm verse without Doxology, the resulting form is:

solo intonation and choral respond

solo verse

choral respond

The melodic construction of the Gradual differs from that of the chants studied heretofore in its use of a formulaic approach, one which uses standardized phrases common to many other Graduals in the same mode. This formulaic approach is similar to one found in oral storytelling, where the poet-singer does not memorize every word but rather uses a common stock of descriptive formulas to flesh out a story remembered in outline. Originally improvised, the Graduals in a given mode came to be highly interrelated by the time they were written down. This may be seen through a partial comparison of two Graduals in authentic Tritus.

The verse of Anthology Example 1, the Christmas Gradual *Viderunt omnes*, makes use of five common melodic formulas. They may be charted as follows (*x* indicating free material):

a   b   c d e   x

Notum fecit Do———minus salutare suum:

e   f   g

ante conspectum gentium revelavit justitiam suam.

Example 2-6 gives a partial comparison of that verse with the verse of another authentic Tritus Gradual, *Omnes de Saba.* Here it can be seen that melodic segments (formulas) b and d are common to both, while formulas a and c, although common to other Graduals in Tritus, are present only in *Viderunt omnes.* In phrase 3, formula d returns in *Omnes de Saba,* while *Viderunt* has nonformulaic material. Formula e is then used by both.[2]

Graduals are found in only five modes: authentic Protus, authentic and plagal Deuterus, authentic Tritus, and authentic Tetrardus; each mode has its own group of melodic formulas. In addition, there is a special group of nineteen highly interrelated Graduals labeled by Apel as the Gradual-type *Justus et palma* (see Apel, pp. 357–62).

Although the formulaic style used in the Graduals is often referred to as "centonization," that term seems to imply a conscious patching together of pieces of melody, an implication more suitable to a literate age than to the oral, nonliterate culture of the Middle Ages. It is better thought of as "formulaic singing," the use and reuse of an appropriate group of melodic formulas within a tightly knit group of chants.

Alleluia.   As Aurelian notes, the word *alleluia* came from the Hebrew as an acclamation of praise. Used as such by the early church, it was later combined with one or two psalm verses.

The first section, sung on the single word *alleluia,* is first stated by a soloist then repeated by the choir, which prolongs the melody with a textless melisma called the *jubilus.* The verse continues with new (but often related) material and, in the great majority of cases, concludes with the melody of either the jubilus or the entire alleluia. After this, the alleluia and jubilus are repeated by the choir with or without the solo beginning:

> Solo alleluia
> Choral alleluia and jubilus
> Solo verse (often with choral conclusion)
> [Solo alleluia]
> Choral alleluia and jubilus

Alleluias do not use the formulaic style of the Graduals. Instead, indicative of their generally more recent origin, they display a highly integrated melodic style with much internal repetition.

This may be seen in Anthology Example 4, the *Alleluia: Angelus domini, Respondens,* for Easter Monday. The alleluia and jubilus consists of three melodic movements: C to G, G to C, and C to G. These may be labeled phrases *a, b,*

---

[2]For a fuller discussion and listing of the formulas, see Apel, *Gregorian Chant,* 344–63. In order to relate the above analysis to the formulas given on pp. 348 and 349 there, it may be noted that *a* equals Apel's i_1; *b,* the first half of M; *c,* the conclusion of M; *d,* the first half of $c_1 0$ and the first half of $a_1 7$; *e,* $a_1 7$; *f,* $F_1 2$; *g,* $F_1 3$; *h,* the conclusion of $c_1 0$.

Phrase 1.

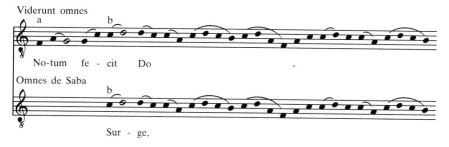

Phrase 3.

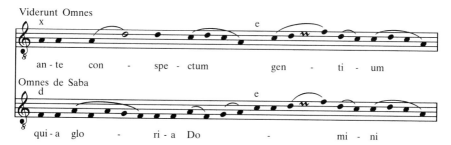

EXAMPLE 2-6. Partial Comparison of Verses, Graduals *Viderunt omnes* and *Omnes de Saba*, following *Mo* H159. For modern versions of the complete chants, see G.R., pp. 48 and 57 or L.U., p. 409 and 459. Melodic formulas are indicated by the letters a through e, while x indicates free material.

and *c* for the purposes of our analysis. Movement throughout the alleluia is stepwise except for the skip in the second phrase (which is filled in most other medieval versions—see for instance the versions contained in the lower voices of Anthology Examples 17 and 26).

Much of the music of the psalm verse is derived from the Alleluia. Twice within the first verse, beginning at the words *et accedens* and again at *et sedebat*, the alleluia and jubilus melody returns. In the first portion of the verse, *Angelus domini* is sung to a variant of alleluia phrase *a*, while the melody of *descendit* moves into a higher register by leaping from the G final to the reciting tone c. The F-G-G cadence at the end of *descendit* reiterates both the cadence of *domini* and alleluia phrase *a*. Finally, *de caelo* outlines the descent of alleluia phrase *b*.

The second verse gives insight into the manner of accommodating chant motives to textual changes. Although this verse is, like the first, in two sections, the first section in verse 2 is longer, containing nineteen syllables instead of the twelve of verse 1. In the musical setting, phrase 1, *Respondens autem angelus*, traces and expands the same movement as the *Angelus domini* of verse 1. Notes are also added to phrases 2 and 3 (*dixit mulieribus: / quem queritus?*).

Changes of a different sort occur in the second half of the two verses. In verse 1, the type of melismatic expansion begun on *descendit* is continued into the phrases on *accedens, revolvit,* and *lapidem*, using the complete alleluia melody. The neumatic style of alleluia phrase 1 is then resumed on *Et sedebat*, leaving *eum* to be sung melismatically to the jubilus melody. In verse 2, however, the use of melisma is avoided entirely and the second part continues in the neumatic style established in the first half. As verse 2 has fewer syllables in section 2 than verse 1 (thirteen instead of eighteen), the text is completed by the end of the alleluia plus jubilus; the jubilus only, without a repeat of alleluia phrase 1, is used to complete the verse. The entire Alleluia can be diagrammed:

	a b c
	Alleluia: ——— .
	a′ d e
Verse 1	Angelus domini descendit de caelo:
	a b c a b c
	et accedens revolvit lapidem, et sedebat super eum——— .
	a″ d′ e
Verse 2	Respondens autem angelus dixit mulieribus: quem queritus?
	a b c b c
	il le autem dixerunt: hiesum nazarenum——— .

Anthology Example 5, *Alleluia: Adorabo ad templum*, shows a less tightly constructed form. The first part of the verse has no direct quotations from the Alleluia. There is, however, internal repetition (in the melisma on [*confi*]*tebor*), and the presence of descending fourths and the melodic shape ◢▙ and its inversion make subtle reference to the motivic material of the Alleluia. The complete Alleluia and jubilus return at the end of the verse on (*no*)*mini tuo.*

Offertory.   Although there is some disagreement, the Offertory should most likely be placed among the responsorial chants. The conflicting evidence centers on Aurelian, who around 843 states that the psalm verse should be sung to a psalm tone, whereas certainly by the tenth century (and possibly earlier—for there is other evidence that contradicts Aurelian) the verses were sung to ornate free melodies, there being sometimes one, more often two or three verses to each Offertory (Anthology Example 6a). The Offertory is also unique among chants in permitting text repetition within the chant.

Originally sung in connection with the receipt of offerings before the Eucharist, when performed complete with verses it can be one of the longest and most beautiful of all the chants. By the twelfth century, however, the Offertory had suffered the same fate as the Communion, and was shorn of its verses in the interest of brevity.

Great Responsory.   Great Responsories are the most important feature of the Matins Office, one being sung after each lesson, a position analogous to the placement of the Gradual after the Epistle reading at Mass.

The Great Responsory differs from the Gradual in using a highly ornate responsorial tone for the verse and in often repeating only the latter portion of the respond, the *repetendum,* between verses. Amalarus of Metz reports the following ninth-century Roman practice:

Respond:	Solo
Respond:	Chorus
Verse:	Solo
Respond:	Chorus
Doxology:	Solo
Repetendum:	Chorus
Respond:	Solo
Respond:	Chorus

This seems to have been simplified in Frankish practice to:

Respond:	Solo intonation and choral continuation
Verse:	Solo:
Repetendum:	Chorus
	or
Respond:	Solo intonation and choral continuation
Verse:	Solo
Repetendum:	Chorus
Doxology:	Solo
Repetendum:	Chorus

(The Doxology is sung only in the last responsory in each nocturn, and then only in shortened form: *Gloria Patri et Filio et Spiritui Sancto.*)

In some cases the repetendum begins later in the respond upon each repetition. This can be seen in the elaborate *Aspiciens a longe* of Anthology Example 7, a Great Responsory with three verses and Doxology drawn from a manuscript in Salisbury Cathedral. In this, the complete respond is sung at the beginning and end, while progressively shortened versions of the repetendum follow each verse and the Doxology. (In performance, this and other Salisbury manuscripts assign the opening "solo" intonation of the respond and also the Doxology to three boys standing on the choir steps, while the verses are sung by one or another of the boys solo. The remainder of the respond and all of the repetenda are performed by the full choir.)

Many respond melodies are constructed, like the Graduals, from common melodic phrases or formulas. Other responds, such as the one of *Aspiciens a longe,* are freely composed without reference to formulas. Another group (including over fifty in plagal Protus) are textual adaptations of a single standard melody.

Verses and Doxology are sung to a set of extremely elaborate *responsorial tones* (given in *NGD* 15:762). The six elements of the authentic Tetrardus tone may be seen in verse 1 of *Aspiciens a longe*: intonation (*Quique*), ornamented reciting tone (*terrigene et*), mediant (*filii hominum*); second intonation (*simul*), ornamented reciting tone (*in unam*), and termination (*dives et pauper*). The succeeding verses and the Doxology are shorter and accordingly less complete:

Verse 1:	intonation, reciting tone, mediant;
	second intonation, reciting tone, termination.
Verse 2:	intonation, mediant;
	second intonation, reciting tone, termination.
Verse 3:	intonation, reciting tone, mediant;
	reciting tone, termination.
Doxology:	intonation, mediant;
	reciting tone, termination.

Unlike the consistent reciting tones of the psalm tones, the responsorial tones use different reciting tones in each half of the verse (c and d in the case of the authentic Tetrardus chant discussed here).

Texts in the Great Responsories differ from the other responsorial forms in being taken largely from the historical or prophetic books of the Bible or early Christian sacred writings, rather than from the psalms.

Short Responsories. In considerable contrast to the Great Responsories of Matins are the Short Responsories used in the brief Offices of Prime, Terce, Sext, None, and Compline. They are syllabic and consist of two short phrases which introduce a half verse of a psalm. The complete Responsory may take the form R R V R′ D R, in which R stands for the complete respond, R′ for its second phrase, V for the verse, and D for the short doxology. Even more concise is the form used at Sext and None: R V D. In recent times three primary melodies were used throughout the year, one each for Advent, the Easter season, and for the rest of the year. The medieval repertoire was considerably more varied.

Tract

The *Tract* is a unique type of psalmody, independent of a surrounding antiphon or respond, called *direct psalmody*. It differs in many ways from the psalm tones, not the least in being soloistic rather than choral.

The Tract, which is not mentioned by Aurelian, is used in the Mass only at certain times of penance, primarily Lent, when it replaces the Alleluia. It is a setting of from two to fourteen psalm verses in an ornate, highly formulaic style.

Tracts appear in only two modes: plagal Protus and plagal Tetrardus. In each, the musical shape of the verse is guided by a predetermined sequence of cadential tones: D, C, F, D in Protus; G, F, G or G, F, G, G (depending on the number of phrases) in Tetrardus. Within each phrase, the melody moves toward the expected cadential goal using common melodic formulas shared with other Tracts of the same mode.

Anthology Examples 8 and 9 present two of the five Tracts for Holy Saturday. These and the other three use the same seven melodic phrases, although not always in the same order, and alter them when necessary to accommodate the changing text.

Comparing the two Tracts phrase by phrase will clarify the structure. *Graduale Romanum* versions have been used to aid comparison with the remaining three Holy Saturday Tracts: *Cantemus Domino* (GR, pp. 186–87; LU, 776R), *Attende caelum* (GR, pp. 189–90; LU, 776U), and *Sicut cervus* (given as Example 2-11 below).

To aid in the analysis, the phrases of the Anthology Examples have been marked with a special set of symbols: G or F to indicate the cadential note of the phrase; subscript 1, 2, or 3 to indicate the first, second, and third phrases with that cadential note; and subscript letters to indicate alternate versions. Accordingly, G_{1a} indicates the first version of the first G phrase, G_{1b} the second version; G_2 indicates the second G phrase (which will normally be the *third* phrase overall).

The first phrase of the initial verse of each Tract begins with an intonation formula unique to this verse (G_{1a}), while verse 2 uses essentially identical phrases cadencing on G (G_{1b}). As an exception, no opening G phrase appears in the third verse of *Vinea*.

The second phrases, cadencing on F, all share a common cadential formula but differ in the first half of the phrase, the second verse of *Laudate* being an ornamented version of verses 2 and 3 of *Vinea,* while verse 1 of each corresponds.

The third phrase (G$_2$) is identical in all verses, and indeed in all five of the Holy Saturday Tracts. The first and second verses of *Vinea* end with this phrase, while the first verse of *Laudate* continues and concludes with a G phrase common to other Tetrardus Tracts (G$_{3a}$). The final verse of each Tract ends with a concluding phrase common not only to all five Holy Saturday Tracts but to all medieval Tracts of the same mode (G$_{3b}$).

Vinea facta est:					
Verse	1	G$_{1a}$	F$_a$	G$_2$	
	2	G$_{1b}$	F$_b$	G$_2$	
	3		F$_b$	G$_2$	G$_{3b}$
Laudate Dominum:					
Verse	1	G$_{1a}$	F$_a$	G$_2$	G$_{3a}$
	2	G$_{1b}$	F$_c$	G$_2$	G$_{3b}$

Special Antiphons

In the Offices, the antiphon normally served as an introduction and conclusion to the singing of a psalm or psalm verse. In the later Middle Ages two types of antiphons without verses developed.

One type comprises the so-called *Marian antiphons,* in honor of the Virgin Mary, added in the thirteenth century to the office of Compline. Some, such as *Salve regina, Alma redemptoris mater, Ave regina coelorum,* and *Regina coeli,* became favorite texts throughout the Renaissance and later.

The second type is associated with processions, which played an increasingly important part in the richly ornate services of the late medieval church. Simple processions to and from chapter house, church, and cloister formed a constant daily event, the procession moving either in silence, to a recited psalm, or to a sung hymn or psalm and antiphon. More elaborate public processions occurred on major feast days in which the richness of ecclesiastical vestments, banners, relics, song, and incense would constitute a public show of religious magnificence. On normal Sundays the procession might remain within the church, proceeding through public areas such as the nave. On more important occasions such as Palm Sunday, the procession could circle the exterior of the building, stopping at various "stations" for short services, or even lead to another church.

For these processions, which were in many ways the most public part of late medieval worship, music could simply be chosen from the office chants for the day, but this was often supplemented with *processional antiphons* especially written for this use, some new, others of ancient, even Gallican, heritage. These were often settings of biblical prose texts without verses, although verses, biblical or newly composed, were on occasion included. (Anthology Example 25 gives a polyphonic setting of the verse portion of one such antiphon.)

Hymns

The history of the hymn in the Western church may be traced back to the time of Saint Ambrose (ca. 340–397), although its widespread use dates from the ninth century, when it began to find a regular place in the Offices. In this context it would be sung by all in attendance, but was still a more intimate expression than the later congregational hymn of the Protestant Reformation.

In structure, a hymn may be defined as a musical setting of a nonbiblical poetic text that is arranged into a number of identically constructed stanzas. Each stanza is sung to the same melody. The hymn represents an early example of strophic construction, in which the individual stanzas are most usually through-composed.

THE CHANTS OF THE ORDINARY OF THE MASS

Chants associated with the Ordinary of the Mass are in general newer than those of the Proper, since the assignment of those chants to the choir took place during the Carolingian period and replaced older congregational chants. The chants of the Proper had been stabilized by the mid-ninth century or before, while the chants of the Ordinary as a rule date from that time forward. Composition of Ordinary chants continued through the fourteenth century and even later.

The musical style of Ordinary chants is definitely post-Carolingian and falls into what is best called *medieval chant,* an idiom that will be taken up in Chapter 3. Nevertheless, for the sake of continuity, the formal structure of those chants will be included here in order to complete study of medieval Mass structures.

Symmetrical Texts

The Ordinary chants, on the whole, display a much more conscious, constructionist approach to form than do the earlier chants of the Proper. Three of the chants of the Ordinary set short texts in symmetrical or semisymmetrical form.

Kyrie. The Kyrie, originally sung by the congregation, immediately follows the Introit. As finally established, it is a prayer of supplication consisting of three lines:

Kyrie eleison
Christe eleison
Kyrie eleison

Lord have mercy
Christ have mercy
Lord have mercy

Each petition is traditionally given a threefold repetition (see Anthology Example 10a), resulting in a composite nine-part form that invites a symmetrical formal structure. Frequent patterns are AAA BBB CCC', AAA BBB AAA', and ABA CDC EFE', in which the final section is the longest. (For a detailed structural analysis of the Kyrie *Clemens Rector*, Anthology Example 10, see "The Chants of the Ordinary" in Chapter 3.) Although many early Kyries appear with additional text (see "Texted Ordinary Chants" in Chapter 3), it is the melismatic form that became established. It is the only melismatic chant in the Ordinary.

Agnus Dei. As Aurelian so poetically describes it, the Agnus Dei was originally sung during the breaking of bread before communion, followed by the Communion chant. It is thus a prayer of supplication.

Similar to the Kyrie, the text of the Agnus Dei has a threefold repetitive structure. Although also sometimes found with additional text in early manuscripts, the earliest standardized form consisted of a threefold repetition of the phrase *Agnus Dei, qui tollis peccata mundi, miserere nobis*. During the twelfth century the ending of the final line was changed to the current form:

Agnus Dei, qui tollis peccata mundi, miserere nobis;
Agnus Dei, qui tollis peccata mundi, miserere nobis;
Agnus Dei, qui tollis peccata mundi, dona nobis pacem.

Lamb of God, who takest away the sins of the world, have mercy upon us;
Lamb of God, who takest away the sins of the world, have mercy upon us;
Lamb of God, who takest away the sins of the world, grant us peace.

Most musical settings do not imitate the AAB form of the text. A simple AAA repetition or an ABA pattern that ignores the contrary pattern of the text is most common (see Anthology Example 11). Other settings modify the ABA form by using the same cadential phrase throughout as a type of musical end rhyme: An; Bn; An; (where n represents the common cadence).

Less florid than the Kyrie, the Agnus Dei moves largely in neumatic melodic movement.

Sanctus. The Sanctus begins with the acclamation of the angels in Isaiah 6:3, "Holy, Holy, Holy, Lord God of Hosts, the earth is full of Thy glory," and then proceeds to the cry of the people attending Christ's triumphant entry into Jerusalem: "Hosanna in the highest. Blessed is he that cometh in the name of the Lord." Like the Kyrie and Agnus Dei, it consists of a series of short phrases, but here the arrangement is less symmetrical:

> Sanctus, Sanctus, Sanctus
> Dominus Deus Sabaoth
> Pleni sunt coeli et terra gloria tua.
> > Hosanna in excelsis.
> Benedictus qui venit in nomine Domini.
> > Hosanna in excelsis.

Like the Kyrie and Agnus Dei, the Sanctus was originally sung by the congregation.

In terms of the text, obvious places for musical repetition are the first three words and the final three phrases; the latter in particular suggests an ABA setting. Some melodies use repetition in both areas, some only in the latter section. Others are through-composed. Indeed, a wide variety of structures may be found. The Sanctus melodies as a whole show a fascinating variety of compositional approaches and are excellent chants for analytic study (see Anthology Example 12 and Example 2-8 below).

The Prose Texts

The Gloria and the Credo are both long prose texts, set musically in syllabic style. The opening intonation is sung by the priest and the remainder by the choir (which is why polyphonic settings traditionally begin with the second phrase). As prose texts, they lack the distinctive organization of the three chants just discussed, and no large-scale formal structure is possible. Unification is achieved by other means, particularly motive or phrase repetition.

Although their outward structure is the same, the two chants have rather different intents and origins in the mass.

Gloria.   The Gloria, which begins with the words of the angels as they proclaim the birth of Christ and continues with a long series of short acclamations, was in Carolingian times reserved for Sundays and festivals in seasons of rejoicing—and even then, with the exception of Christmas, only when a bishop was present to give the opening intonation. This special relationship to the presence of a bishop was relaxed during the course of the eleventh and twelfth centuries until it merely became a matter of deference to the bishop if one was present.

The tenth-century Gloria of Anthology Example 13 gives a good example of formal construction. The text, consisting as it does of short phrases with occasional parallelism, permits no large formal design; unity is achieved through the repetition of a number of melodic cells or motives, all less than a phrase in length, but having a recognizable melodic shape. In this Gloria, six melodic fragments are intermixed with each other and nonrelated material (phrase numbers given in parentheses):

a: *Et in terra pax* (2) = *Agnus Dei* (10) = *Qui sedes* (13).
b: *bonae voluntatis* (2) = *agimus tibi* (7) = *Domine Deus* (8) = *Domini Fili* (9) = *Domine Deus* (10) = *(pec)cata mundi)* (11) = *(pec)cata mundi* (12) = *solus Altissimus* (13).
c: *te* (6) = *gloriam tuam* (7, slightly altered) = *miserere nobis* (11) = *(depre)cationem nostram* (12) = *(mi)serere nobis* (13).
d: *Rex caelestis* (8) = *unigenite* (9).
e: *Jesu Christe* (9) = *Jesu Christe* (16) = *Cum Sancto Spiritu* (17).
f: *Filius* (10) = *Patris* (10).
g: *Qui tollis peccata mundi* (11) = *Qui tollis peccata mundi* (12), both enclosing a statement of motive b.

This may be seen in Example 2-7.

It will be noticed that text repetition (*Jesu Christe, Qui tollis* . . .) and parallel constructions (*Dominus Deus / Dominus Fili / Dominus Deus*) often result in melodic repetition. Not all textual parallelisms are reflected in the music, however. The sequence of motives *b + d + e* in phrases 8 and 9 make melodic parallelism out of texts that are only partially so, while phrase 10, which is closer to phrase 8 in construction, deviates.

EXAMPLE 2-7. *Gloria IV*, Motivic Analysis, G. R., pp. 725–26.

The motive *c*, which has a cadential function, makes end rhymes out of phrases 6 and 7, and phrases 11, 12, and 13. Even more pervasive are the frequent occurrences of two basic cadential figures: 𝄞⎯⎯ and 𝄞⎯⎯.

Credo.   Although the Nicean creed was established in the fourth century, the singing of it became accepted only gradually—in the Carolingian world by the ninth century, in Rome by the eleventh. Credo melodies are medieval in style (see Anthology Example 14), with a formal organization like that of the Gloria.

The Dismissal Formulas

Ite, missa est (Go, the mass is over) and *Benedicamus Domino* (Let us bless the Lord) are alternate dismissal formulas at the end of Mass; the use of one or the other depends on the season. The *Benedicamus Domino* has a much more important role as the concluding formula for the Offices. Both texts possess a rich legacy of chant settings, and the *Benedicamus Domino* in particular came to receive frequent polyphonic settings in the twelfth and thirteenth centuries because of its use in Vespers and Matins.

Practicum

PLAINCHANT ANALYSIS

This section is designed to provide an opportunity to analyze in detail selected examples of plainsong styles. Plainchant encompasses several structural types, each of which requires its own analytical approach to formal structure and melodic technique. Viewed in this way, we can discern three broad categories: melodies involving internal repetition and design (most Ordinary chants and many Alleluias); formulaic melodies, which demand comparison with other chants of the same genre and mode (Gradual, Great Responsory, and Tract); and realizations of melody types, which demand comparison with a wide range of other similar chants (Introit and Office antiphon).

In the space possible here, the first of these categories is easiest to analyze, for each example is self-contained, and the analysis is exclusively an internal one. The second is more difficult to pursue, unless comparison is confined to a circumscribed group of chants. For this reason another Holy Saturday Tract is provided in Example 2-11 for comparison with the two included in the Anthology. Study of the third category demands a large, wide-ranging group of examples and thus is not possible here.

Discussion in this chapter has given considerable attention to these three structural types, and the relevant sections should be carefully studied before attempting analysis here. Each example should be considered in terms of its particular genre and style.

Nonetheless, certain general principles pertain throughout. Consideration should first be given to large structure and to major divisions, which often coincide with major divisions of the text. These may be designated by capital letters, unless other terms, such as *antiphon, respond,* or *verse,* are more appropriate. Smaller divisions or subphrases should be designated with lowercase letters. A superscript (¹) may be used to designate closely related variants. Be always conscious of the medieval penchant for end rhyme, which can also affect analytical interrelationships.

Begin by transcribing the assigned chant into modern notation—but study the original as well, for motivic shapes are sometimes easier to spot in the original neumatic notation. Contrariwise, note that identical melodic shapes may at times appear in different notational form because of different text underlay.

The musical analysis should be shown directly on the music and also briefly summarized in written form. Always include an analysis of the modal structure in a manner appropriate to the chant involved.

Assignments

Transcribe and analyze one or more of the following chants for mode and formal and melodic structure: Examples 2-8, 2-9, 2-10, 2-11, and 2-12. Additional chants may be chosen from the *Graduale Romanum* or the *Liber Usualis.*

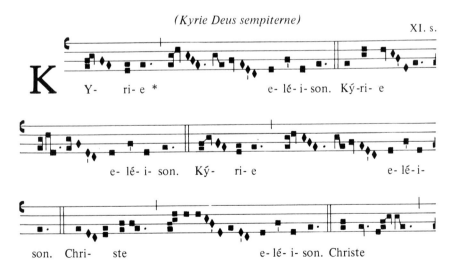

EXAMPLE 2-8. *Kyrie Deus sempiterne,* G.R., pp. 718–19. © Abbaye Saint Pierre de Solesmes, France, 1974, reprinted with permission.

e- lé- i- son. Chri-   ste   e- lé-i-

son.   Ký- ri- e   e- lé- i- son.   Ký-ri-

e   e- lé- i- son.   Ký- ri- e

e- lé- i- son.

EXAMPLE 2-8 *continued.*

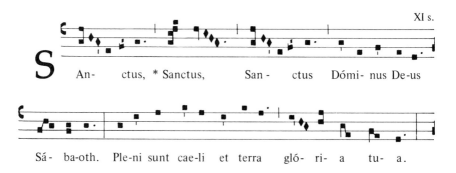

San-   ctus, * Sanctus,   San -   ctus   Dómi- nus De-us

Sá- ba-oth. Ple-ni sunt cae-li et terra   gló- ri- a tu- a.

EXAMPLE 2-9. *Sanctus* IV, G.R., p. 727. © Abbaye Saint Pierre de Solesmes, France, 1974, reprinted with permission.

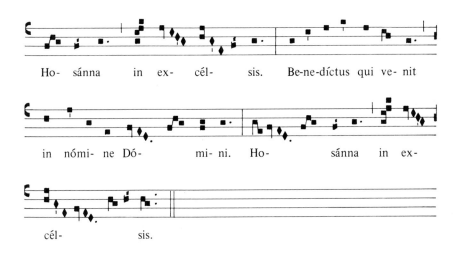

Ho- sánna in ex- cél- sis. Be-ne-díctus qui ve- nit

in nómi- ne Dó- mi- ni. Ho- sánna in ex-

cél- sis.

EXAMPLE 2-9 *continued.*

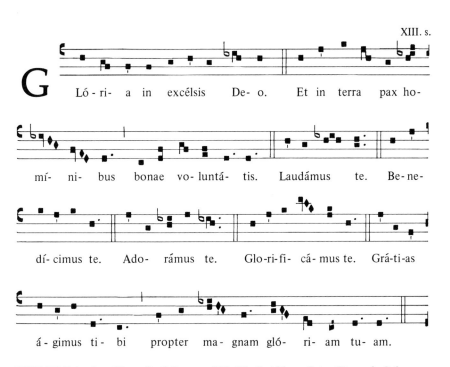

XIII. s.

G Ló - ri- a in excélsis De- o. Et in terra pax ho-

mí- ni- bus bonae vo- luntá- tis. Laudámus te. Be-ne-

dí- cimus te. Ado- rámus te. Glo-ri-fi- cá- mus te. Grá-ti-as

á - gimus ti - bi propter ma-gnam gló- ri- am tu- am.

EXAMPLE 2-10. *Gloria II*, G.R., pp. 715–17. © Abbaye Saint Pierre de Solesmes, France, 1974, reprinted by permission.

Dómi- ne De-us, Rex cae- léstis, De-us Pa- ter omní- pot- ens.

Dó-   mi- ne Fi- li u- ni- gé- ni- te Ie- su Chri-ste.   Dómi-

ne De-us, Agnus De- i,   Fí- li- us Pa- tris.   Qui tol-

lis peccá- ta mundi,   mi- se- ré- re no-bis.   Qui tol- lis pec-

cá- ta mundi,   súsci- pe depre- ca- ti- ó- nem nostram.   Qui se -

des ad déx- te- ram Pa- tris,   mi- se- ré- re no-bis.   Quó-ni-am

tu so- lus sanctus.   Tu so-lus Dó- mi-nus.   Tu so-lus Al- tís-

EXAMPLE 2-10 *continued.*

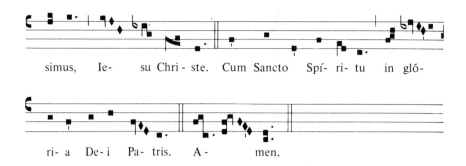

simus, Ie-   su Chri - ste.   Cum Sancto   Spí- ri- tu   in gló-

ri- a   De- i   Pa- tris.   A -   men.

EXAMPLE 2-10 *continued.*

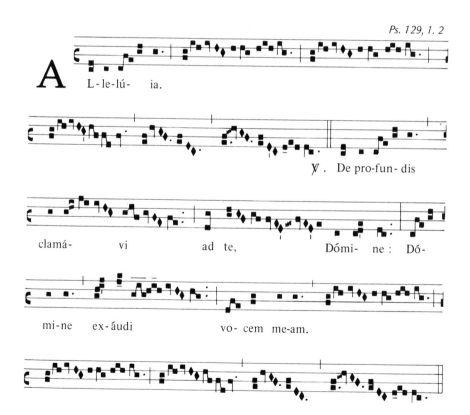

AL - le-lú-   ia.

℣ . De pro-fun- dis

clamá-   vi   ad te,   Dómi-   ne :   Dó-

mi- ne   ex- áudi   vo- cem me-am.

EXAMPLE 2-11. *Alleluia: De profundus,* G.R., pp. 367–68. © Abbaye Saint Pierre de Solesmes, France, 1974, reprinted by permission.

EXAMPLE 2-12. Tract *Sicut cervus*, G.R., pp. 190–91. (Three verses, four phrases per verse, compare with Anthology examples 8 and 9.) © Abbaye Saint Pierre de Solesmes, France, 1974, reprinted by permission.

cte, dum dí- ci- tur mi- hi per síngu- los di-

es : U- bi est De- us tu- us?

EXAMPLE 2-12 *continued.*

BIBLIOGRAPHY

Music and Theory

See Chapter 1.

Readings

Andrew Hughes, *Medieval Manuscripts for Mass and Office: A Guide to Their Organization and Terminology* (Toronto: University of Toronto Press, 1982), gives encyclopedic coverage and is essential for anyone engaging in an in-depth study.

Concerning the liturgy and its origins and development, see Cyrille Vogel, *Medieval Liturgy: An Introduction to the Sources,* rev. and ed. W. G. Storey and N. K. Rasmussen (Washington, D.C.: Pastoral Press, 1986); Cheslyn Jones et al., *The Study of Liturgy* (Oxford: Oxford University Press, 1978); and A. G. Martimort et al., *The Church at Prayer,* 4 vols. (Collegeville, Minn.: Liturgical Press, 1986–87).

Older sources include Josef A. Jungmann, S.J., *The Early Liturgy to the Time of Gregory the Great,* Liturgical Studies 6 (Notre Dame, Ind.: University of Notre Dame Press, 1959) and *The Mass of the Roman Rite,* 2 vols. (New York: Benziger, 1951–55); and S. J. P. van Dijk, O.F.M., and J. Hazelden Walker, *The Origins of the Modern Roman Liturgy* (London: Darton, Longman & Todd, 1960).

The rhymed Office is discussed in Andrew Hughes, "Chants in the Rhymed Office of St. Thomas of Canterbury," *EM* (1988): 185–201.

3

Medieval Chant

When Charlemagne died in 814, he was succeeded by his only surviving legitimate son, Louis the Pious, a moderately competent ruler who nonetheless did not have the ability to keep together the multifarious kingdoms and peoples temporarily united by the force of his father's personality. In 817 Louis divided his authority among his three sons, only to have another son born the next year. This resulted in a further division of the empire and inevitable family quarrels. The situation remained unresolved until 843 when, in the Treaty of Verdun, the essential boundaries of modern Europe were struck. Louis the German received the German-speaking East Frankish kingdom, Charles the Bald the Romance-speaking West Frankish kingdom, and Lothair northern Italy and an unstable corridor separating East and West Francia (see Map 2-1).

This division established the territorial and linguistic foundations of France, Germany, and Italy. It influenced music as well, for within a basically unified chant idiom, there would soon occur regional dialects affecting matters of detail, such as the German preference for c as an upper neighbor to a, rather than the b or b flat favored in France.

The newly divided empire did not find itself in peace, for not only was there internecine warfare, but Christian Europe was suddenly confronted with new barbarian invasions on all sides: the Vikings (Norsemen) attacking England and France, the Muslims occupying the Mediterranean islands and raiding Italy, and the Magyars sweeping from the plains of Hungary through much of Germany as far as the Rhine Valley (see Map 2-1). It is amazing that a strong and vital ecclesiastical musical life could survive the turmoil of those centuries. However, the musical life that developed during this time initiated a long and productive period of later medieval chant composition that would last into the sixteenth century.

This new chant is sufficiently different from the earlier Roman-Gallican idiom to warrant a distinctive designation as *medieval chant.* It is an indigenous

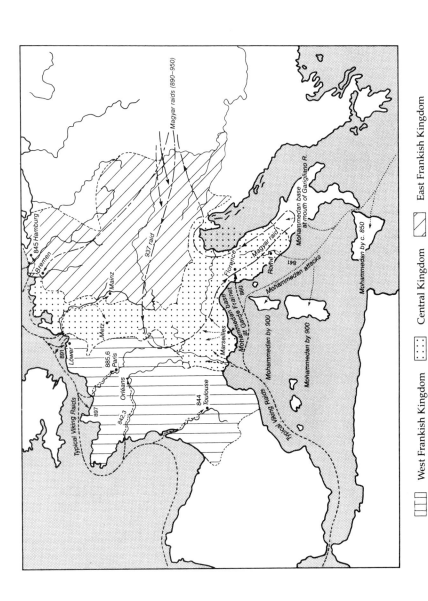

Map 2-1. The breakup of the Carolingian Empire at the Treaty of Verdun (843) and Viking, Mohammedan, and

chant idiom growing largely within the Frankish territories and is indicative of the spirit of post-Carolingian Europe.

ORGANIZATION AND STRUCTURE

By the mid-ninth century the chants of the Proper had become an established repertoire in the Roman-Gallican tradition. As a result, the new medieval chant was forced to find its expression elsewhere: in new settings of Ordinary chants (replacing the older, congregational ones) and in the new Carolingian forms—the sequence, trope, and prosula.

Characteristic of medieval chant are sharply defined melodic segments, clearly articulated phrases, and a modular or fixed design making considerable use of melodic and motivic repetition. This is distinctly different from the earlier idiom, for while repetitive structures do occur in Roman-Gallican chant—one need only think of the alternation of antiphon and psalm verse—the repetitive element tends to be deemphasized and the sections less articulated, with the melodic connections leading smoothly from one section to the next.

The sharply etched sectionalism of much medieval chant is clearly evident in settings of such symmetrical texts as the Kyrie, Agnus Dei, and Sanctus, and equally so in the favorite new genre, the sequence, where the text (often newly written to fit the music) complements a modular musical pattern. The clearly defined larger form coupled with a coincident manipulation of smaller motivic fragments in medieval chant gives the impression of a more conscious, intellectual compositional approach (in distinction to Roman-Gallican chant, which began its life in an improvisatory environment, only later to be captured and "frozen" in notation). As we shall see, this change in compositional approach was coincident with changing concepts of tonal organization and modality.

The Chants of the Ordinary

A new approach to structure is apparent in the various chants of the Ordinary. All of these chants make use, in one way or another, of repeated melodic segments.

The Kyrie illustrates the modular approach particularly well, showing not only a large-scale symmetrical structure, but the use of a variety of more subtle means of unification.

One of these procedures is the use of identical or alternating phrase endings throughout the chant as a musical end rhyme. Using *n* and *o* to indicate the phrase endings, they could be diagrammed:

n		n
n		o
n	or	n
n		o
etc.		etc.

A second approach uses motives or subphrases in a pattern of internal repetition within the formal phrase structure. These modular approaches can be seen in the Kyrie *Clemens rector* (see Anthology Example 10a), which will serve in this chapter as a paradigm for a variety of medieval chant techniques.

Considering first the larger organization of the chant, we notice that the structure of the text is duplicated by nine distinctly articulated sections, each ending with the identical Protus cadence C-D-D. The musical sections do not, however, merely duplicate the simple AAA BBB AAA parallelism of the text, but instead create their own pattern of interrelationships: sections 1 and 3, 2 and 5, and 4 and 6 are identical to each other and form the modular pattern ABA CBC.

Confining our attention for the moment to these same six sections, a more intricate lower-level structure begins to appear when each section is divided into its component motives (indicated by the phrase marks on the top staff line in the transcription). These phrases and motives can be charted:

MAIN PRASE	MOTIVES
A	a a b
B	c d c′
A	a a b
C	e f b
B	c d c′
C	e f b

Section A consists of a repeated ten-note motive followed by a seven-note cadential one. B begins with an eight-note motive that returns as a cadential pattern following a contrasting six-note motive. C consists of two motives, the second of which flows into the seven-note cadential motive of phrase A. These three sections (six, with repetitions) display both an interlocking larger structure and a more intricate web of interior motives.

The three concluding sections enlarge on the components of the initial three. D expands the first motive of A by prefixing a two-note beginning, repeats it, adds two new motives, and ends with the cadential motive of B. E begins with the cadential motive of A (with a two-note prefix), followed by the second and third motives of B. D′ is like D, but with an additional internal repetition. The entire Kyrie may be diagrammed:

SECTION	MOTIVES					
A	a	a			b	
B	c	d			c′	
A	a	a			b	
C	e	f			b	
B	c	d			c′	
C	e	f			b	
D (A′)	a′	a′	g	h		c′
E (B′)	b′	d				c′
D′ (A″)	a′	a′	g	g	h	c′

Also important in this analysis is the interlocking pattern of cadential phrases —musical end rhyme—and the sense of increasing complexity as the form reaches its climax in the final phrases.

Motivic (or sub-phrase) repetition and rearrangement within a less symmetrical overall form may be seen by reexamining the Gloria analysis in Chapter 2. There, returning melodic motives are intermixed with freer, nonrepetitive material.

Embellishments of the Liturgy

Musical vitality in this new age found a somewhat limited outlet in the composition of chants for the Ordinary (there are after all only five different texts). The greater thrust was in the creation of new forms to embellish the now established liturgy. No sooner, it seems, had the newly received liturgy and chant been standardized throughout the Carolingian empire than musicians and poets began to ornament it.

The great medieval inclination was not to discard but to improve—not to challenge received learning but to explain or "gloss" it, even if that gloss subtly changed the received meaning. So it was with the service of the worship of God, a desire not to change but to embellish and thus make even more meaningful the texts of the Mass and Office.

Although loosely and generically called "tropes" in much of today's literature, the process of musical and textual embellishment is more properly divided into two categories: *prosulas* and *tropes*, with texted Ordinary chants fitting uneasily in between.

Prosula.   Simplest of these categories is the prosula, which adds a text to an already existing but nontexted chant melisma. The textual addition is designed to underline or enrich the meaning of the original chant.

A common form of the prosula adds text to the melismatic jubilus of an Alleluia, one syllable per note, or even adds new text to the entire Alleluia. This procedure can also be applied to other melismatic chants, such as the responsories of the Offices. Anthology Example 6 illustrates the conversion of the respond of an Offertory, *Stetit angelus,* to the prosula *Stetit Michael patronus noster.* The prosula text is in prose and amplifies considerably the original thought. It is placed (with rare exceptions) syllable by syllable on each note of the original melody. The text is so shaped as to incorporate the words of the original text at their appropriate places.

Tropes. Whereas a prosula does not change the musical shape of the original chant, a trope does, either through the addition of musical melismas (a melodic trope) or text and music (a textual trope). The function of both types is illustrated in relationship to the Easter Introit *Resurrexi* in Anthology Example 2.

In the melodic trope, long melismas of joy extend each line to embellish and make the chant more ornate for festivals and other special occasions. As seen in Anthology Example 2b, each line of the chant is extended through textless melisma, often doubling the original length.

In the textual trope, the addition of text and music serves in the first instance to introduce the chant and to make its text more specific to the service of the day. Usually this is followed by additional lines of text and music, which are interspersed between the remaining lines of text in the chant in order to introduce those lines, further amplify the original psalm text, and, if necessary, make it liturgically specific.

The process may be seen in the textual trope to *Resurrexi* (Anthology Example 2c). Here the antiphon text "I am risen and am still with thee" applies to Christ in a prophetic sense. The trope introduction, "Rejoice and be glad because the Lord is risen," leaves no doubt as to its application to Easter while simultaneously exhorting the worshipers to praise. Similarly, the interspersed lines amplify the text by alluding to the events of the Resurrection (the great earthquake, the descent of the angel to the tomb, the swooning of the guards from fear).

Many tropes might be written for a particular chant; the tropes in Anthology Example 2 are only two of a large number that are applicable to the *Resurrexi* chant.

Tropes may be added to any of the chants of the Proper or Ordinary. An Agnus Dei trope may be seen in Anthology Example 11b. There the introductory trope serves to relate a very general text to the specific occasion of Christmas, while the interior trope lines amplify on the majesty of Christ. In this case, however, the trope lines partially *replace* the normal text, a peculiar feature of many Ordinary tropes that will be discussed below.

Melodic structure in the trope is determined equally by its own text and by the structure of the chant it is embellishing; it must fit the sections that precede and follow. An appropriate relationship is achieved through the correspondence of mode and range. Chant and trope become a new unity, with the composite structure enriching and expanding the original, both musically and in a religious context. A medieval musician would consider the trope not a strange, parasitical growth surrounding the chant (as some twentieth-century commentators view it), but rather a positive means of enlarging, of making a grander entity out of a simpler original.

Texted ordinary chants.   Many Ordinary chants, especially Kyries, appear simultaneously in texted and melismatic form in early manuscripts, making it difficult to determine whether the texted version is a prosula of an earlier melismatic original or if the melismatic form is a simplification of an earlier texted version. While the recent tendency has been to assume the melismatic setting to have been the earlier, this is not clear in all cases. In addition, the fact that the liturgical text itself may be partially supplanted in the texted version further sets the texted Ordinary chant apart from the more easily categorized trope and prosula. (The freedom of application of even those procedures to Ordinary chants can be seen in the troped Agnus Dei of Anthology Example 11b, where the second *Agnus Dei qui tollis peccata mundi* phrase is suppressed, to be replaced by two appearances of its conclusion, *miserere nobis*.)

A representative example of a texted Kyrie may be seen in the Kyrie *Clemens rector* (Anthology Example 10). The melismatic version in 10a gives the expected nine-part Kyrie. The texted version in 10b precedes each melismatic phrase with a fully texted version of the melody, resulting (if the manuscript layout is indicative of performance procedure) in a composite eighteen-part Kyrie of alternating texted and melismatic lines. The additional text either largely (as in section 1) or completely (as in section 2) replaces the expected liturgical text.

Two other texting procedures also occur in medieval manuscripts. One places the additional text on the melisma between the words *kyrie* and *eleison* (a prosula technique *if* the melismatic version actually preceded the texted one): "Kyrie, *fons bonitatis, Pater ingenite, a quo bona cuncta procedunt,* eleison." The final procedure retains the word *eleison,* but replaces the word *Kyrie* with new text, the technique of section 1 of *Clemens rector,* but used throughout and without melismatic alternation.

Texted Ordinary chants often cross the boundary between trope and prosula as we try to reconstruct those medieval procedures. The various forms in which they occur suggest that distinctions between techniques may not have been as clear-cut as we would like them to be.

The Sequence

The *sequence,* or *prose,* although often loosely classed with tropes and prosulas as an embellishment to the liturgy, should more properly be considered a chant in its own right. It began in the mid-ninth century as an addition to the Proper and became a favorite form of the later Middle Ages. Of some 4,500 sequence texts, all but four were eliminated in the sixteenth century as an aftermath of the Council of Trent (a fifth was reinstated later).

In medieval terminology, the word *sequentia* appears most often to refer to a long textless melisma that could be added to the jubilus of the Alleluia, the term *prosa* to a text added to the sequentia, the whole being called *sequentia cum prosa*. Modern terminology rather loosely uses either *sequence* or *prose* interchangeably to refer to the entire composition.

Notker Balbulus, a late ninth-century monk from St. Gall who is our only early witness concerning the composition of sequences, speaks of setting new texts, one syllable per note, to *sequentia* melodies brought by a monk fleeing the Vikings. This, along with the appearance of multiple texts for individual melodies, suggests that the norm in sequence composition would have been to add text to already existing melodies.

Liturgically, the sequence occurs after the Alleluia and before the reading of the Gospel (see the Mass diagram in Chapter 12). It thus became a third expansive chant between the Epistle and Gospel, a moment of reflection in which music has a major role. Some sequences are melodically related to the Alleluias they follow, this relationship being evident in the opening phrase. Others, however, bear no such melodic relation, which seems to have been a completely optional feature.

The sequence is built in a series of couplets, paired lines identical to each other in length and grammatical construction, sung to a repeated melodic phrase. Typically, the series of couplets is preceded and concluded by a single line. At its simplest and most regular it would be diagrammed as follows, where the paired letters indicate the couplets and A and X respectively indicate the beginning and concluding single lines: A BB CC DD . . . X.

This simple outline hides a wealth of artistic possibilities: the length of text and music, the relationship of line lengths to each other, and, in the early sequence, the presence of occasional single lines within the body of the sequence, for example, A BB CC D EE FF . . . X.

Anthology Example 15, *Regnantem sempiterna*, is a sequence from the tenth century. It begins with a short quotation of the opening of the *Alleluia: Laetatus sum*, the Alleluia that would immediately precede it in the Mass for the second Sunday of Advent. The *Regnantem* text, which expostulates on Christ as a merciful judge, is appropriate to Advent but bears no direct relationship to the text of the Alleluia, which states "I was glad when they said unto me: let us go into the house of the Lord." This casual relationship between Alleluia and sequence is typical.

Unusual in this case is the inclusion of the word *alleluia* itself: more usually, a quotation of an Alleluia melody, if present, would be set to the beginning words of the sequence. (Note Facsimile 3-2, a later version, in which the *alleluia* is omitted.)

Also unusual in *Regnantem sempiterna* is the appearance of two single lines before the regular series of parallel couplets takes over. Although held together by the syntax of the text, the long second line seems musically divided into five short phrases: a first pair, *a + a* (*Regnantem sempiterna = per saecla susceptura*), followed by an asymmetrical second pair in *b, c + b* pattern (*concio devote concrepa / divino sono / factori reddendo debita*). Couplets then proceed in typical fashion, each differing in length from its neighbors, sometimes considerably so. In terms of syllable lengths, lines 3–8 may be diagrammed:

3. ———————————————— 19 syllables

4. ——————— 8

5. ———————————————— 19

6. ————————————— 14

7. ———————————— 12

8. ——————————— 11

The text is in prose, but of a literary type that takes on some of the attributes of poetry. This is evident in the assonant *a* that ends each line (we would call it rhyme, but the Middle Ages defined rhyme as encompassing one or more complete syllables, as in lines 4 [a and b]: judi*cia* / poten*tia*, *c* and *t* being pronounced identically in these words). It is also apparent in the lilting rhythm, which is never carried throughout the line as it would be in poetry.

The move toward a fully poetic text occurred in the twelfth century and found expression in the sequences of Adam of St. Victor. These use the rhymed rhythmic poetry that will be discussed in full in Chapter 6 and set a standard for the late medieval sequence.

Liturgical Drama

Liturgical drama has its roots in the same desire for enrichment and expansion that led to trope, prosula, and sequence—and indeed to rhymed Offices. The enactment of tiny dramatic scenes such as, for instance, the Easter story of the angel appearing to the three Marys at the tomb (the most widespread of the dramas, with over seven hundred different versions still existing today), was one more form of embellishment to the service:

After the third responsory [of Matins] three of the brothers [shall come forward] in the semblance of women. One of them in a red cope, between the two others, shall carry a thurible; the others on each side, wearing white dalmatics, shall carry vessels resembling pyxes. They shall stand by the candleholder and sing in a low voice making this complaint:
"O God, who shall roll back the stone for us from the entrance to the tomb?"
From there they shall go forward slowly to the door by the altar, and a single brother standing by the "sepulchre" in the semblance of an angel shall reply:
"Who are you seeking in the sepulchre, O worshipers of Christ?"
The Women: "Jesus of Nazareth the crucified, O dwellers in heaven."
The Angel: "He is not here, he is risen, as he had foretold. Go, announce that he has risen, saying:"
The Women: "Alleluia, the Lord has risen."

The Angel: "Alleluia, the Lord has risen."
The Women to the People: "Alleluia, the Lord has risen."
The Angel to the Women: "Come and see the place where the Lord was laid."
The Women to the People: "The Lord has risen from the sepulchre, he who for us
   hung upon the cross."[1]

Just as the "women" are monks in liturgical garb, the role of the angel is taken by another monk. The music they sing (for it is sung throughout) is largely taken from Office antiphons, only direct dialogue being new.

The drama, in this case performed near the end of Matins and followed by the singing of the Te Deum, would be one more embellishment to an already elaborate service of worship. It is not theater in the modern sense, nor is it necessarily particularly public; many such enactments were intended primarily for the priests and monks.

On the other hand, this kind of Easter dialogue could also function as a type of trope preceding the Introit *Resurrexi* at mass, or, more public, be performed at a station in the procession preceding the Mass.

In addition to numerous plays on Easter and Christmas subjects, other plays are found on Old Testament (Isaac, Joseph, Daniel) and New Testament (the Wise and Foolish Virgins, the Raising of Lazarus, the Annunciation) subjects. One of the best and most elaborate of these is the thirteenth-century *Ludus Danielis* (The Play of Daniel), which portrays the story of Daniel under both King Nebuchadnezzar and King Belshazzar, intertwined with prophecies of the coming of Christ. Here, liturgical chant is combined with such later forms as Sequence and Conductus in a panorama of broad musical and dramatic scope lasting over forty-five minutes in performance.

MODAL THEORY

Evolving Modal Theory

A move toward the new structural principles of medieval chant was accompanied by a change in modal concepts. Carolingian musicians had brought about an accommodation between a body of European liturgical chant and a modal system based on Byzantine practice. The next generation began the final accommodation necessary to fulfill the medieval quest for ordering all knowledge into one grand plan: the reconciliation of medieval practice to the ancient Greek musical system as it had been conveyed by Boethius and others.

This accommodation, which began about 900 in Hucbald's treatise *De harmonica institutione* (Melodic Instruction) and in the anonymous *Alia musica,*

---

[1]From a fourteenth-century processional from the Benedictine Abbey of Fécamp in northwestern France, trans. John Stevens in *Words and Music in the Middle Ages: Song, Narrative, Dance and Drama, 1050–1350*, Cambridge Studies in Music (Cambridge: Cambridge University Press, 1986), 331–33.

was carried on and completed by eleventh-century theorists such as Guido of Arrezo, Berno, and John of Affleghem. The results of this accommodation would alter modal thinking for coming centuries, for this accommodation moved away from the concept of mode as melodic formula and toward one of mode as scale structure.

A first step was taken by Hucbald, who, after charting correctly the ancient Greek system of descending conjunct and disjunct *tetrachords* (scale segments encompassing a fourth), inverted that configuration by beginning with the lowest note, thus creating at a stroke a scale pattern of *ascending* tetrachords that precisely defines the medieval gamut. The pattern consists of two pairs of *conjunct* tetrachords (tetrachords joined by a common tone) in *disjunct* relationship to each other (separated by a whole tone), topped off with an added note to complete the double octave:

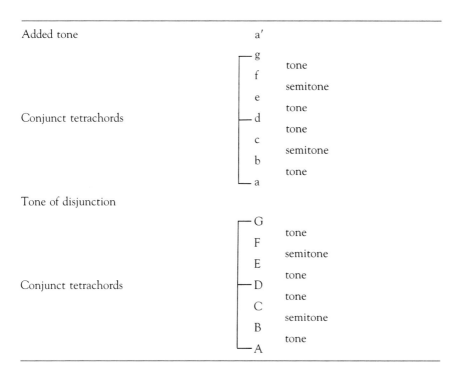

Added tone	a′	
	g	tone
	f	semitone
	e	tone
Conjunct tetrachords	d	tone
	c	semitone
	b	tone
	a	
Tone of disjunction		
	G	tone
	F	semitone
	E	tone
Conjunct tetrachords	D	tone
	C	semitone
	B	tone
	A	

This system would remain in place throughout the medieval period and would underlie most later theoretical thought. Only the range would subsequently be expanded through the addition of G̲ at the lower end (signified in writing by the Greek letter *gamma* Γ) and through additional notes above.

The final element of Hucbald's de facto medieval gamut is the introduction of the tone b flat, accomplished through the introduction of a third conjunct tetrachord with the Greek name *synemmenon*:

	c	tone
(Synemmenon tetrachord)	b♭	semitone
	a	tone
	G	tone
	F	semitone
Conjunct tetrachords	E	tone
	D	tone
	C	semitone
	B	tone
	A	

From this time on, there was theoretical justification for the use of b flat (but not B flat) as an optional tone within the system. It was only in the twelfth century that other accidentals began to be introduced, and then only in non-chant repertories.

Simultaneous with Hucbald's formulation, the anonymous *Alia musica* introduced the Greek names (Dorian, Hypodorian, etc.) to the theoretical literature by equating the modes to the Greek octave species.

Species of tetrachords and pentachords. More important, however, was the introduction in the *Alia musica* of the concept of *species* of tetrachords and pentachords—scale segments of a fourth or fifth—a concept that became of primary importance in both melodic composition and modal theory. These species are defined by the placement of the semitone within the scale segment (see Example 3-1).

These species could be combined to define modal scale structure. The first species of each, when combined, creates the Protus scale, the second species Deuterus, and the third species Tritus. For Tetrardus, the fourth species of pentachord is combined with the first species of tetrachord, there being no fourth species of the latter (see Example 3-2).

As Example 3-2 shows the relative placement of the pentachord and tetrachord defines the authentic and plagal ranges: the tetrachord above the pentachord gives the authentic mode, the tetrachord below, the plagal. In this way, it is the pentachord that defines what might be called the modal nucleus, the portion of the mode that is common to both plagal and authentic forms and that is most closely allied with what is distinctly "modal" about each scale's structure.

Practical application. The modular use of the pentachord and tetrachord in melodic construction became an element in much, although not all, subsequent modal writing. This is particularly clear in the same Kyrie *Clemens rector* (An-

Pentachords   Tetrachords

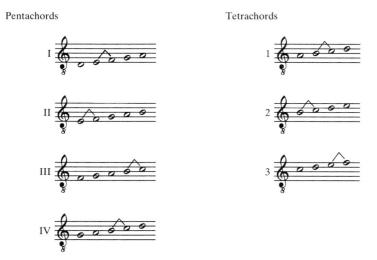

EXAMPLE 3-1. Species of Pentachords and Tetrachords.

thology Example 10) whose structure was analyzed above. The present analysis will proceed section by section.

Section 1 (also section 3) lies within and defines the first-species fifth, the characteristic Protus pentachord D-a (with the always allowable auxiliary tones above and below). It thus establishes the fundamental modality.

Section 2 (also section 5), in contrast, sets *Kyrie* and *eleison* in the plagal tetrachord A-D, while permitting the melismatic extension of the first word to move into the lower part of the pentachord. The first three phrases thus combine to establish the plagal Protus mode.

Section 4 (also section 6) begins abruptly in the authentic tetrachord a-d before ending with a scalewise pentachordal descent from a to D. In this way, it defines the authentic octave range by first establishing the authentic tetrachord and then extending it down through the pentachord. (Extended ranges such as this are uncommon in the medieval chant repertory.)

Section 7 (also section 9) begins, as did section 1, in the pentachord and remains there until the concluding plagal tetrachord. It therefore reestablishes a plagal range.

Section 8, with a strong relationship to section 2, remains in the lower part of the pentachord and the plagal tetrachord.

All of these sections operate within clearly definable scale segments equivalent to the pentachord and tetrachord. The pivotal tones of the phrases are A, D, a, and d, the points of demarcation between the pentachord and the two tetrachords. Although often less clear than here, the tendency to conceive melodies in this manner is found on into the Renaissance.

EXAMPLE 3-2. Construction of the Modal Scales from the Conjunction of Species of Pentachords and Tetrachords.

The Fully Developed Theory

The Middle Ages did not think in terms of octave scales: a mode was a conjunction of a pentachord and a tetrachord. Eleventh-century modal theory, notably that of Guido of Arezzo, Berno, and John of Affleghem, amplified and systematized the teachings of the *Alia musica* and Hucbald into what became the "classical" form of modal theory, influencing music through the Renaissance and beyond.

In this final form, the pitches to be used for interior cadences and, especially, the concept of reciting tones (borrowed from the psalm tones but now applied to all types of chant), added to a new, larger definition of mode. Example 3-3 codifies the modal scales in their late eleventh-century form, with the reciting tones represented by whole notes, finals as breves (|◙|), and optional range extensions shown within parentheses.

The application of these additional concepts can be seen in Anthology Example 10. The chant, firmly established on D, is definitely Protus, but the extended range, encompassing both plagal and authentic, makes further classification difficult. The medieval theorist would look further at the structure. The most prominent tones throughout are A, D, a, and d, with D and a the most important. The emphasis on a, the reciting tone of Protus authentic, rather than F, the reciting tone of the plagal, makes the classification Protus authentic.

All of the Ordinary chants in the Anthology show the same emphasis on the final, the same tendency toward sharply etched motives, and, to the extent

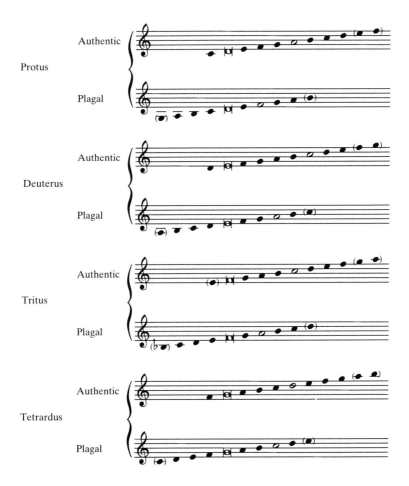

EXAMPLE 3-3.   The Fully Developed Modal System.

possible, an arrangement of the structure into clearly discernible components. A quick comparison with the earlier approach to modal organization may be had by comparing two plagal Deuterus chants, the Roman-Gallican Introit *Resurrexi* (Anthology Example 2) and the twelfth-century Sanctus (Anthology Example 12).

As discussed in Chapter 1, the tonal organization of *Resurrexi* is based on the third chain D-F-a, with F as the most prominent tone throughout. E occurs primarily as a neighboring tone to D or F and only twice, at the end of the first and third *alleluias*, at important structural points. The E final is incidental to the tonal structure of the chant as a whole.

The Sanctus is profoundly different in conception. All phrases end on the final E, which is thus central to the chant throughout. The motive used for the first and third *sanctus* and the *gloria* stresses the plagal Deuterus reciting tone c and begins with the characteristic intonation figure G-a-c found in Deuterus psalm tones, a figure repeated on *benedictus*. Although the D-F-a coloring that often appears in Deuterus (and that dominates in *Resurrexi*) occurs in passing over *Deus, Pleni,* and (*Ho*)*sanna*, it is immediately resolved back to an orientation on E.

The affinal.   We have noted that medieval musicians did not think in terms of an octave scale and that the nucleus of the mode resided in the pentachord. Eleventh-century theory went beyond this to suggest that it was the four or five notes immediately surrounding the final, the portion that was common to both the authentic and plagal modes, that held the real kernel of modal quality.

Hucbald had previously noticed that the tonal surroundings of any given note were duplicated at the fifth (although he spoke in terms of tetrachords), and Guido, around 1030, expanded this into the doctrine of the *affinal,* in which the note a is considered a possible replacement for D, b for E, and c for F. As seen in Example 3-4, the arrangement of tones and semitones is identical within a fourth or fifth in each of these cases. G has no affinal, as the tonal space around

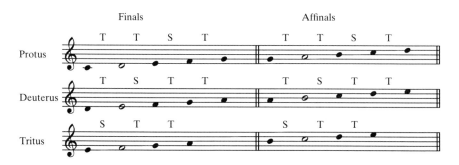

EXAMPLE 3-4.   Affinals.

its fifth, d, is not sufficiently comparable to that around G (d-e-f is a tone-semitone pattern rather than the required tone-tone pattern of G-a-b).

Medieval musicians found this identity so close that at times the affinal is found as an alternate cadential tone. Accordingly, an authentic Protus chant, notated D to d, *may* end a phrase or even the entire chant on the affinal a (see the chant used as the lower voice in Anthology Example 19).

Modal transposition.   Even though the modal system described in Chapter 1 was able to accommodate the great majority of the inherited Roman-Gallican chants, a small but significant number of troublesome anomalies still remained: chants whose tonal structure could not be easily accommodated in an eight-mode system based on the finals D, E, F, and G.

Some simply wandered from mode to mode and were either classified by the tone of their final or were amended by later theorists to be more modally consistent. Others, whose inherent scale structure did not fit into the normal eight modes, became a problem as notation evinced an ever greater concern with pitch.

The introduction of b flat solved many problems, and there is no mode that does not have at least a few chants requiring it. Some chants went beyond this, however, and used scales that, if notated on any of the normal finals, would require B flat, E flat, or F sharp, notes foreign to the notation of the time. Eleventh-century theory accommodated this through the theories of *transposition* and *transformation*, notating the chant not on the normal final but, by substitution, on a tone a fourth or a fifth higher, thus permitting the use of b flat and b natural to accommodate these abnormal notes within the modal system. *Transposition* is the term used to indicate notation a fifth higher on the affinal (for example, Protus on a). Notation at this pitch permits b flat to become a replacement for E flat and F for low B flat. *Transformation* is the term used until the thirteenth century to indicate notation up a fourth, on the basis that the necessary b flat in that transposition *transforms* G Tetrardus into G Protus. Transformation permits b flat and b natural to function as replacements for F natural and F sharp, respectively.

This technique may be seen in the Communion *Surrexit dominus* (Anthology Example 3), listed as Tetrardus plagal in Mo H159, but notated on c instead of G. The process may be explained as "Tetrardus transposed up a fourth," or simply as "Tetrardus on c." The normal transpositions were Protus on a, Deuterus on b, and Tritus on c, while the common transformations were Deuterus on a and Tetrardus on c.

Tonal consistency.   There is some evidence to suggest that medieval musicians tended to organize and hear music in relatively short segments without the long-term tonal awareness we take for granted. One such indication is the sheer possibility of an affinal acting as a substitute final in chants notated in the normal range. Another can be found in manuscript variants, where individual phrases are sometimes found transposed upward or downward anywhere from a second to a fifth without affecting the shape or pitch of the remainder of the chant.

This procedure can be seen by comparing the texted and untexted versions of Anthology Example 10. Section 7 in the modern composit version of 10a remains in the plagal Protus range throughout. The medieval version in 10b, however, transposes the first half of that section (from *Respice* to *excelsis*) up a third, with only minor changes, then resumes the normal pitch for the remainder. Another medieval manuscript retains that transposition and adds to it the transposition of section 5 up a fifth, ending on the affinal a. Such transpositions of chant portions seem to be an acceptable "norm."

NOTATION

Early notation served as a memory aid to those who already knew the melody. As such, its emphasis was on the indication of nuances of performance: ornaments, vocal articulations related to text, speed, and slowness. But gradually the impetus of a changing society moved toward a desire for a more precise pitch notation—a notation, in short, that made fewer demands on memory. In the process, the variations in neume shapes that indicated performance nuance were reduced to simple pitch-oriented designs. Of the many special neumes formerly in use, only the quilisma and the liquescent were retained.

Hucbald, who in his treatise advocates a letter notation for pitch precision, states the need for precise pitch indication this way:

> As the sounds and differences of words are recognized by letters in writing in such a way that the reader is not led into doubt, musical letters were devised so that every melody notated by their means, once these signs have been learned, can be sung even without a teacher. But this can scarcely happen using the signs which custom has handed down to us [the neumes] and which in various regions are given no less various shapes, although they are some help as an aid to one's memory, for the markings by which they guide the reader are always indefinite. . . . Looking at the first mark, which appears to be rather high, you may easily sing it at any pitch in your range. But when you try to connect it to the second note, which you observe is lower, and you inquire by what interval you should do so—whether the second should be one or two or even three steps away from the first—you cannot even vaguely detect how this was prescribed by the composer unless you get it by ear from someone.[2]

---

[2]Warren Babb, trans., *Hucbald, Guido, and John on Music,* ed. Claude V. Palisca (New Haven: Yale University Press, 1978), 36–37.

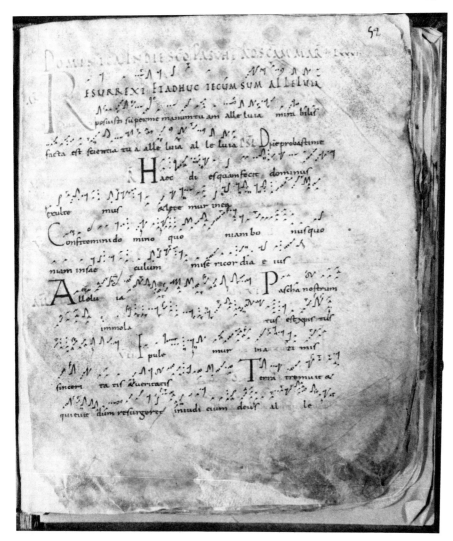

Facsimile 3-1. Diastematic Neumes. Laon, Bibliothèque municipale, MS 239, fol. 52, ca. 930.

Although theorists such as Hucbald proposed letter type notations, the trend in practical manuscripts was toward a more careful placement of neumes on the page, so that the height of the neume above the text and the vertical relationship of one neume to the next would indicate the interval more precisely. This use of *diastematic* or heightened neumes was to prove the basis for future notational developments (see Facsimile 3-1, where a diastematic version of the Introit *Resurrexi* in Anthology Example 2 appears at the top of the page).

Although more precise, diastematic neumes still lack two essentials for the exact notation of pitch: indications of the pitch of the starting tone and of the placement of semitones. The natural use of scribal guidelines, where the scribe would scratch a line on the parchment as an aid to properly aligning the notes, suggested the way to the staff.

The first theoretical exposition of the staff is by Guido of Arrezo (ca. 1030). His is a rudimentary two-line staff, with a red line for F, a yellow one for c. From this, the two lines expanded to four, and the letters C and F, rudimentary clef signs, replaced the colored lines. Thus was formed the four-line staff with moveable C and F clefs that was to serve for chant until the present day.

Facsimile 3-2 shows the beginning of the sequence *Regnantem sempiterna* (Anthology Example 15) and is from an English Troper-Graduale of around 1140. The sequence follows the *Alleluia: Laetatus sum,* notated on the previous page, and is identified in the manuscript by the abbreviated word *sequentia* in red ink at the end of the first line of folio 59'. A flat sign in the space for b is used as a clef, changing to a natural on the same space when b actually begins to appear in the music (line 5). A comparison with the transcription in the Anthology will show, aside from the omission of the opening alleluia, only the sort of minor variance of pitch, as at *divino sono,* that is common in alternate medieval versions of chant.

Despite the precision of the new staff notation, its widespread use came slowly. Most eleventh- and twelfth-century manuscripts still use staffless diastematic neumes, indicative of the continued reliance on memory in medieval musical life.

Medieval notation conveys only relative, not absolute, pitch. The notated pitch level is simply that which avoids the use of accidentals; it in no way indicates the performance pitch level. Thus a Tetrardus chant notated G to g might well be sung at the same pitch as a plagal Protus chant notated a seventh lower.

All chant is related to the singer's comfortable range. The same would have been true of early polyphony.

TEACHING AIDS

The Hexachords and Solmization

Coincident with the impetus toward notational precision is the development of techniques to enable the quick learning of melodies. Earliest was the use of the monochord, a one-stringed instrument that, through the use of a movable bridge, was able to play the successive intervals of a chant.

A less cumbersome system using solmization syllables is attributed to Guido. He used a familiar hymn to Saint John, *Ut queant laxis,* in which each phrase begins on the succeeding note of an ascending scale, as a means of tonal ori-

Facsimile 3-2. Four-line Staff. London, British Library, Roy. 2 BIV, ca. 1140, fol. 59′.

entation. From the first syllables of these six lines were abstracted the syllables *ut, re, mi, fa, sol,* and *la,* making a six-note scale or *hexachord.* Like its descendent, modern solmization with movable *do,* Guido's system allows transposition, though to only three positions: hexachords beginning on C (the *natural* hexachord), F (the *soft* hexachord, with a b flat) or G (the *hard* hexachord), see Example 3-5.

In singing melodies that extend beyond the six notes of the hexachord, the singer *mutates* into the next appropriate hexachord, a process discussed in detail in the Practicum at the end of this chapter.

The principal importance of the hexachord system for the singer is in its definition of a scale segment containing a single semitone, always between *mi* and *fa.* It became an all-pervasive teaching system that stood apart from the modal system and was adaptable to music of various organizational approaches. Its influence on music was strong throughout the Renaissance.

The Gamut

As hexachords can be formed on <u>G</u>, C, F, G, c, f, and g, it is apparent that they will overlap in a recognizable pattern. This is codified in the *gamut,* which arranges in composite order an ascending series of seven hexachords (see Example 3-6). Specific tones could be identified by naming all the applicable syllables: e.g., D re-sol, or d re-sol-la. The lowest note, *gamma-ut,* gives the gamut its name.

EXAMPLE 3-5. The Hexachords.

EXAMPLE 3-6. The Gamut.

The gamut serves as a definition of usable tonal space, one roughly equivalent to the male singing voice (including the male alto voice). It was largely a theoretical construct until the full range began to be exploited in the polyphony of the thirteenth and fourteenth centuries. It remained the notated definition of musical space through the male-oriented polyphony of the late Renaissance, although it only designated relative, not absolute, pitch.

The Hand

Another teaching aid attributed to Guido, but probably in use earlier, is the so-called Guidonian Hand, a visual sight-singing device in which each joint of the hand represented a particular note of the gamut (see Figure 3-1). The leader would indicate the correct syllable, and thus the correct interval, by pointing to the appropriate spot on his upheld hand.

Practicum

SINGING WITH THE HEXACHORDS

Practice in sight-singing with the hexachords is one of the quickest ways to begin to assimilate the thought process of the medieval musician. In the later Middle Ages and the Renaissance, hexachordal analysis is often the most effective way to solve problems of musica ficta.

The hexachord process is not complex and is an excellent one to use in the singing of plainchant. As a teaching aid, it is similar to (and ancestor of) the modern system of movable *do,* but with the following differences:

1. The syllable *ut* is used instead of *do.*

2. It encompasses only six notes (medieval musicians did not think in terms of octaves).

3. As b flat is the only allowable chromatic, the "movability" of the hexachords is confined to the tones C, F, and G (and their octaves).

4. The three hexachords are the *natural* on C, the *soft* on F, and the *hard* on G (see Example 3-7).

In this system, *mi-fa* represents a semitone, all other syllables whole tones. Singing begins in the hexachord into which the first phrase most naturally fits. If the melody exceeds the limits of the hexachord that is in use, shift or *mutate* to the next higher or lower one. This is done by mentally exchanging the

Figure 3-1. The Guidonian Hand. Milan, Bib. Ambrosiana, MS D.75.INF.

appropriate syllable name of the old hexachord for the proper one in the new. Accordingly, in Example 3-8 G is approached as *fa* in the soft hexachord, but left as *sol* in the natural.

the *natural* on C:

ut re mi fa sol la

the *soft* on F:

ut re mi fa sol la

and the *hard* on G:

ut re mi fa sol la

EXAMPLE 3-7. The Three Hexachords.

Initially, for practice, it is wise to say both names. Later it will become a mental process and only the second name need be sung. The following examples, in which the syllables are given, should be practiced until the concept is clear (Examples 3-9a–d).

Assignment

Practice singing the following melodies (Examples 3-10 to 3-12) in hexachord solmization as assigned. Begin with the examples here, which, for simplicity, are notated in the transposing treble clef. Subsequently, apply solmization to the examples in chant notation in Chapter 2 (Examples 2-7–11).

Soft: fa re mi re=
Natural: sol mi re mi

EXAMPLE 3-8. Example of Mutation.

a.   Mutation from the soft to the natural hexachord

Ut re fa mi re=   re mi sol fa mi=
        sol mi fa mi re fa sol=   la re mi re.

EXAMPLE 3-9. Examples of Mutation Procedures   *(continued)*

b.   Mutation from the hard to the natural hexachord

Ut mi fa sol fa re mi re   re fa mi re ut.
                la mi fa re mi fa sol la

c.   Alternate mutation possibilities. Often there are several possible points of mutation. Either of the given methods of solmization is correct, although the one under the staff, remaining in each hexachord as long as possible, is probably preferable. Note that, when possible, *ut* is avoided as a point of mutation.

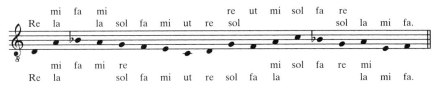

d.   Mutation into all three hexachords

EXAMPLE 3-9 (*continued*)

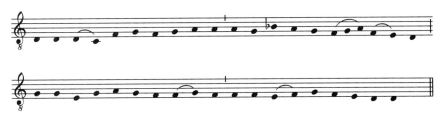

EXAMPLE 3-10.   Antiphon *Dum esset*, Antiphonale Monasticum, p. 741. © Abbaye Saint Pierre de Solesmes, France, 1974, reprinted by permission.

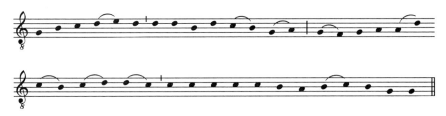

EXAMPLE 3-11.   Antiphon *Lucia Virgo, Antiphonale Monasticum*, p. 770. © Abbaye Saint Pierre de Solesmes, France, 1974, reprinted by permission.

EXAMPLE 3-12. *Alleluia: Haec est virgo*, G.R., p. 501. © Abbaye Saint Pierre de Solesmes, France, 1974, reprinted by permission.

BIBLIOGRAPHY

Music

Chant sources are given in the Bibliography for Chapter 1. Twenty-two dramas, some not otherwise available, are given in chant notation in Edmond de Coussemaker, *Drames Liturgiques du Moyen Age* (Rennes, 1860, rpt. Geneva: Slatkine Reprints, 1975). Versions in modern notation, with performance suggestions, include a series of individual publications by Oxford University Press, all edited by William L. Smoldon: *Herod* (1960), *Visitatio Sepulchri* (1964), *Peregrinus* (1965), *Planctus Marie* (1965), *Officium Pastorum* (1967), and *Sponsus* (1972). *The Play of Daniel* has received two modern editions, one edited by William L. Smoldon and revised by David Wulstan (Sutton, Surrey: The Plainsong and Medieval Music Society, 1976) and the other by Noah Greenberg (New York: Oxford University Press, 1959).

Theory

The *Alia musica* has been cited in Chapter 1. Three other key theorists are found in translation in Warren Babb, *Hucbald, Guido, and John on Music*, also cited there. Two additional writings of Guido are given in Strunk, 117–25, as is the *Dialogus de musica* (*Enchiridion musices*) of Pseudo-Odo (103–16). The treatise *Musica* by Hermanus Cantractus is translated in Leonard Ellinwood, *Musica Hermanni Contracti*, Eastman School of Music Studies No. 2 (Rochester: Eastman School of Music, 1936).

Readings

Concerning troping in general, see Richard L. Crocker, "The Troping Hypothesis," MQ 52 (1966): 183–203.

Richard Crocker, *The Early Medieval Sequence* (Berkeley, Cal.: University of California Press, 1977), is the definitive study of the early sequence and includes editions of much of the early repertoire. John Stevens, "The Sequence," *Words and Music in the Middle Ages: Song, Narrative, Dance and Drama, 1050–1350,* Cambridge Studies in Music (Cambridge: Cambridge University Press, 1986), 80–109, covers the early, middle, and late sequence.

Concerning the trope, see Paul Evans, *The Early Trope Repertoire of Saint Martial de Limoges* (Princeton, N.J.: Princeton Univ. Press, 1970); Nicole Sevestre, "The Aquitanian Tropes of the Easter Introit: A Musical Analysis," *JPMMS* 3 (1980): 26–40; Alejandro Planchart, *The Repertory of Tropes at Winchester,* 2 vol. (Princeton, N.J.: Princeton University Press, 1976); Charles M. Atkinson, "The Earliest Agnus Dei Melody and Its Tropes," *JAMS* 30 (1977): 1–19; David Bjork, "Early Settings of the Kyrie Eleison and the Problem of Genre Definition," *JPMMS* 3 (1980): 40–49; and Alejandro Planchart, "On the Nature of Transmission and Change in Trope Repertories," *JAMS* 41 (1988): 215–49.

William L. Smoldon, *The Music of the Medieval Church Dramas* (London: Oxford University Press, 1980), is a basic study of liturgical drama, while another recent survey is in John Stevens, *Words and Music,* pp. 308–71. Also pertinent are the essays in Thomas P. Campbell and Clifford Davidson, eds., *The Fleury Playbook* (Kalamazoo: Western Michigan University, 1985).

Detailed discussion of modal transposition may be found in Dolores Pesce, *The Affinities and Medieval Transposition* (Bloomington, Ind.: Indiana University Press, 1987). An exposition of hexachordal theory through the Renaissance is contained in Gaston G. Allaire, *The Theory of Hexachords and Solmization and the Modal System,* MSD 24 (AIM, 1969).

4

Early Polyphony

Many musical cultures make use, in some limited or accidental way, of different pitches sounded simultaneously, but only in Europe was the practice cultivated and made the foundation of a whole musical culture. The cause of this is one of the great mysteries of music history and musical aesthetics. For the astonishing fact is that the first manifestation of a systematic polyphonic practice is recorded at the very same time and in the very same milieu as Europe's first codification of plainchant and of the new development of a system of notation. It is as if, with the earliest Carolingian musical documentation, we enter the theater in the middle of the second act—we find ourselves in a musical milieu in which every aspect of later European musical development is present, at least in embryo, but we know little about how this came to be.

In the first detailed account of polyphony, that of the anonymous late ninth-century *Musica enchiriadis* (Manual on Music) and its companion *Scholia enchiriadis* (Commentary on the Manual), we are already presented with two distinct types. One, *parallel organum*, is more an expansion of texture than true polyphony in the usual modern sense: it is simply the duplication of the chant at a perfect fifth, fourth, or octave. The second, *oblique organum*, was initially also an expansion of texture, but in the use of oblique as well as parallel motion and the coming together of the voices in a unison cadence, it already contains the seeds of future development.

We can only surmise that the formative period of these styles stretches back into the eighth century or possibly even earlier, for these first descriptions of polyphony discuss it not as something new but as an established practice. The practice of polyphony was probably already developing in the seventh and eighth centuries, or even in the sixth, during the period before musical notation, and possibly as much in secular as in church music, for one of the early theoretical examples of polyphony sets a secular text at a time when virtually no other secular music was being recorded. What we do know is that by the late ninth century two approaches to polyphony existed, of sufficient importance to warrant detailed theoretical discussion.

The practice of parallel and oblique organum remained an important part of musical activity for quite some time, judging from Guido of Arezzo's detailed description of it in his *Micrologus* (ca. 1026–28) some one hundred and fifty years after *Musica enchiriadis*. Its lifespan was actually much longer, since it probably predated *Musica enchiriadis* by a century or two and lasted, at least in outlying areas, into the fifteenth century.

Tracing the prehistory of polyphony lies in the realm of conjecture, but certain primitive practices can be surmised to have played a role.

One is the normal divisions of the human voice, which as often as not lie a fifth rather than an octave apart—one need only consider the relationship of soprano to alto and tenor to bass. This, coupled with the acoustical consonance of a perfect fifth, can easily induce the untrained singer to parallel the melody not at the octave but at the fifth or fourth (even today, and even against the harmonic accompaniment of an organ or campfire guitar!).

Another is the widespread use in many musical cultures—and in medieval musical instruments—of the drone, a sustained note or notes above which the melody moves and which gives an undefinable sense of fullness or "harmony" to the melody.

The third general procedure is *heterophony*, the casual melodic differences that occur when different versions of the same melody are performed together, the differences occurring either through variance in the remembered versions of the melody or through deliberate ornamentation.

A fourth, less sure influence may have been the medieval organ, derived from the Roman *hydraulis*. In tenth-century accounts it is described as having several pipes per key, possibly arranged in octaves and fifths like a mixture stop. Whether this was influenced by, or an influence on, vocal singing is a matter of conjecture, but it seems significant that the same Latin term was used interchangeably for both instrument and early vocal polyphony.

All of these practices except the last occur naturally in folk idioms around the world. It is only in Europe that musicians took them beyond casual practice and developed them into a conscious musical system.

PARALLEL ORGANUM

The simplest form of organum is that in which the added voice parallels the original melody in perfect fourths, fifths, or octaves. The voice carrying the original melody is called the *vox principalis* (principal voice) while the added voice is called the *vox organalis* (organizing voice). Three forms of simple parallel organum are given in Anthology Example 16. In theoretical discussions about this style the organizing voice, shown in black noteheads in the transcription, is considered to be *below* the principal voice.

Composite parallel organum—in which one or both of the voices is doubled at the octave and, according to the *Scholia enchiriadis*, even in a second octave—

was apparently more common in actual practice than these simple forms. As described in the *enchiriadis* treatises, the variety of possible doubling is considerable (Example 4-1) and often results in simultaneous parallel perfect fourths and fifths. When to these is added the further possibility of the doubling, by boys or instruments, at a third octave, the concept of parallel organum becomes slightly less simple.

Although such parallelism may seem sterile to a "sophisticated" twentieth-century listener, think instead of its effect within a liturgical service otherwise sung in unison chant, and, especially, heard by listeners not conditioned by a millennium of harmonic complexities. Performed slowly, as the *Scholia enchiriadis* specifies, in the resonance of a stone church, in the variety of possible doublings given, the result can be impressive. As the added text of a trope enriches and embellishes a chant monophonically, so sonorous doubling can enrich a chant through pure sound.

Another feature that can also take this "simple" parallelism into a richer domain is the extemporaneous ornamentation of one or more of the upper lines, a practice specifically discussed by thirteenth- and fourteenth-century theorists and undoubtedly used long before.

Parallel organum was seldom committed to writing, but it remained an improvised performance idiom through the fifteenth century. It merged with other concepts to form the practice of "fifthing" in the thirteenth and fourteenth centuries (an offshoot of organum at the fifth) and the fauxbourdon of the fifteenth (incorporating parallel movement at the fourth).

OBLIQUE ORGANUM

The ninth-century *enchiriadis* treatises give equal emphasis to the parallel and oblique types. By the time of Guido's treatise of around 1026–28, though, taste has changed, for Guido calls parallel organum "hard" (*durus*), while the preferred oblique style he calls "smooth" (*mollis*).

His treatment of oblique organum is not only more extensive than earlier treatments, but also betrays a greater awareness of its subtlety and of the qualities of discrete individual intervals: "In [organum] we do not permit the semitone or the fifth, but we do permit the tone, the major third, the minor third and the fourth; and of these the minor third ranks lowest and the fourth highest."

Octave doubling, still expected in parallel organum, has no place in Guido's oblique style. Instead, instruction for composition is described in terms of individual intervals: "The accompanying voice should not descend lower than the *tritus* [the third note of the tetrachord system] either when phrases end on it or when the tritus is next below such an ending." These rules are illustrated with a series of examples (see Example 4-2).

Guido's *tritus*, the third note of each tetrachord in Hucbald's series of tetrachords (see Chapter 3), is normally C or F. When the chant to be harmo-

1.   The *vox organalis* is doubled an octave higher:

2.   The *vox principalis* is doubled an octave lower:

3.   The *vox organalis* is doubled an octave lower:

4.   The *vox principalis* is doubled an octave higher:

5.   The *vox principalis* is doubled at the octave and the *vox organalis* is sung, not at pitch, but two octaves higher:

6.   The *vox principalis* and the *vox organalis* are both doubled an octave higher:

7.   The *vox principalis* is doubled an octave below, the *vox organalis* an octave above:

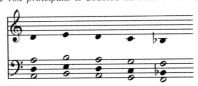

EXAMPLE 4-1.   Composite Organum Doublings from the *Enchiriadis* Treatises.

o = *vox principalis*

● = *vox organalis*

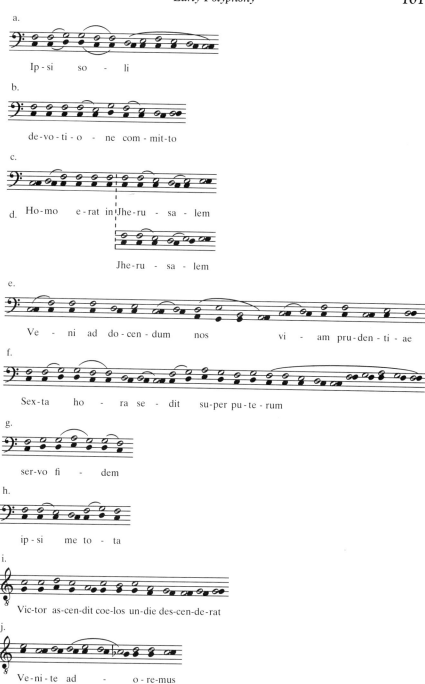

EXAMPLE 4-2. Oblique Organum Examples from Guido's *Micrologus.*

(continued)

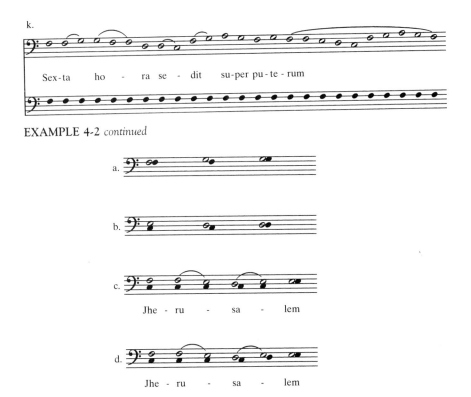

k.

Sex-ta   ho - ra se - dit   su-per pu - te - rum

EXAMPLE 4-2 *continued*

a.

b.

c.

Jhe - ru - sa - lem

d.

Jhe - ru - sa - lem

EXAMPLE 4-3.   The Use of the Second at Cadences.

nized lies close to either of those pitches, the *vox organalis* acts as a drone, remaining stationary on that pitch. When the melody is high enough, the *vox organalis* moves in parallel fourths with it.

Other alternate stationary pitches are also used: G̲ when the chant goes below C (see Example 4-2e), G when a chant in that range uses b natural.

The result is an organum that combines drones with oblique and parallel motion. This gives, far more than does the purely parallel style, a suggestion of polyphonic independence.

Possibly most important, however, is the concern Guido gives to what is a rudimentary concept of cadence—*occursus* in his terminology: "This coming together [*occursus*] on the final is preferably by a tone, less so by a major third, and never by a minor third." In his view the coming together of the voices is preferably on a unison: always so at the end of a piece, preferably so on interior phrase endings. The *occursus* encompasses two intervals, the final and the penultimate. It is their relationship that creates the sense of *occursus*. A fourth resolving inward to a unison is possible, but weak. A major third resolving inward is better. Best is the dissonance of a major second resolving by oblique motion.

Although tastes change radically from age to age, this is the first intimation of the desire for tension and resolution that has marked European cadence structures ever since (although it would take nine centuries to regain the appreciation for the major second!).

Various options are given in Example 4-3. Chants cadencing on G or D can be nicely harmonized with a precadential dissonance of F or C. Deuterus chants on E may cadence on a unison via a skip of a third from C (Example 4-3c), but will preferably close in the third through what amounts to parallel seconds (Example 4-3d).

THE SOURCES

Information about parallel and oblique organum is tantalizingly scarce; our discussion to this point has been based entirely on the explanations of organum given in a handful of theory treatises. These provide rules and short musical examples. The advantage of these examples is their notation in letters or some other system that permits reliable transcription. Their disadvantage is their fragmentary nature and their having been chosen to illustrate theoretical rules which, like theoretical precepts at any time, probably tend to be more rigid than actual musical practice.

The only glimpse we have into an actual performance repertoire is regrettably incapable of such precise transcription. This is the so-called Winchester Troper, an important manuscript now located at Cambridge University, where it has the shelf number of Corpus Christi College, 473. It derives from the important medieval liturgical center of Winchester in what was then Anglo-Saxon England and contains a collection of 174 two-voiced organa that may be largely the compositions of Wulfstan, cantor there from around 990 to 1010. Notation is in nondiastematic neumes, with some letter notation that may imply instrumental accompaniment or performance.

Although the nondiastematic neumes of the manuscript make precise transcription impossible, recent research has shown it possible to re-create at least the broad contour of the music, even if we cannot verify each pitch.

As can be seen in the transcription by Holschneider of the *Alleluia: Angelus domini; Respondens* (Anthology Example 18), the general procedures of Guidonian-style oblique organum are followed, but with the freedoms that one might expect from experienced improvisors. (A facsimile of the organal part may be seen in *NGD*, 13:801.)

The most notable deviations from the rules of Guido are the use of an upper drone, as at the beginning of the polyphonic *Alleluia* and the opening of the verse, and the use of the interval of a fifth at the beginning of some phrases, the organal voice holding the drone until the *vox principalis* merges with it in a unison. The element of voice crossing that ensues, the *vox organalis* being temporarily above the *vox principalis*, may also be seen in a short ninth-century treatise known as the "Paris" organum treatise.

Also noticeable is the use of the minor third as a precadential dissonance, a progression avoided by Guido and other earlier organum treatises (see for instance the cadences to the second *alleluia* phrase and to those beginning *revolvit, eum*).

Practicum

COMPOSITION AND IMPROVISATION

Parallel Organum

Parallel organum consists of consecutive parallel intervals. It is simple in theory, except for the problem of the tritone, for in singing perfect fifths or fourths throughout the octave, *one* of the two voices will have to alter a tone somewhere in the scale (for example, an F sharp to match a B or a B flat to match an F). The result is a kind of primitive bimodality that may disturb the modern singer used to a consistent tonality. Presumably this caused no problem for the medieval performer, who at this time thought in an almost totally linear fashion, merely singing the chant, from memory, at whatever pitch was given. This bimodality does, however, create problems when the style must be notated, for the tritone can only be avoided if the *vox organalis* is written with one additional flat in organum at the fifth or one additional sharp in organum at the fourth.

Parallel organum was important in the development of medieval music because it cultivated sonority for its own sake and explored the effects of intervals and intervallic doubling. It also established in the medieval ear three intervals—the fourth, fifth, and octave that would remain the workhorse consonants through the thirteenth century.

To appreciate the special effect of this parallel style it is necessary to perform and notate examples, using both simple and composite forms.

Assignments. Using Examples 4-8–4-11 below or any of the Anthology chants:

1. Perform, as a class or one on a part, examples of simple and composite parallel organum at the fifth and fourth.

2. Notate examples of each.

Oblique Organum

Although the rules for oblique organum given by medieval theorists are based on the tetrachord, the modern student, unfamiliar with the tetrachord system, will most easily grasp the practical aspects of oblique organum through reference to the system of hexachords. Accordingly, although the preliminary discussion earlier in the chapter speaks in more neutral terms, the explanation here will refer to the hexachords as a practical matter. The unspoken relationship between oblique organum and the hexachords may be described in the following manner.

The sustained "drone" notes spoken of by Guido (G̲, C, F and G) are also the bottom notes of the standard hexachords: the hard on G̲ and G, the natural on C, the soft on F. Guido's usage is also parallel: F when b flat is present, G when b natural, C when the melody ranges from C to a. The range of the principal melody above that lowest sustained note is also limited to a sixth or rarely a seventh, coinciding in practical terms with hexachord range. A cross section of Guido's examples was given in Example 4-2.

Restating oblique organum procedures in terms of hexachord equivalents will in most cases clarify the practical procedures of composition and improvisation.

1. The *vox organalis* is below the *vox principalis* and will not descend below *ut* of the hexachord in which the *vox principalis* phrase lies. If the *vox principalis* changes hexachords, so will the *vox organalis*. When a phrase or phrase segment of the *vox principalis* can be interpreted in either of two hexachords, there arises a rare chance for "artistic" choice. Example 4-2g interprets the notes F G a G F as being in the natural hexachord, harmonizing them in parallel fourths, while the conclusion of Example f treats the same notes as belonging to the soft hexachord, deliberately shifting from the natural in order to conclude on a unison cadence.

2. Phrases may begin on either a unison or a fourth.

3. Phrases will proceed in parallel fourths when possible, but otherwise, the *vox organalis* will remain stationary on *ut*. Obviously, the range of the *vox principalis* within the hexachord will affect this: parallelism is possibly only when the main melody lies in the upper half of the hexachord.

4. Cadences deserve special attention. All major phrases end on a unison, although less important interior phrases *may* end on a fourth. In approaching a cadential unison, neither a minor second nor a minor third should be used. This eliminates the cadential possibilities of Example 4-4.

Cadential movement of a major third to a unison is good. A major second to a unison is better. A perfect fourth to a unison should be used only at a final cadence, and then only if no other option is available. Acceptable cadential progressions are given in Example 4-5.

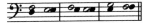

EXAMPLE 4-4. Incorrect Cadential Progressions.

To the tone A:

To the tone C:

To the tone D:

To the tone E:

To the tone F:

To the tone G:

To the tone a:

To the tone b:

EXAMPLE 4-5.   Acceptable Cadential Movement.

In explaining the preference for a major second to a unison cadence, Guido mentions three special applications of this progression, illustrated earlier in Example 4-3. In Example 4-3a, the effect of the final G is enhanced by the retention of the F and its resolution through oblique motion. In Example 4-3b, the same concept is used to embellish what is essentially a third-to-unison movement, retaining the C of the *vox organalis* as a type of suspension. The two alternate settings of *Jherusalem* (Examples 4-3c and d) show that even parallel seconds might be used as a precadential dissonance.

The above rules work perfectly when the principal voice lies in the G, C, or F hexachords. When the melody lies in the G hexachord, however, although the normal sustained tone is G, an F may be used in the *vox organalis* to harmonize G and A, as in Example 4-2i. This is particularly useful at cadences.

The same rules seem to apply to the transposed modes, for Guido cites Example 4-2j as plagal Tritus, which implies a transformation up a fourth from F to b flat. He then treats the whole passage as if it were a transposition of the previous example, c acting as the organal sustained tone, while b flat accompanies c and d at the cadence.

In approaching composition or improvisation in this style, begin by determining, preferably through singing, the correct hexachord solmization for the chant, and then relate the organal voice to it.

The process involved may be seen in Example 4-6, a sample oblique organum setting of the Gradual respond *Bonum est*. The chant and organal setting are given on the first staff, a few possible variants on the second staff. The third staff in system 1 illustrates a seemingly logical yet prohibited movement.

Most notes in the *vox organalis* are dictated by the organum rules. Only the few artistic options need comment:

1. Phrase 1 is best begun on a fourth, although, as the initial phrase of the piece, a unison is possible. A stepwise movement away from that unison is, however, prohibited because of the minor second that would result.

2. Phrase 2 could begin in the C hexachord and shift within the phrase. The option of staff 1, remaining within the same hexachord, is possibly more idiomatic.

3. The interior cadence of phrase 2 is made more definite by the version on staff 1, but the version on staff 2 would unify the melisma into one long phrase if that should be desired.

4. The exact shift in a change of hexachords may occasionally be a matter of choice, as in phrase 4b.

As the melody of *Bonum est* tends to lie in the upper range of the hexachord, it permits a relatively high ratio of parallel motion. Other chants permit very little. A case in point is the opening of the Sanctus in Example 4-7.

The entire example lies within the C hexachord and does not even rise to *la*. C is the lowest organal tone and, in the simple setting on staff 1, seldom leaves the tones C and D. The options on staff 2 alleviate the drone effect somewhat. Guido does not mention parallel unisons, but they are used in other treatises and are an option when the phrase beginning or ending is on one of the three lowest notes of the hexachord. The optional cadence for phrase 4 is a favorite of Guido's.

Assignments

1. Write oblique organum settings of Examples 4-8–11. These examples have been chosen for their suitability for oblique organum practice and are arranged in approximate order of difficulty.

EXAMPLE 4-6. Sample Oblique Organum Setting. (Gradual respond *Bonum est con-fiteri*, G.R., p. 327.)

EXAMPLE 4-7. Oblique Organum Setting of *Sanctus ad libitum*, G.R., pp. 795–96.

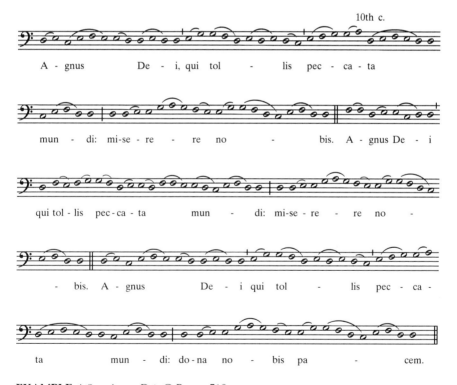

EXAMPLE 4-8. *Agnus Dei*, G.R., p. 718.

2. Perform the notated solutions, singing the organal part in hexachord syllables.

3. When familiar with the principles of oblique organum through notation and performance, improvise examples in and out of class. As an aid in this process, it may be helpful first to "improvise" organal parts to chants previously worked out in notation, using only the chant melody as a guide.

4. Improvisation may also be based on chants in modern chant notation. Those in the Practicum of Chapter 1 are particularly suitable.

BIBLIOGRAPHY

Music

No precisely transcribable music of the period exists except for short examples in theory treatises, about half of which are included in this chapter and the Anthology.

Guido's *Micrologus* is available in translation in Babb, *Hucbald* (see Chapter 1), and the organum portion of the *Scholia enchiriadis* in Strunk, 126–38. Both the *Enchiriadis* treatises are translated in Richard Holladay, "The 'Musica Enchiriadis' and 'Scholia Enchiriadis': A Translation and Commentary" (Ph.D. diss., UMI No. 78-5855).

All of the early organum treatises are published in Latin with German translation in Ernst Ludwig Waeltner, *Die Lehre von Organum bis zur Mitte des 11*

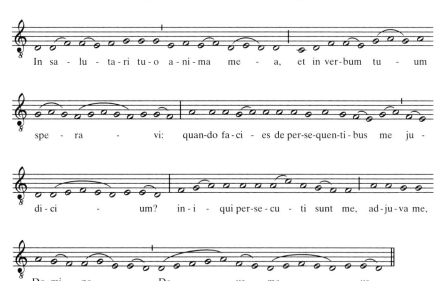

EXAMPLE 4-9. Communion Antiphon *In salutario*, G.R., p. 350.

EXAMPLE 4-10. Communion Antiphon, *Data est mihi*, G.R., p. 213–14.

Jahrhunderts, vol. 1 (Tutzing: Hans Schneider, 1975), although the examples have been altered to eliminate notated tritones and other supposed anomalies. The *enchiriadis* treatises have received a new edition in *Musica et Scolia enchiriadis una cum aliquibus tractatulis adiunctis recensio nova post Gerbertinam altera ad fidem omnium codicum manuscriptorum,* ed. Hans Schmid, Bayerische Akademie der Wissenschaften: Veröffentlichungen der musikhistorischen Kommission 3 (Munich: Bayerischen Akademie der Wissenschaften, 1981), which should be used, however, with reference to a review by Nancy Phillips in *JAMS* 36 (1983): 128–42.

The Winchester Troper is discussed at length, with carefully reasoned transcriptions, in Andreas Holschneider, *Die Organa von Winchester* (Hildesheim: George Olms, 1968). A few more transcriptions may be found in Alejandro Planchart, *The Repertory of Tropes at Winchester* (Princeton: Princeton University Press, 1977). One of the Holschneider transcriptions is available as OAMM 38.

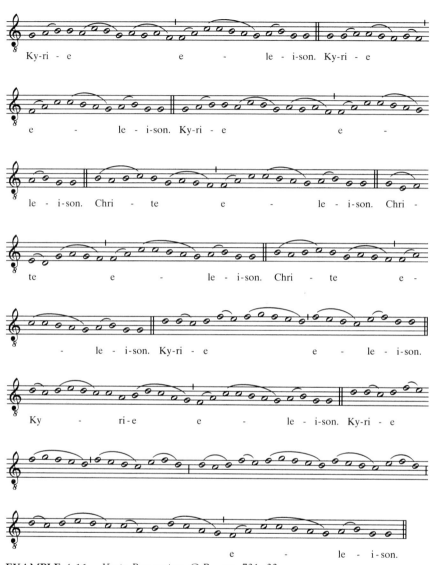

EXAMPLE 4-11. Kyrie *Rex genitor*, G.R., pp. 731–32.

Part II

THE FLOWERING OF STYLE
1050–1250

Introduction

There can be little doubt about the beauty and artistry of Carolingian plainchant: it remains one of the glories of Western civilization. The same cannot be said for the rough charm of Carolingian polyphony, for organum to 1050 remained a rudimentary art. It lay to the next age to bring to flower the art of polyphony, to create a new monophonic sacred repertoire, and to introduce a new courtly secular monophony.

While the new monophony can be seen as a merging of traditional procedures with a new rhythmic poetry, the seed of later polyphony lies in the seeming simplicity of *free organum*, for it was in this new development in the late years of the eleventh century that the fundamental concept of contrary-motion discant was established, the fundamental principle on which the Aquitanian versus, the Notre Dame conductus and organum, the motet of the thirteenth and fourteenth centuries, and the subsequent French and Italian song forms are based. Even beyond, contrary-motion discant underlies the counterpoint of the Renaissance and merges with later harmonic thinking to form the basis of part-writing in Baroque and Classical times.

Because of this, it is especially important to examine closely the music of these early formative periods, proceeding from the simple principles of free organum to the more artistic use of those ideas in the polyphony of Aquitania and the culmination of the period in the expansive organa and the conductus of Notre Dame.

Stylistic change is rarely marked by a special signal event; more commonly, it creeps forward gradually, and at different rates in different idioms. For the study of history, however, lines of demarcation between style periods must be set arbitrarily. Such is the case in the change from the Carolingian and post-Carolingian Romanesque style to the incipient Gothic style of the twelfth century.

In the field of monophony, medieval chant received its fullest modal explication in the mid- and late eleventh century and continued throughout the later Middle Ages and beyond as a compositional genre. Coincident with this codification of the old, however, is the appearance of powerful new forces connected with the setting of the new rhythmic poetry: new forms of sacred music, such as the versus and the conductus, and the explosion of secular courtly music in the newly developing Germanic and Romance languages.

A somewhat parallel situation is found in polyphony. There is every evidence that the earlier simple forms of organum continued throughout the succeeding centuries as an improvised form, seldom committed to writing, while important new activity was leading toward greater and greater refinement and artistic potential. This new idiom began as the free organum of the late twelfth century and grew into the melismatic and discant forms of Aquitanian and Parisian polyphony.

The geographical center of the activity we have recounted in Part 1 lay within the central areas of the Frankish kingdoms, particularly western Germany and France, with some important theoretical input from northern Italy in the eleventh century. In this new historical age the center of activity remains in France—first in the wealthy, civilized South of Aquitania, then in the intellectual and artistic capital of Paris.

The great political event of the age, the Crusades, that series of romantic (and not so romantic) attempts to wrest the Holy Land from the Infidel that began in 1096, had limited success in its avowed purpose. It did, however, bring medieval Europe into direct contact with the Byzantine and Muslim cultures of the Middle East.

Closer to the heart of musical development were another series of crusades: those that occurred throughout the eleventh century against the Muslims in Spain and that gradually increased the area of Christian Spain, and the one against the Albigensians of southern France, waged between 1209 and 1229 at the pope's bidding by northern French knights, which ended both the political independence and the unique civilization of the South.

Despite the drain on Europe caused by the Crusades, the constant internecine warfare between feudal barons, and the jockeying for position of popes and kings, the twelfth and thirteenth centuries were marked by a flowering of knowledge and artistic endeavor that would result in the founding of the great medieval universities, the creation of Gothic art, and a no less impressive expansion in the art of music.

Like the political energy unleashed in the wake of the First Crusade (1095–99), this expansive musical energy made itself openly apparent at the beginning of the twelfth century. But, just as the First Crusade could not have occurred without the earlier confluence of many seemingly disparate events, so the artistic expansion of the twelfth century was the result of a new direction in musical thought that took shape in the latter part of the eleventh century.

That initial growth was international, observable both in the songs of the wandering minstrels and in a new organum style that has left traces from England to Italy. Soon, however, artistic leadership was assumed by the rich civilization of southern France, for it is here that, by 1100, we find both an artistically enriched polyphony and a new courtly monophony. Indeed, in the twelfth century, southern France became an artistic source from which musical ideas spread like waves to Spain, northern France, Germany, and Italy.

If this phase belonged to southern France, the culmination of the era occurred farther north, especially in Paris and the Île-de-France, for it is here that the miracles of Gothic architectural construction were born and where the same breadth of artistic vision led to the expansion of musical texture to three and even four concurrent lines, while simultaneously laying the groundwork for the systematized codification of rhythm.

Most obvious as a symbol of the new age is the Gothic cathedral. The earlier Romanesque style is based on heavy stone walls, rounded arches, few and small windows, and a ceiling whose height is curtailed by the engineering methods involved. The composite effect is of a beautiful but earthbound structure. Gothic style, in contrast, is one of vertical expansion, of walls pierced by numerous windows that through the art of stained glass become luminous wall paintings, and of a seemingly weightless construction in stone that balances force against counterforce so that each smaller part forms a harmonious relationship to the whole. It may not be an accident that the Île-de-France, with Paris at its center, should have created both Gothic architecture and mensural polyphony within the same century.

Gothic style was established in 1144 in the reconstructed choir of the abbey church of Saint-Denis near Paris. It was emulated in grandiose style in the next generation through the construction of the Cathedral of Notre-Dame in the heart of Paris, the exact environment in which worked Leonin, Perotin, and the anonymous composers who brought melismatic organum to heights rivaling the building in which it was performed. It is one of the few times in history when musical and architectural styles are known to have grown in such close contiguity.

If assigning a date to the opening of this artistic period is an uncertain task, assigning one to its close is nearly impossible, for the ramifications of the new artistic impulse spread unevenly throughout Europe. The main thrust of southern French activity ended around 1210, although its monophonic afterglow lasted throughout the thirteenth century, interrelated with the monophonies of Spain and Italy. German Minnesinger tradition begins by the mid-twelfth century, but continues, in evolving but unbroken fashion, until the very beginning of the Baroque. In northern France the tradition of the trouvère continued until the end of the thirteenth century, while the polyphonic composition of conductus and organum reached an end around 1240, overlapping the germination of the early motet.

5

Free Organum

STYLE

We have seen that Guido, in his detailed discussion of oblique organum in the early eleventh century, paid considerable attention to discrete intervallic quality and, especially, to the need for making a good cadence, even including contrary motion. His style was succeeded in the second half of the century by a new one that capitalized on these ideas, but which, most importantly, incorporated contrary motion as an important principle not just at cadences but throughout.

Given a normal time for genesis, the new style probably began to develop around 1050 or slightly earlier, for it appears in theoretical treatises around 1100. Further, it appears as an international style, extant fragments deriving from as far apart as England and Italy. Although all of these examples use the same technical construction, the difference in aural effect is vast, due, primarily, to two distinct definitions of acceptable vertical sonority, which we can call *Style 1* and *Style 2*.

Style 1, taught in the anonymous treatise *Ad organum faciendum* and shown in Anthology Examples 19–21, virtually excludes the third, creating an aural effect based on pure fourths, fifths, and octaves. Style 2, preserved in the Chartres manuscript and a scrap from England (Anthology Examples 22–25), includes the third as a consonance and presents a sonority rich in thirds, with voices that move in closely entwined sinuous lines.

This stylistic distinction does not figure in the first part of this chapter, which deals with matters of structure based on the *Ad organum faciendum*, whose examples are all in Style 1. The comparison of the two styles is resumed in the second portion, a discussion of medieval concepts of consonance and dissonance.

Stylistic Concepts

The new style is called *free organum* (or, occasionally, "new organum"). Its emphasis on contrary motion laid the foundation for all subsequent polyphonic development. Although outwardly simple and "primitive," when considered in terms of its ramifications it is possibly the most important of all medieval polyphonic styles and warrants very careful study.

Free organum is characterized by independence of voice movement in what is still note-against-note polyphony. Although parallel, similar, and oblique motion are still used, contrary motion is not only present but basic to the style. In addition, voice crossing is permitted, and the *vox organalis* more often than not lies above the *vox principalis*.

Parallel and oblique organum are conceived with the chant in the upper and most audible position. The parallel type is little but a textural expansion of the chant through intervallic doubling. In oblique organum, the *vox organalis*, though less strictly dependent, is still placed below the *vox principalis* and is melodically less interesting.

Emphasis on intervallic doubling and the subordination of the added voice to that of the chant gives way in free organum to an increased awareness of the quality of the individual interval and of the artistic possibilities of the added voice. The move toward this new concept is already observable in the account of Guido, who, unlike the ninth-century *Scholia enchiriadis*, omits any discussion of octave doubling in oblique organum and instead stresses the unique quality of individual intervals. Free organum completes this shift: octave doublings are no longer mentioned and the two voices move within the same tonal space, the *vox organalis* now above, now below the *vox principalis* in a less subservient relationship to it.

The Changing Place of Polyphony in the Service

Change in organum style goes hand-in-hand with an important change in the liturgical use of polyphony. Parallel and oblique organum were initially used to set choral portions of the liturgy. Only with Guido and the Winchester Troper do we begin to find the solo portions of chant set, but as yet with no change of style. Choral singers, accompanying chant in an improvisatory or quasi-improvisatory manner, must have simple rules, ones the whole choir can follow. Even oblique organum meets that criterion. Most organal notes are precisely dictated by the movement of the chant, and what few matters of choice remain can be easily settled beforehand.

Free organum, in contrast, is used exclusively to set solo chants or solo portions of chants, particularly the solo portions of Alleluias. The implications of the change are profound. A soloist can sing more difficult music and can also make up or alter his part as he sings. Although these possibilities were not immediately realized to their fullest, the fruitful seeds were planted.

In brief, free organum is characterized by:

1. an emphasis on independent voice movement

2. contrary motion and voice crossing

3. the frequent placing of the added voice above the chant

4. performance by solo singers

5. an expansion of the awareness of intervallically controlled polyphony

The eleventh and twelfth centuries are still in the era of oral culture. Little music was notated, and most polyphony was improvised within the guidelines of the style. Occasionally a more or less fixed composition might evolve from repeated improvisations and be written down, but this was rare. Only a few notated sources exist, and most of these are fragmentary. In addition, only about five of the sources can be accurately transcribed, for although staff notation had been developed, most manuscripts continue to use diastematic or nondiastematic neumes. Of those capable of precise transcription, notation is either in letters or through neumes placed on a dry-point staff (one in which the lines have been scratched into the surface of the parchment, but left uninked). Much of that repertoire is given in Anthology Examples 19 to 25.

Our information about the polyphony of this period is accordingly based on a scattering of fragmentary manuscripts and the descriptions in a few short theory treatises.

Theoretical Concepts

The earliest theoretical descriptions of the new style are the *De musica* of John of Afflighem (also known as John Cotton) and the anonymous *Ad organum faciendum* (How to construct organum). John's account warrants partial quotation:

We now wish to discuss diaphony briefly and succinctly, so as to satisfy the reader's eagerness about this subject as well, as much as we can. Diaphony is the sounding together of different but harmonious notes, which is carried on by at least two singers, so that while one holds to the original melody, another may range aptly among other tones, and at each breathing point both may come together on the same note or at the octave. . . .

Different musicians practice this differently. The simplest method for it is when the various melodic progressions are borne carefully in mind, so that wherever there is an ascent in the original melody, there is at that point a descent in the organal part and vice versa. . . .

You should take note, too, that although I have set a syllabic organum against syllabic motion, it is allowable for anyone making organum to double or triple the syllabic progressions if he wishes, or to build them up suitably in any way whatever. May this little that I have said about diaphony suffice.[1]

An example appended to John's discussion, Example 5-1, succinctly illustrates his method. The element of independence of melodic line and the use of contrary motion is clear. The two voices move within the same musical space, a characteristic of all polyphony prior to the fourteenth century.

The idea of consonance and dissonance and goal-oriented movement needs further explication. Although normal consonances in this period are unisons, fourths, fifths, and octaves, with the third a kind of semiconsonance whose importance seems to vary from area to area, this short example contains not only two thirds, but a second and a seventh. The explanation is in the concept of goal-oriented movement: melodic resolution on either a unison or an octave at the end of each word or phrase, points of arrival indicated by the arrows in Example 5-1.

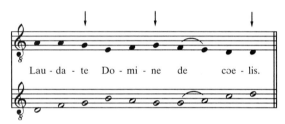

EXAMPLE 5-1.   John of Affleghem, Organum Example.

Analyzing the thirds in John's example in terms of melodic motion, it can be seen that the first third results from the holding of the a in order to resolve on G (Lau*da*te), while the second third occurs as a passing interval aiming also at G. Likewise, the interval of a second results from a passing motion and the seventh from an anticipation of the modal final, the end of a logical melodic motion.

The Organum Modes

Free organum is treated more systematically in the second treatise, the *Ad organum faciendum*, which introduces as a teaching technique five compositional procedures or *organum modes* (not to be confused with the earlier use of the word *mode*). Beyond their immediate application to free organum, these procedures are far more important in establishing a fundamental analytical concept that has been in use, consciously or unconsciously, ever since: the division of a phrase into a beginning, a middle, and an end. Organum modes 1 and 2 deal with

[1]Warren Babb, trans., *Hucbald, Guido, and John on Music*, ed. Claude V. Palisca (New Haven: Yale University Press, 1978), 159–61.

phrase beginnings, 3 and 4 with continuation. Organum mode 5 mentions the possibility of other than note-against-note style. Cadence (*copula* in his terminology) is mentioned throughout.

Collating these organum modes with explanations given in other treatises and a study of existing fragments of free organum results in the following set of generalities.

General style. The counterpoint is, with rare exceptions, note against note. Contrary motion is standard, although similar motion is frequent and two or, at most, three parallel intervals may occur in a row.

Both voices operate within the same tonal space, although the *vox organalis* usually exceeds the *vox principalis* in overall range, a tenth or eleventh being common.

Phrases tend to be short (from two to twelve notes), and cadences are frequent. Phrase length is determined by the text being set; a single word or even syllable often determines the phrase limit.

Phrase structure. Phrases are divided into an initial interval (*prima vox*), the intermediate ones (*medie voces*), and the last (*ultima vox*).

The *prima vox* may be either a unison or an octave (organum mode 1), a fifth or a fourth (organum mode 2), or, exceptionally, a third or sixth (see the discussion of consonance and dissonance below).

Medie voces may move in parallel or similar motion using fifths and fourths (organum mode 3), or in contrary motion using unisons and octaves as well (organum mode 4). Depending on the style of consonance use, thirds and sixths may also be used as *medie voces*.

The *ultima vox* is always a unison or an octave.

The penultimate note of the phrase should be carefully joined to the phrase ending to form a two-note *copula* or cadence. Most common as cadential movements are a fourth to a unison and a fifth to an octave. Less frequent are a third to a unison and a sixth to an octave.

Short phrases may not contain all these elements. A two-note phrase is merely a two-note *copula*. A three-note phrase would contain a *prima vox* and a *copula* consisting of a single *media vox* and the *ultima vox*.

Examples. The *Ad organum faciendum* includes as didactic examples five settings of an identical Alleluia (Example 5-2).

Example 5-2a, organum mode 1, contains two phrases, of five and seven notes respectively. The second phrase begins on a change of syllable within the melismatic chant. Each phrase, as an illustration of organum mode 1, begins on an octave. Both cadences are on the unison. The *medie voces* alternate between fifths and fourths, but include two sets of parallel fourths and one set of parallel fifths. Both cadences are a fourth to a unison.

Example 5-2b, organum mode 2, illustrates phrases beginning on a fourth (phrase 1) or fifth (phrase 3). The second phrase is merely a two-note *copula*, beginning on a fourth. The *medie voces* of the first phrase follow organum mode 3 (parallel motion), those of the third phrase organum mode 4 (contrary motion). (The division of the syllable *lu* into two phrases is unusual and probably a pedagogical device to permit a third phrase.)

Example 5-2c is an illustration of organum mode 3, phrase continuation using parallel and oblique motion. Here the *vox organalis* is set as an extended phrase using fourths and fifths in parallel and similar motion. Intervals alternate, and series of two and three parallels occur. The first note must be considered an isolated one-note phrase.

Example 5-2d, organum mode 4, is the most important of the organum modes, encapsulating the new concept of contrary motion within the phrase. Phrase 1 moves entirely by contrary motion. Phrase 2 mixes contrary motion with the parallel motion of organum mode 3.

Example 5-2e, organum mode 5, illustrates the use of several notes in one voice against one in the other. No rules are given as to when or why this should happen, and its occurrence is rare in notated examples of free organum. Apart from the cadential flourish in the *vox organalis*, the organum is conceived in a single phrase similar to Example 5-2c.

a. First organum mode

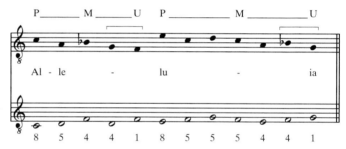

b. Second organum mode

EXAMPLE 5-2.   The Organum Modes of the *Ad organum faciendum.*
P = *prima vox*
M = *medie vox*
U = *ultima vox*
— = *copula* or cadence

c. Third organum mode

d. Fourth organum mode

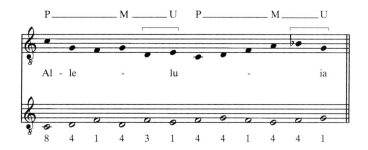

e. Fifth organum mode

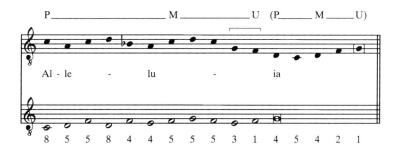

The usual cadence in these examples is a fourth resolving inward to a unison. A counterpart to this, when the range is wide, is a fifth moving out to an octave (Anthology Examples 19–21). Less common cadences are a third to a unison and a sixth to an octave (see the section on thirds and sixths below).

CONSONANCE AND DISSONANCE

The Medieval System of Classification

For the medieval musician, to whom the entire concept of the simultaneous sounding together of notes was new and fresh, the precise quality of each interval had an importance we can scarcely comprehend. Free organum codified this awareness in a basic categorization that would influence all subsequent music. Each interval had a place in a successive progression of most to least consonant in a manner roughly equivalent to their relative acoustical complexity.

In considering this, it may be useful to think in terms of relative degrees of tension rather than a black-and-white polarity of consonance and dissonance. The unison and octave are the purest intervals and were classed alone as the two perfect consonances. The fourth and fifth have a high degree of consonance, yet less than a unison or octave, and were considered intermediate consonances (note the distinction between the first and second organum modes). Thirds and sixths, more complex again, were more an element of controversy, going in and out of fashion until their final acceptance in the fourteenth century.

The medieval continuum of consonance and dissonance may be approximated as follows with the caveat that the third would at times be classed as an imperfect dissonance:

Consonance:	perfect:	unison and octave
	intermediate:	fourth and fifth
	imperfect:	thirds
Dissonance:	imperfect:	sixths
	perfect:	seconds, sevenths, tritone

Although written two hundred years later, Franco's explanation from around 1280 defines the medieval continuum as well as any while leaving to subjective interpretation the intervals to fit each category:

Concords are called perfect when two sounds are so combined that because of their consonance one is scarcely perceived from the other.

Concords are called intermediate when two sounds are combined to produce a concord better than imperfect, yet not as good as perfect.

Concords are called imperfect when the ear hears that two sounds differ considerably, but are not discordant.

Discords are called imperfect when the ear hears that two sounds agree with one another to a certain extent, yet are discordant.

Discords are called perfect when two sounds are so combined that the ear hears them to be incompatible with each other.

Although nowhere stated by the theorists, study of the music reveals a further important feature of the imperfect consonances and dissonances: imperfect *dissonances* are most often intervals that function well as precadential dissonances, as in the progression sixth to octave. (After 1250, when the resolution of a minor seventh to a perfect fifth became common, the seventh also became classed as an imperfect dissonance.) Imperfect *consonances* are intervals that can serve that purpose (e.g., third to unison, third to fifth) while also being consonant enough to appear sparingly within a phrase. Medieval theory lacks terminology to discuss such relationships, but Franco comes as close as any when he states "it should be known that all imperfect dissonance concords well immediately before a consonance."

Pythagorean tuning. An additional factor that weighs heavily on the medieval perception of consonance and dissonance is the Pythagorean tuning that was used throughout the Middle Ages. In this system, fourths and fifths are pure and beatless, while major thirds and sixths are distinctly wider than pure, minor thirds and sixths smaller. Thirds and sixths thus do not have the smooth cohesion of a pure interval, or even of the modern tempered variety, but possess a degree of bite. (It is undoubtedly more than a coincidence that the complete acceptance of thirds and sixths in the fifteenth century was matched by a shift to a tuning system that favored pure thirds.)

The Individual Intervals

A discussion of the individual intervals as they appear in free organum will prove useful not only in understanding of that style, but also in setting basic principles on which to judge subsequent change of style. A tabulation of intervallic frequency in five free-organum manuscripts capable of precise transcription is given in Table 5-1. Although a relatively small sample, the tabulation at least suggests a number of important concepts in the handling of intervals.

The two distinct styles of consonance treatment we will find are represented in Anthology Examples 19–21 and 22–25 respectively. As we shall see, the primary difference lies in the acceptance of the third.

The unison and octave. These perfect consonances make up from 31 to 44 percent of all intervals in free organum and are basic to the style. Given the narrow range of most free organum, unisons predominate over octaves.

The fourth and fifth. Although equal in consonance, these intervals are not equal in degree of use. We have noticed the preference for the fourth over the

The Flowering of Style

Table 5-1   **Percentage of Intervals in Five Free-Organum Manuscripts.**

	Ad organum faciendum	Autun 40B	Lucca 603	Oxford 572	Chartres 109
Number of Intervals:	349	94	47	70	241
Octaves:	16.4%	24.5%	10.6%	2.9%	3.7%
	39.9%	43.6%	38.3%	31.4%	32.3%
Unisons:	23.5	19.1	27.7	28.5	28.6
Fifths:	28.6	15.9	17.0	8.6	6.2
	55.4*	39.3	42.5	25.7	26.1
Fourths:	26.8	23.4	25.5	17.1	19.9
Thirds:	3.4	2.1	8.5	25.7	27.8
Sixths:	1.1	13.8	4.3	4.3	4.1
Seconds:	0	0	6.4	12.0	9.5
Sevenths:	0	1.0	0	.8	0

*This percentage includes one eleventh and one twelfth.
Percentages may not total exactly 100%.

fifth in oblique organum. This preference continues into free organum; only one free organum source, the *Ad organum faciendum* treatise and its accompanying examples (Anthology Examples 19–20 and Example 5-2 above), shows an equal use of fourths and fifths. All other sources favor the fourth, a preference even more pronounced (a two-to-one ratio) in manuscripts favoring the third.

The third.   As intimated above, the third is the most volatile of any of the intervals used in free organum. Some manuscripts virtually exclude it, while in others it represents a full 25 percent of all intervals present (as against 30 percent perfect and 25 percent intermediate consonances). The use or avoidance of the third distinguishes two styles of consonance treatment.

In *Style 1*, represented by Anthology Examples 19–21, the third is virtually absent, being limited either to a third-to-unison cadence pattern or to the occurrence of a single third (and rarely more than one to a piece) as a *media vox* in a passing- or neighboring-tone configuration or as an alternate interval in avoiding a tritone. These manuscripts seem to treat the third as an imperfect dissonance.

In *Style 2*, the third appears as a type of consonance, an interpretation supported by two small anonymous treatises known as the *Montpellier Treatise* and *Berlin B*. In these the third is recognized not only as a good precadential interval, but as a legitimate interval for a *prima* or *media vox*. Indeed, *Berlin B* goes further and recognizes series of two or three parallel thirds within the phrase. This style is illustrated in Anthology Examples 22–25. There is no apparent distinction made between major and minor thirds.

The sixth. In the Middle Ages the sixth was not, as it is to us, an inverted third, since the concept of inversion was foreign to earlier thinking. Thus the sixth was heard as a distinct interval with its own unique properties. It is aurally more complex than the third and is less stable as an isolated interval. Accordingly it took longer to receive general acceptance.

It appears only sparingly in free organum. The most common use, present in both styles, is in a sixth-to-octave cadence, as an occasional replacement for the more usual fifth-to-octave progression. In manuscripts that also favor the third it occasionally appears as a *media vox* and, in one manuscript, as a *prima vox* (Anthology Example 21). *Berlin B* recognizes it in both of these positions.

The extent to which the avoidance of the sixth in most manuscripts should be attributed to taste or simply to the relatively narrow compass cannot be determined with certainty. At best, the sixth is an unusual and infrequent interval.

The second. In spite of the preference given it by Guido, the second is excluded from use by all free organum theorists. Nevertheless, it appears in some settings, often those emphasizing the third, where its use is essentially that which was found in oblique organum and is an apparent carry-over from that style. It may appear as a precadential dissonance (second to unison or parallel seconds to unison) or as a free or strict passing or neighboring tone.

HISTORICAL CONSIDERATIONS

There is a world of difference between the organum of Guido and that of the *Ad organum faciendum*, even if the seeds of the latter can be found in the former. As long as contrary motion within a phrase is avoided, the added voice is a derivative, dependent on the cantus firmus. The simple extension of contrary motion to movement within the phrase makes possible the formation of a really independent melody. It is only from this time that true counterpoint and polyphony can be said to exist.

In considering this, it is instructive to compare the Winchester and Chartres settings of the *Alleluia: Angelus Domini* in Anthology Examples 18 and 24.

Evident in both is the frequent movement to cadence points, identical in each setting, often culminating in seconds between the voices (compare the cadences on *descendit, accedens,* and *lapidem* in Anthology Example 18 with those on *Domini* and *accedens* in Anthology Example 24; although we cannot verify each pitch in the Winchester example, there seems little doubt about this feature, present also in Guido). Although the free organum of Chartres moves largely in contrary motion, moments of parallelism occur, as at the beginning of the word *Angelus.*

Nevertheless, the contrast between the two organal voices is startling. Winchester is static and subservient, Chartres melodic and independent. In spite of the rhythmic simplicity, there can be little doubt concerning the in-herent artistic advances of the newer organum style.

The final element needed for the development of a truly artistic polyphony is rhythmic independence between voices. This development took place in southern France, and it is to that geographical area that we must turn in Chapter 6.

Practicum

COMPOSITION OF FREE ORGANUM

Composing in the style of free organum greatly facilitates the understanding of this seminal style. Fundamental principles include frequent cadences on ei-ther the unison or octave and a phrase structure utilizing contrary, parallel, or similar motion between voices. Rhythm is note-against-note. Consonances are unison, fourth, fifth, and octave in Style 1 and those intervals plus thirds and, to a lesser degree, sixths in Style 2.

Style features of free organum have been outlined earlier in the chapter and are summarized here as compositional procedures. **The special allowances per-missible in Style 2 will be given in parentheses and bold type.** These instruc-tions relate to the common practice of the period. Advanced students may discover exceptional procedures through careful analysis of Anthology Examples 19–25.

1. Establish cadence points for the entire composition, bearing in mind text placement and the usual length of an organum phrase.

2. Notate two-note cadences at the places chosen. Cadential progressions are standardized, and exceptions are rare. The normal progressions in Style 1 are a fourth to a unison when the *vox principalis* ascends either a second or a third, and a fifth to an octave when the *vox principalis* descends a second or a third. **(In Style 2 the ascending second may use either a fourth- or a third-to-unison cadence. The descending second *may* be harmonized with a fifth or a sixth to an octave, but *much* more often is accompanied with an *inverted* [the *vox organalis* being below the *vox principalis*] third-to-unison or even fourth-to-unison cadence [see Example 5-3]. This is probably due to the predominantly narrow range of this style.)**

When the *vox principalis* has two identical pitches at a cadence there is little standardization, a fourth to a unison being possible in Style 1 **(a third to a unison or sixth to an octave in Style 2).** It is also possible to treat the first of the two tones as a dissonance, seventh to octave or, more frequently, an in-verted second to a unison, the *vox organalis* approaching the *vox principalis* from

STYLE 1   STYLE 2

Ascending Second:

                             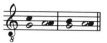

Ascending Third:

Descending Second:

                             Rare

Descending Third:

Unisons:

EXAMPLE 5-3. Normal Cadential Progressions.

below. See Example 5-3 for standard cadential progressions. In the case of voice crossing, the progressions may be inverted, the *vox organalis* taking the part marked here for the *vox principalis*.

3. Establish a *prima vox* for each phrase.

4. Harmonize the *medie voces* using organum modes 3 and 4. Use similar, parallel, and contrary motion, remembering that purely parallel motion is applied only to the intermediate consonances—fourths and fifths. Individual unisons or octaves should be considered normal in passages of contrary motion.

Taking the composition as a whole, perfect and intermediate consonances should appear in about equal proportion. **(In Style 2 fourths and thirds will be the most-used intervals, with an occasional fifth or sixth. Two or three thirds may occur in succession. In this style perfect, intermediate, and imperfect consonances should be used in approximately equal proportion.)**

5. The *vox organalis* should be limited to a range of a tenth or eleventh, using the same basic range as the *vox principalis*. The melodic contour of the added voice should be a consideration, but on the whole, this seems to be less important than the intervallic relationships of the two voices. Voice crossing may occur. **(In Style 2, the range of the *vox organalis* is the same, but the voices tend to remain quite close, with never more than an octave interval between them, and voice crossing is very common.)**

Assignment

Compose free organum using the melodies in Examples 5-4–5-7. Begin with Style 1, proceeding to Style 2 only when the procedures are clearly understood. Settings should be strictly in one or the other of the two styles. The range of the added voice may extend from the lowest note of the *vox principalis* to an eleventh above it. Caution should be taken to avoid melodic or harmonic tritones. Indicate cadences with a bar line.

BIBLIOGRAPHY

Music

Most of the repertoire capable of precise transcription is printed in the Anthology. A study of those and other sources, with facsimiles and attempted transcriptions of some examples in nondiastematic neumes, is contained in Marion Sibley Gushee, "Romanesque Polyphony: A Study of the Fragmentary Sources" (Ph.D. diss., UMI order no. 65-9676).

Theory

The John of Affleghem treatise is included in Babb, *Hucbald, Guido, and John on Music*, cited in Chapter 1. The *Ad organum faciendum* may be found in

Be - ne - di - ca - mus   Do - mi - no.

EXAMPLE 5-4. *Benedicamus Domino, Antiphonale Monasticum,* p. 1247. © Abbaye Saint Pierre de Solesmes, France, 1974, reprinted by permission.

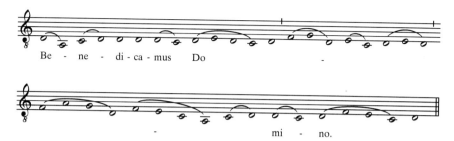

EXAMPLE 5-5. *Benedicamus Domino,* Antiphonale Monasticum, p. 1244. © Abbaye Saint Pierre de Solesmes, France, 1974, reprinted by permission.

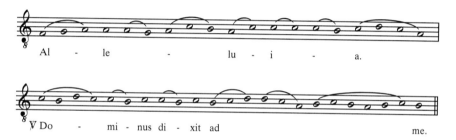

EXAMPLE 5-6. *Alleluia: Dominus dixit* (Paris, B.N., lat. 1235, fol. 182′), extract from *Music at Nevers Cathedral* par Nancy van Deusen avec permission de l'Institut de musique médievale.

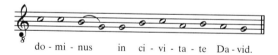

EXAMPLE 5-7. Antiphon *Natus est nobis* (Paris, B.N., lat. 1235, fol. 42), extract from *Music at Nevers Cathedral* par Nancy van Deusen avec permission de l'Institut de musique médievale.

Jay A. Huff, trans. and ed., *Ad organum faciendum and Item de organo*, Music Theorists in Translation 8 (Brooklyn: Institute of Medieval Music, 1969) and the Montpellier Treatise in Fred Blum, "Another Look at the Montpellier Organum Treatise," *MD* 13 (1959): 17–24.

The original Latin of John of Affleghem is available in J. Smits van Waesberge, ed., *Johannis Affligemensis, De Musica cum tonario*, CSM 1 (AIM, 1950), while all the other treatises are included in Hans Heinrich Eggebrecht and Frieder Zaminer, eds., *Ad Organum Faciendum: Lehrschriften der Mehrstimmigkeit in nachquidonischer Zeit*, Neue Studien zur Musikwissenschaft 3 (Mainz: B. Schott's Söhne, 1970).

Readings

There is little in English about this neglected formative period. Mark Lindley, "Pythagorean Intonation and the Rise of the Triad," *RMA-RC* 16 (1980), 4–61, gives insight into the role of tuning systems in music.

6

The Sacred Music of Southern France

Guido wrote his definitive description of oblique organum around 1028, before the development of free organum, yet by around 1100, a scant seventy-five years later, we find in southern France a sophisticated polyphonic music related to, but startlingly in advance of, those earlier styles. We do not know how this artistic leap occurred, and why in southern France, but it is that region that dominates the first half of the twelfth century in monophonic and polyphonic music and in secular as well as sacred music. It is part of an artistic impulse that had already made itself apparent through the development of a regional chant dialect and through becoming one of the centers for the lively composition of tropes and sequences.

Although the region was nominally subject to the Capetian kings in Paris, the ties were loose, and the South had for centuries developed a distinctive Mediterranean civilization in easy affinity with other southern cultures, particularly those of Christian Spain and northern Italy. The poets and musicians of southern France were welcomed at Spanish and Italian courts, and Provençal, the poetic language of southern France, was embraced as one of the chief literary languages of Spain and northern Italy.

The cultural division of northern and southern France was reinforced linguistically, as the various medieval French dialects fell into two broad groups: Old French or *langue d'oïl* in the North and Provençal or *langue d'oc* in the South (*oïl* and *oc* being their respective words for "yes"). In this linguistic division, Provençal had as much affinity with the Catalan of Spain as with the *langue d'oïl* of the North. This linguistic division helps define the boundary of the two cultures around the river Loire (Map 6-1).

There is no all-inclusive name for this southern territory, embracing as it does many feudal fiefdoms. In modern literature the area tends to be called

8

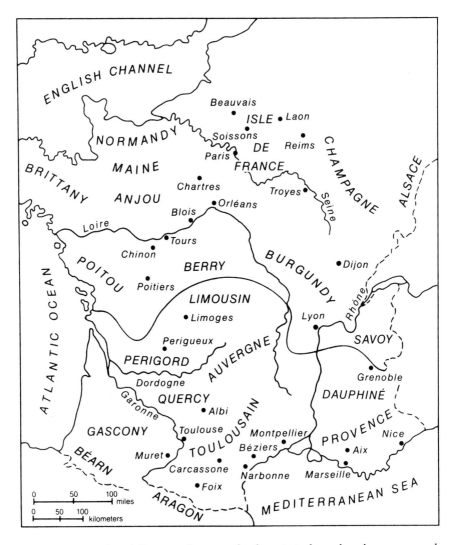

Map 6-1. Medieval France, showing the linguistic boundary between north and south, twelfth century.

Aquitania when sacred music is being discussed, *Provence, the Languedoc,* or *Occitan* when the music of the troubadours is the topic. In addition, the sacred polyphony is often named *Saint Martial,* a geographically limiting designation named from the abbey where many of the early manuscripts were collected. For clarity, Aquitania or simply southern France will be used here.

The twelfth century was a period of growing wealth and trade in the South. The Crusades served to open up a demand for the goods of the orient, and trade soon followed. Italian ships arrived at southern French ports to supply the markets of Toulouse and Beaucaire. Trade, the growing wealth of the cities, the genial climate and fertile soil, a time of relative peace—all led to an affluent culture in which developed the leisure and the taste for the cultivation of the arts, above all poetry and music. Southern France became for a time the richest and most civilized area of Europe.

This flowering civilization came to an abrupt end in the Albigensian Crusade of 1209–29, one of the more infamous episodes in European history. At that time Pope Innocent III instigated a crusade on the part of the northern French knights, not against the infidels, but against the Albigensian Christians of Aquitania, who denied certain tenets of the accepted faith and thus were classed as heretics. The opportunity was seized upon by the northern nobles less for Christian zeal than as an opportunity for plunder and political aggrandizement.

The North amassed an overwhelming army. The first city attacked, Béziers, gave up without a struggle: all sixty thousand inhabitants—men, women and children, priests, nuns, heretics and orthodox alike—were put to the sword. This was to be the story of the Crusade. In the ensuing years over three hundred towns and two hundred castles were stormed or burned and their inhabitants massacred. By the end, the independent civilization of the South had been brought effectively to a close and an era had ended.

THE SOURCES

The sources of Aquitanian sacred music lie in four composite manuscripts that comprise what may have been nine original sources. The earliest of these, Paris, Lat. 1139, dates from around 1100 or shortly thereafter, while two other Paris manuscripts, Lat. 3549 and 3719, are midcentury. The final manuscript, London Add. 36881, is of late twelfth- or early thirteenth-century origin. Taken together, these manuscripts record three chronological layers of Aquitanian composition encompassing a repertoire of approximately sixty-five monophonic and seventy polyphonic items, a considerable improvement on the mere handful of fragments we have noted in earlier periods.

The three manuscripts now in Paris were in the possession of the Abbey of Saint Martial in Limoges in the early thirteenth century, and it is from this fact

that the common designation of *Saint Martial* arose for this repertory. It is
doubtful, however, if all portions of those manuscripts originated in the abbey
(the librarians there were notorious collectors), and the fourth manuscript,
carrying much of the same repertoire, comes from near the Franco-Spanish
border, possible Narbonne. It is therefore more correct to think of a southern
French or Aquitanian style rather than one limited to Saint Martial.

The various manuscripts provide a good guide to the practical use of notation in the period. The earliest, from around 1100, uses carefully heightened
neumes around a single, dry-point line. The midcentury manuscripts rule the
page from top to bottom with closely spaced dry-point lines, the scribe using as
many as necessary at any given time to notate the music. Only the final source,
from around 1200, takes the step to inked staves. None of the notation has
rhythmic significance.

THE MONOPHONIC VERSUS

By the twelfth century the liturgy and the chants of the Mass and Office
were well established, but the impetus for religious composition continued unabated. Much of this impetus found outlet in the continuing composition of
tropes, prosulas, and sequences, but it also began to find other means of expression. As John of Affleghem exclaims:

> Since not only are the previously mentioned official sacred chants sung in the holy
> church, but shortly before our time there existed other composers of chant, I do
> not see that it should be forbidden for us to compose songs. For even if new
> melodies are not necessary in the church we can still exercise our ingenuity in
> singing rhythmic poetry and the plaintive versus of the poets.

Setting rhythmic poetry became a dominant feature of twelfth-century music. It found immediate expression in the sacred paraliturgical form of the versus,
governed the music of the troubadours, and by the end of the century would be
a primary feature of the sequence.

The *versus* may be described in general terms as a musical setting, monophonic or polyphonic, of a poem written in rhymed, rhythmic verse. Its use
within the church is varied and difficult to define. Often it seems to have served
as processional music in church or within the monastery or to have been used to
cover liturgical movements within the service (such as the movement of the
deacon or subdeacon to the appointed place for scripture reading). Another
major group served as poetic substitutes for the Benedicamus Domino, the
dismissal formula for the Office and some masses. Others have no clearly defined
use and may even have served for recreational edification within the monastery.

Musical settings of these poems may be strophic or through-composed. They
involve a variety of modal techniques, old and new. They at times introduce a
newer, more structured phraseology, involving elements of repetition and of

antecedent-consequent phrases. Above all, they exhibit a variety of text-setting techniques, from concise syllable settings to elaborate, effusive ones.

Aquitanian composers mixed these various techniques within individual versus and applied them to both monophony and polyphony. Choice of style may have been partly a matter of taste, or may relate to the function of the particular versus: a song designed to be sung by monks in procession would suggest a simpler, more rhythmic style than one designed to accompany an elaborate liturgical action on a high feast day.

Poetic Structure

The starting point for a study of the versus is not, however, the musical setting, but the poem to which it is set. No longer is the text prose, as in most chant and early tropes and sequences. It is in a structured, rhythmic, rhymed verse that suggests a new musical response. As this is the dominant style of poetry throughout the remainder of the Middle Ages—the Latin versus, conductus, and later sequence; the chansons of troubadour and trouvère; the rondeau, virelai, and ballade of Machaut; and the madrigal, ballata, and caccia of Italy, we will begin our discussion here with a rudimentary explication of the principles of that poetry, then proceed to the Aquitanian responses to it.

For this purpose, the four Aquitanian monophonic versus of Anthology Examples 26–29a have been chosen as paradigms. Analysis of these will focus first on concepts of poetic structure, and then on elements of texture, phrase structure, and mode.

Classical Latin poetry was constructed by manipulating long and short syllables in discernable patterns or *feet*, a poetic technique known as *ars metrica*. The long and short syllabification of classical Latin had disappeared long before the twelfth century, and both Latin and the Latin-derived dialects of northern and southern France used syllables that were now equal in duration. Poetic attention shifted to the larger concept of line length.

In this new poetic procedure, known as the *ars ritmica*, syllables are equal in length and are arranged into lines of equal or varying numbers of syllables. Poetic lines are determined by syllable count. The end of each line is distinctly indicated by rhyme and end-of-line accent.

At its simplest, as in the versus *Novum festum celebramus* (Anthology Example 29a), it may be merely a regular series of four eight-syllable lines in an A A B B rhyme pattern. In this poem, the rhymes encompass two syllables each, forming what is known as *rich rhyme* (in which the final *two* syllables rhyme) and each line has an identical end-of-line accentuation (on the penultimate or next-to-last syllable: a *trochaic* cadence in medieval terminology, a feminine one in that of today):[1]

---

[1] This excerpt also illustrates the fact that, while accent was often regular in the early part of the poetic line, it need not be consistently so:

	SYLLABLES	RHYME
Novum festum celebrémus	8	A
Novus cantus et cantémus	8	A
Facta rerum novitáte	8	B
In nova sollemnitáte	8	B

In more complicated poems, line length may change to form structure within the poem (Anthology Example 26):

	SYLLABLES	RHYME
Congaudeat ecclésià	8	A
Per hec sacra sollémpnià	8	A
Et gaudet cum letítià	8	A
Letti ducat tripúdià	8	A
Ergo gaude gaúdiò,	7	B
Juvenilis cónciò,	7	B
Ac de patris fóliò	7	B
Virginis in grémiò	7	B
Christo, Dei fíliò	7	B
Náto.	2	C
Nova puerpériò	7	B
Fácto.	2	C
Gaudeat hómo.	5	C

Here the poet has set up a series of eight-syllable lines followed in the second half of the stanza by a seven-syllable series with a new rhyme. Even shorter lines punctuate the conclusion of the stanza. The eight- and seven-syllable lines place the chief accent on the antepenultimate (third-from-last) syllable with a lighter, secondary accent on the ultimate or last syllable (a dactylic cadence in medieval terminology, a masculine one in modern terminology). The short final lines change to a trochaic or feminine cadence.

More intricate relationships are possible (Anthology Example 27):

Plebs dóminì,		4	A
Hac díe		3	B
Letáminì,		4	A
Sed píe		3	B

(*Continued*)

    Nóvum féstum cèlebrémus
    Nóvus cántus et cantémus
    Fácta rérum nòvitáte
    In nóva sollèmnitáte
Medieval writers about poetry concern themselves only with end-of-line accent.

Laus vírginì	4	A
Maríe	3	B
Et córdibùs	4	C
Et vócibùs	4	C
Et áctibùs	4	C
Prométur.	3	D

Here we find on the surface a patterned alternation of four- and three-syllable lines, each marked by end rhyme. At the same time, however, the alternation of dactylic and trochaic (masculine and feminine) cadences in the first six lines serves to combine each pair into a larger entity, a composite line of seven syllables:

Plebs domini	hac díe	7 (4 + 3)
Letamini	sed píe	7 (4 + 3)
Laus virgini	Maríe	7 (4 + 3)

The poet at this point, having set up an expected regularity, deviates from it for rhetorical effect; three parallel four-syllable phrases interrupt the pattern before the three-syllable conclusion:

Et córdibùs		4
Et vócibùs		4
Et actibus	prométur	7 (4 + 3)

The refrain of the poem further plays on the ambiguity of line length by beginning with a composite (four-plus-four) eight-syllable line in which the four-syllable components are not set off by rhyme, followed by first a distinct eight-syllable line and then a pair of undivided seven-syllable ones:

Mariam vox, Mariam cór	8 (4 + 4)	E
Mariam sensus, mens, vigór	8	E
Proclament hac in díe	7	B
Et filium Maríe.	7	B

Internal rhyme, associated with a *caesura* (pause) after a set number of syllables, is a common feature of rhythmic poetry.

From the above analysis certain large principles of twelfth-century poetry become evident:

1. Poetic form is established through line length (that is, the number of syllables per line).

2. Individual lines are set off by rhyme in a pattern that helps establish poetic form.

3. More complex composite lines with an internal caesura often marked by internal rhyme are frequent.

4. Line ends are further distinguished by end-of-line word accent.

5. Regular patterns of accent in the earlier portion of the line may or may not occur, but are never mentioned by medieval theorists to be a necessary part of the poetic structure.

Texture and Phrase Structure

Syllabic and neumatic styles.   Following the pattern established in our discussion of Roman-Gallican chant, we can divide melodic style into syllabic, neumatic, and melismatic. With the versus repertoire, however, the syllabic and neumatic styles become closely intertwined, and we will find it necessary to distinguish a florid and a melismatic style.

The setting of *Congaudeat ecclesia* (Anthology Example 26) begins with a section in neumatic style, followed by one in syllabic. The interrelationship of music and poetry is shown by the coincidence of the change of musical style with the poetic change from the opening group of four eight-syllable lines to the succeeding group of seven-syllable ones.

In phrase structure the initial group of four eight-syllable lines are set as a musical entity in antecedent-consequent relationship and with phrases 1, 2, and 3 being further united by identical phrase endings, a musical end rhyme: ax | bx | ax | by. It is only the nonfinal ending of the fourth phrase that opens up the form and invites musical continuation.

As the versus continues, now in syllabic style, the first two phrases form an antecedent-consequent pair, while the next two repeat the first. The fifth and short sixth phrases combine to form an expansion of the same musical shape: c | d | c | c | c'.

The refrain is even more tightly organized, being based completely on an ascending three-note scale (related to the beginning of phrase c) and its inversion, which is augmented to a fourth in the final phrase: e | e' | e | f | e''.

As illustrated here, poetic lines of equal length may result in an antecedent-consequent phraseology or in more or less exact melodic repetition. This does not always happen, however, for freedom in the application of procedures is characteristic of much Aquitanian music and is one of its charms.

Plebs domini (Anthology Example 27), also syllabic, displays a little of this freedom. The composite seven-syllable line is chosen as the musical phrase length, and the first two phrases are set to virtually identical melodies. In spite of the continued parallelism in the poem, the musical setting breaks off at this point to present a musically unrelated third phrase.

The musical setting of the next two four-syllable lines is ambiguous, but for tonal reasons may be considered two separate phrases. Although this series of *et* phrases suggests a sense of poetic urgency, it is not concluded, as one might expect, in an immediate cadence, but is released through an expansive cadential melisma on the verb *prometur*. In this case the composer has bypassed simple phrase parallelism between phrases 2 and 3 in favor of using phrase 3 to open up a larger unit that carries the as-yet verbless sentence inexorably on to its expansive conclusion on the verb of action. (As we will see later, the tonal structure also leads forward to this moment of culmination.)

The florid and melismatic styles.   Some Aquitanian compositions move predominantly in short melismas of from two to six notes per syllable; others are even more expansive, having melismas of up to twenty notes. The dividing line between these two styles, and indeed between the florid and neumatic, is often difficult to draw with precision, for no one piece follows one or another style exclusively.

Novum festum celebremus (Anthology Example 29a) is a case in point, a versus that hovers on the borderline between the neumatic and florid styles. The effusive melody somewhat obscures the regularity of the poetic structure. There is no phrase parallelism, and the only large-scale structural elments are the alternation of phrase endings between d and G and the similarity of the sequential melismas in the final two phrases over the words *novitate* and *sollemnitate*. Melismas are built through the sequential use of short melodic shapes and their inversions. The motivic material used is not unique to this versus, but is part of a common stock of melodic motives freely transferable from one such melisma to another. Compare, for instance, the use of the same motive in the final melisma of *Plebs domini*. The same motivic material is also found in the polyphonic versus.

A fully melismatic style is apparent in the sweeping arches of the second verse of *Letabundi jubilemus* (Anthology Example 28), a three-stanza versus set in an ABA form. This and similar melismatic melodies avoid direct repetition and concise motives; instead, another, more flexible procedure is at work: the shaping and reshaping of a basic melodic contour. Immediately noticeable are the scalewise ascents to a' in the first phrase of the verse and the use of sequence there and, especially, in the long ascent on the syllable *ter*, an ornamented expansion of the original ascent. The ascents to the high b' in the concluding portion of the verse (from the word *Arcanum*) can be seen equally as a shape in itself and as an intensification of the previous rise to a'. The melodic contours of the melismatic style are not arbitrary; mode in particular plays an important role in shaping these seemingly free melodies.

Tonal Structure and Mode

The modes received their classical formulation around 1100 following the writings of Guido, Berno, and John of Affleghem. These modal criteria go beyond range and final to consider tones used for interior cadences, the division of the scale into species of pentachord and tetrachord, the incorporation of characteristic melodic motives, and the use of the modal reciting tone as an important structural tone (see "Modal Theory" in Chapter 3).

The liturgical modes were intended to serve primarily the style of music the name suggests: liturgical music for the service. Once adopted, the modes had direct influence on the composition of tropes, sequences and late chants for the Ordinary. They had a more diffuse effect on the paraliturgical versus and other, less liturgical music, where their influence was one among many.

Modality as displayed in the versus entails a somewhat broader conception embracing (as did Roman-Gallican chant) third-chain and pentatonic structures as well as newer concepts. (To signify the distinction between the liturgical modes and the modes of the Aquitanian versus, we will refer to the latter simply by the name of the finalis.) The existing Aquitanian repertoire, monophonic and polyphonic, virtually excludes the modes on E and F (liturgical Deuterus and Tritus). The favored modes are D and G, each of which has its own characteristic procedures.

The D mode.   The D mode encompasses a range of third-chain, pentatonic, and tonic-fifth organizational procedures. Third-chain melodies are familiar from Roman-Gallican chant. The chain of thirds is a pervasive idiom found in many medieval repertoires, but not all melodies that contain thirds or triadic formations are necessarily third-chain melodies. What is important is the use of the notes of the primary third-chain as key structural tones and, most characteristically, the emphasis on the seventh rather than the eighth scale degree as the upper pivot.

In the versus *Plebs domini* (Anthology Example 27) the tension lies between a principal chain built on the finalis and a secondary chain, built on the subfinalis, that seeks resolution in the principal chain (Example 6-1). The first two phrases explore the lower range of each chain, while the third opens up the higher portion of the principal chain. Various portions of the two chains are explored in the three *Et* phrases, culminating in the exposure of the whole primary chain in the precadential melisma on *prometur*. In this way, the composer has reinforced the syntactical arrangement of the poem, for, as the poet has reserved the verb *prometur* for the end of the statement, the composer has reserved for that word the exposition of the complete third chain.

Pentatonic structure in relatively unobscured form may be seen in the opening stanza of *Letabundi jubilemus* (Anthology Example 28). The pentatonic scale is the same as that found in Roman-Gallican chant, notated an octave higher—a, c, d, f, g, and a'. The tone b is missing entirely, and e is generally treated as a passing or neighboring tone. Opening with an a-c-d progression, typical of pentatonic melodies, an unadorned pentatonic sequence is revealed in phrase 3. Phrases 4 and 5 are more diatonic, but pentatonic structure returns in phrase 6.

EXAMPLE 6-1.   Third-Chain Analysis of *Plebs Domini*, Phrases 1 to 6.

Stanza 2 represents a still different type of modal organization. Range is from a to a′, with finalis on d: the range of plagal Protus, but notated an octave higher. Organization of the melody distinctly follows the division of the octave into pentachord and plagal tetrachord, the pentachord governing all of the melismatic phrases, while the central syllabic phrases fall into the tetrachord (setting them apart in both style and range). Nonetheless, the stanza begins with the plagal Protus intonation formula c-d-f, leading to an expectation of a plagal Protus quality that is not followed in the remainder of the stanza. Instead, the melody is organized around two basic pivots, the finalis d and the fifth a′ which are established in the second phrase segment and which then form the outer boundaries of the subsequent melodic expansions of that phrase (Example 6-2).

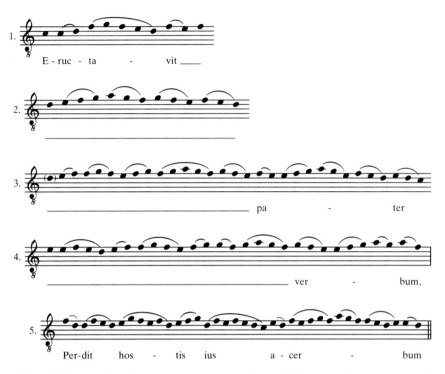

EXAMPLE 6-2.   Free Expansion of a Melodic Shape (*Letabundi jubilemus*, phrases 10 and 11).

The compositional process at work here is one of molding a melodic shape to a particular tonal context. It is probably less a conscious constructionist approach (as will be observed in the music of northern France) than one resulting from an improvisatory idiom that exploits basic shapes in a free but artistic manner. (Evidence for this is in the lack of exact symmetry in the sequential passages and the frequent disagreement in matters of detail from source to source, the shape rather than the specific detail being the essential element.)

The G mode.   In contrast to the diversity of the D mode, that on G displays fairly standardized procedures. Melodic organization is diatonic and excludes pentatonic and third-chain structures. The plagal or authentic range of the melody often indicates which reciting tone will be favored as chief structural tone. This can be seen clearly by comparing the plagal *Congaudeat ecclesia* (Anthology Example 26) with the authentic *Novum festum* (Anthology Example 29a).

In *Congaudeat* the melody moves within the narrow range common to both the plagal and authentic forms of the G mode. The important structural tones are G, c, and d (the finalis and the reciting tones of the plagal and authentic Tetrardus). Almost throughout, however, the G-c fourth controls the melody, acting as the pivot notes in phrases 1, 3, 5, 7, 8, 9, and 15 and, in the guise of the plagal Tetrardus psalm-tone intonation, initiating phrases 5, 7, and 8. Even phrases 2 and 4, which begin on d, give prominence to the c by placing it as point of departure for a leap and as the highest pitch in the concluding portion of the phrase. Only phrases 6 and 14 unequivocally set up d as a contrasting structural tone.

Novum festum, in the authentic range, emphasizes finalis and fifth, with only passing reference to c near the end of the second phrase.

Although these two versus on G have a strong modal relationship to the liturgical Tetrardus, their sharply defined phrase structures are distinctly unchantlike.

THE POLYPHONIC VERSUS

Interesting and innovative as the monophonic versus may be, the most exciting developments lie in Aquitanian polyphony. Here the promise implicit in free organum receives speedy fulfillment in an organum that exploits rhythmic as well as melodic independence. The range and sophistication of this repertoire as well as its close relationship to the monophony of the same manuscripts may be seen in a brief survey of the styles.

Syllabic Style

Simplest is a syllabic style in which the voices move in note-against-note fashion, as in phrases 2–6 of *Orienti oriens*, Anthology Example 30. In analogy it can be seen to be a transference into polyphonic idiom of the syllabic style we have noted above in *Plebs domini* and the latter half of *Congaudeat ecclesia* (Anthology Examples 26 and 27). Occasionally the syllabic style may be decorated through neumatic movement in the upper voice, but only in neumes of two or three notes (for instance, Anthology Example 31, phrase 4, on the syllables *tes, cli, pre*).

The note-against-note style is that of free organum. Later twelfth-century theorists would call it *discant*, especially when, as here, it uses the contrary-motion principle of organum mode 4. We will use the term hereafter in this sense.

Aquitanian discant owes much to free organum and often resembles it closely, as can be seen in Example 6-3.

Phrases begin on the unison or octave (organum mode 1), fourth or fifth (organum mode 2), or third (acceptable in Style 2). The interior of the phrase moves largely in contrary motion (organum mode 4), but similar and parallel motion may also be seen. Intervals are predominantly the unison, fourth, fifth,

a. *Annus novus,* phrases 1 to 3 (Paris, B.N. lat. 1139, f. 36')

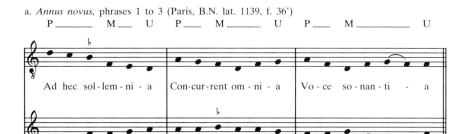

b. *Noster cetus,* phrases 1 to 3 (Paris, B.N., lat. 1139, f. 61)

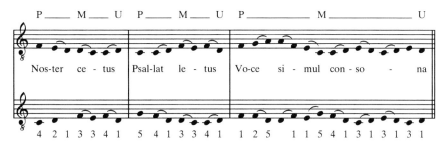

c. Res jocosa, phrases 1 to 3 (London, add. 36881, f. 21')

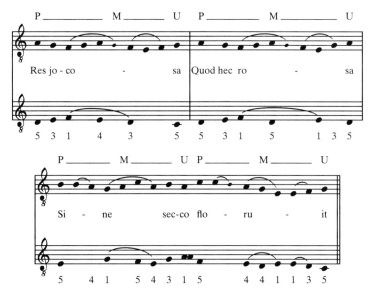

EXAMPLE 6-3.   Free Organum Structure in Aquitanian Versus.

and octave of Style 1, but the third is used with some freedom (as in Style 2). The intervals of the second or seventh may occur as a discant interval when demanded for reasons of voice leading (for examples of the second, see Anthology Examples 22–24; for the seventh, Anthology Examples 21 and 22).

There is only one basic change in concept between the Aquitanian syllabic style and free organum: the acceptance of the fifth as a suitable interval for interior and final cadences. As we shall see, this has great importance in the formation of a stable tonal structure.

Other cadences in common use are the usual ones of free organum, although the fourth-to-unison cadence rapidly loses precedence to the third-to-unison cadence of Style 2.

Melodic structure is similar to that of the monophonic versus, with antecedent-consequent and repetitive phrasing often apparent.

The Florid and Melismatic Style

While many Aquitanian versus are in syllable style, it is those that explore the florid and melismatic styles that make a unique advance on the concepts of free organum. Although flourishes of up to twenty notes may occur over a single syllable, most flourishes consist of from three to six notes and fall into what may be called the florid style (see Anthology Example 32 and the first two phrases of both 29b and 31). The style is not unlike that seen in the opening verse of *Letabundi jubilemus* (Anthology Example 28). Characteristically the rate of ornamentation does not remain constant; neumes of varying length alternate with single-note declamation.

Flourishes longer than this fall into the melismatic style. An instance is Anthology Example 33, in which the upper voice carries up to eighteen notes to one in the lower. The melodic technique of the melismatic voice is similar to that of the second verse of *Letabundi jubilemus* discussed on page 143 above.

A distinct boundary between the florid and melismatic styles is difficult to draw, but may be noticed when consistently longer melodic flourishes are used in distinction to the more usual two- to six-note ones.

The theoretical foundation.   The florid and melismatic styles are present in the earliest of the Aquitanian manuscripts, around 1100. For their theoretical foundation we need look no farther than free organum theory, although the potential for melodic ornamentation is only hinted at there, when John of Affleghem says "although I have set a syllabic organum against syllabic motion, it is allowable for anyone making organum to double or triple the notes over the syllabic progression, or to expand them suitably in any way whatsoever."

Later twelfth-century theorists are similarly reticent about any but the most basic concepts, but an early thirteenth-century treatise, the *Vatican Organum Treatise* (probably from Paris, but now in the Vatican library), illustrates through a series of examples the procedure of ornamenting simple discant. In each instance the basic discant motion is given and then illustrated with a series of melodic embellishments of the basic motion. This may be seen in Example 6-4, which is accompanied with the instruction "If the cantus [the lower voice] ascends a second and the organum begins at the octave, the organum should descend a third to form a fifth." (The fourth version incorporates both the element of sequence and of delayed resolution on the final note that are common features in both the Aquitanian and Parisian styles.)

Alternate manuscript versions of a given composition suggest that this type of melodic elaboration was the result of a fundamentally improvisational approach. Although the fundamental discant structure remains the same, the details of melodic embellishment constantly vary, as in Example 6-5.

Underlying Structure

The florid style.   The florid style consists of an underlying discant structure embellished with melodic flourishes of varying lengths. The underlying discant is consonant and uses the third as a structural interval only in the cadential progressions 3–5 and 3–1. Dissonance occurs only as an incidental element within the melodic flourishes or as a quickly resolving appoggiatura-type dissonance at the beginning of a new tenor note (Example 6-5b).

The melismatic style.   In contrast, the controlling element in the melismatic style is no longer the intervallic structure, but the highly ornamented upper part. Discant movement is largely abandoned in favor of parallel perfect inter-

The basic progression

EXAMPLE 6-4. Discant Examples from the Vatican Organum Treatise.

a. *Omnis curet*

b. *Lux refulget*

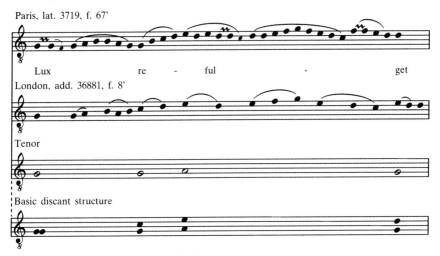

EXAMPLE 6-5.   Alternate Melodic Ornamentation.

vals, which serve as a stable underpinning for the freely melismatic upper voice. Example 6-6 extracts the underlying intervallic structure from the counterpoint in a melismatic setting.

Neume-Against-Neume Melisma

A special idiom in the Aquitanian style is the neume-against-neume me-lisma, which is like discant in its note-against-note structure, but which is melismatic in terms of text (see Anthology Examples 30, phrase 7, and 31, phrases 4, 6, and 8). The voices are notated as neume-against-neume rather than note-against-note, each neume embracing a melodic pattern or a segment

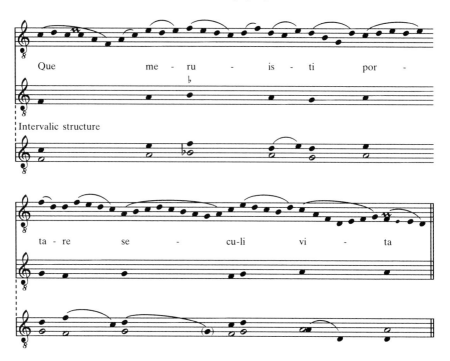

EXAMPLE 6-6. Parallel Intervalic Structure in the Melismatic Style (*Inviolata Maria*, phrase 1, second half: Paris B.N., lat. 3719, f. 81′).

thereof. The voices tend to move in mirror image, but the mirror image is often approximate rather than exact (for instance, a downward fourth may answer an upward fifth). Also, while equal-length neumes are normally placed against one another, unequal ones may occur, as in the melisma of phrase 6 of Anthology Example 31. Here, presumably, the singers adjusted the neumes to each other according to procedures unknown to us. This patterned, sequential type of melisma can be seen in monophonic idiom in the concluding melisma of *Plebs domini* and the third and fourth phrases of *Novum festum celebremus* (Anthology Examples 27 and 29a).

Although contrary motion is the norm in Aquitanian polyphony and is the surface feature of the neume-against-neume melisma, the underlying structure is very often that of ornamented parallel motion, generally descending stepwise to the final, and acting as a reinforcement of the final as "tonic." An illustration of this may be seen in the two melismas in Example 6-7: in the first a series of parallel fourths alternate with a series of parallel unisons; in the second parallel unisons alternate with parallel fifths. In each case the final is the point of arrival of the parallel unisons.

This type of sequential, mirror-image melisma is frequent in both the discant and florid styles of polyphonic versus.

a. *Noster cetus* (Paris, lat. 1139, f. 61)

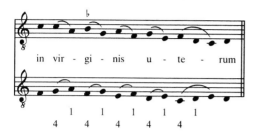

b. *Cantu miro* (London, add. 36881, f. 12')

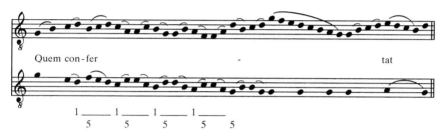

EXAMPLE 6-7. Parallel Motion in Neume-Against-Neume Melismas.

TONAL ORGANIZATION

With the versus we come upon the first polyphonic compositions in which every element of composition is under the composer's control. All previous polyphony has been molded on a cantus firmus, a preexistent melody whose shape and duration inevitably give form to the composition and whose melodic structure controls the intervallic space through which the upper voice travels. Now, in the polyphonic form in which both voices are newly composed, there exists the opportunity for the conscious shaping of all elements of the composition.

The traditional church modes, in many ways not applicable to the monophonic versus, are even less applicable to polyphony, where the problem is not merely one of a single line relating to a tonal center, but of two melodies relating to each other as well.

No medieval theorist attempts to apply the church modes to polyphony, and Grocheo, around 1300, specifically states that the modes are applicable only to plainchant. In looking for procedures of tonal organization, we should therefore disregard modality and look for a process growing from the concept of two-voiced intervallic organization.

Successive Composition

Polyphony in the Middle Ages was built up through the addition of voice to voice. In cantus firmus composition, this procedure is axiomatic; the borrowed voice already exists, the new one is added to it. In versus composition, the composer also began with the lower voice, but now one newly composed to fulfill polyphonic requirements. In the course of the twelfth century these melodies came to have a strong tonal focus on final and fifth, establishing a tonal polarity between these two scale degrees.

Like Aquitanian monophony, the polyphonic versus relies entirely on the D and G modes, a reliance characteristic of other twelfth-century repertoires as well.

Versus in G

Versus in G are about twice as numerous as those in D, and seem to have achieved tonal stability sooner. While the four examples in the earliest source (ca. 1100) do not show a consistency of tonal organization, all but two of the twenty-three from the middle or latter part of the century are firmly rooted on a "tonic-fifth" G-d polarity. It is established, if not from the first, at least from the second or third note; it is the principal and often the only internal cadential interval (relieved with cadences on the unison or octave G or the unison d); and it or the unison G forms the final cadence. Indeed, although the concept would have been foreign to a medieval musician, many versus can be viewed as an ornamental prolongation of that single interval, without even the establishment of a secondary center as contrast.

Tonal unification.   The consistency of cadential tones became a primary compositional technique, strongly supported by the lower voice. The process of tonal unification may be seen in Anthology Example 30, *Orienti oriens*. The lower voice distinctly hinges on G and d, cadencing on one or the other of those tones and, except in phrase 5, clearly pivoting between those two notes. The complementary function of the upper voice is seen in phrases 1, 2, and 5 where, the lower voice cadencing on the fifth, the upper voice crosses under to sound the G. The ensuing cadence structure is one of total consistency:

Upper voice:	G G d d G d d
Lower voice:	d d d G d G G

The neume-against-neume melisma often powerfully reinforces this tonal stability. Here the concluding melisma, moving in loosely constructed parallel unisons and fifths, begins its descending unison movement on the fifth and culminates, after touching the subfinal, on the final, the upper voice leaping up to cadence on the fifth.

In the polyphonic setting of *Novum festum*, Anthology Example 29b, we see a more sophisticated procedure. Here the melisma on *solemnitate* in the last phrase is an expansion of the melisma on *novitate* in the phrase preceding. The lowest note of the descending fifths reaches the final in the last phrase, while the similar movement in the preceding phrase is deflected upward as a kind of "deceptive" phrase end (G as "tonic" has been well established throughout).

The alternation of b naturals and b flats that occurs in these and similar melismas, needed to avoid the tritone in sequential passages, has little effect on tonality: it is heard as an incidental element of a broader structural movement, one that by providing a highly ornamented scalewise descent to the final further emphasizes the tonality.

Versus in D

Just as Aquitanian monophony in the D mode is more nebulous than that in G, so too is Aquitanian polyphony in D less stable tonally, at least in the first half of the twelfth century. Only two of the seven surviving versus in D from the early and midcentury sources show tonal unity. The seven versus from the end of the century, however, use a process analogous to that for the G mode.

CANTUS FIRMUS SETTINGS

Although the bulk of Aquitanian polyphony consists of versus, there do exist a few cantus firmus settings, which suggest important things for the future. Eight are florid polyphonic settings of monophonic sequences. Two are respond prosulas in an extremely florid style, and the remaining two, a *Benedicamus Domino* and an *Ora pro nobis*, are melismatic in style. It is noteworthy that none of these cantus firmus compositions are in the syllabic or neumatic style, and that these ten compositions together make up a majority of *all* the florid and melismatic compositions in the Aquitanian repertoire. This implied division of styles anticipates the clear division in Parisian polyphony between the syllabic discant of the conductus and the melismatic organum style of Leonin.

Also worthy of mention are two Benedicamus Domino tropes in verse form that are superimposed over the regular liturgical Benedicamus chant and text, which appear in the earliest of the Aquitanian sources (Example 6-8). These tropes mark the first appearance of polytextuality in music and seem a special extension of the concept of troping. This concept will reappear again in a different context in the motet of the thirteenth and fourteenth centuries.

RHYTHM

Twelfth-century notation lacks rhythmic significance and no contemporary account of performance sheds any light on the question of rhythm. What few clues we have must be drawn from the versus themselves and what we know of their performance environment.

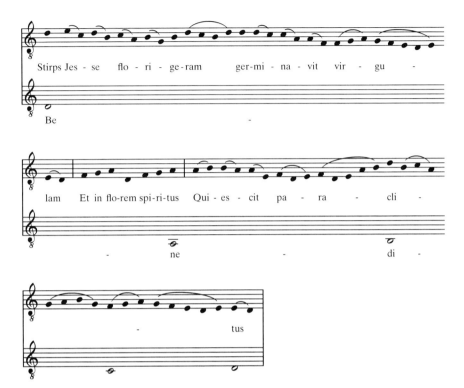

EXAMPLE 6-8. *Stirps Jesse—Benedicamus Domino* (Paris, B.N., lat. 1139, f. 60′).

In versus in syllabic-neumatic style, the regularity of phrase construction and the tendency toward symmetrical phrase grouping, frequently mirroring the text, suggests an accommodation of the music to the rhythm of the poetic phrase lengths. This can be accomplished by giving an equal length to each syllable and accommodating the melodic notes to suit (cadential melismas being treated more freely when necessary). Such an interpretation permits the text and line rhythm to be heard clearly and would certainly be most appropriate for processional use.

In the florid, melismatic songs it is apparent that the melodic element takes precedence over a regularized declamation of the text: the natural poetic rhythm, which clearly controls the simpler idioms, is sacrificed to musical virtuosity. If sung, as is likely, by the same solo singers who would perform the similarly melismatic Gradual and Offertory verses, the style may have been essentially the same, the "equal note value" performance that had apparently been standard in chant since around 1050.

Beyond this, little can be said. Various attempts at mensural versions have been made, but all remains hypothetical. We may assume rhythmic conventions were in use, ones passed from performer to performer by oral tradition, but we have no knowledge of their nature.

Practicum 1

POETIC ANALYSIS

Rhymed, rhythmic poetry as introduced in this chapter remains standard throughout the later Middle Ages. Its thorough understanding now will greatly facilitate subsequent study.

Assignment

Following the method outlined in "Poetic Structure" above, analyze one or more poems from Anthology Examples 30–33 in terms of line length, rhyme, and end-of-line accent.

Practicum 2

COMPOSITION IN THE FLORID STYLE

Fundamentals of composition in the florid style are not complex, although a complete assimilation of the correct melodic style requires greater study. The ensuing discussion is aimed primarily at an understanding of the guiding principles of the style. Concluding remarks will point the way toward the more idiomatic aspects of style.

Basic Procedures

1. Composition of a polyphonic versus begins with the composition of the lower voice. This will be a setting of the first verse of the poem in the case of a strophic versus, the complete poem in the case of a through-composed one. (A cantus-firmus setting of course omits this step, as the lower voice is a preexistent melody.) To simplify the initial stages of composition in this style, two potential lower voice melodies are given at the end of the unit. More advanced students may compose their own. The lower voice of a versus should be a pleasing melody in its own right, but, in the mature Aquitanian style of the mid-twelfth century, it also plays an important part in the establishment of a stable tonality. Accordingly, it is written with a clear sense of tonality and will consistently cadence on the final or the fifth. The upper voice will, in contrast, be more tonally diffuse.

2. When the lower voice is established, a basic discant structure (which will become the skeletal structure of the upper voice) is added to it. The procedure is identical to that of the free organum composition practiced in

Chapter 5, with the following differences that reflect midcentury style:

    a. Composition may begin on the fourth or fifth as well as the unison or octave.

    b. Cadences occur only at the end of each phrase of the text.

    c. Cadences are uniformly made on the final and fifth of the mode or, less often, on one of those tones doubled.

    d. The final cadence may be on the final and fifth or on the unison final.

3. The discant intervals in the upper voice are incorporated into a free-flowing melody in florid style by the addition of melodic passages that connect those skeletal tones. These passages may contain from two to eight notes, but their length is constantly varied as the phrase progresses; two flourishes of identical length seldom follow one another. Melodic motion is predominantly stepwise, relieved through the occasional use of a third and through tone repetition (see "Melodic Progression" below).

All melodic motion may be directed from one consonance to another. (This procedure is illustrated in Example 6-9, where the same discant structure is fleshed out in two different florid settings.) The discant interval is consonant, but intervening passagework may be freely dissonant against the lower voice.

4. In the procedure outlined in step 3, all motion was directed from one consonance to another. In true Aquitanian style, however, many of the discant tones, excepting only the initial note of the phrase, may be subject to dissonant treatment. This will normally be of an ascending or descending appoggiatura type, involving either single or double appoggiaturas. The most characteristic

a. Lower voice and chosen discant structure.

Clar-ra so-nent or - ga - na

b. Version one.

Cal - ra   so   -   nent   or   -   ga   -   na

c. Version two.

Cla   -   ra   so - nent   or   -   ga   -   na

EXAMPLE 6-9.   Sample Versions.

forms are given in Example 6-10. (It should be remembered that the sixth is an imperfect dissonance and the third is generally avoided as a structural interval.)

The dissonant interval is normally approached through stepwise motion or by anticipation, as in Example 6-11a. More rarely the descending appoggiatura may be approached through ascending leap, Example 6-11b. Appoggiaturas below the main melody are rare.

Three different applications of these concepts may be seen in Example 6-12, all based on the general outline of Example 6-9b.

Melodic Progression

A true assimilation of Aquitanian style can be gained only through considerable study of the extant repertoire, for the melodic style is free and not subject to precise definition. The following rules are therefore only a general guide to the most common features of style.

1. *Stepwise progression* is the norm.

2. *Repetition of a tone* may serve to emphasize a particular pitch. It is also the only way of notating a pitch of longer duration.

a. Descending appoggiatura figures

Single note

Double note

b. Ascending appoggiatura figures

Single note

Double note

EXAMPLE 6-10.   Appoggiatura Forms.

EXAMPLE 6-11.   Approach to the Appoggiatura.

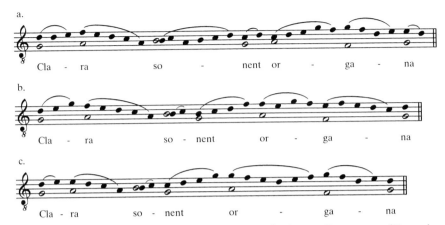

EXAMPLE 6-12. Sample Compositions, Based on the Discant Progression of Example 6-9.

3. *Thirds* are the most common melodic interval other than seconds. They typically occur in one of two configurations, either as an incidental element within a scalewise passage of a fifth or more (as in Example 6-13 a–c) or, in passages of limited range, as an intervallic movement normally answered by a melodic movement in the opposite direction (Example 6-13 c–g).

4. Fourths and fifths are rare, but (along with even rarer larger intervals) may be found in both ascending and descending form. They may occur between

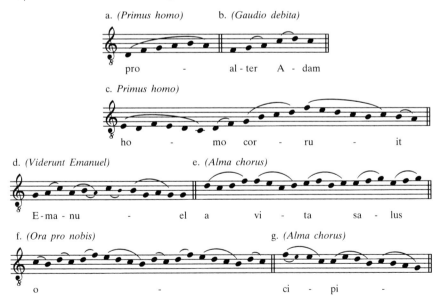

EXAMPLE 6-13. Use of the Third.

phrases or, within the phrase, when the florid melodic movement is interrupted through the introduction of one or more notes of simple discant (Example 6-14a). Their use within a totally florid idiom is harder to categorize, but one common use is in regaining a pitch level just abandoned. This usually involves an ascending leap, but descending ones do occur (Example 6-14 b–e).

Assignments

1. Compose a florid organum setting using one of the lower-voice melodies of Example 6-15.

2. Compose a complete versus, beginning with a newly composed lower voice.

The compositions should be performed and evaluated for closeness to style.

BIBLIOGRAPHY

Music

The complete body of Aquitanian polyphony has been published in a controversial rhythmic interpretation in Bryan Gillingham, *Saint-Martial Polyphony*, Musicological Studies 44 (Henryville, Pa.: Institute of Medieval Music, 1984). Much of the same repertoire is available in a more rhythmically neutral notation in volume 3 of the Sarah Fuller dissertation mentioned below. Individual polyphonic examples may be seen in the following anthologies: AMM, nos. 29, 30; HAM, no. 27a; OAMM, nos. 40, 41; *Masterpieces of Music before 1750*, ed. Carl

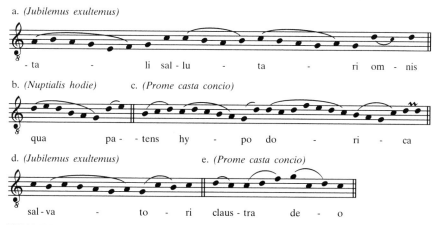

EXAMPLE 6-14. Melodic Intervals of Fourth and Fifth.

a.

Om - nis   sal - tus   Li - ba - ni   Mul - to   sple - det   de - co - re

A   du - ce   pre - no - bi - li   Re - ga - li   fac - ta   mo - re.

b.

Ver bum pa - tris hu - ma - na - tur   Dum pu - el - le   sa - lu - ta - tur

Sa - lu - ta - ta   de - cun - da - ta   Vi - ri nes - ci - a

E - y - a   no - va   gau - di - a.

EXAMPLE 6-15. Lower Voices for Compositional Practice.

Parrish and J. Ohls (New York: Norton, 1951), no. 8; *Music Scores Omnibus*, ed. William J. Starr and George F. Devine (Englewood Cliffs, N.J.: Prentice-Hall, 1968), no. 15; and *Examples of Music before 1400*, ed. Harold Gleason (New York: Appleton-Century-Crofts, 1942), nos. 30–32.

The monophony is largely unpublished, although a small selection may be found in the dissertation by Leo Treitler mentioned below.

Facsimiles of the manuscripts may be found in Bryan Gillingham, ed., *Paris Bibliothèque nationale, fonds latin 1139; Paris Bibliothèque nationale, fonds latin 3719;* and *Paris Bibliothèque nationale, fonds latin 3549 and London, British Library, Add. 36,881,* PMMM 14–16 (Ottawa: Institute of Mediaeval Music, 1987).

Theory

The Vatican Organum Treatise is available in translation and facsimile in Irving Godt and Benito Rivera, "The Vatican Organum Treatise: A Colour Reproduction, Transcription, and Translation," in *Gordon Athol Anderson In Memoriam,* vol. 2 (Henryville, Pa.: Institute of Medieval Music, 1984), 264–

345. The various medieval treatises on Latin poetry may be found, in Latin, in Giovanni Mari, *I Trattati Medievali Di Ritmica Latina*, Memorie del Reale Instituto Lombardo di scienze e lettere: Classe di lettere, scienze storiche e morali, 20 (Milan: Ulrico Hoepli, 1899).

Readings

Two dissertations that deal with the musical style in some detail are Leo Treitler, "The Aquitanian Repertoire of Sacred Monody in the 11th and 12th Centuries" (UMI no. 67-09613), and Sarah Ann Fuller, "Aquitanian Polyphony of the Eleventh and Twelfth Centuries" (UMI no. 70-13051).

Jens Bonderup, *The Saint Martial Polyphony: Texture and Tonality* (Copenhagen: Dan Fog, 1982), is a wide-ranging discussion of aspects of Aquitanian polyphony, while articles in the *NGD* on "Versus," "St. Martial," and "Early Latin Sacred Song" represent up-to-date scholarship in concise form. Also informative are Sarah Fuller, "The Myth of 'Saint Martial' Polyphony: A Study of the Sources," *MD* 33 (1979): 5–27; James Grier, "The Stemma of the Aquitanian Versaria," *JAMS* 41 (1988): 250–88; and Leo Treitler, "Musical Syntax in the Middle Ages: Background to an Aesthetic Problem," *Perspectives of New Music* 4 (1965): 75–85. The only detailed discussion of the theoretical structure of the polyphony is in German: Gunther Schmidt, "Strukturproblem der Mehrstimmigkeit im Repertoire von St. Martial," *Mf* 15 (1962): 11–39.

For Latin poetic style see Margot E. Fassler, "Accent, Meter, and Rhythm in Medieval Treatises 'De Rithmis'," *JoM* 5 (1987): 164–90; and Stevens, *Words and Music*, Chapters 2 and 12, although Chapter 1 gives the needed basic information about syllable count and other matters.

Standard texts on medieval poetry are those of F. J. E. Raby, *A History of Christian-Latin Poetry from the Beginnings to the Close of the Middle Ages*, 2nd ed. (Oxford: Clarendon Press, 1953), and *A History of Secular Latin Poetry in the Middle Ages*, 2 vol., 2nd ed. (Oxford: Clarendon Press, 1957), and Peter Dronke's more recent *Medieval Latin and the Rise of the European Love-Lyric*, 2 vols., 2nd ed. (Oxford: Clarendon Press, 1968), and *The Medieval Lyric*, 2nd ed. (London: Hutchinson, 1978), which also include translations and musical examples.

7

Secular Monophonic Music

A rich heritage of Aquitanian secular music forms an essential counterpart to the sacred music. Both developed simultaneously and represent opposite but interrelated faces of a bountiful musical culture.

Church musicians, working within the well-ordered world of the monastery or cathedral, were generally the best trained of the age, their knowledge often extending beyond performance to matters of theory and notation. On the other hand, secular musicians were, by and large, a more rough and ready sort, whose skills, if a minstrel or jongleur, could extend from dancing, clowning, juggling, and mime to slight-of-hand, acrobatics, fire eating, feats of strength, and performing with trained monkeys or bears. Musical training took the form of a practical apprenticeship and involved learning to sing and to play a variety of instruments.

Opportunities for secular music making in the Middle Ages were manifold: a day in the country might call for songs or for dancing to outdoor instruments such as shawm, pipe and tabor, or bagpipe. Journeys (and they were long in those times) included singing to while away the time, and some nobles took jongleurs with them to ease the boredom of travel. Banquets called for professional music making, vocal and instrumental, both as dinner music and for dancing, using indoor instruments such as the vielle, harp, psaltery, recorder, and flute. In private quarters, or as after-dinner entertainment, would come the singing of more serious chansons. An evening's festive entertainment could include a variety of colorful performers:

The jongleurs now arose,
Each striving to make sure
He was heard.
Out rang the melody
Of many tunes,
And they made trial
Of songs new-written for the vielle,
Essaying chant, descort and lay,
Each at his best did strum and play.
The Honeysuckle legend rang
From one, one of Tintagel sang;
One the True Lover's Tale related,
And one the tale of Yvain created.
One played the harp and one the vihuela,
And one the pipe and one the flute.
Some played the fythel and some the rote,
Some sang the words, some twanged the note,
Some on bagpipe, some on shawm,
Some with mandura, others the strings
Of psaltery and monochord.
While one with puppets contrives
Good sport, another juggles knives.
One tumbles, while another leaps
And somersaults, yet nimbly keeps
His feet. Some dive through hoops.
Each man performs as best he can.[1]

Secular music of widely varied types existed from classical times, but what little is known of music of the first thousand years A.D. derives from the desire of the church to preserve and pass on its traditions. No trace at all exists of the much more ephemeral music of secular life: the popular, folk, and dance idioms of the people, the more sophisticated music of the court. That such music existed is nevertheless abundantly clear—Europe has always had a lively secular culture that lived a life apart from the church:

It must be banned, this artificial music which injures souls and draws them into feelings sniveling, impure and sensual, and even a Bacchic frenzy and madness. One must not expose oneself to the powerful influences of exciting and languorous modes, which by the curve of their melodies lead to effeminacy and infirmity of purpose. Let us leave coloured harmonies to banquets where no one even blushes at music crowned with flowers and harlotry.[2]

---

[1]*The Romance of Flamenca,* ed. Marion Porter, trans. Merton Hubert (Princeton: Princeton University Press, 1962), lines 593–615, with instrument names corrected. The poem is from thirteenth-century Aquitania.

[2]Clement of Alexandria, around 312, trans. Alec Robertson, in *The Pelican History of Music,* vol. 1 (London: Penguin Books, 1960), 147.

Concrete evidence of medieval Latin secular song, however, dates from the ʒenth century, and from that time we begin to find major collections of Latin ʉlar poems clearly intended to be sung, the most important of which are the ʒlfth-century *Cambridge Songs* and the thirteenth-century *Carmina Burana.* ʒgrettably, few of the melodies were notated, and most that were are in ɑdecipherable unheightened neumes. The subject matter may be religious or ɑoral, but more often reflects the worldly spirit of the age: the joys of eating, drinking, gambling, springtime and love. The practitioners, commonly called *Goliards,* were wandering scholars and clerics who were active throughout most of Europe from the late tenth to the mid-thirteenth centuries. Learned men, many were teachers, while others were associated with courts. Their Latin poetry follows the rhymed, syllable-counting procedures discussed in the last chapter, but far too few recoverable melodies exist for conclusions to be drawn on their musical style.[3]

Simultaneously, we begin to find references to secular music in the developing Romance languages of Western Europe, and we know that *chansons de geste,* long epic poems in French declaimed to memorized melodic formulas, existed from at least the tenth century.

SOUTHERN FRANCE: THE TROUBADOURS

Not until around 1100 do we have our first preserved songs in the vernacular, those of Guillaume, ninth count of Poitou and seventh duke of Aquitaine, history's first known troubadour. He died in 1127 and it is almost ten years before the next troubadours receive recorded attention: Cercamon, Marcabru, and Jaufre Rudel. From that time on the troubadour tradition becomes established.

The background of that tradition has already been lightly touched upon: the rich, genial, cultured life of southern France, influenced by the culture of Christian and Moorish Spain, for as Aquitanian troubadours sojourned in Spanish courts, so Moorish singers, instrumentalists, and dancers were welcomed in the courts of Christian Spain and southern Europe. Of greater influence, however, was Christian sacred song, for the poetry of the early troubadours is closely related to that of the versus, and similar modal and melodic characteristics are often evident.

The music and poetry of the troubadour was aristocratic, yet not all troubadours were knights. Marcabru was a foundling, Perdigon the son of a fisherman, Bernart de Ventadorn the son of a kitchen maid, Cercamon a vagabond.

---

[3]The earliest known Goliard melody, *O admirabile Veneris idolum,* may be found in NOHM 2:221, while its sacred contrafact, *O Roma nobilis,* is printed in William J. Starr and George F. Devine, *Music Scores Omnibus* (New York: Prentice-Hall, 1964), 1:13. A Latin secular song that appears alongside the monophonic and polyphonic versus of the second of the Aquitanian manuscripts is given as AMM 40.

What mattered most was skill and the ability to assume the requisite aesthetic stance. For the art of the troubadour concerned *courtly love,* a poetic cultural fiction embraced by an aristocratic society whose wealth and ease made leisure pursuits possible.

Courtly Love

The idea of courtly love that lies behind so many troubadour lyrics is difficult to comprehend today. It is possibly most easily understood as a game-playing counterpart to the actual world of chivalry and feudalism. The knight pledged his homage and loyalty to the noble lady. He became her liege man; she his suzerain. His duty was to offer service; hers to offer protection and, in the end, reward his service.

If it was a poetical fiction, it was a convenient one, and one that fit the age. Marriage among the nobility was contracted for political purposes, not love. Expression of romantic love of necessity took place outside marriage, and the theatricality of the courtly love convention gave an aura of respectability to a relationship that was by implication adulterous.

In the original twelfth-century concept, the poetic fiction of the forlorn lover praying for favors from his distant lady became a convenient cover for the type of sexual freedom that the nobility has always considered its special prerogative. The Albigensian Crusade of 1209–29 changed all that, for it destroyed the wealth and culture of the South, and the subsequent establishment of the Inquisition served to eliminate, through fear of torture and the stake, the public expression of any but the most orthodox of Christian thoughts. Now the conceit of courtly love became generalized and abstract, the worship of an idealized lady from whom the worshiper can at best hope for a glance or smile.

This change in poetic ideology marks the division of the two periods of troubadour activity. The first, from the early twelfth century to the advent of the Albigensian Crusade, was one of richness and variety. The second, through the thirteenth century, finds troubadours writing at home under the cloud of the Inquisition or living in dispersion in Spain, Italy, Sicily, and elsewhere. With a few exceptions, it is a pale reflection of an earlier, happier time.

The Sources

Preservation of the troubadour repertoire is in distinct contrast to that of the Aquitanian sacred repertoire. Whereas the versus were copied in the twelfth century, while the repertoire was a living one, the troubadour heritage appears only in retrospective collections, after 1250 for the poetry, 1300 or later for the music. It is also striking that emphasis in preservation is on the poetry, not the music, for, while about 2,600 troubadour poems survive, there are only about 275 melodies.

Principal sources for the melodies are two chansonniers: one, the *Chanson-nier d'Urfe,* Paris, B.N. frç. 22543, originating in Aquitania; the other, Milan, Bib. Ambrosiana, R,71,sup., in Northern Italy. A smaller number of melodies are included in a few North French chansonniers devoted primarily to the music of the trouvères. The manuscripts give the appearance of having been assembled as collectors' items, and many contain *vidas*—accounts, often fanciful, of the lives of the troubadours—and miniature "portraits" of them. There is little evidence that either is based on historical fact.

Music of the troubadours is in this respect more difficult to study than the versus. Not only was the music notated long after its composition, but, as we know that new melodies were written for older poems and new poems written for older melodies, it is impossible to separate historic layers with certainty. Although the poems can be approximately dated, the music cannot.

The Poetry

Troubadour verse is constructed on the same *ars ritmica* principles as the versus: line length, marked by end-of-line rhyme. Word accent, to the extent it occurred in the French dialects of that day, was systematic at the end of the line, changeable in the early part.

Troubadours were, above all, poets and rhetoricians. Their poems are crafted with great ingenuity and virtuosity. Any real understanding of troubadour art must accordingly begin with an understanding of the poetry.

Most important is that the poems were designed for the ear, not the eye; to be heard, not read. In approaching troubadour poetry, therefore, the student is encouraged to read aloud, for silent reading cannot convey the richness of the poet's intention. Even in translation, the act of verbalization forces performance decisions on the speaker, matters of inflection, stress, length of pauses, emotional coloring of words. Further, in oral performance stanzas vary, sometimes widely, in verbal nuance. So would the coloration and nuance of the singing, even if to the same strophic melody. Troubadour art is first and foremost a poet's art—an art of words and wordplay—and the music and the performance are a vehicle for that art, for we know that performances could be dramatized, the troubadour or his jongleur assuming the persona of the lover and underlining with gesture and facial expression the changing emotional implications of the song.

The simple poetic style, the *trobar leu,* may be seen in Bernart de Venta-dorn's *La dousa votz* (Anthology Example 34). The poem deals in relatively straightforward manner with the poet's rejection by one he had served long (the "traitress" of stanza four: in the etiquette of courtly love the loved one is not named, only alluded to). It uses lines of seven and eight syllables with the rhyme scheme—a b a c d d c b—repeated, in the poetic form of a *coblas unissonans,* in the same order throughout the six stanzas. Even the customary final short stanza, called an *envoy* or *tornada,* retains the same rhymes.

In Bertran de Born's *Rassa, tant creis* (Anthology Example 35) the first six lines of each stanza end in an identical rhyme, which changes with each stanza. The second portion of the stanza (lines 7–11), however, uses a second rhyme, which is not abandoned but returns for the last five lines of each succeeding stanza, plus the *envoy*, a total of thirty-two lines ending with the rhyme *or* with only five repetitions of words.

Most complex of all the Anthology examples is number 36, Arnaut Daniel's *Lo ferm voler*, a poem that will give insight into the intricacy of intellectual wordplay. A practitioner of the *trobar ric*, the rich, difficult style, Arnaut has set a virtuoso task. Using a poetic form of his invention known as a *sestina*, six rhyme *words* are chosen: *intra* (enter), *ongla* (fingernail), *arma* (soul, spirit, or, to arm), *verga* (rod or branch), *oncle* (uncle), and *cambra* (chamber). They appear at the end of the six lines of stanza one and then reappear in scrambled but carefully contrived order in each succeeding stanza. A final three-line *envoy* combines the six words as the final two of each line.

Although seemingly unrelated, the words have been carefully chosen for their emotive connotations. The poem deals with the wish to *enter* the *chamber*, symbolic of erotic love. *Rod* or *branch* is a multifaceted word symbolizing in turn punishment (stanzas 1–3), passive frailty (stanza 4), the Stem of Jesse (the genealogy of Christ), and finally desire. *Soul* carries with it a connotation of spiritual rather than carnal love, while the same term in verb form symbolizes combat. *Fingernail*, both weapon (stanza 1) and means of clinging (stanza 6), can also picture closeness in its intimate relationship to the finger (stanzas 3, 4, 5). *Uncle* in medieval imagery was often a guardian and here, by extension, guardian of morality and obstacle to the fruition of love.

From these mixed images and other evocative connotations Arnaut calls to mind the various levels of love, carnal and spiritual, while conveying a multi-layered mood of frustrated passion. That this can be accomplished while maintaining the requisite syllable count and the intricate rhyme scheme ordained by the form is an indication of great technical virtuosity.

Poetic forms.   Troubadour poetry was of varied types, and certain names became attached to particular poetic idioms. These should *not* be equated with the concept of musical form, a mistake often encountered in modern histories and anthologies.

Vers (Latin *versus*) was the name given by the first troubadours to their poems. It is an early name for a courtly poem in rhymed, rhythmic poetry designed to be sung. *Canso* (northern French *chanson*) was the later name to designate a *vers*. *Serventes* referred in a specific sense to any poem composed in imitation of another, and thus was written to fit a borrowed melody. Later it came to mean a poem, often satirical, about a moral or political subject.

Pastorela, *alba*, and *tenso* refer to specific poetic scenes or situations involving dialogue. The *pastorela* portrays the often witty dialogue between a shepherdess and a knight who tries to seduce her. The *alba* was a "dawn song," sung by a faithful watcher, or the lovers themselves, when the approaching dawn forces them to part. The *tenso* represents a poetic debate, often with alternate verses by opposing troubadours. The *balada* and *dansa* were dance songs, often with a refrain.

Musical Style

Most troubadour melodies are syllabic or have only moderate ornamentation, often at the end of lines (compare Anthology Examples 35 and 36 with Example 34). Expression of the poetic declamation is the most important element, and melodic phrase lengths follow poetic line lengths.

Modality.   As with the monophonic versus, modality is a variable element in troubadour song. Melodies employ third-chain, pentatonic, and tonic-fifth schemes and rely at times on the church modes or liturgical recitative. Some melodies have a strong tonal center throughout. Others oscillate between two tonal centers or shift in a linear fashion from one center to another. It is quite possible for variant manuscript versions of a chanson to begin on the same note, but end on quite different finals.

Troubadour chansons were passed on by oral or a mixed oral and written tradition in the years before the existing manuscripts. (It is surmised that there may have been manuscript rolls or sheets specifically copied for performers, but, if so, none have come down to us.) Variants that one finds are those that one would expect in such an environment. The two versions of Bernart de Ventadorn's *La dousa votz* given in Anthology Example 34 illustrate the divergence of this transmission. The basic structure of both versions is the third chain D-F-a-c, in which the most active elements are the F and a, the D appearing only in phrases 2 and 8, the c functioning structurally only in phrases 5, 6, and 7. The melodic contour is the same in each version, and both versions clearly convey the same melody, but with many obvious variants.

Greatest stability is apparent in the phrase beginnings, precisely the elements that would be easiest to memorize and recall. Much more variation occurs in matters of ornamentation and the manner in which the text is fitted to the music. Greatest difference occurs at phrase endings, where varied melodic ornamentation often directs the melody toward different cadence tones, even in the final phrase. Should this melody be considered D mode or E?

Troubadour music was disseminated by public performance. If a song was appealing, others learned it and performed it, or their version of it, elsewhere. A jongleur in another town might remember the poem, but vary the melody, either deliberately or due to a faulty memory; there existed no absolute relationship between a poem and its musical setting.

Scale types.   Within the troubadour repertoire there are many approaches to tonal organization, and only rarely can a melody be said to be in a definite mode. It is more appropriate, then, to speak of generalized scale patterns rather than mode, even in the broad sense in which that term was applied to the versus.

Like the versus, the troubadour repertoire avoids the use of E as a final, but unlike the versus it sometimes places the final on C, which in medieval modality would be considered a transposition of Tritus.

Given the medieval penchant for notation without the use of any accidentals except b flat and the lack of any connotation of absolute or even relative pitch, the scribe's choice of one or another final would be based on the desire to notate the melody with a minimum of accidentals. Notation on D permits a minor-sounding scale with a flexible sixth scale step (D-E-F-G-a-b flat / b-c-d). As b flat is consistently avoided in chansons notated on G, that scale represents a major scale type with a lowered seventh scale degree (G-a-b-c-d-e-f-g). To this, the troubadour repertoire adds a major type notated on C: a major scale with a raised seventh scale degree (C-D-E-F-G-a-b-c).

If the few pieces notated on a are combined with those on D, and the few on F are combined with those on C, we arrive at the following frequency of use:

Minor type with flexible sixth degree	133
Major type scale with lowered seventh	65
Major type scale with raised seventh	68

"Minorish" and "majorish" scale patterns exist in approximately equal proportion, and the majorish scale options include raised as well as lowered sevenths. The seventh step, raised or not, seldom functions as a leading tone in the modern, tonal sense, however. Rather, the scales notated on C, F, and G are aspects of generalized "major" idiom that encompasses flexible fourth and seventh scale degrees. For instance, both an upper b flat and a lower B natural occur in Anthology Example 36, a chanson notated on C. In other cases, actually more frequent, such chromatic alterations will result in a whole tone below the final and a major seventh above it.

Musical Form

Troubadour chansons are strophic; that is, the same melody is repeated for each verse. In considering melodic form, Dante, writing about troubadour song in the late thirteenth century, lists four basic designs, of which only two are commonly found: the *oda continua* and the *pedes cum cauda*.

The *oda continua* ("continuous song") is equivalent to our more common term *through-composed*. About 75 percent of the troubadour chansons fall into this classification, although the varied techniques it encompasses are so numerous as to make the term a mere generality.

Organization may be totally unrepetitive or permit varied amounts of unstructured repetition. Even the absence of obvious repetition does not mean that more subtle means of unification are absent. Anthology Example 35 attains unity through an elaboration of basic shapes. Phrase 1 begins like a liturgical recitation on c, and phrase 2 can be seen as an ornamental approach to that tone followed by an ending identical to phrase 1. In phrases 3, 5, 8, 9, and 10 the recitation tone changes to a, while phrases 4, 6, and to some extent 7, reflect the rising and falling fourth of phrase 2. Without literal repetition, there is nonetheless a high degree of unity and cohesion.

Dante's second form, the *pedes cum cauda* (literally "feet with tail," referring to a repeated section plus a continuation), accounts for most of the remainder of the repertoire. It is a bipartite form in which the first portion contains an internal repeat; although the form is diagrammed AAB, the B section is as long or longer than the two A sections combined.

Despite these definitions, musical form in the troubadour chanson is a fluid procedure, and the simple terms above can hide a wealth of specific procedures. This fluidity may extend even to variant versions of the same chanson. Compare the two versions of *La dousa votz* given in Anthology Example 34. The first is in perfect AAB form—Dante's *pedes cum cauda*—the two A sections having in characteristic fashion open and closed endings:

A		A		B			
a	b	a	b′	c	d	e	f

The second version b negates this through its free approach to phrases 3 and 4. It is an *oda continua*, a through-composed chanson (unified through the identical beginnings of phrases 1–4, 7, and 8).

Rhythm

Like the Aquitanian versus, troubadour chansons are notated without indication of rhythm even though at the time of their copying, ca. 1300 and later, a rhythmic notation was well known and practiced. It would appear from this that a fixed rhythm was not integral to their performance, an interpretation supported by the theorist Grocheo, writing about 1300, who states that only polyphony is precisely measured.

Nevertheless, considerable controversy has arisen within this century regarding the rhythm of troubadour chansons, with many transcribers attempting to apply the rhythmic modes of thirteenth-century Parisian polyphony to this southern French monophonic repertoire, part of which dates from a hundred years before the known development of the rhythmic modes. The appearance of several trouvère chansons in a somewhat inconsistent mensural notation within a few late manuscripts is often cited as evidence for this procedure.

Against this evidence must be placed the fact that the overwhelming majority of all notated chansons (trouvère as well as troubadour) are in nonrhythmic notation, even in fourteenth-century chansonniers. There is also such specific evidence as the Adam de la Hale manuscript, where the scribe notates the chanson repertoire in nonrhythmic notation, while using rhythmic notation for the polyphony and the dancelike songs of the play *Robin et Marion.*

Application of the rhythmic modes in troubadour music has now been largely abandoned in favor of a flexible, unmetered performance that emphasizes poetic structure and its expression through the music. The troubadour was primarily a poet, writing in the same *ars ritmica* as the Aquitanian versus, a poetry based on syllables of equal length, with a rhythmic structure based on length of line and rhyme. This, plus what we know about performance context, suggests a freer, more rhetorical performing style than that of the sacred versus, one based on an interpretation in equal syllable lengths, but colored by the interaction of poetic declamation and melodic movement. The resulting performance style, demanding an intimate knowledge of both the language and the music, would not be unrhythmic, but would incorporate rhythms far too subtle to be captured in medieval (or modern) notation.

NORTHERN FRANCE: THE TROUVÈRES

Music of the troubadours reached the North when Eleanor of Aquitaine, married to King Louis VII of France in 1137, brought southern troubadours to Paris. By around 1160 northern French practitioners of the art, called *trouvères,* were writing in the *langue d'oïl.* As in the South, the early trouvères lived and wrote within an aristocratic environment, even though not all trouvères were aristocrats. This slowly began to change during the thirteenth century as the growing prosperity of the town created a new middle-class clientele. While the first half of the thirteenth century saw many aristocratic trouvères—most notably Thibaut de Champagne, Roi de Navarre—the trouvère movement of the second half was dominated by bourgeois poets and composers who gathered in guilds and organized assemblies or *puys* to judge new songs.

Trouvères, like troubadours, were trained rhetoricians but amateur musicians. A rare exception is Adam de la Hale, one of the last of the trouvères and a trained musician who also wrote motets and polyphonic rondeaux. Adam's death in 1288 (or 1302?) brought the trouvère movement to a virtual close, although it did not end the composition of secular monophony in France: it was followed by the monophonic *ballades* and *rondeaux* of the *Roman de Fauvel* and of Jehan de Lescurel and the important *lais* and *virelais* of Machaut.

The Sources

The music of the trouvères is considerably better preserved than that of the troubadours. In all, about 2,400 poems and 1,700 melodies have survived in two dozen chansonniers. This large body of song has yet to be adequately studied. Like the sources of troubadour music, these chansonniers all date from the mid-thirteenth century or later: retrospective collections after the movement had largely run its course.

The Poetry

The poetry of the trouvères follows the same *ars ritmica* as does that of the troubadours. Poetic forms are also those found in the South, to which the trouvères added a few special types: the *chanson de toile* or spinning song, the *malmariée* or song of the unhappy wife complaining of her husband and longing for a young lover, and the *reverdie* or song of longing for spring and love.

Musical Style

Most of the remarks made about troubadour song are equally applicable to the trouvère repertoire. In formal structure, however, the trouvères, although maintaining considerable flexibility, tend toward greater use of the AAB form (possibly 75 percent of the chansons), with most of the remainder being through-composed.

Notation and Tonality

In notation, the trouvère manuscripts tend to make greater use of accidentals (known as *musica ficta* when they are foreign to the mode), including E flat, F sharp, C sharp, and even G sharp. However, this is often an orthographic difference, for, while the appearance on the page looks more "modern," by and large the melodies show the same lack of concern with precise tonality as in the troubadour tradition. Application of musica ficta differs from manuscript to manuscript, reinforcing the appearance of casualness in the approach to modality. Approximately 25 percent of the repertoire appears in modal variants in the sources.

There has been no overall survey of the entire literature, but a study of 321 songs reveals the same preference for scale patterns as in the South.

MONOPHONIC SONG OUTSIDE OF FRANCE

Germany

The Minnesingers ("singers of love") appeared in Germany at approximately the same time as the trouvères in northern France. They were in many ways direct counterparts to the trouvères and wrote about the same subjects. Like them, the early Minnesingers were aristocrats, coming from all parts of the German territories, from Holland to Austria to Switzerland to the Rhineland. Outstanding among them were Wolfram von Eschenbach and Walther von der Vogelweide. Regrettably, almost no melodies have survived for these poems, making musical analysis nearly impossible. Some poems imitate French models; attempts have been made to apply the French melodies to the German poems, but there is no medieval evidence for such a practice. Indeed, medieval German poetry operated on a distinctly different principle than that of France, making such melodic borrowing highly unlikely.

German poetry differs from French in being definitely accentual in nature, with strong and weak syllables following the natural accents of the language. Line lengths are determined by the number of accents rather than the number of syllables. Consider, for example, the following three lines, extracted from different poems:

> Ĭn | eínem̆ | zwível|lĭchĕn | wãn
> nãh | mĭmĕ gĕ|séllen̆ | ĭst mĭr | wḗ
> | Dú bĭst | mĭn, | ích bĭn | dĭn

Each is poetically equal in containing four accented syllables, forming four poetic feet (indicated by the vertical lines). The syllable count of each is different, however, due to the addition or suppression of weak syllables, a procedure that is particularly evident in the early Minnesinger poems.

This style of poetry inevitably calls for a different type of musical rhythm than that of the troubadours and trouvères. Its nature remains conjectural, however, as the German manuscripts, like the French, are without rhythmic indications. It is complicated by the fact that, even in later manuscripts, not even the first stanza is underlayed under the notes of the melody and, as the number of notes and the number of syllables often do not match, the exact application of the text to the music is problematic. (Subsequent music of the German Meistersingers, from the fifteenth century on, tends to ignore the natural stress of the language and return to syllable counting, often leading to a bad mismatch between melodic and poetic rhythm.)

The first definite Minnesinger melodies we have are those of Neidhart von Reuenthal (ca. 1190–after 1236), but here confusion arises through their inclusion among other melodies that most editors consider to be later imitations (there are probably seventeen authentic melodies). Of the two authentic melodies readily available in anthologies (AMM 48 and 49), *Ine gesach die heide* is through-composed, while *Owê, lieber sumer* is in *bar* form, the German equivalent to Dante's *pedes cum cauda*. In German terminology, the *Aufgesang* (first section) is divided into two *Stollen*, followed by the *Abgesang*. It is not uncommon for the *Abgesang* to contain material from the *Stollen*: when this material occurs at the end (for instance, abc abc defa), it is commonly called *rounded bar form*. (Other Minnesinger examples may be seen in HAM 20 [c and d are not authentic Neidhart songs] and SSMS 16.)

The first period of Minnesinger activity ended around 1220, after which, as in France, bourgeois composers become increasingly important as the thirteenth century progressed. Minnesinger tradition continues to the mid-fifteenth century, when it merges into the Meistersinger guilds of the fifteenth and sixteenth centuries. The long duration and wide dissemination of the monophonic idiom in Germany may be seen in the numerous examples of monophony in the various late fifteenth-century *Liederbücher* designed for domestic music making.

Spain

A close relationship between southern France and Spain was maintained throughout the later Middle Ages, with the troubadour movement strongly influencing Spain: both Spanish and Catalan poets wrote poems in the *langue d'oc* of Aquitania. In addition, the native languages of the area were used and six early thirteenth-century Galican-Portuguese love songs by Martin Codax survive with music, our only trace of this early activity.

The *Cantigas de Santa Maria,* compiled under the direction of King Alfonso the Wise of Castile in the late thirteenth century, are a major collection of differently oriented monophonic songs, also in Galican-Portuguese. Devoted to retelling the stories of the seemingly numberless miracles worked by the Virgin Mary on behalf of her devoted worshipers, the *Cantigas* represent a popular religious expression that was maintained into the Renaissance and may be seen in many sixteenth-century villancicos.

Form in many melodies tends to approximate the pattern *refrain-verse-refrain-verse-refrain, etc.,* with part of the verse using the music of the refrain. It may be diagrammed, capital letters indicating the music of the refrain:

Refrain	Verse	Refrain	Verse	Refrain (etc.)
A	b b a	A	b b a	A

This form, also found in a few Italian lauda, anticipates and may be the forerunner of the fourteenth-century French virelai (see AMM 51, HAM 22, SSMS 18).

Like other thirteenth-century repertoires, the vast majority of melodies falls into the three standard scale classifications, but with the major type on C being notated on F with a b flat. The resulting modes are thus D, F with b flat, and G, with D being over twice as numerous as the two "major" types.

Unlike the other monophonic repertoires, the late thirteenth-century *Cantigas* are notated in a semimensural notation that is capable of rhythmic transcription. The resulting rhythms are often not those of the Parisian rhythmic modes. This is not immediately apparent in the published transcription by Anglès, who transforms many nonmodal rhythms into modal ones.

Italy

Courts in northern Italy had been open to troubadour culture throughout the twelfth century, and the dispersion of troubadour poets after the Albigensian Crusade found many sojourning there and in southern Italy and Sicily and influencing native-born *trovatores.* Unfortunately, none of these early melodies survive.

A more indigenous Italian idiom is the *laude spirituali,* a type of hymn popular during several periods of widespread religious zeal in the century between 1250 and 1350, penitential reactions to the repeated devastations brought on Italy by recurring war and pestilence (*AMM* 50, *HAM* 21, *SSMS* 17).

Laude are preserved in several collections dating from the late thirteenth and early fourteenth centuries in a nonrhythmic notation. Like the *cantigas,* some of them hint at the form that was to become the *ballata* in Italy and the *virelai* in France.

England

Secular song in English is rare. Norman-French was the language of the court (which was troubadour influenced), and Latin was that of the church. Little music exists in the vernacular of the people. Among the few remains are three religious songs by Saint Godric (d. 1170) and seven from the thirteenth century, three religious and four secular. Of the secular songs, two, *Worldes blis* and *Man mai longe lives,* lament the shortness of earthly joys, while *Brid one breere* and *Miri it is while sumer ilast* refer to love and the passing of summer (*HAM* 23, *AMM* 52, *SSMS* 19 and 20).

BIBLIOGRAPHY

Music

An excellent introductory anthology of troubadour and trouvère song, with commentary, translations, and recorded performances, is *The Medieval Lyric: Anthology I* (South Hadley, Mass.: Mount Holyoke College, 1988). There is no suitable anthology of Latin songs. Friedrich Gennrich, ed., and R. G. Dennis, trans., *Troubadours, Trouvères, Minne- and Meistersinger,* Anthology of Music 2 (Köln: Arno Volk Verlag, 1960) gives a cross section of French and German styles, but in the editor's mensural versions.

Troubadour.   There are two good editions of the extant troubadour melodies: Ismael Fernández de la Cuesta and R. Lafont, eds., *Las Cançons dels Trobadors* (Toulouse: Institute d'estudis occitans, 1979), and Hendrik van der Werf and G. A. Bond, eds., *The Extant Troubadour Melodies: Transcriptions and Essays for Performers and Scholars* (Rochester: privately printed, 1984), which also contains important essays on style.

A facsimile of one of the important chansonniers has been published: Ugo Sesini, ed., *Le melodie trobadoriche nel Canzoniere provenzale della Biblioteca Ambrosiana R.71 Sup* (Turin: G. Chiantore, 1942).

Trouvère.   Hendrik van der Werf, ed., *Trouvère-Melodien I–II,* Monumenta Monodica Medii Aevi 11 and 12 (Kassel: Bärenreiter, 1977–79), which gives parallel versions of the melodies for eleven trouvères in mostly unmeasured notation, and Samuel N. Rosenberg and Hans Tischler, eds., *Chanter m'estuet* (Bloomington: Indiana University Press, 1961), a critical edition of over two hundred texts with extant music transcribed in modal rhythm, are the best introductions to the trouvère repertoire.

Five of the chansonniers are available in facsimile: Pierre Aubrey, ed., *Le Chansonnier de l'Arsenal* (Paris: P. Guethner, 1909–12); Jean Beck, *Les Chansonniers des Troubadours et des Trouvères, Le Chansonnier Cangé* (Paris, 1927; rpt. New York: Johnson, 1965); Jean Beck, *Les Chansonniers des Troubadours et des Trouvères, Le Manuscrit du Roi* (London: Pennsylvania Press, 1938); A. Jeanroy, *Le Chansonnier d'Arras* (Paris, 1925; no publisher given); and P. Meyer and G. Raynaud, eds., *Le chansonnier français de Saint-Germain-des-Pres (Bibl. nat. fr. 20050),* (Paris: Didot et Cie, 1892; rpt. New York: Johnson Reprint Co., 1968).

Minnesingers. Ewald Jammers, ed., *Ausgewählte Melodien des Minnesangs* (Tübingen: M. Niemeyer, 1963) contains a selection of 131 songs. Ronald Jack Taylor, ed., *The Art of the Minnesinger,* 2 vol. (Cardiff: University of Wales Press, 1968), is an edition, in modal rhythm, of all songs up to 1300.

Friedrich Gennrich has published two collections in facsimile, *Die Jenaer Liederhandschrift,* Summa Musicae Medii Aevi 11, and *Die Colmarer Liederhandschrift,* Summa Musicae Medii Aevi 18 (Frankfurt: Langen, 1963 and 1967).

Spain. The seven Martin Codax songs are available in facsimile and transcription in Pedro Vindell, ed., *Martin Codax: Las Siete Canciones de Amor* (Madrid: [Imprenta de la Sucesora de M. Minuesa de los Rios], 1915), while the *Cantigas de Santa Maria* are similarly treated in Higinio Anglès, ed., *La música de las Cantigas de Santa Maria del Rey Alfonso el Sabio* (Barcelona: Diputación Provincial de Barcelona, Biblioteca Central, 1943–64).

Italy. Fernando Liuzzi, ed., *La Lauda e i Primordi della melodia italiana* (Rome: La Libreria della Stato, 1935) presents a main *lauda* manuscript in facsimile and transcription.

England. E. J. Dobson and Frank Lloyd Harrison, *Medieval English Songs* (London: Faber and Faber, 1979) contains the complete early English repertoire (including polyphony) with extensive critical notes, but in often overly imaginative musical versions. A smaller selection, with cassette recording, may be found in *The Medieval Lyric: Anthology III* (South Hadley, Mass.: Mt. Holyoke College, 1989).

Readings

Troubadour and Trouvère. A useful introduction into the diverse facets of troubadour and trouvère song is Howell Chickering and Margaret Switten, eds., *The Medieval Lyric: Commentary Volume* (South Hadley, Mass.: Mt. Holyoke

College, 1988). Stevens, *Words and Music* contains a good treatment of the poetic-musical relationship, with a summary of the rhythmic problem. Hendrik van der Werf, *The Chansons of the Troubadours and Trouvères: A Study of the Melodies and Their Relation to the Poems* (Utrecht: A. Oosthoek, 1972) gives an excellent overview with alternate versions of thirty-three chansons with translations. Also important is the article "Troubadours and Trouvères" by John Stevens and Theodore Karp in *NGD* and the articles on individual troubadours and trouvères there.

Aspects of performance are considered in Ian Parker, "The Performance of Troubadour and Trouvère Songs: Some Facts and Conjectures," *EM* 5 (1977), 184–207. Christopher Page discusses the applicability of instrumental participation in detail in *Voices and Instruments of the Middle Ages: Instrumental Practice and Songs in France 1100–1300* (Berkeley and Los Angeles: University of California Press, 1986).

More analytical articles include Theodore Karp, "Borrowed Material in Trouvère Music," *AM* 34 (1962), 87–100; idem., "Modal Variants in Medieval Secular Monody," in *The Commonwealth of Music, in Honor of Curt Sachs,* ed. Gustav Reese and Rose Brandel (Glencoe, N.Y.: Free Press, 1964), 118–29; Ian Parker, "Troubadour and Trouvère Song: Problems in Modal Analysis," *RBM* 31 (1977), 20–37; Robert H. Perrin, "Discant and Troubadour Melodies: A Problem in Terms," *JAMS* 16 (1963), 313–24; idem., "Some Notes on Troubadour Melodic Types," *JAMS* 9 (1956), 12–18; Hendrik van der Werf, "Recitative Melodies in Trouvère Chansons," in *Festschrift fur Walter Wiora zum 30 December 1966* (Kassel: Barenreiter, 1967), 231–40.

Spain.   Higinio Anglès, "Hispanic Musical Culture from the Sixth to the Fourteenth Century," *MQ* 26 (1940), 494–528 is still a good introduction, as is Isabelle Pope, "Medieval Latin Background of the Thirteenth-Century Galican Lyric," *Speculum* 9 (1934), 3–28. Gerardo V. Huseby's dissertation "The 'Cantigas de Santa Maria' and the Medieval Theory of Mode" (UMI no. 83-07167) gives an excellent analysis of that aspect of the Cantigas. Rhythm and notation are discussed in Hendrik van der Werf, "Accentuation and Duration in the Music of the *Cantigas de Santa Maria,*" in *Studies on the Cantigas de Santa Maria: Art, Music, and Poetry,* ed. Israel J. Katz and John E. Keller (Madison, Wis.: The Hispanic Seminary of Medieval Studies, 1987), 223–34.

8

Other Polyphonic Styles

THE *LIBER SANCTI JACOBI*

A fascinating manuscript from the twelfth century is the *Liber Sancti Jacobi,* also known as the *Codex Calixtinus* or Compostela manuscript. Long regarded as Spanish, more careful research suggests that the manuscript was in fact compiled in northern France and that its musical contents represent a cross section of midtwelfth-century northern French polyphony. This makes possible a comparison of northern and southern styles in the crucial period just before the burgeoning development of the Parisian polyphony of Notre Dame.

The *Liber Sancti Jacobi* uses the notation of east-central France and appears to have taken shape at Saint Jacques de la Boucherie in Paris and the Benedictine abbey of Cluny. The manuscript was designed, however, for presentation to the Spanish cathedral of Compostela, which, with its reputed possession of the bones of Saint James, was one of the great pilgrimage centers of medieval Europe, surpassing in importance all but Rome and Jerusalem.

As such, the manuscript is completely centered on Compostela-related subjects: an elaborate plainsong Mass and Office for the Feast of Saint James, accounts of his twenty-two miracles, tracts concerning the moving of his bones to Santiago de Compostela, a humorous guide to the various pilgrimage routes therewith, a fabulous account of Charlemagne's campaigns in Spain, and, most important to us here, an appendix of polyphony to be used in the Mass and Office given earlier in the manuscript.

The *Liber Sancti Jacobi* was definitely copied before 1173, probably around 1160. Accordingly its polyphony represents a midcentury practice roughly contemporary with the middle Aquitanian sources and just before the first or Leonin period of Parisian development. The liturgical context of the polyphony is northern French, emphasis being placed on polyphonic settings of the same items northern French composers had earlier set as free organum: the solo portions of responsorial chants and troped items from the ordinary, items neglected in the Aquitanian repertory.

Unexpectedly, in an age when anonymity in church music was normal, attributions are given for all the musical settings. These ascriptions have been much debated and, indeed, must be judged carefully. For instance, much of the monophonic Mass and Office, and much of the nonmusical content of the manuscript as well, is attributed to "Pope Calixtus," who, it appears, is not Pope Calixtus II (pope from 1119 to 1124), but a pseudonym used by the chief author and compiler of the manuscript. It is this which led to the alternate designation of the manuscript as the *Codex Calixtinus.*

The other musical inscriptions can be taken more seriously, however, and, while it is doubtful that all the bishops and archbishops named were actual composers, they may well represent the titular suppliers of the music, the composition deriving from the repertoire of their diocese or from a musician under them.

The polyphony is attributed to both known and unknown personages, practically all from central and northern France: Chartres, Paris, Soissons, Troyes, Bourges, Vezelay. We seem to have, then, a kind of anthology of northern French polyphony.

Of the twenty-one polyphonic pieces in the manuscript, two are known from the Aquitanian repertoire, but they appear here with new texts in praise of Saint James. One of these, *Noster cetus,* was apparently a popular piece, occurring in all three layers of Aquitanian manuscripts. The attribution is to the archbishop of Bourges, a city lying close to Aquitania, which could have been the city of transmission and where the new text could have been written. The second, *Ad honorem,* appears only in the last of the Aquitanian manuscripts and may well have originated with the *Liber Sancti Jacobi.*

Conductus

The term *conductus* is found in the plainsong Mass and Office and in the polyphonic appendix. In each case it refers specifically to processional pieces, presumably the original meaning of the term. Later northern French manuscripts use the term in a more general sense that is an almost exact equivalent to the southern French use of the term *versus.* In the ensuing discussion we will use the term in that broad sense.

Seven of the polyphonic pieces in the *Liber Sancti Jacobi* fit this definition. They are settings of rhymed, rhythmic verse and utilize the same scale systems as the Aquitanian versus, being on either D or G. They are consistently in discant or only moderately florid style and, unlike some versus, are all strophic in form. Most use a small number of motives in a tightly woven melodic fabric.

This element, tight melodic construction, is the chief difference between these pieces and the Aquitanian style, for, typically, the upper voice will weave a small number of stock figures into a highly integrated structure.

In *Jacobe sancte tuum* we find a succinct example (Example 8-1). Here, three simple shapes form much of the upper voice's melodic material. The motives are

EXAMPLE 8-1. The Old Bishop of Benevento, *Jacobe sancte tuum* (*Liber Sancti Jacobi*, f. 131).

not memorable in themselves, and all occur in other pieces as part of the common melodic idiom of the day. It is the consistency of their use and the way they permeate a given melody that make them functional.

In Anthology Example 37, *Regi perhennis*, the tenor establishes an ABCB pattern (disguised in the notated phraseology of the manuscript). The upper voice both adheres to and overrides this structure for, while the B sections are identical, the C section is so permeated with motives from B that no sense of departure and return occurs: all is a prolonged B section. Five of the seven conductus display a similar tight melodic construction.

Cantus Firmus Settings

Eleven cantus firmus settings in the *Liber Sancti Jacobi* follow northern French liturgical preference. Included are four settings of solo portions of Office responsories, one with an appended prose, a Mass Gradual and Alleluia; two troped Kyries and three untroped *Benedicamus Domino* settings. All but one are in the florid style, a preference we have already noticed in cantus firmus settings in the Aquitanian repertoire.

A comparison of one of these settings, *Alleluia: Vocavit Jhesus Jacobum* (Anthology Example 38), with any of the free organum Alleluias (Anthology Examples 20, 21, 23, and 24) will show immediately the greater expansiveness of the style. A small stock of motives musically unifies the upper voice. Three of these appear in conjunction at the beginning of the Alleluia (Example 8-2) and return as an entity at the beginning of phrases 3, 8, and 12. Motive *b*, which we have already seen in the discant idiom of Example 8-1 (where it formed

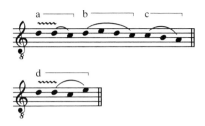

EXAMPLE 8-2.   Motives from *Alleluia: Vocavit Jhesus Jacobum.*

motive *c*), appears by itself or in conjunction with *c* in phrases 2, 3, 4, 7, 9, 16, and 17 and as a connective between phrases 4 and 5.

Phrases 10, 11, 15, and 23 have a more intimate relationship: 10, 11, and 23 all begin with a fusion of *a* and *b*, and 11 and 23 are identical throughout. Phrase 15 begins with a different conjunction of *a* and *b*, yet is identical (in notes 2–15) to the concluding portions of phrases 11 and 23 (notes 6–19).

Motive *d* appears unnoticed in phrase 2, but then becomes a significant sequential figure in phrases 13, 20, and 22, its close relationship to *a* being shown by their juxtaposition in phrases 20 and 12. The concluding neume-against-neume melisma of phrase 24 is a result of the structure of the twelfth-century chant composed by our anonymous "Pope Calixtus."

Melodic style is quite different from the relatively free-flowing Aquitanian idiom, where unity comes, in as far as it exists at all, from the exploration of large, generalized melodic shapes. Here, it is the recombination of discrete motives. Both can grow out of an improvisatory idiom, but each displays a distinctly different concept of melodic organization.

This close-knit melodic organization is characteristic of the remainder of the repertory as well. Of the cantus firmus settings most readily available in anthologies, the responsory *Huic Jacob* (AMM 31) and the Kyrie trope *Cunctipotens genitor* (HAM 27b) both draw from the same stock of motives as the Alleluia just discussed. The Gauterius *Benedicamus Domino* setting (HAM 28b) makes use of motives *a* and *b* of Example 8-2 in combination with an exploitation of a more generalized melodic shape, the movement from a to c followed by a scalewise descent to D.

Three-Voiced Composition

One composition in the *Liber Sancti Jacobi*, the *Congaudeunt catholici* of Master Albertus, appears to be the earliest known three-voice composition in discant style (in distinction from the mere octave duplication of the composite forms of parallel organum). The notation and relative amount of dissonance have caused much comment, and it is not universally accepted as a genuine three-voice composition (Example 8-3).

Nonetheless, considering the amount of dissonance that can occur in the slightly later Parisian three-voice conductus, there seems no compelling reason not to accept *Congaudeunt catholici* as an early venture into three-voice texture. Perhaps significantly, the composition is attributed to a Master Albertus of Paris, and an Albertus was on the rolls of Notre Dame as a singer between 1147 and 1173.

PRIMITIVE POLYPHONY

The twelfth-century polyphony we have so far studied represents a repertoire of music worthy of being preserved in notation. Probably far more prevalent in the period was the more-or-less artistic improvisations of singers of varying levels of ability, singing service music week after week, music not preserved nor meant to be preserved, music for the moment.

An anonymous English writer of the late thirteenth century describes such singers, dividing them into three types: those who are "plain or new" and sing largely in parallel motion; those partially experienced, who sing sometimes in parallel, sometimes in contrary motion; and the "true" singers of discant, who are skilled in the use of contrary motion.

That an improvised idiom should have used forms of parallelism as late as the twelfth and thirteenth centuries may seem surprising from the twentieth-century point of view, but should not when viewed from the medieval perspective. The liturgical singer of medieval times would first be required to know the year's chant repertoire from memory. Then, as a singer of organum, he would be required to improvise a suitably harmonious melody to a chant simultaneously recalled from memory (singers may at times have had the chant in front of them, but there is no evidence that this was at all common). What could be more normal than that the novice improviser would rely on a fair degree of parallelism, and that even a more skilled one might rely on it at times? We must

EXAMPLE 8-3. Master Albertus of Paris, *Congaudeunt catholici,* beginning (*Liber Sancti Jacobi,* f. 185).

remember that parallelism was not an unattractive sound to the medieval ear, and that even "artistic" free organum permits up to three parallel perfect intervals in a row.

It is not usual to find this type of music in notation, but occasional examples appear, as in Example 8-4, drawn from Aquitanian manuscripts. They would seem to be representative of the second of the three types of singers described above.

The longevity of the parallel style, especially in less artistic centers, may be seen in the Epistle setting of a German antiphonal of 1426 given in Example 8-5.

HISTORICAL CONSIDERATIONS

This survey of the *Liber Sancti Jacobi*, along with that of the Aquitanian repertoire in Chapter 6, permits a consideration of the state of polyphonic music in France in the midtwelfth century, on the eve of the remarkable explosion of activity that was to take place in Paris in the second half of the century.

There is no proof of a direct link, but certainly the ideas that lay behind the first or Leonin stage of Parisian polyphony were in the air by midcentury. All of the relevant styles of polyphony, from note-against-note or neume-against-neume discant to florid or even moderately melismatic organum, were in use in northern and southern France in the first half of the century. Although less severely categorized, even the application of these styles is largely anticipated:

a.

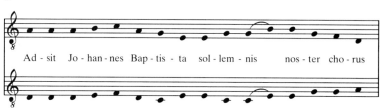

b.

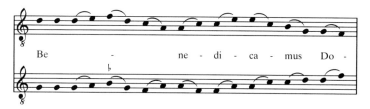

EXAMPLE 8-4.   Examples of Improvisatory Styles.
a. *Adsit Johannes Baptista* (Paris, B.N., lat. 3549, f. 160)
b. *Benedicamus Domino* (Paris, B.N., lat. 3719, f. 46)

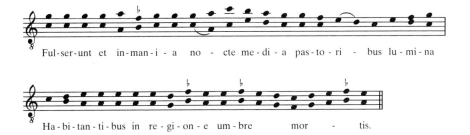

Ful-ser-unt et in-man-i-a no - cte me-di-a pas-to-ri - bus lu-mi-na

Ha-bi-tan-ti-bus in re-gi-on-e um-bre mor - tis.

EXAMPLE 8-5. Fifteenth-Century Improvisatory Style (Breslau, Universitatsbibli., 505, f. 206', excerpt). Reprinted with permission from Theodor Göllner, *Die Mehrstimmigen Liturgischen Lesungen* (Tutzing: Hans Schneider, 1969), p. 155.

discant or a moderately florid texture for the versus or conductus, florid or melismatic style for cantus firmus settings.

Evidence of alternate, non-Parisian styles is observable into the thirteenth century and serves to place the Parisian development in perspective. Not only were there the forerunners just discussed, but there is evidence of a continued non-Parisian polyphony into the thirteenth century in the Beauvais circumcision office of around 1225–30, and in the Saint Victor manuscript, which contains, from the same period, a repertoire different from yet technically as advanced as that of Notre Dame.

The polyphony of Paris did not win ascendancy at once, but at first competed with other regional styles. That it eventually won out over them and became the international standard is a test of its artistic superiority.

BIBLIOGRAPHY

Music

There are two editions of the music of the *Liber Sancti Jacobi*. Volume 2 of W. M. Whitehall, G. Prado, and J. C. Garcia, *Liber Sancte Jacobi, Codex Calixtinus*, 3 vol. (Santiago de Compostela, 1944), gives the music in facsimile and transcription, while Peter Wagner, *Die Gesänge de Jakobusliturgie zu Santiago de Compostela*, Collectanea Friburgensia, n.s., pt. 20 (Freiburg: Kommissionsverlag, 1931), gives the music transcribed into square notation. A color facsimile of the polyphonic section is in José López-Carlo, *La Musica Medieval en Galicia* (La Coroña: Barrie, 1982). Paul Helmer, *The Mass of St. James*, Musicological Studies 49 (Ottawa: The Institute of Medieval Music, 1988), gives a transcription of a complete Mass from the manuscript, including tropes and three polyphonic pieces. A few examples are available in anthologies: *HAM* 27b and 28b, *AMM* 31 and 32, and *OAMM* 42.

Many examples of primitive polyphony are given in Theodor Göllner, *Die Mehrstimmigen Liturgischen Lesungen*, 2 vol. (Tutzing: Hans Schneider, 1969).

Readings

A detailed discussion of the *Liber Sancti Jacobi*—the manuscript, the music, and the ascriptions—is in C. Hohner, "A Note on Jacobus," *Journal of the Warburg and Courtauld Institutes* 35 (1972): 31–80.

9

Sacred Music in Paris

THE MUSIC OF NOTRE DAME

The growing importance of Paris as a cultural and artistic center in Europe came about through the confluence of various political, religious, and educational events. An important actor in this was Eleanor of Aquitaine, the remarkable lady mentioned in Chapter 7 as an agent in the northward spread of troubadour culture. Born in 1122, Eleanor was heiress to all of Aquitaine, that vast southern fief encompassing about one-third of all France. In 1137 she became the wife of the French king Louis VII, bringing with her to Paris a love of the troubadour art (she was the granddaughter of the first of the troubadours, William IX of Aquitaine). She played her role in the cult of courtly love with a bit too much realism for the king; after several prominent affairs and, maybe more importantly, failing to bear the king a son, the marriage was annulled, apparently by mutual consent. (It took the king three wives to achieve the required male heir.)

Within several months of the annulment Eleanor married Henry, duke of Normandy and count of Anjou. Two years later, having been queen of France, Eleanor became queen of England when Henry acceded to the English throne. Her inheritance, along with other English holdings in France, gave England control of northern and western France: Normandy, Brittany, Maine, Anjou, and Aquitaine. It is only due to the astuteness of Louis and his successor Philip II that the French kingdom was able to not only hold its own against the English but grow.

The situation remained largely a stalemate during the reigns of the English kings Henry II and Richard, as Philip of France waged alternate war and intrigue against them. The accession to the English throne of the weak King John, however, gave Philip his chance, and by 1205 the French crown had gained control of much of the territory of France, an ascendancy that was further confirmed in the aftermath of the Albigensian Crusades. As a result, the French monarchy succeeded in strengthening its own central position, even during these years of fending off a stronger English foe. With this went greater prosperity and importance for the capital, Paris, and at the same time, a great expansion in its importance as a center for education and the arts.

Since Carolingian times, education throughout Europe had been in the hands of the monastic and cathedral schools. Of these, that attached to the Cathedral of Notre Dame in Paris began to attract special attention when, in the late eleventh century, William of Champeaux began to attract attention as a teacher, to be followed by his pupil Peter Abelard and by Hugh of Saint Victor and Peter the Lombard, bishop of Paris, establishing Paris as an international mecca for thought and inquiry. Abelard, a brilliant yet egotistical teacher around whom students flocked, brought to new heights the study of dialectic: the attempt to resolve arguments or opposite points of view by setting forth in great detail all possible arguments, pro and con, and weighing one contradiction against another in the search for truth. When in his *Sic et Non* (Yes and No) he brought this reasoning to bear on articles of Christian faith, he opened to a not too happy church a world of questioning thought.

The clergy provided the teachers for this growing endeavor. It also provided leadership and direction in the simultaneous artistic explosion of architecture and music. The most highly educated men in Europe were those who came through this system of church-related education, people who were expected to be masters of many things.

One of these, the multitalented Suger, rose from peasant status to become abbot of the royal abbey of Saint Denis and advisor and virtual prime minister to the king, regent of France while the king was on crusade. Between 1141 and 1144, in his carefully planned and closely reasoned reconstruction of the choir of Saint Denis, Suger virtually single-handedly created Gothic architecture.

Then there was Leonin, canon at the Cathedral of Notre Dame and its associated church of Saint Benoît from the 1150s to 1201, the apparent year of his death. Well educated, with a master's degree probably in arts or theology, he was a poet of distinction, a priest with important administrative duties at Notre Dame and Saint Benoît, and, in his composition of the *Magnus liber organi*, the originator of the Parisian style of composition that was to dominate Europe for the next hundred years and more.

Leonin (or Leoninus, as he was also called) worked at Notre Dame during the second half of the century, during the exact time when the new Gothic cathedral was rising to take the place of the just demolished Romanesque one. It is seldom in music history that a compositional and an architectural style have seemed so closely wedded.

Gothic architecture is one of vertical thrust, of slender pillars reaching great heights, of pointed arches arranged in an intricate arrangement of thrust and counterthrust, of luminous stained-glass windows coloring all. The accomplishment of Leonin and his successors is no less—long arches of melisma, articulated by phrasing and sequence over lengthy pedal tones; contrasting sections of discant; expansion into three- and even four-voice counterpoint; and matching it all, a development of a codified rhythmic system and a means of notating it.

The known roots of Notre Dame's involvement in musical composition can be traced back to at least the beginning of the century. Adam of Saint Victor (died ca. 1145) was an important composer of sequences who established the fundamental style of the late medieval rhymed sequence and who held the twin positions of precentor at Notre Dame and canon at the nearby abbey of Saint Victor. Next came Albertus, cantor at Notre Dame until around 1177, whose two- or three-voice *Congaudeunt catholici* we have noted in the *Liber Sancti Jacobi*. From these roots the new style developed.

The records of twelfth- and thirteenth-century Paris can be informative in intellectual and political matters. They are not so in musical matters, and what little information we have about musical development in Paris comes, almost a century after the fact, from an anonymous English writer of the 1270s or 1280s whose treatise has already given us information about the quality of liturgical improvisation. This work was the fourth in a series of anonymous treatises published by Edmund Coussemaker in the nineteenth century. Anonymous IV, as the author has come to be called, gives a retrospective glimpse into Parisian music history:

> It should be noted that Master Leoninus, who, as was pointed out, was the best composer of organum, made the *Magnus liber organi* (Great book of organa) from the gradual and antiphonal for the augmentation of the divine service. This was in use until the time of the great Perotin, who edited the book, and who made many very fine clausulae and puncta, since he was the best composer of discant and better [in this] than Leonin. This cannot be said regarding the technical fine points of his organa, etc.
>
> This same Master Perotin wrote the best quadrupla (four-voice organa), such as *Viderunt* and *Sederunt*, with an abundance of the beauties of harmonic music. Likewise, many outstanding tripla (three-voice organa) such as the *Alleluia: Posui adiutorium, Nativitas*, etc. He also composed conductus for three voices such as *Salvatoris hodie* and for two voices such as *Dum sigillum summi patris*, even for one voice, as *Beata viscera* and others.
>
> The book or books of Master Perotin were in use until the time of Master Robert of Sabilone and in the choir of the major church of the Blessed Virgin in Paris, and from his time until the present day.

The "major church of the Blessed Virgin" is, of course, the Cathedral of Notre Dame, whose great Gothic structure was rising at precisely the time of the events to which Anonymous IV refers: construction took place between 1163 and 1267, with the first phase completed by 1182.

The exact years of Leonin's musical activity is not known, but we are probably safe in assuming the 1160s and 1170s for the composition of the *Magnus liber organi*, with Perotin's activity a generation later, possibly a decade before or after 1200. Their activity is thus contemporaneous with the last phase of Aquitanian composition. The vogue of the organum and conductus of the type described by Anonymous IV was over by 1240.

Paris, with Notre Dame at its heart, became the source of an international style that remained dominant until the fourteenth century. It had its genesis in the music and liturgy of Notre Dame, but subsequently spread elsewhere. The later codification of rhythmic notation was probably the work of composers associated with the new University of Paris. With this in mind, the somewhat more inclusive term *Parisian* will sometimes be used interchangeably with the more common term *Notre Dame*.

The Sources

Slightly later in his treatise, Anonymous IV describes a series of volumes of Parisian music arranged by type: *quadrupla* (four-voice organa); *tripla* (three-voice organa); *organa dupla* (two-voice organa); three-voice conductus with caudae (textless melismatic passages); two-voice conductus with caudae; two-, three-, and four-voice conductus without caudae; and monophonic conductus.

The main sources of Parisian music are indeed arranged into fascicles or sections much as indicated by Anonymous IV. Four primary manuscripts of this type are known collectively as the Notre Dame manuscripts. As we shall see, they are not all Parisian manuscripts. They also stand in a different chronological relationship to the repertoire they contain than do the earlier polyphonic manuscripts we have studied. Those were copied concurrently with the active use of the repertoire recorded; they bear witness to a still-living art form. The Notre Dame manuscripts (like those of the troubadours and trouvères) were copied after the fact; they are massive retrospective collections of music no longer in fashion. The four manuscripts are:

F. The manuscript Florence, Bib. Laurenziana, Pluteus 29.1, commonly known by the abbreviation *F*, is the only manuscript positively identified with Paris. It was copied around 1245–55 and contains the largest collection of music in all the categories mentioned by Anonymous IV.

W_1. The manuscript Wolfenbüttel, Herzog August-Bibl., 677, known as W_1, was copied in the 1240s, not in Paris but in Great Britain, most probably in Saint Andrews, Scotland. It is nonetheless largely devoted to the Parisian repertory, testifying to the close relationship between French and British liturgical centers at that time and also to the international spread of the Parisian style.

W_2. A third manuscript, Wolfenbüttel, Herzog August-Bibl., 1206, known as W_2, is likely from Paris or nearby, but dates slightly later, probably around 1260–75.

Ma. A slightly smaller manuscript that is often included as a fourth Notre Dame source, Madrid, Bibl. Nac., 20486, is Spanish in origin and appears roughly contemporary with W_2.

All of these manuscripts, as well as the numerous smaller fragments and collections that also exist, treat the existing repertoire in a heterogeneous manner, freely mixing earlier and later pieces and, especially in the organa, often carrying variant versions of the same composition. It is impossible to tell from the manuscripts themselves the chronological order of the pieces they contain.

Also, the manuscripts transcribe the music as it was performed at the time of their copying (1240 or later), after a period of some seventy years of rapid change, particularly in the field of rhythm. They may or may not faithfully represent the state of that music at the time of its composition.

THE DEVELOPMENT OF RHYTHM

From all theoretical accounts, the rhythmic procedures of Notre Dame organum had their beginning in the discant sections of otherwise melismatic organum. We will trace that development here before discussing the larger form of which it was a part, concentrating first on the tenor (the part holding the preexistant chant) and then on the duplum (the added upper voice).

The First Stages

The apparent earliest stage lay in discant sections, called *discant clausulae*, of the type shown in Example 9-1 and seen in *Alleluia: Adorabo ad templum* (Anthology Example 39) in sections 5 (W_2 and the second tenor statement in F) and 6 (W_1 and F).

Above the evenly moving plainchant tenor is placed a duplum in slightly ornamented discant. This ornamentation is simple, with only the cadence calling for more than two notes for each note of the tenor. In Parisian fashion, as we will presently discuss, the ornamentation fits into a ternary subdivision of the beat. This discant uses unisons, fourths, fifths, and a single third in a manner clearly descended from free organum. Punctuation within the series of tenor notes is determined solely by the length of the various duplum phrases. The aural effect is of an irregularly interrupted, ongoing pulse: the even note durations convey a sense of beat, but the uneven phrase lengths negate any feeling of larger metric organization.

This style presumably developed in the later years of the twelfth century, long before the complete codification of the system of rhythmic modes. It in fact represents only a slight elaboration of the rhythm of free organum. (Because of this, the rhythm of the duplum is often called "premodal trochaic"—*trochaic*

EXAMPLE 9-1. Clausula *re*, *W1*, f. 47' (from the *Alleluia: Justus germinabit*).

being the term used in metric poetry for a long-short rhythm—while the tenor is considered to move in *cantus planus* or plainchant style.)

The Rhythmic Organization of the Tenor

As the style of the discant clausula developed, it tended more and more toward a systematic upper-voice phraseology, often resulting in balanced four-beat phrases. This procedure, generally associated with Perotin and his generation (ca. 1190–1210), affected the tenor structure as well, and in this style we frequently find the tenor divided into groups of three notes divided by a rest. Compare, for instance, Examples 9-2a and b, both drawn from section 5 of *Alleluia: Adorabo ad templum* and showing a likely chronological development of this concept.

EXAMPLE 9-2.   Clausulae from *Adorabo ad templum.*
   a. W$_2$
   b. F

Although seemingly insignificant, this change was one of great importance, for the regularity of the phrasing, reinforced by the regular pattern of the tenor, provides a sense of larger organization missing from the earlier style. The steady discant structure supplies the beat, the predominantly four-beat phraseology supplies the meter, and the ornamentation of the duplum supplies the ternary subdivision of the beat.

A special feature of this rhythm is its lack of accent. Modern rhythm depends on the use of strong and weak beats differentiated by the use of consonance and dissonance. In modal rhythm each beat is equal in consonance and stress in accordance with the rules of discant. Dissonance occurs between the beats, resolving to consonance on the beat. The grouping of beats (meter) occurs not by the accentuation of one of the group, but by the opposite, a regularly recurring silence or lessening of sound that creates an audible grouping of beats, which the ear identifies as meter. In the vast majority of cases the resulting meter is duple, although occasional triple or ambiguous groupings occur.

Although simple tenor patterns such as that of Example 9-2 remained popular throughout the period, they were soon augmented by tenors using the mode of the upper voice(s) or employing a more stylized pattern combining two modes (for example, ♩· ♩ ♪ ♩ ♪ ♩ ♪ or ♩ ♪ ♩ ♪ ♪ ♩· ♩ ♪). Whatever the pattern, the result is of a kind of short rhythmic ostinato that pervades the composition and contributes in an important way to its metric organization.

The Rhythm of the Upper Voices

All the evidence suggests that the earliest clausula and motet dupla moved in a premodal trochaic rhythm, broken at times with bits of faster ornamentation or occasional longer notes (compare Examples 9-1 and 9-2). In the first quarter of the thirteenth century, alternate methods of beat subdivision developed; by around 1240 these were codified into a system called the *rhythmic modes*.

The authoritative exposition of the system is that of Johannes de Garlandia, whose treatise *De musica mensurabilis*, although often dated as early as 1240, was probably written around 1250–60. The rhythmic modes relate only to the ornamental subdivision of the beat, the fastest layer of rhythmic activity in the clausula. Garlandia lists six modes:

1. A long and a short
2. A short and a long
3. A long and two shorts
4. Two shorts and a long
5. All longs
6. All shorts

The first mode is a codification of the trochaic rhythm of the early clausula; mode 2 represents an alternate short-long subdivision. These and mode 6 represent all the possible manners of ternary beat subdivision, while mode 5, mostly confined to tenors and conductus, represents the beat itself.

Mode 3 is a more complex two-beat pattern. Accordingly, it is called *ultra mensuram*, "beyond [normal] measure," by Garlandia. Many writers today believe that there had been an earlier form of this mode with the rhythmic configuration (generally called "alternate third mode" by today's writers), which had changed to Garlandia's pattern by the time he wrote. The fourth mode, in contrast to the others, seldom appears in practical use. It was probably included in the formulation to give the outward appearance of symmetry that was so prized at the time.

In normal practice a given mode permeates a voice part throughout a clausula. In combining voices, only similar rhythmic types would be used. Blend, not contrast, was the guide. The long-short rhythm of mode 1 could be used with modes 5 and 6, but not with the short-long patterns of modes 2, 3, and 4. Mode 2 is compatible with all modes except the first.

The Ordo

An *ordo* (pl. *ordines*) is defined concisely by Anonymous IV as "the number of notes before a rest." As such it could measure the length of any modal pattern, but was particularly applied to tenor patterns. A complete first ordo of the first mode would comprise one complete modal pattern plus a note equivalent to the starting note: ♩ ♪ ♩ ♩. Second ordo would include two patterns: ♩ ♪ ♩ ♪ ♩ ♩. Third ordo of first mode would be: ♩ ♪ ♩ ♪ ♩ ♪ ♩ ♩.

NOTATION

The Notre Dame manuscripts represent the first generation of manuscripts written in a rhythmic notation, where the rhythm of the music can be deduced, at least partially, from the design of the notes themselves. Anonymous IV tells us that rhythmic notation began "about the time of Perotin and not much before." If so, it would place the beginnings of rhythmic notation in the last years of the twelfth century.

The notation makes use of the square note forms that had been developed by that time for the notation of plainchant (and which are still used in modern plainchant notation):

	9th cen.	12th cen.	13th cen.
Clivis			
Podatus			
Climacus			
Scandicus			
Porrectus			
Torculus			

The earliest datable manuscript to use these forms in a mensural context was copied after 1227, and the earliest theoretical account probably dates from near midcentury. At this stage of development, the note groups—now called *ligatures* rather than *neumes*—have no absolute value in themselves, but take on rhythmic meaning according to context.

As an illustration, we may consider the value of the three-note ligature in each of the following configurations:

1. ♪♪ ♩ ♫ = ♩ ♪♩ ♪♩ ♪♩ ♪

2. ♫ ♩ ♪♪ = ♪♩ ♪♩ ♪♩ ♪

3. ♪♪ ♫ = ♩· ♪♩ ♩· ♪♩ ♩· ♪

In each case the value is determined not by the shape of the ligature, but by its place in a series of such ligatures. As Anonymous IV says, "because the written notes were the same, . . . they were performed by understanding alone, saying, I understand that note to be long, I understand that note to be short; and they used to labor long before they would know anything well."

This earliest stage of rhythmic notation, often called *modal notation*, operated by suggesting a particular rhythmic mode through the particular combination of two- and three-note ligatures. It is a notation specifically designed to show rhythm in a melismatic context:

COMBINATION	EXAMPLE	TRANSCRIPTION
1. 3 2 2 2	◢ ♪♪ ♩	♩ ♪♩ ♪♩ ♪♩ ♪
2. 2 2 2 3	♩ ♪♪ ♪♪	♪♩ ♪♩ ♪♩ ♪
3. 1 3 3 3	▪ ♩ ♫	♩· ♪♩ ♩· ♪♩ ♩· ♪
4. 3 3 3 1	♪♪ ◢ ♪	♪♩ ♩· ♪♩ ♩· ♩· ♪
5. 3 3 3	♫ ♫	♩· ♩· ♩· ♪ ♩· ♩· ♩·
6. 4 3 3	♪♪♪ ♪♪	♫♫♫ ♫♫♫ ♪

Although simple in the abstract, this system can be ambiguous in practice. It works well in melismatic music when voice parts move in relatively unbroken modal rhythm. It becomes increasingly problematic when the regular patterns are broken for any reason, such as the necessity of repeating a pitch within a ligature or through the introduction of an occasional longer note or faster ornamentation. It is totally useless in syllabic music because individual note shapes have no rhythmic value in themselves and the patterns of ligatures cannot be used.

An example of this style of notation may be seen in Facsimile 9-1, the W_2 version of the organum *Alleluia: Adorabo ad templum* transcribed in Anthology Example 39. The great economy of space possible in this type of melismatic notation is immediately apparent—the entire organum, taking many pages in

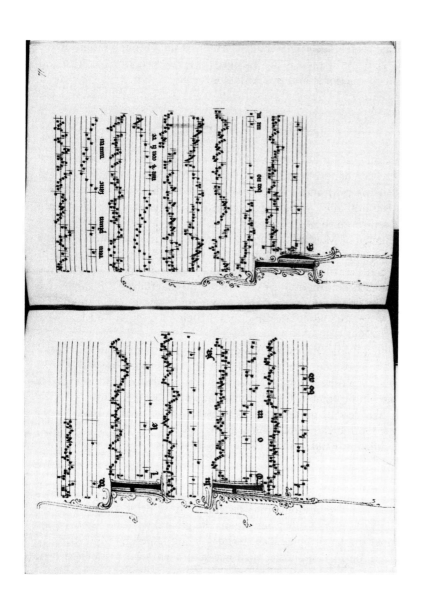

Facsimile 9-1. Modal Notation; Wolfenbuttel, Herzog August Bibliothek: Cod. Guelf. 1099 Helmst., fols. 70ʹ–71.

the Anthology transcription, is concisely carried on two pages of music. The Alleluia begins with the capital A of the second system of folio 70' (the left-hand page), with the verse beginning at the capital A two systems below. The two voice parts are written in score form, with the text entered under the tenor. The short vertical lines on the staff often indicate rests, but may also, ambiguously, indicate merely a syllable change. The rhythmic interpretation of the notation, particularly in the discant sections, may be seen through a careful comparison of the facsimile and the Anthology transcription.

ORGANA DUPLA

The repertoire of Notre Dame organa consists of settings of the solo portions of the responsorial chants of the Mass and Office (Mass Graduals and Alleluias and Office responsories) and a few *Benedicamus Domino* settings. Polyphonic versions of items from the Ordinary, present in free organum and the *Liber Sancti Jacobi*, are absent from the Parisian repertoire.

The monumental *Magnus liber organi*, identified by Anonymous IV as the work of Leonin, is a setting in extensive two-voice organum of the principal responsorial chants for the entire church year and was clearly meant to adorn the services of the cathedral then under construction. Regrettably, it is impossible to reconstruct its original form; as noted above, the Notre Dame manuscripts, copied seventy or more years later, indiscriminately mix earlier and later sections.

As presented in those manuscripts, an organum setting cannot be considered a unified composition, the representation of a single composer's thoughts. Rather, it is a composite structure consisting of a number of interchangeable segments that can be combined and recombined from one performance to the next, much like certain modern aleatoric pieces. More to the point is the analogy of the Gothic cathedral, which might be constructed over a period of centuries by different hands and in ever-changing styles.

General Style

We have noticed that Aquitanian cantus firmus settings and those of the *Liber Sancti Jacobi* operate in that flexible middle ground we have labeled florid and melismatic: the upper voice may shift easily and imperceptibly within the phrase between longer and shorter melismas and even an occasional syllabic note. The Notre Dame idiom, in contrast, juxtaposes opposites more rigidly. Thus Johannes de Garlandia states: "It should be known, therefore, that of organum in its general sense there are three species, namely discant, copula, and organum." Of these, the first and third had already been defined by a late twelfth-century anonymous theorist: "Between discant and organum, however, one judges in this way: while a discant corresponds to its cantus with an equal number of notes . . . , an organum is joined with its cantus not with an equal number of notes, but with an unbounded multiplicity and also a kind of wonderful flexibility."

In other words, *discant* is the note-against-note style derived from free organum, while the term *organum* is now applied to the florid and melismatic styles. In this concept discant and organum become opposites rather than part of a continuum. The *copula* is a middle ground between the two.

Organum purum.   In the late twelfth and thirteenth centuries, the term *organum* still referred in a general way to any kind of polyphony, while in a more specific sense it also indicated polyphony based on a cantus firmus. In a still more precise manner, it subsequently came to designate a particular style of melismatic two-voice composition. To clarify this latter meaning, thirteenth-century theorists frequently use the terms *organum purum* or *organum per se.*

Organum purum is characterized by a melismatic upper voice—now called the *duplum* (second voice)—over a sustained-note *vox principalis*, now called the *tenor*. Although an outgrowth, direct or indirect, of the florid styles of the earlier part of the century, Notre Dame organum purum possesses distinct characteristics of its own, most noticeably the great extension of the melismas and their distinct division into a series of phrases over the now much more extended, dronelike notes of the tenor. It is a truly melismatic style.

Thirteenth-century theorists set organum purum apart from strict modal rhythm or any clearly definable system. This is confirmed by the notation, for while the ligature patterns are for the most part clear and unambiguous in discant sections, they are irregular and ambiguous in sections of organum purum. Thus, while scholars have often considered the rhythm of the duplum in these organum purum sections to have been modal, recent research suggests rather a flexible, not precisely measured performance.

Discant.   Discant, as we have noted, was the late twelfth-century name to describe the essentially note-against-note, contrary-motion style first introduced in free organum. With the advent of Notre Dame polyphony, a rhythmic element became integral to the definition.

In this thirteenth-century sense, discant consists of a precisely measured upper voice (or voices) moving in a rhythmic mode over an also measured lower voice. It is distinguished from organum purum both by the precise measurement of the duplum and the relatively rapid, measured movement of the tenor. It follows earlier discant theory in placing the consonant discant interval at the beginning of each pattern, forming a regular series of consonant beats. Ornamentation and passing dissonance occurs between these on-the-beat consonances.

Copula.   Often misinterpreted by twentieth-century writers, the copula represents a middle ground between organum purum and discant. It may be found when the normally freely constructed duplum of two-voice organum temporarily takes on a patterned, sequential organization. It then abandons its free rhythm and takes on, for the duration of the passage, a measured rhythm related to the rhythmic modes. The resulting passage accordingly has the upper voice of discant, but the sustained-tone tenor of organum purum.[1]

Given the late dates of surviving sources, it is difficult to reconstruct the historical sequence of style development. The statements of Anonymous IV and other corroborating evidence, however, suggest three broad stages of compositional activity:

1. The composition of the *Magnus liber organi*, either largely or totally in organum purum, by Leonin and possibly others of his generation;

2. The composition by Perotin and his generation of shorter discant sections (*clausulae*) to replace sections originally in organum purum, commonly called *substitute clausulae*;

3. The composition of longer, more musical discant clausulae to replace some of the shorter, more utilitarian clausulae of phase 2 or, possibly, to function as independent compositions.

Although phases 2 and 3 undoubtedly overlapped to some extent, and some organum purum is probably later than phase 1, this outline probably resembles the broad progression of historical movement.

Alleluia: Adorabo ad templum

The best way to comprehend these layers of accretion is to view the transmission of a single organum duplum, the *Alleluia: Adorabo ad templum* (Anthology Example 39). Each of the three primary Notre Dame manuscripts—W_1, F, and W_2—contain settings. The W_1 version (in the Anthology it appears on the lowest two staves of each system) contains the largest amount of organum purum and may be closest to Leonin's original. The version carried in F is given on the next two staves, and that of W_2 above that. Substitute discant clausulae are noted on the top system. (The motet texts notated within the discant clausulae of section 6 are not part of the original complex, but were added later to those clausulae when they were converted into motets.)

The plainchant on which this organum is based is given in Anthology Example 5 and was briefly discussed in Chapter 2. In the Notre Dame setting, as in free organum, it is the solo sections that are performed in polyphony, the choral sections remaining in plainchant. In structure, the Notre Dame setting divides the chant into six sections:

---

[1]Note that the term *copula* is used differently here than in free organum.

1. *Alleluia*

2. *Ado-*

3. *rabo*

4. *ad templum*

5. *sanctum tuum*

6. *et confitebor*

As can be seen from the breaking up of the word *adorabo*, the structural divisions are made on musical, not textual grounds.

Section 1.   This begins in organum purum in all sources. W_1 and F agree, while the setting in W_2 differs. W_1 and F continue largely in copula, returning to organum purum before the plainchant conclusion common to all three. The copula section is tightly structured: an ascending passage; a distinctive motive in sequence; a second motive in varied repetition; a return of the ascending passage. The ligature pattern suggests and permits a reading in the first rhythmic mode.

W_2 is largely dissimilar, but does coincide with W_1 and F in the first sequential passage of the copula. It is otherwise in organum purum.

The three-note opening figure in the duplum of all versions, a seventh resolving to an octave above the first tenor note, is a typical opening motive. Theorists suggest that the entrance of the tenor was delayed to coincide with the octave in the upper voice.

Section 2.   The verse *Adorabo* begins in organum purum in all versions. W_1 and F are again identical (except for slight differences of ornamentation), while W_2 has a considerably condensed version of the same melodic material.

Section 3.   This section is based on a melismatic portion of the original plainchant (see Anthology Example 5). As such, it is a typical place for the introduction of discant. Nonetheless, W_1 retains what may have been the original organum purum setting, followed by copula.

The three other settings may well represent three additional chronological layers. Earliest would be that of the substitute clausula given on the top two staves. In form it represents the second of the three stages outlined above, the composition of short clausulae in discant style to replace original but longer sections in organum purum. The clausula, although shorter, is nonetheless liturgically complete, containing all the required notes of the plainchant cantus firmus.

The third stage—the replacement of shorter, functional discant sections with longer, more artistic ones—is represented by W_2. Here, length is attained by the common practice of repeating the tenor chant segment (liturgical propriety giving way to musical expediency).

An intermediate, transitional practice is represented by F, for here the complete organum purum and copula of W_1 is given, *followed* by a second setting of the same tenor, partly in discant, partly in organum. This adding of disparate sections to one another may have first suggested the type of tenor repetition seen in W_2.

Section 4.   Here, unlike the preceding sections, it is F and W_2 that generally agree, joining in a short copula section. W_1 retains a setting in organum purum.

Section 5.   The melismatic setting of *sanctum tuum* in the original chant again invites discant clausula settings. W_1 carries the organum setting, for which the substitute clausula represents a replacement. The discant settings of F and W_2 are not single clausulae with an internal repetition of the tenor, but are combinations of two distinct shorter clausulae. This is shown by the definite change in tenor patterns and duplum styles at the point of repetition (indicated by the double bar in the tenor).

Section 6. Another plainchant melisma, the final section of the chant, is given a different setting in each of the manuscripts. This plainchant segment was in fact one of the more popular ones in the early thirteenth century, and while only one substitute clausula is included in the Anthology, an additional six can be found in the substitute clausulae collections in F. The plainchant melisma on the syllable *te* of *confitebor* is a lengthy one: fifty notes. W_1 and F set it once, but W_2 and the substitute clausula from F set it twice.

The concluding phrase of the verse is choral plainchant, followed by a repeat of the opening alleluia in W_1 and W_2; F supplies a new setting in discant style.

Alleluia: Adorabo ad templum is a multiform composition: there are at least two alternate settings for each section, and ten exist for section 6. The version in W_2 has almost nothing in common with that of W_1, and F has passages in common with both. Each manuscript presumably carries the local performing tradition at the moment of copying, with ample substitute discant clausulae available elsewhere in the manuscript for substitution as desired.

Further evidence of this flexible approach is seen through a comparison of these three settings with those of *Alleluia: Posui adiutorium*, another setting of the same tenor melody in the same manuscripts. Instead of repeating the same polyphony, the W_1 version is different throughout, using much of the music found in the W_2 version of *Adorabo ad templum* plus two discant clausula found in F. The two settings in F are also different, relating much more to W_2 in *Posui adiutorium* than in *Adorabo ad templum*. Only W_2 is consistent.

Many organa are transmitted with less variation than this, but the principles outlined here hold throughout the repertoire.

Before leaving *Adorabo ad templum*, it may be well to compare it in length and style with the immediately preceding Alleluia setting in the Anthology, that of the florid-style Goslin *Alleluia: Vocavit Jhesus Jacobum* of the *Liber Sancti Jacobi* (Anthology Example 38). The expansiveness of the Parisian Alleluia is immediately apparent. It is equally apparent in performance, for while the Goslin setting can be performed in four minutes, W_1 takes nine.

ORGANA TRIPLA AND QUADRUPLA

Composition in three and even four voices took place before the end of the twelfth century. If, as seems probable, Perotin's masterful four-voice organa *Sederunt* and *Viderunt* were composed in 1198, the move into this more complex idiom was quick and assured. Four-voiced composition remained the exception, however; only three such compositions are known, while thirty-two organa and seventeen substitute clausulae in three voices are preserved in Notre Dame manuscripts.

Except for a handful of *Benedicamus* settings, the extant repertoire is the same as that of the organa dupla. The compositional process is also the same: the solo portions of the chant are set polyphonically, and the choral sections remain in plainchant. There is also the same alternation of discant and sustained-tone organum and the same sectional approach to construction.

The primary difference in style is due to the innate difference between two- and three-voice performance: a single soloist can sing in flexible rhythm over a long-held tenor tone, but two or three soloists singing different lines must coordinate their parts. As a result, organum tripla and organum quadrupla have only two contrasting styles: one in which the upper voices move in measured modal rhythm over a sustained-tone tenor (similar to two-voiced copula, but without the required ingredient of sequence) and discant clausulae—there is no counterpart to the organum purum style. This may be seen in Anthology Example 40, the *Alleluia: Posui adiutorium* which, as already noted, is based on the same melody as the *Alleluia: Adorabo ad templum*. The Alleluia portion is set in sustained-tone style, except for a short clausula on the syllable *lu*. The verse alternates sustained-tone and discant styles. (For ease of comparison, the section numbering used in *Adorabo ad templum* is retained here. The main deviations in the chant melody are the interpolated four notes for the word *Posui* and a shortened section 4. Further analysis of this organum is given on p. 218 below.)

Sonorities

As in two-voice organa, the upper voices at no time exceed the interval of an octave above any given tenor note. The result is a close-knit texture in which three or four voices intertwine within the octave. Voice crossing in the upper voices is accordingly normal.

Consonant sonorities are those typical of late twelfth century theory, vertical mixtures of the perfect and intermediate consonances, particularly the combinations of octave and fifth and octave and fourth. The tendency is strongly toward the former, a sonority that occurs almost invariably at the beginning and ending of each organal passage and which occurs repeatedly therein. The octave-fourth combination is confined to the interior of phrases and is often treated like combinations containing imperfect consonances or dissonances: as a passing, unstable sonority. Triads or other combinations including a third occur more often than one would expect, particularly in four-voice writing, where the limitation of an octave between outer voices requires either doubling or the use of the third.

Tonal Structure

Large-scale tonal organization is a function of the preexistent plainchant, not of the polyphony added to it. Nonetheless, three- and four-voice organa do create a special sense of temporary tonality over each long-held tenor note, even if this does not relate to a long-term goal. The effect is not unlike the tonal saturation of some Aquitanian versus, in which the composition constantly emphasizes the tonic-fifth relationship. The technique used here, however, is one in which that relationship is realized audibly through the sustained pedal point of the tenor and the recurring octave-fifth sonority of the upper voices.

In the discant passages, dissonance is treated as in two-voiced discant: passing or neighboring tones between the beats. In the sustained-tone organal passages, they are used as ornamental notes around the prolonged octave-fifth sonority established above the tenor, clashing temporarily before resolving again on a consonant tone. These passing dissonances drive and color the three- and four-voice organa.

MONOPHONIC CONDUCTUS

The Notre Dame conductus is, in general terms, equivalent to the Aquitanian versus. Both are settings of rhythmic, rhymed poetry. Both may be monophonic or polyphonic. Both were used in and out of church. But the conductus took in a wider range of subject matter, including political events (such as the martyrdom of Thomas à Becket, or coronation ceremonies) and the *admonitio*, a poem of censure, condemning the evils of the world or the corruption of the church.

Musical Style

Structure in the conductus is more formalized than in the versus. All texted parts are in syllabic or neumatic style (discant when polyphonic). Textless melismas, now called *caudae*, are not haphazardly placed within the composition, but will occur when present on the first or next-to-last syllables of phrases and, more particularly, at the beginning and end of the conductus. The melisma may vary in size from a short concluding flourish to a long passage that completely dwarfs the texted portion. As an extreme, as much as 75 percent of the conductus can be cauda.

As was the case with the versus, the conductus is typically completely original, although there are occasions in which the tenor or even both voices are borrowed. Such exceptions emphasize the flexibility with which medieval musicians viewed musical "categories."

Conductus also appear in various guises: monophonic in one manuscript and in two or even three voices in another. As we shall see, the addition or subtraction of voices is common practice in all forms of late medieval music and emphasizes the multiform nature of medieval composition and performance.

As in the Aquitanian versus, settings of multiversed poems may be either strophic or through-composed, although many conductus set poems of only one verse. The music for the individual verse may be through-composed, AAB, or more rarely AABB. Through-composed settings may contain a limited amount of unsystematized repetition or may adopt the paired-line structure of the sequence.

Veste nuptiali (Anthology Example 41) is a simple conductus without caudae. The texture is almost completely syllabic. The poem, expanding on the biblical story of the wise and foolish virgins (Matthew 25:1–13), uses lines of varying lengths, with seven syllables the recurring norm. (The two pairs of shorter lines combine to make a larger composite.)

Veste nuptiáli,	6	A
Splendore figuráli	7	A
Non tam corporáli	7	A
Quam habitu mentáli	6	A
Nuptias intróeàs	7	B
Sic fúlgeàs	4 ⌐ 8	B
Ut sédeàs	4 ⌐	B
In sede speciáli	7	A
Cáveàs	3 ⌐ 7	B
Ut hábeàs	4 ⌐	B
Inhabitu te táli	7	A
Quod non éxeàs	5	B
De domo pulsus regáli	8	A

The first two pairs of lines, in the pattern 6 + 7, are set as antecedent-consequent phrases, the first pair having an open or nonfinal ending, the second a closed one. Together they comprise the two A sections of an AAB form,

Dante's *pedes cum cauda* and the Minnesinger bar form. The B section is longer than the two A sections combined and continues in a truly through-composed fashion to the end. Three stanzas are set strophically to the same melody.

   O curas hominum (Anthology Example 42) is an example of a *conductus cum cauda* also set in strophic form. The poem is an *admonitio*, decrying in allegorical language the greed of the papal court: anything may be purchased there, from high position to forgiveness of sin, and he who has no money has no chance of advancement. The text is set in syllabic-neumatic style, but the regularity of the poem is interrupted by caudae on the first and penultimate syllables of the stanza, and also by one on the first syllable of line 3, a relatively common position for caudae.

Modality.   Like the Aquitanian versus and the conductus of the *Liber Sancti Jacobi*, the Parisian conductus, whether monophonic or polyphonic, shows a preference for two scale systems, those on D and G, *but* with the D mode often notated on G with a b flat, in what the Middle Ages considered a *transformation* of Tetrardus into Protus. In this case it uses a fixed b flat and an optional e flat (as a counterpart to the b flat of the untransposed scale). In other words:

$$D \ E \ F \ G \ a \ b\flat/b\natural \ c \ d$$
becomes $G \ a \ b\flat \ c \ d \ e\flat/e\natural \ f \ g$.

   In general, this seems to be a mere graphic difference, but occasionally advantage is taken of the common final to shift or "modulate" from one modal configuration to another (Example 9-3). The procedure occurs sparingly, but its relationship to a modern "change of mode" is obvious.

   Of the eighty-three monophonic conductus in *F*, seventy-six are in the G and D modes (transposed and untransposed). Only five are notated on F; of these, four use constant b flats, and the other alternates b flat and b natural. Six of the conductus in the G mode make use of f sharp, but only intermittently and without any clear implication of a leading tone. D mode is more consistently

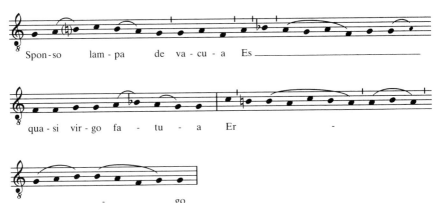

EXAMPLE 9-3.   "Change of Mode" in the Monophonic Conductus (from *Ad cor tuum*, *F*, fol. 421).

finalis-fifth oriented than it was in the Aquitanian versus, while the E mode continues to be ignored.

Rhythm.   Modal rhythm grew within the environment of Parisian polyphony. There is no indication, either on the part of theorists or from the notation, that it was applied to monophony. Grocheo, writing about 1300, states that monophony is "not precisely measured." Notation of the melismatic caudae, where modal notation could have been used to good advantage to show a precise rhythm (and where it is so used in the polyphonic conductus), is generally haphazard in the monophonic conductus. Since the same scribes notated both, and in the same manuscripts, the distinction appears intentional. The fact that a few of these compositions appear in mensural notation in later manuscripts (ca. 1300 or later) tells us how they were performed at that later time, but offers no sure guide to an evolving mensural practice one hundred or more years before.

The Rondellus/Rondeau

An early thirteenth-century form that was later to take on considerable importance is called *rondellus* when the text is Latin, *rondeau* when the text is French (later in the century, however, *rondellus* could also mean a composition based on voice exchange). Initial examples of this form appear in F (see "The Sources" above) immediately following the monophonic conductus just discussed. French-language rondeaux appear at approximately the same time; sixteen are in the *Roman de la Rose* of around 1228.

As seen in this early stage, the form is extremely flexible; the one common element is the use of a recurring refrain. The poems are strophic, with the refrain recurring in the same pattern in each verse.

The most frequent early type took the form a A a b A B, with the capital letters indicating repetition of both text and music.

The form may be understood most easily by considering Anthology Example 43, the rondellus *Omnes gentes*. The poetic refrain consists of two lines, the first of which makes sense on its own: "Sing songs to the crucified King, For, crucified, he conquers and reigns."

The poem itself consists of three verses. The text of each verse completes a thought:

> O clap your hands, all ye people,
> Chant a hymn to God,
> For he was conquered, who had conquered us.
>
> Hung from the tree,
> And unjustly killed,
> He restores what had been lost.
>
> Sing praises to God,
> Who reopens for his people
> The way of lost liberty.

The refrain, with a subtlety that is much easier to discern in the original language, comments on and amplifies that thought, while being subtly reinterpreted itself. The composite musicopoetic form is carefully balanced and interrelated.

Later in the century the two-line refrain was used to begin as well as end the verse, and the form came to approximate the later fourteenth-century form:

A B a A a b A B.

The rondellus/rondeau may have developed from a type of song meant to accompany dancing and seems to belong to the sphere of the entertainer, although modern references sometimes incorrectly link it with the trouvères. It is also closely associated with polyphony; the second half of the century saw the composition of three-voice rondeaux, the frequent quotation of rondeau refrains in motets, and even composition of motets in rondeau form.

THE POLYPHONIC CONDUCTUS

The majority of Parisian polyphonic conductus, one hundred thirty four, are in two voices, while a smaller but substantial number (about sixty) are in three voices. Three are in four voices.

Musical Style

Notre Dame polyphonic conductus differs from Aquitanian style more markedly than does the monophonic conductus in texture, form, and tonal organization. Most important is the matter of rhythm.

Rhythm. The modal notation of the Notre Dame manuscripts, though effective in notating the rhythm of the melismatic discant clausula, is equivocal in notating the rhythm of texted conductus. As a result, the reconstruction of conductus rhythm is one of the most difficult tasks in the transcription of medieval music. Modal notation conveys rhythm through a pattern of ligatures. In conductus this can happen only in the melismatic caudae. The texted portion, which must be notated in single notes or ligatures in irregular order, is necessarily ambiguous. Therefore, while conductus caudae can be transcribed with reasonable assurance, the syllabic portions are open to conjecture and a great amount of editorial opinion.

In attempting to reconstruct this aspect of conductus rhythm, editors and performers may consider the following information, all of which is nonetheless equivocal in nature: (1) later sources from the late thirteenth or early fourteenth century in a fully rhythmic notation (which may or may not correctly preserve the earlier tradition), (2) the meter of the poetic text (which may or may not be reflected in a rhythmic mode), (3) the placement of ornamentation in the upper voice (which may be irregular, suggesting even-length syllables, or tend to appear primarily on either even or odd syllables, suggesting that one of those syllables may be longer), and (4) the rhythm of the cauda in the few cases where there is a musical identity between a cauda and a texted passage (complicated by the fact that the cauda itself sometimes reappears in a changed rhythmic mode).

A careful use of all these guides has established fairly standard procedures for the transcription of the polyphonic conductus. However, a glance at variant transcriptions of numerous conductus will show that often not even the experts agree. The rhythm of the syllabic portion of a conductus transcription must always be considered an informed editorial opinion.

The history of the development of rhythm within the polyphonic conductus is difficult to establish. Most probably, progression would start from the concept of equal syllable length, as fits the equal syllable length of the rhythmic verse. In simple and slightly ornamented discant this would represent an even pulse, as it would have in the first stage of discant clausula rhythm (see "The Development of Rhythm" above). In the modal system this would be indicated by the use of the fifth rhythmic mode, and indeed this is the mode most used in the later mensural transmissions of conductus. From this beginning, two changes may have come about as the new rhythmic process coalesced: the originally free ornamentation may have regularized into triple patterns and the newly evolved modes 1, 2, and 3 may have come to be used in the composition of new conductus.

A consideration of *Ver pacis aperit* (Anthology Example 44), one of the earliest datable polyphonic conductus, will permit some speculation on the early stages of this process. *Ver pacis*, a political conductus, was written for the coronation of Philip Augustus in 1179. It has no cauda to suggest a rhythmic mode. A simple transcription of the rhythmically noncommittal notation (Example 9-4a) has an appearance not unlike that of an Aquitanian versus (and indeed, the whole melodic, contrapuntal, and tonal idiom is close to that of a versus). If transcribed in a slightly more rhythmic notation, one can suggest a simple performance based on equal syllable lengths (Example 9-4b).

Adjustment to a ternary measurement of the ornamentation is a simple procedure (Example 9-4c). The result would be described in modal terms as fifth mode with the ornamentation using first- and sixth-mode patterns.

The larger concept of a counterpoint of phrase lengths is also a major innovation of the Notre Dame composers. Whereas all earlier polyphony had been based on a simultaneity of phrase lengths between upper and lower voices, Parisian polyphony began to exploit contrasting phrase lengths between voices and, in effect, to create a rhythmic counterpoint at that level. Overlapping phrases, particularly evident in the caudae of three-voice conductus, result in a more continuous structure, subtly articulated by individual rests in the separate voices. This can be seen in the caudae of Anthology Example 46, *A solis ortus cardine*.

Tonal organization. Again, the G and D modalities are dominant, and again the D idiom is usually transformed to G with a mandatory b flat. A change of mode similar to that of some monophonic conductus occasionally occurs (see Anthology Example 45).

The normal "majorish" scale is that on G. A small number of compositions make use of either F with a b flat or G with an f sharp. As in the secular repertoire, however (see Chapter 7), the resemblance to the modern major scale is deceiving. The scale on F generally avoids the semitone below the final, and a scale based on C is missing from the repertoire. Pieces on G may raise the upper seventh but not the lower subfinal. What emerges is a scale form that inflects the seventh degree upward but, with rare exceptions, retains the whole tone as a subfinal (see, for instance, Anthology Example 46). The concept of a leading tone is a fourteenth-century development.

The Notre Dame conductus expands upon the tonal techniques of the versus. Most important is the construction of a highly tonal lower voice and a consistent use of what we have called the "tonic-fifth"—the final and its fifth, or either in unison, at key cadences throughout. In addition, whether because

EXAMPLE 9-4. *Ver pacis aperit,* Three Rhythmic Notations (F, f. 355).

of the greater length of the conductus or because of an increasing ability to control tonality, contrasting secondary tonal centers now emerge.

Taking *Quod promisit ab eterno* (Anthology Example 45) as an example, note the firm establishment of the transposed D mode (G "minor") at the beginning and its constant cadential reinforcement in the first nine phrases. The shift to the fifth F-c at the end of phrase 10 marks the beginning of a recurring area of contrast that also includes references to D and b flat. The G "tonic" returns at the end of phrase 14 and is reaffirmed throughout the remainder of the first verse and at the beginning of the second. Contrasting sections occur in phrases 26–27 and 38–41. The other sections are firmly rooted in the "tonic-fifth," with the tonality fluctuating between the "major" and "minor" idioms in phrases 42–47, with the "major" being established in the long concluding melisma.

Form. As with the monophonic conductus, there are two basic classes of conductus: *conductus simplex*, without caudae, and the more ornate *conductus cum cauda*. The variety of form, especially within the second class, is immense, and it is impossible to cite a "typical" conductus. They range from thirty to over four hundred measures in length when notated in $\frac{6}{8}$, dwarfing by far the longest of the Aquitanian versus. The caudae may be short appendages or completely engulf the syllabic portion: in *Quod promisit ab eterno*, two-thirds of the conductus is given over to melisma. The caudae usually bear no melodic relation to one another or to the syllabic portions, although there are exceptions (see for instance "Modal Transmutation" later in the chapter).

POLYPHONIC TECHNIQUES

The twelfth century saw the development of a number of specific polyphonic techniques that became standard contrapuntal procedures throughout the thirteenth century and beyond. Most appeared first in Aquitanian polyphony, then became more developed in the Parisian style. In the twelfth and thirteenth centuries they rarely appear as the dominant technique in a composition, but rather as one among others. They are most apparent on the phrase or subphrase level, only rarely becoming a large-scale structural device. They appear frequently in conductus and in three- and four-voice organa. Insofar as possible, the following examples are drawn from pieces in the Anthology, thus permitting the viewing of these short excerpts in their larger context.

Literal Repetition

Literal repetition often occurs in otherwise through-composed compositions. It may occur directly, as in Example 9-5a, or after intervening material, as in Example 9-5b.

a.

b.

EXAMPLE 9-5. Literal Repetition
  a. Without intervening material (*Quod promisit*, phrases 54 and 55).
  b. With intervening material (*Quod promisit*, phrases 40 and 41).

Repetition with Open and Closed Endings

At times a more formal ministructure may occur, resembling antecedent-consequent phrases (Example 9-6).

Repetition in One Voice

Often the repetition occurs in only one voice, usually the tenor, while the other voice or voices continue with new counterpoint (Example 9-7).

Repetition with Voice Exchange

The technique of repetition with voice exchange, sometimes called by the German designation *Stimmtausch*, becomes increasingly common as the thirteenth century progresses, especially in English music, where it forms the basis for the English rondellus. In voice exchange, a passage is repeated literally, or largely so, but with the parts interchanged. The aural effect is of a change of timbre (Example 9-8).

Melodic Sequence

Already conspicuous in Aquitanian style, melodic sequence is even more prevalent in Notre Dame polyphony. It may involve only a single voice or a polyphonic complex of two or more voices, as in Example 9-9.

Motivic Interchange and Interrelationships

The use of interwoven motives, a feature of the earlier *Liber Sancti Jacobi*, continues as a frequent but not constant element in later Parisian polyphony. As seen in Example 9-10, the technique is intermixed with the use of melodic sequence.

EXAMPLE 9-6. Repetition with Open and Closed Endings (*Quod promisit*, phrases 33 and 34).

EXAMPLE 9-7. Literal Repetition in One Voice with New Counterpoint (*Ver pacis aperit*, phrases 1-4).

a.

b.

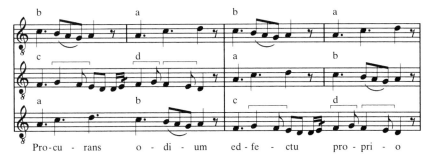

Pro - cu - rans   o - di - um   ed - fe - ctu   pro - pri - o

EXAMPLE 9-8.   Repetition Using Voice-Exchange.
   a. Two-voice texture (*Quod promisit*, phrases 15-18)
   b. Three-voice texture (*Procurans odium*, F, f. 226)

EXAMPLE 9-9.   Sequence: Two Voices, Phrases 44-45a; Tenor only, Phrases 45b-46 (*Quod promisit*, phrases 44-46a).

EXAMPLE 9-10.   Motivic Interchange, Combined with Sequence (*Quod promisit*, phrases 43-46).

EXAMPLE 9-10 *continued*

a.

b.

EXAMPLE 9-11. Imitation.
    a. Canon (*Soli nitorem*, first cauda, F, f. 327′)
    b. Imitation (*O felix bitura*, F, f. 209)

Imitation and Canon

Although not a common feature of the Parisian style, occasional examples of imitation and even canon can be found. Example 9-11a shows a rare occurrence of canon. Example 9-11b is a particularly dense passage involving the imitation of shorter and longer motives.

Modal Transmutation

One means of adding variety to the repetition of a cauda in the Parisian conductus is to change the rhythmic mode upon the return of the cauda in a later part of the composition. The usual procedure is to change modes 1 or 2 into modes 3 or 5, but other interchanges may occur. Example 9-12 shows the second and the last caudae from the conductus *Soli nitorem*, in which the mode changes from 1 to 5. The entire conductus may be seen in AMM, no. 37.

Aside from this use within the conductus, the more usual thirteenth-century use of modal transmutation was in alternate performance possibilities: entire motets and hockets may at times be found in different rhythmic modes in different manuscripts and the Anonymous of Saint Emmeram, writing in 1279, explains the procedures for alteration in performance.

Hocket

Hocket, a much-used technical device in the thirteenth and fourteenth centuries, consists of dividing a melodic line between two singers so that each will alternate single notes and rests. The resulting vocal effect is aptly illustrated by the name itself, which means "hiccup." Example 9-13a shows two hocket passages and the melodic line from which the hocket voices derive. Example 9-13b implies a harmonic rather than a melodic progression. In Example 9-13c the two lower hocket voices underlie a triplum in continuous rhythm.

Anthology Example 40 illustrates most of these techniques within the confines of a single organa tripla. There, mixed with freer passages, they serve particularly to unify the sustained-tone sections:

1. Repetition in a single voice with varied counterpoint in the other (duplum phrases 3 and 5 of section 7);

2. Repetition in a single voice with open and closed endings (duplum phrases 3 and 4 in section 1);

3. Repetition in both voices with open and closed endings (section 1a);

4. Repetition with voice exchange (beginning of section 4).

Melodic sequences abound throughout.

EXAMPLE 9-12. Repetition With Modal Transmutation (*Soli nitorem*, F, f. 327').
  a. Second cauda — mode 1
  b. Fourth cauda — mode 5

THE RHYTHMIC CONTEXT
OF PARISIAN POLYPHONY

There is evidence that plainchant was performed in some kind of a measured manner in the ninth and tenth centuries, although there is disagreement about the specific rhythms involved. The shift to chant performance in equal note lengths apparently came about in the eleventh century, probably becoming general by around 1050. The reason for this shift is unknown, but seems paralleled by a change in notational style from one emphasizing performance nuance to one giving greater indication of precise pitch. Both phenomena seem to indicate a definite shift in taste in performance.

Plainchant by around 1050 or thereabouts had lost its small-scale rhythmic nuance as seen in the concept of longer or shorter note values, but retained the large-scale rhythm of melodic ebb and flow with an attendant, often asymmetrical phrase rhythm. This is also the prime characteristic of dupla in florid and melismatic polyphony. A trained liturgical singer, used to performing plainchant melismas in the equal note values then current in chant performance, might well apply the same procedure to the similar melismas of polypony. In a similar manner, the singer accustomed to an equal-note performance of syllabic plainchant might well apply the same procedure to simple discant.

It is this reasoning that is behind the suggested equal-syllable-length performance of the simpler versus and conductus and the essentially equal-note performance of the florid and melismatic styles of Aquitanian polyphony and the *Liber Sancti Jacobi*, although this equality might be tempered by an amount of interpretive freedom.

a.

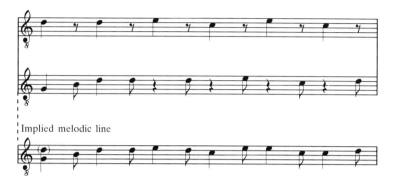

Implied melodic line

b.

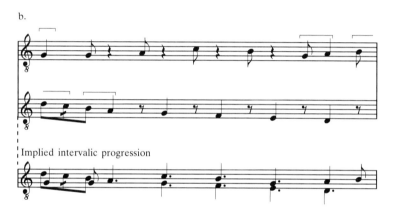

Implied intervalic progression

c.

EXAMPLE 9-13. Hocket.

    a. Single melodic line divided between two voices (*Dic Christe veritas*, F, f. 203)

    b. Implying an intervalic progression (*Transgressus legum Domini*, F, f. 214)

    c. Two-voice hocket under a continuous voice (*Parens patris natique filia*, F, f. 252′)

That some type of flexibility was present in the melismatic idiom of Notre Dame organa is shown by the difficulty thirteenth-century theorists had in describing its rhythm. The Anonymous dictus Saint Martial speaks of "a kind of wonderful flexibility." Anonymous IV describes longs that were too long and shorts that were too short: in other words, note values that were not in necessary mathematical ratio to each other, but determined *ex contingenti*, by the context in which they were found.

In this historical view, a performance of the dupla of the original *Magnus liber organi* (and possibly those of the preceding styles) in essentially equal notes could be envisaged, an equality of note values that however became tempered in performance through the requirements of good cadencing and the ever-changing consonant-dissonant relationship of the moving duplum over the stationary tenor. Johannes de Garlandia and other theorists suggest the lengthening of notes consonant with the tenor, but without specifying the amount of lengthening. Anonymous IV, in discussing organum purum, lists a plethora of note names and values that would seem to defy the possibility of any strict mathematical ratio.

A shift to a more standardized relationship between notes may have first occurred in sequential passages, those that were subsequently called copula, where there would be a tendency to retain the rhythmic as well as the melodic shape of the sequential motive, regardless of potential dissonant clashes with the tenor.

The need for a fully systematized procedure would have come about in the discant clausulae of the next generation of Notre Dame composition. Here the need is for the precise coordination of upper and lower voices. The point of departure would be discant, with its evenly marching series of on-the-beat consonances, ornamented with passing between-the-beat dissonances.

With the organa dupla of Notre Dame we have a final meeting of old and new concepts. The freer performance practice evidenced in organum purum became an increasingly alien one as the thirteenth century progressed, to be virtually forgotten by the early fourteenth century. Conversely, the more precise rhythms of the discant clausula would, through the medium of the motet, become the chief conveyor of the new system of precise mensural rhythm.

BIBLIOGRAPHY

Music

The complete body of two-voice organa is transcribed in modal rhythm in Hans Tischler, ed., *The Parisian Two-Part Organa: A Complete Comparative Edition* (Stuyvesant, N.Y.: Pendragon Press, 1989). The W_1 version of the

Magnus liber is transcribed, also in modal fashion, in William G. Waite, *The Rhythm of Twelfth Century Polyphony*, Yale Studies in the History of Music (New Haven: Yale University Press, 1954), which also contains a detailed account of early mensural notation. The three- and four-voice organa are available in two older transcriptions: Heinrich Husmann, ed., *Die drei- und vierstimmigen Notre-Dame Organa*, Publikationen älterer Musik 11 (Leipzig: Breitkopf und Härtel, 1940; rpt. Hildesheim: Georg Olms, 1967), and Helmut Schmidt, ed., *Die drei-und vierstimmigen Organa* (Kassel: Bärenreiter, 1933).

The complete conductus repertoire has been edited by Gordon A. Anderson, ed., *Notre-Dame and Related Conductus: Opera Omnia* (Henryville, Pa.: Institute of Medieval Music, 1979–). Equally worthy of study are Ethel Thurston, ed., *The Conductus Collections of MS Wolfenbüttel 1099*, 3 vol., Recent Researches in the Music of the Middle Ages and Early Renaissance 11 (Madison, Wis.: A-R Editions, 1980), and Janet Knapp, ed., *Thirty-Five Conductus for Two and Three Voices*, Collegium Musicum 6 (New Haven: Yale University Department of Music, 1965).

The most important Notre Dame manuscripts are available in facsimile: W_1: James H. Baxter, *An Old St. Andrew's Music Book* (London: St. Andrews University Publications, 1931); W_2: Luther Dittmer, *Wolfenbüttel 1099 (1206)*, PMMM 2 (Brooklyn: Institute of Mediaeval Music, 1960); *F*: Luther Dittmer, *Firenze, Pluteus 29.1*, 2 vol., PMMM 10 and 11 (Brooklyn: Institute of Mediaeval Music, n.d.).

Theory

Garlandia's *De mensurabili musica* is translated in Stanley H. Birnbaum, *Johannes de Garlandia, Concerning Measured Music (De mensurabili musica)*, Colorado Springs Music Press Translations 9 (Colorado Springs: Colorado College, 1979). Anonymous IV is translated in Jeremy Yudkin, *Anonymous IV: De mensuris et discantu*, MSD 41 (AIM, 1985).

Readings

There is an extensive literature on the Notre Dame styles. Apel, *Notation*, and Parrish, *Notation*, should be consulted about notational procedures.

Problems of rhythm and performance in the organa are taken up, with varying points of view, in Jeremy Yudkin, "The *Copula* According to Johannes de Garlandia," *MD* 34 (1980): 67–85; idem., "The Rhythm of Organum Purum," *JoM* 2 (1983): 355–76; idem., "The Anonymous of St. Emmeram and Anonymous IV on the *Copula*," *MQ* 70 (1984): 1–23; Edward Roesner, "Johannes de Garlandia on *Organum in Speciale*," *EMH* 2 (1982): 129–60; idem., "The Performance of Parisian Organum," *EM* 7 (1979): 174–89; Ernest Sanders, "Consonance and Rhythm in the Organum of the 12th and 13th Centuries," *JAMS* 33 (1980): 264–86; Theodore Karp, "Towards a Critical Edition of Notre Dame Organa Dupla," *MQ* 52 (1966): 350–67.

Rhythm problems in the conductus are discussed from different points of view in Janet Knapp, "Musical Declamation and Poetic Rhythm in Notre Dame Conductus," JAMS 32 (1979): 383–407; and Gordon Anderson, "The Rhythm of *cum littera* Sections of Polyphonic Conductus in Mensural Sources," JAMS 27 (1973): 288–304.

Particular technical matters are discussed in Sarah Fuller, "Theoretical Foundations of Early Organum Theory," AM 53 (1981): 52–84; Gordon A. Anderson, "Mode and Change of Mode in Notre Dame Conductus," AM 40 (1968): 92–114; Norman E. Smith, "Tenor Repetition in the Notre Dame Organum," JAMS 19 (1966): 329–51; Hans Tischler, "The Structure of Notre-Dame Organa," AM 49 (1977): 193–99; Vincent J. Corrigan III, "The Style of the Notre-Dame Conductus," 2 vols. (Ph.D. diss., UMI no. 80-20022; three- and four-voice conductus only).

For biographical information about Leonin, see Craig Wright, "Leoninus, Poet and Musician," JAMS (1986): 1–35; about Adam of Saint Victor, Margot E. Fassler, "Who Was Adam of St. Victor? The Evidence of the Sequence Manuscripts," JAMS 37 (1984): 233–69.

Discussions of manuscript dating and provenance may be found in Rebecca Baltzer, "Thirteenth-Century Illuminated Miniatures and the Date of the Florence Manuscript," JAMS 25 (1972): 1–18; Edward H. Roesner, "The Origins of W_1," JAMS 29 (1976): 337–80; and Julian Brown, Sonia Patterson, and David Hiley, "Further Observations on W_1" JPMMS 4 (1981): 53–81.

More general matters are included in Manfred Bukofzer, "Interrelations between Conductus and Clausula," AM 1 (1953): 65–103; Gordon A. Anderson, "Texts and Music in 13th-Century Sacred Song," MM 10 (1979): 1–27; Edward H. Roesner, "The Problem of Chronology in the Transmission of Organum Duplum," EMH (1981): 365–99; Hans Tischler, "The Evolution of the *Magnus Liber Organi*," MQ 70 (1984): 163–74; Heinrich Husmann, "The Enlargement of the Magnus liber organi and the Paris Churches St. Germain l'Auxerrois and Ste. Geneviève-du-Mont," JAMS 16 (1963): 176–203.

Part III

THE ERA OF THE MOTET
1200–1400

Introduction

By the beginning of the thirteenth century Paris was well on its way to becoming the artistic and intellectual capital of Europe. The first phase of the building of the Cathedral of Notre Dame, the construction of the chancel, had been completed in 1183. The nave was completed by the beginning of the century, and the transepts and facade by 1267. Leonin died, or at least disappeared from the rolls, in 1201, while Perotin remained active possibly into the 1220s.

The University of Paris, growing out of the cathedral schools of Notre Dame, was formally constituted by 1200, with written statutes dating from 1208 and papal confirmation by 1215. By 1219 students were so numerous that they had to be divided into four "nations," groupings according to place of origin: France (including Italy), England (including German students), Picardy, and Normandy. In 1210 Guillaume le Breton remarked, "Never before in any time or in any part of the world, whether in Athens or Egypt, had there been such a multitude of students. The reason for this must be sought not only in the admirable beauty of Paris, but also in the special privileges which King Philip and his father before him conferred upon the scholars."[1]

There were as yet no university buildings. Teaching took place in the houses of the masters, which by this time had spread onto the Left Bank, in what is now the Latin Quarter, and where the present University of Paris buildings are located. The area then was a mixture of masters' and students' houses, mixed among other elements of city life. Only gradually did students come to live and study together. Generally students would choose the master under whom they wished to study and arrange for their own place of lodging. Lectures were in Latin. Study led first to the Bachelor of Arts and then Master of Arts, the degree that provided authorization to teach. Further study, for those that undertook it, could be in law, medicine, or the "queen of sciences," theology; this might take thirteen years of study beyond the Master of Arts degree.

Students need books, and by the second half of the century a professional book trade was firmly established among *stationarii*, who copied the books, and *librarii*, who sold them, all licensed and supervised by the university. Manuscript copying was a laborious and time-consuming task. Careful and artistic copying could take months: a New Testament of 1333, containing 278 folios (556 pages), took six months to copy. The commercial book trade obviously needed faster methods. Books were divided up into small sections assigned to different copyists, each of whom would copy and recopy one particular small portion.

---

[1]Trans. in Joan Evans, *Life in Medieval France*, 3rd ed. (London: Phaidon Press, 1969), 128.

Growing familiarity with the text would speed copying so that it eventually could be done virtually from memory. Sections were then assembled, and if certified correct by the university's examiner, the books were sold or, more often, rented to students (who might well make their own copies in turn).

An important explosion in manuscript production in the latter part of the century included, among other things, the copying of important collections of music, gathering up the repertoires of the past century and a half. Music copying was more lengthy and complicated than straight text. The parchment had to be lined with dry-point guidelines to help the copyist keep the lines of text even and to indicate margins. Staves had to be drawn in and the text copied. Then the musical copyist added the notes, and finally the rubricator would draw the ornate initial that would start a manuscript section or an individual composition, often incorporating it into elaborate marginal illustrations (see Facsimile 11.1 below). These would be drawn in brightly colored inks—often blue and red—and in sumptuous volumes further decorated with gold leaf. Many *ateliers* or workshops produced specific styles that today serve to identify the date and place of origin of a manuscript.

The prodigious copying of music manuscripts in the second half of the thirteenth century represents a landmark in the gradual shift from the purely oral culture of the early Middle Ages to the literate one of the late Renaissance. It was as if there suddenly appeared a desire to capture in writing the rich heritage of the past hundred years or more: *all* of the troubadour and trouvère manuscripts, *all* of the retrospective Notre Dame manuscripts with their massive collections of organa and conductus, and the motet collections, copied while the music was relatively new.

Paris was still a center of musical activity of all kinds. The cathedral, the other churches in the city, and the many monasteries in and around the city all had their own corps of highly trained musicians: clerks and priests dedicated to the musical worship of God. The court had its own royal minstrels, nine of whom are identified in a roster of 1288. Other, more common minstrels could live in the Rue de Jugleors (Street of the Jongleurs) or elsewhere around Paris, making their living catering to the aristocratic, bourgeois, and popular tastes of the city. By 1321 a confraternity of "minstrels, jongleurs, and jongleresses" had been formed. By this time Paris is thought to have reached a peak population of sixty thousand or possibly much more (depending on how the documents are interpreted), making it a city of first rank, about the same as such southern cities as Florence, Venice, and Milan, and larger than London, Genoa, or Cologne.

Long before, royal power had been established in and around Paris, and a number of strong kings had gradually increased the amount of territory under their direct rule. By 1259 much of northern France was under the control of the French crown, but Aquitaine and Gascony, which had become a fief of the English crown through the marriage of Eleanor of Aquitaine to England's Henry II in the midtwelfth century, remained as a source of friction between the

French and English kings. The situation came to a head in 1337, launching the so-called Hundred Years' War between France and England.

Throughout the fourteenth century the tide ebbed and flowed, with the low point for the French coming after 1415 when, Burgundy having entered the war on the side of the English, the English-Burgundian allies controlled over half of France, including Paris itself, with the French king insane and under the control of the duke of Burgundy. The miraculous turnabout in events that would drive the English from the continent started with the sudden appearance in 1429 of Joan of Arc, who sparked a sense of national patriotism in the French. The English ascendency rapidly declined, and by 1453 they retained only the town of Calais on the English Channel.

The long war was fought on French soil, and the French bore the brunt of the devastation. Time and again the countryside was ravaged by English armies who, scourging the peasants' unarmed lands, carefully avoided attacking the fortified cities. Both sides employed large bands of mercenaries, and in times of truce these mercenaries, no longer paid, raided the countryside as lawless brigands, becoming a scourge worse than war. To this devastation was added, at midcentury, the Black Death, a terrible epidemic of bubonic plague that started in China and swept across Europe between 1347 and 1350, wiping out one-third of the population of Europe.

Nonetheless, in spite of devastation and turmoil, French artistic life continued unabated. France retained a hegemony of sorts in the arts throughout the period, although her primacy was shared in the fourteenth century with Italy and, to a lesser extent, with England.

The motet was the dominant musical form of the thirteenth and fourteenth centuries. Originating in Paris at the beginning of the thirteenth century as a troped form of discant clausula, it had become an international style by midcentury. It retained its ascendancy until the mid-fourteenth century, after which it was gradually replaced by the new polyphonic song forms. The time of the motet comes to an end in the lengthy ceremonial motets of Dunstable and Dufay as the Middle Ages shifts into the Renaissance.

It is proper, therefore, to designate the period from 1200 to 1400 as the era of the motet, realizing that its inception overlapped the culminating stage of organum and that it would gradually give up its supremacy after 1340. Between those years, however, it remained the musical form par excellence.

Within fifty years of its origin, the motet had spread to England, Spain, and Germany, and even to Poland and Czechoslovakia, a broad circle surrounding its place of birth. Nevertheless, northern France remained the center of artistic innovation in the motet throughout the thirteenth and fourteenth centuries. Development of Franconian and Petronian rhythmic styles, musical organization based on the principle of isorhythm, increasingly intricate systems of rhythmic notation to define the specifics of rhythm—all are manifestations of the continued ascendancy of northern France. Peripheral areas were, in general, more conservative and less prone to polyphonic complexities in their approach to the motet.

England—for hundreds of years the meeting ground between the culture and music of France and that of the rougher Danes and Norse—is the only one of the non-French lands to evidence an indigenous compositional style, one particularly evident in the latter years of the thirteenth and the early years of the fourteenth century.

The progression of motet composition and style was continuous throughout the more than two hundred years of its development. Only for clarity of presentation is it broken here into succcessive periods, each marked by a predominate style and form of notation.

10

The Early Motet
(ca. 1200–1270)

The motet consists of one or more texted voices above a tenor drawn from a melismatic segment of plainchant, all proceeding in a measured rhythm. In origin it is a discant clausula to which text has been added. In its earliest manifestation the added text functioned as a textual elaboration of the subject of the tenor chant, a "trope" in the larger sense of the word. This is the probable impetus behind the formation of the motet: the desire to superimpose elaborating text and melody over the basic chant in a polyphonic idiom. Already an application of this concept is apparent in the earliest of the Aquitanian manuscripts (see Chapter 6), but it is only with the conjunction of trope and discant clausula that the motet form per se took shape.

The time when this occurred can only be surmised, but it must have been preceded by the establishment of the discant clausula as a distinct genre, a development usually associated with the second or Perotinian generation of Parisian composers. A date of around 1200 or shortly thereafter is therefore not unreasonable.

DEFINITIONS

Johannes de Grocheo, writing around 1300, defines the motet as "a composition in several voice parts having several texts or many varied syllables sounding harmoniously together." The distinctive feature of the motet is thus a multiplicity of texts—at least one, often two, and occasionally three in addition to the implied text of the chant melisma used in the tenor.

The resulting variety of procedure can be codified through the use of the following modern terms:

231

Two-voice motet—one texted upper voice and a tenor;

Single-texted motet—a three- or four-voice motet in which all the upper voices share the same text and rhythm, creating a conductus-like texture above the tenor, from whence comes the common but misleading term *conductus-motet*;

Double motet—a three-voice motet with a different text in each upper voice;

Triple motet—a four-voice motet in which each of the three upper voices has its own individual text.

The terms *single, double,* and *triple* refer not to the number of voices, but to the number of texts that are present (the single syllable of the tenor is not considered a text). Later in the century we will find a three-voice triple motet in which two upper voices are placed above a fully texted French chanson tenor. Additional classifications relate to the language of the upper voices: Latin, French, or bilingual (when one upper voice is in Latin, the other in French).

The clausula duplum, now carrying text, is renamed *motetus* (from the French term for *word*), from which the entire composite form takes its name.

A motet must be considered a multiform composition in conception and practice, for as copious examples demonstrate, texts can be changed and voices added, replaced, or omitted at will. A Latin motet may become French through the substitution of a new text (a practice known as *contrafactum*). Through the process of addition, a three-voice motet may be made out of a two-voice one, or a triple motet out of a double. A new triplum may be written to replace an older one. Conversely, a double motet may be reduced to two-voice form, or a triple to a double.

The core of a motet is the music of the motetus and tenor. All else could be subject to alteration, even the text of the motetus. As a given motet may appear in many guises in many manuscripts, it is advisable to think in terms of motet families, in which many variants may appear around that basic core.

In medieval usage, a motet was ordinarily identified by the opening words of the motetus. In twentieth-century practice it is more usual to identify a motet with, in turn, the opening words of the triplum, motetus, and tenor: *Veni, virgo—Veni, sancte—Neuma* (see Anthology Example 50).

THE SOURCES

Originating in Paris, the motet spread rapidly, becoming an international genre well before the middle of the thirteenth century. This, coupled with the remarkable upsurge in manuscript copying that began around midcentury, has left a rich trove of motet material: over one-hundred manuscripts, stemming not only from France but also from Spain, Italy, Germany, and Poland—in effect, all of Europe north of the Alps, with some inroads into northern Italy. These manuscripts carry four-hundred and fifty motet families from before 1270, with about twice that number of individual variants.

The bulk of this repertoire is contained in eight main manuscripts, while many smaller manuscripts tend to carry copies or alternate versions of the main repertoire. The most important of the principal manuscripts may be divided into two groups: those completely devoted to the early motet repertoire, and those also encompassing an end-of-century repertoire.

The first group, manuscripts totally devoted to the early, pre-1270 motet repertoire, include:

F—a Notre Dame source: 77 mostly two-voice and single-texted motets in addition to conductus, organa, and clausulae (Parisian, ca. 1250);

MüA—Munich, Bayerische Staatsbibliothek, Gallo-rom. 42: fragments of a collection of 36 motets (central French, ca. 1250);

W_2—220 motets, mostly two-voice but some double, including French as well as Latin texts (central French, ca. 1260–75);

Ma—40 two-voice motets as well as conductus and organa (Spanish, ca. 1260–70);

Cl—"La Clayette," Paris, B. N., nouv. acq. frç. 13521: a collection of 55 motets (central French, ca. 1270–80).

The second group, manuscripts carrying a later as well as an early repertoire, include:

Mo—The Montpellier Codex, Montpellier, Fac. de Médecine, H 196: the largest and the most sumptuous of the motet manuscripts, Mo includes almost 350 motets, of which the first 250 pertain to the early period. These are contained in the first six fascicles (sections) of the manuscript and are often called the "old corpus" of the manuscript. They were probably copied around 1270–80, while fascicles 7 and 8 probably date from around 1300. Fascicles 1–7 are Parisian, while fascicle 8, originally a separate manuscript, is probably French provincial in origin.

Ba—The Bamberg Codex: Bamberg, Staatliche Bibl., Lit. 115: a collection of 100 three-voice motets (of which approximately two-thirds belong to the early period) followed by seven untexted hocket compositions. The geographical provenance of Ba is much disputed, opinions ranging from western Germany to Paris itself. It was probably copied around 1285–90.

Tu—Turin, Bibl. naz., vari 42: a smaller manuscript of 31 motets, about three-fourths of which are later. The manuscript is from Liège, around 1300–10.

Hu—The Las Huelgas Codex; Burgos, Monasterio de Las Huelgas: a Spanish manuscript from around 1325, *Hu* contains a conservative, liturgically oriented collection of 61 Latin motets, many two-voice, with some single-texted motets and some double motets. Half relate to the early period, while many others are later works in conservative style.

NOTATION

Rhythmic and notational procedures that began in the discant clausula were taken over and developed in the early motet. As we have noted, modal notation grew with the melismatic clausula and is ideally suited to it. It is of little use in conveying the rhythm of either a texted conductus or the texted voice of a motet. Nevertheless, it is the notation of all the motet manuscripts to *Cl* and *Mo*, including the main Notre Dame manuscripts *F* and *W*$_2$. Fortunately, the rhythm of a texted motet voice can be easily determined through its relationship to the tenor which, being untexted, can use modal ligature patterns.

Distinct methods of notating texted passages do not show up in the manuscripts until *Cl* and *Mo* (ca. 1270), although the procedure for differentiating individual note shapes is discussed in the treatise of Garlandia some ten to twenty years earlier. The procedure established there forms the basis for all subsequent rhythmic notation: the shape of the note designates relative length.

There are four note shapes:

the duplex long:	◥
the long:	▌
the breve:	■
the semibreve:	◆

Note shape denotes relative value only; precise value is still determined to an extent by context. For example, a long followed by a breve takes on its *recte* (correct or true) value of two *tempora* (time units); when followed by another long, however, it becomes *ultra mensuram* (beyond usual measurement) and contains three tempora.

Similarly, the breve normally equals one tempus (half of a normal long), but will equal two tempora if it is the second of a pair of breves between two longs (thus permitting the notation of mode 3). The duplex long is stable in equalling two *ultra mensuram* longs (six tempora), while the semibreve appears normally in ornamental groups of two or three per breve, but is not given a precise value.

The use of these individual note shapes in indicating the rhythmic modes is as follows:

Mode 1	♩ ▪	♪ ♪
Mode 2	▪ ♩	♪ ♪
Mode 3	♩ ▪ ▪	♪· ♪ ♪·
Mode 4	▪ ▪ ♩	♪ ♪ ♪·
Mode 5	♩ ♩	♪· ♪·
Mode 6	▪ ▪ ▪	♪ ♪ ♪

CHRONOLOGICAL DEVELOPMENT

The early history of the motet, like that of Parisian organum, must be re-created by deduction, for the earliest of the motet manuscripts dates from at least forty years after the inception of the motet as a form. Evidence suggests that there are three broad stages of development.

The Trope-Oriented Motet

In its beginning, the motet was closely related to its parent organum. Motet texts typically troped the organum chant, as in section 6 of *Alleluia: Adorabo ad templum* (Anthology Example 39), where the text *Locus hic terribilis* has been added to the clausula of W_2. The entire chant relates to the dedication of a church, and it is on this subject that the new text expands. In addition, it ends in typical fashion with a quotation of the specific text of the tenor melisma, *et confitebor*.

Other trope-related examples employ assonance, making prominent use of the vowel sound of the tenor melisma. This may be seen in Anthology Example 47, on the melisma *go* from the complete word *Virgo*. The motet text quotes the complete word at beginning and end, and begins many of its phrases on the *o* vowel sound sustained by the tenor: Oculus, Porta, Oleum, Nomen, Pro-pelleuma. Later lines use it at the beginning and end: Nova grant hora, Oper-arios, Dies hos Egyptios, Propter filios.

These very early motets took on two outward forms, either simply retaining the two voices of the source clausula (the majority) or adding a third voice (called the *triplum*) with the identical text and phrase structure as the motetus. The latter is illustrated in the triplum of Anthology Example 47. The two-voice source clausula is transmitted in W_1. The added triplum of the single-texted three-voice motet follows the first-mode rhythm of the motetus virtually without deviation while sharing the same text.

The Independent Motet

The second and decisive stage of motet development is marked by a freeing of the motet from its close liturgical relationship, the introduction of the French language and secular subject matter, and the development of the double motet. The motet now takes on an independent existence.

Separation of the motet from its liturgical roots may have begun with the performance of motets outside of the service. Latin texts were then free to relate to more general religious subjects, including doctrinal questions, public and churchly morality, and above all, the then-growing worship of Mary.

The introduction of the French language into the motet is a larger jump. Given the close relationship between church and court, however, with clerics holding office in civil governments and church officials often ruling as virtual temporal rulers, the migration of motet from monastery and cathedral to court is not surprising. Indeed, there is at least some evidence that the earliest French motet texts may have been translations of Latin sacred ones, and a few such can be found. By and large, however, the subject of the French motet came to be that most courtly of subjects, courtly love in all of its ramifications (with as a subspecies the *Pastourelle*, a knight-and-shepherdess drama). An example of the progression from clausula to Latin motet to French contrafactum (substitute text) may be seen in the already-mentioned section 6 of *Alleluia: Adorabo ad templum*: clausula in W_2; Latin motet in F; the French motet *Traveillié du mau d'amer* in *Mo*.

We also have little specific knowledge concerning the genesis of the double and triple motet. The single-texted, three-voice motet seems to have been a relatively short-lived phenomenon, except in outlying European territories. The double motet apparently arrived as a replacement early in the century. A few of these early double motets simply put a new text to the triplum of a single-texted one. More often, they are motet versions of three-voice clausulae or expansions of two-voice ones.

An additive process can be seen in the substitute clausula of section 6 of *Adorabo ad templum*. Here, a two-voice clausula has been converted into a two-voice motet through the addition of the text *De virgula, veris initio* in W_2. The later manuscript *Hu* carries an added triplum with the words *O Maria, decus angelorum*, creating a three-voice double motet. The texts deal with different aspects of the praise of Mary.

Another process, the replacement of a voice, may be seen in *O Maria, virgo—O Maria, maris stella—Veritatem* (Anthology Example 48b), where the original first-mode triplum of the single-texted, three-voice motet (48a) has been replaced with a new melody and text in the sixth rhythmic mode. This motet is a particularly good illustration of the complexity of motet redaction in the thirteenth century. Its earliest preserved form, in *F*, is as a three-voice, single-texted motet. Five later manuscripts carry it in reduced two-voice form (motetus and tenor only), while *Hu* adds a new triplum to create a second single-texted, three-voice motet. *Mo* and four other manuscripts carry the double-motet version given here. In addition, W_2 carries the music of the original motet but with a French religious text, and *Hu* adds a new triplum. A collation of thirteen of these sources can be seen in *NOHM* 2:393. Appropriate to the Feast of the Assumption of the Blessed Virgin Mary, the chant and the texts are all Marian, the original motetus text also troping the text of the tenor melisma, *veritatem = in veritate.*

Midcentury Styles

Early stages of motet composition seem to have occurred within the first thirty or forty years of the century, giving way to new tendencies by around 1240. By that time two opposing tendencies are apparent: the two-voice motet moved toward a simpler, more popular idiom, and the double motet toward greater complexity.

The two-voice motet. The two-voice motet became increasingly influenced by secular monophony. It appears in trouvère chansonniers, at times notated without the tenor, suggesting a possible monophonic performance of the motetus.

Anthology Example 49, *Quant je parti—Tuo*, is representative of this rapprochement between secular chanson and midcentury, two-voice motet. The text is typical of courtly love. The motetus melody, which could stand on its own, takes advantage of a partial repetition in the otherwise through-composed tenor (measures 1–2 = 5–6) to assume a typical AAB or *Pedes cum cauda* form. A sense of popular idiom pervades the motet.

The double motet. In contrast, the double motet now becomes the main line of musical development, and many motets begin to use one or the other of the two rhythmic developments that would eventually undermine modal rhythm. The first of these involves an increase in ornamentation in the upper voices, a practice that tends to hide the modal pattern of the melody in nonmodal rhythmic movement, as in the triplum of Example 10-1. When this happens, the concept of modal rhythm is conveyed only by the pattern of text declamation. This transfer of the function of the rhythmic modes from determiner (or codifier) of melodic rhythm in the clausula and early motet to determiner of textual rhythm within a freer melodic context in the later motet marks a gradual weakening of the modal rhythmic system.

The second development—the use of a triplum in mode 6 over a first- or second-mode motetus and, often, a fifth-mode tenor (Anthology Example 48b)—created distinct rhythmic layers and a greater degree of voice differentiation. Although present in less than 10 percent of all early double motets, a long-term result of this style was the exploitation of faster triplum rhythms and the creation of the characteristic motet idiom of the latter part of the century. (The rhythmic style of Anthology Example 48b, with a sixth-mode triplum in which the first breve is divided into two texted semibreves, is often incorrectly designated as *Franconian*, whereas it is in reality a *pre-Franconian* idiom, existing well before—but leading into—the rhythmic changes later codified by Franco.)

EXAMPLE 10-1. Modal Textual Declamation Regulating Non-Modal Melodic Motion. *Mo* no. 140, beginning (fol. 190′-191).

FORM AND STYLE

Johannes de Grocheo's account of motet compositional procedures in his *De musica* of around 1300 serves as a useful point of departure in a consideration of form:

> A motet is a composition in several voice parts having several texts or many varied syllables sounding harmoniously together.
>
> The tenor is that part upon which all the others are based, just as the parts of a house or building are placed upon a foundation. And it regulates them and gives them their quantity, just as the bones [support] the other parts [of the body].
>
> The motetus is the melody that is arranged immediately above the tenor. And it most often begins at the interval of the fifth and continues at the same interval with which it began or ascends to the octave.
>
> The triplum is the melody which should begin an octave above the tenor and continue at the same interval as much as possible. I say "as much as possible" because sometimes it descends into the range of the motetus or the interval of the fifth for the sake of euphony, just as the motetus sometimes ascends to the octave.
>
> The quadruplum is a melody that is added to some pieces in order to complete the consonance.

Wishing to compose this type, one should first arrange or compose the tenor and give it mode and measure. The principal part should be formed first, since by its means the others are afterwards shaped. I say "arrange" since in motets and organa the tenor is from an older, previously composed melody, but is set out skillfully by mode and in more correct measure. I say "compose" since in conductus the tenor is completely made anew and is modified and extended according to the will of the composer.

The tenor having been composed or arranged, the motetus should be composed or arranged above it.

But finally the triplum ought to be superimposed on these.

The following discussion takes up elements of Grocheo's description in turn.

Rhythmic Style

The function of the tenor. We have already seen that the rhythm of the tenor is a major determinant of the rhythmic and metric structure of the clausula and motet. It also serves in other ways to "regulate and give quantity."

Chant melismas chosen to serve as motet tenors vary considerably in length and in many cases would result in very short motets. The problem of length was solved in the clausula by the simple expedient of repeating the tenor melody (see, for example, the three W_2 clausulae in *Alleluia: Adorabo ad templum*). This practice continued and was expanded in the motet, three-quarters of which contain two or more presentations of the tenor melody.

Repeating the tenor several times had latent structural import for the motet, for the tenor repetitions, if reflected in the other voices of the motet, had the power to create a strophic form in the motet. Except for the very earliest of the motets, however, the structural importance of tenor repetition is not systematically emphasized until the end of the century. Rather, the emphasis throughout the mainstream of early motet activity is to disguise tenor repetitions through the devices of through-composition and phrase overlap in the upper voices.

Before passing to these, however, it may be noted that, in most instances, the length of the tenor melody coincides with the end of its rhythmic pattern, so that each succeeding repetition of the tenor melody is in the same rhythmic guise. When they do not coincide, so that the tenor melody would be rhythmically displaced upon repetition, the tenor pattern is normally adjusted to fit the length of the tenor melody by shortening or lengthening the final notes. Occasionally, however, it is not, so that the repeat of the melody is permitted to assume a different rhythmic form than the first presentation (see Anthology Example 50).

Upper-voice phrase structure. Some very early motets are written with a close correspondence between tenor and upper voice(s), between the upper voices themselves, or both. This is especially true in the early single-texted three-voice motet, where the two upper voices have identical phrase lengths (disguised occasionally by a link between phrases in one voice) generally related to a multiple of the length of the tenor pattern. In the single-texted motet version of Anthology Example 48a the motetus and triplum move in synchronous declamation and rhythm (relieved only by ornamentation) in consistent sixteen-beat phrases. Each upper-voice phrase spans two tenor patterns, resulting in a completely homorhythmic motet. Although the term *isoperiodic* ("equality of phrases") is usually applied to considerably later English and continental motets, it could as well be applied here to describe this early and passing phase of motet construction. It can be seen in slightly more flexible form in Anthology Example 47, both in the three-voice single-texted motet and in the parent clausula.

Soon, however, simple isoperiodic phrase structure was abandoned in favor of constantly overlapping phrase lengths. An example of this is the double motet version of Anthology Example 48, where the newly written triplum consistently overlaps motetus and tenor rests, giving a continuous flow to the whole. This technique became the standard throughout the remainder of the century, as may be seen in Anthology Examples 50 and following. Phrases seldom relate in any rational order, a constantly changing flux being the norm.

An elementary stage may also be seen in Anthology Example 50, where the motetus phrases coincide with those of the tenor until the extended sixth phrase (which carries not two but three poetic lines). That this deviation is a conscious compositional device is shown by the manner in which the triplum is manipulated. It begins in regular six-beat patterns, setting up a counterpoint of phrase lengths with the motetus. The triplum's pattern would coincide with the tenor every twelve beats, as at the end of the second phrase, but this is deliberately avoided at the end of the fourth phrase through the rhythmic extension of the final word *Maria*.

Anthology Examples 51 and 52 and the new triplum of Anthology Example 48a show the fully developed stage of this development. In Anthology Example 51, the motetus and tenor always cadence on an even-numbered beat, while the triplum is designed to cadence on an odd-numbered beat, ensuring continual overlap. In Anthology Example 52, the recurring three-beat triplum phrases, the five-beat motetus phrases, and the two-beat tenor phrases ensure a continual overlap from beginning to end; a continuous web of sound lightly articulated by occasional two-voice cadences. The new triplum of Anthology Example 48b, with its advanced sixth-mode rhythm and offset phrasing, seems specifically designed to counteract the regularity of the original motetus and tenor.

An interesting juxtaposition of the two approaches may be seen in the clausula Go of Anthology Example 47a. The clausula contains two statements of the tenor cantus firmus, both in the same fifth-mode rhythm pattern. During the first statement, the clausula duplum is designed to coincide with the tenor in multiples of the four-beat tenor pattern. Thereafter, however, the composer interposes a single long and a rest to throw the duplum out of phase with the tenor for the remainder of the clausula, creating an overlapping phrase structure. There is a striking contrast between the sectional first half and the continuous second half.

In the motet version, the triplum duplicates the motetus's phrasing. By overlapping the beginning of the tenor repetition in the upper voices, the composer negates whatever structural importance the tenor repetition may have. While occasionally in the early motet the upper voices cadence at the end of the tenor statement and begin anew on the repeat, it is by and large a rare procedure. The impetus during most of the century was toward continuousness rather than sectionality, ignoring the inherent structural importance of tenor repetitions.

Melodic Style

General principles of melody writing are, aside from the element of rhythm, not markedly different from those of the twelfth century. Motion is overwhelmingly conjunct and movement is within a narrow range.

According to Grocheo's instructions each voice would be composed in turn: tenor, motetus, triplum, quadruplum (if present), in the traditional medieval additive method of composition. Nonetheless, occasional occurrences of a close relationship between the voices suggest that the compositional process was not always so simple.

Voice crossing.   In theory, each voice occupies its own range above the tenor, but in practice the upper voices constantly cross, though the triplum tends to be higher than the motetus more of the time. Grocheo is correct, nonetheless, in placing the motetus a fifth and the triplum an octave above any given tenor note, or vice versa, because the fifth and octave is the most usual vertical sonority.

Melodic writing.   All melodic activity is circumscribed within a very narrow range and the total range of a voice part seldom exceeds a tenth. As a result, melodic motion is basically stepwise, relieved through the occasional introduction of thirds and fourths. Larger skips are extremely rare, except between phrases, where they are accepted.

Melodies tend to descend. Ascending passages do occur, but are generally contained and counterbalanced within the phrase. Melodic range within the phrase is typically a fifth or a sixth, although it may vary from a second to an eleventh.

Limited range, conjunct motion, and constant voice crossing between the upper voices (and occasionally the tenor) work together to prevent the creation of memorable melodic lines in the upper voices. Rather they coordinate with each other in composite interaction.

There is no attempt to integrate music and text emotionally. Rather, the melody is a musical element governed by its own rules onto which text is placed. Accordingly there is no difference in melodic style among the various types of motet, and there is no attempt at tone painting.

Melodic structure.   In terms of formal structure, an individual voice may be completely through-composed without obvious devices of unification, or may be unified through phrase or motivic repetition. The distinction is not always easy to make, for the pervasive modal rhythm, constant conjunct motion, and limited range combine to create a melodic idiom that inevitably uses and reuses a common stock of melodic shapes, conveying a sense of unity even without the presence of conscious devices.

The deliberate use of repetition or the quotation of well-known melodies within the motet is probably largely a midcentury development. In thirteenth-century theory, these devices w∪re discussed under the heading of *color* (pl. *colores*): "Put colores where there are relatively unknown phrases and the melody will be noted more and, if noted, please. Similarly, put as a color anywhere a known melody, a phrase or a passage, descending or ascending instrumental runs, or a phrase of a song." This passage, from a later, edited version of the Garlandia treatise, refers in the first instance to melodic repetition within a voice part, a not uncommon feature in the midcentury motet.

It can occasionally result in a patterned form, such as the *pedes cum cauda* noted in Anthology Example 49. More often it is evidenced through the device of motivic repetition. In such a case, it serves not only to unify the motet, but to make the melodic material more obvious and accessible.

A good example is Anthology Example 50, *Veni, virgo—Veni sancte—Neuma*, in which all the motetus phrases begin with the identical motive

either at pitch or transposed a tone higher or lower. The motive also permeates the triplum, beginning phrases 2, 5, 6, 8, and 10, and appearing within phrases 7 and 8, leading occasionally to imitation between the voices (compare the beginnings of motetus phrases 4, 6, and 7 with the following triplum phrases, triplum phrase 6 with the following motetus one).

Imitation is never a dominant feature of the motet. It may occur through such a device as motivic repetition, but only within an otherwise nonimitative context. Other examples of imitation may be seen in Anthology Example 51, over the fifth to eighth tenor phrases (highlighted by the identical words of the two texts) and also over the sixth tenor phrase before the end.

Both Latin and French motets use the technique of motivic repetition of various kinds. The French motet may also quote short popular melodies, known as *refrains*, in the triplum or motetus. An example is the motet just cited, which begins with simultaneous refrain quotations (shown by the italicized words) in the triplum and motetus. The motet ends with the same two refrains, but with the voices exchanged and with added ornamentation. More extensive refrains may be seen in the motetus of *Trop sovent—Brunete—In seculum* (Anthology Example 52), which is in fact little more than a chain of refrains.

Voice Relationships

Rhythmic relationships. In the modal system, a given rhythmic mode dominates a voice part throughout, and concurrent voices have compatible modes. This led to the dominant style of the period, in which the upper voices move in an essentially equal rhythmic motion in modes 1, 2, or 3, over a slightly less active, rhythmically patterned tenor (see Anthology Examples 47, 50, 51, and 52).

A second, contrasting style appears sporadically, but most commonly near the end of the period. This places a mode 6 triplum above a mode 1 or 2 motetus and (usually) a mode 5 tenor to create a stratified rhythmic structure (see Anthology Example 48b). Appearing in small numbers in the early motet repertoire, these "mode 6" motets contain the seeds of the important rhythmic expansion at the end of the century.

Two- and three-voice composition. The two-voice motet is the simplest form of motet writing. In effect it is an accompanied song, for although the motet is based on a cantus firmus, the attention of the listener is on the new motetus melody and text. Three-voice composition is considerably more complex, requiring the intermingling of two upper voices, each with their own text, within the octave of the tenor.

Four-voice composition. Four-voice motets form a small but interesting subgroup among the early motets, a series of seventeen appearing in fascicle 2 of *Mo*. These motets compound the problems of the three-voice ones, for now not two but three upper voices must intertwine within the octave space delineated by the tenor. Though often considered to belong to the middle period of early motet composition, the advanced rhythms displayed in some suggest a later composition. By the end of the period, however, four-voice writing disappears on the continent, to be revived in a different format and in an enlarged tonal space in the fourteenth century.

Harmonic Style

Consonance. The thirteenth-century definition of consonance is similar to that of the preceding century. Garlandia gives the following tabulation:

Perfect:	Unison and octave
Medium:	Fourth and fifth
Imperfect:	Thirds (major and minor)

In practice, however, the fourth is no longer equal to the fifth. The latter is now the standard medium consonance; fourths are used little more than thirds. Acceptance of three-voice writing as the norm is the most likely cause of the demise of the fourth, which became more marked as the century progressed. A fourth may function as well as a fifth in two-part counterpoint, but the octave-and-fourth sonority is less stable than the octave-and-fifth. Fourths are considerably more common in two-voice motets, although even here the fifth is used more. Thirds were favored in the earliest group of motets, but fell out of favor thereafter.

Dissonance.   Any combination of dissonant intervals is permitted between the beats. Garlandia's only stipulation is that a dissonant tone "fit in melodically with the preceding and following tones in the manner of some ornament"; in other words, vertical, between-the-beat dissonance is largely controlled by horizontal melodic considerations.

Harmonic rhythm.   One of the important functions of the tenor—part of its role as foundation mentioned by Grocheo—is to establish the series of discant sonorities that will control the upper-voice motion, inasmuch as it is, with rare exceptions, the lowest voice. By "arranging" (to use Grocheo's term) a given borrowed melody now in fifth mode, now in first, second, or third, or in a rhythmic pattern incorporating one of the latter modes with fifth, greatly changed sequences of discant sonorities can be set up. Example 10-2 demonstrates the variety of intervallic progressions possible through the rhythmic rearrangement of the same cantus firmus. Determining an intervallic sequence is, in effect, the initial stage of composition, one that will determine the field through which the upper voices will move.

Since the discant sonority tends to change on each beat, the early motet moves in what may be called (to borrow modern terminology) a rapid but undirected harmonic movement.

Tonality

We have already noted the general inapplicability of the church modes to polyphonic writing. This inapplicability is made even more evident when contemplating the motet repertoire; as the tenor is only a melismatic segment of a longer chant, it seldom displays the modality of the complete chant and may be modally ambiguous within itself. Furthermore, the upper voices may not relate to whatever modality the tenor may suggest and are frequently modally unclear themselves.

Anthology Examples 50 and 52 illustrate the diversity to be found in the motet repertoire. The former is tonally stable much like the versus and conductus: beginning and ending on the "tonic" and constantly referring to it internally. It is saturated with the D sonority and based on a tenor segment with distinct tonal stability—indeed, the tenor is simply a standard modal formula that expresses the Protus plagal.

Anthology Example 52, in contrast, pays little attention to composite tonal unity. Here the chosen tenor lacks a central tone, wandering from c to F. The

EXAMPLE 10-2. Various Rhythmic Configurations for *Et gaudebit* and their harmonic implications.

upper voices go their own way, centering and cadencing on c without regard for the tenor's movement to F, resulting in tonal ambiguity.

Because the tonality is the by-product of the tenor chosen and the choice of tenor is the first act of composition, the tonal instability of much of the motet repertoire can only be attributed to deliberate choice. In fact, the tonally ambiguous *In seculum* tenor of Anthology Example 52 is one of the most frequently used of all thirteenth-century tenors.

THE TEXTS

Thirteenth-century poetry is constructed on the same principles as that of the twelfth, although its application in the motet is different from its use in the earlier forms. Versus, conductus, and troubadour chanson are all musical settings of preexistent poetry. The reverse is true in the motet: newly constructed poetry must be fitted to preexistent music. This is patently so when text is added to a preexistent clausula, or when a French text is written to replace a Latin one. It apparently remains the normal practice in motet composition throughout the thirteenth and fourteenth centuries.

Now the task of the poet is different. He must compose poetry to fit irregular musical phrase lengths that may or may not relate to any logical pattern. Syllable counting of equal-length lines accordingly gives way to a flexible poetic structure where lines of varying lengths are punctuated, as in normal poetic style, by rhyme.

Locus hic terribilis—Te, the W_2 Latin motet formed by the addition of words to the discant clausula *Te* (*Alleluia: Adorabo ad templum*, section 6, Anthology Example 39), illustrates an early stage of this process. Here, a new text is fitted syllabically to the clausula duplum, resulting in a poem with the following unsymmetrical form:

	SYLLABLES	RHYMES
Locus hic terríbilìs,	7	A
Sacrátus,	3	B
Mundus venerábilìs,	7	A
Ornátus,	3	B
Iúbilìs,	3	A
Fundo petre stábilìs,	7	A
Firmátus	3	B
Per longitúdinèm,	6	C
Tenditur fidéi,	6	D
Per altitúdinèm	6	C
Erígitùr	4	E
Spéi	2	D
Habens latitúdinèm,	7	C

Qua diffúnditùr	5	E
Amore próximì	6	F
Et Déi	3	D
Ígitùr	3	E
Ut in hac ecclésià	7	G
Bene pláceàm	5	H
Éi,	2	D
Déleàm	3	H
Vítià	3	G
Et confitébor.	5	I

Another example of the adaptability of thirteenth-century rhythmic poetry to the needs of motet writing may be seen in the newly composed motet *Veni, virgo—Veni, sancte—Neuma* (Anthology Example 50).

The triplum text honors the Virgin Mary, the motetus text the Holy Spirit; the tenor, as has just been observed, is a modal formula or *nuema*. Poetic subjects of newly composed motets need not relate to each other or to the subject of the tenor chant. (Amusingly, the scribe of one manuscript, *Ba*, punningly relates the tenor to the motetus by spelling the tenor chant designation not *Neuma* but *Pneuma*, Greek for "spirit.")

In the motetus of this example, the poet matches the regular eight-beat (seven beats plus a rest) phrases of the first-mode melody with an equally regular juxtaposition of paired lines of thirteen (seven plus six) syllables:

	SYLLABLES	RHYMES
Veni, sancte spíritùs,	7	A
Veni, lux grátiè,	6	B
Veni, reple célitùs	7	A
Tue famíliè	6	B
Pectora radícitùs,	7	A
Pater poténciè,	6	B
Et extirpa pénitùs	7	A
Labem neqúiciè.	6	B
Da nobis divínitùs,	7	A
Pater, sic víverè,	6	C

Subsequently, when the composer extends the phrase length, the poet complies with lines of $7 + 8 + 8$ syllables, followed by a final one of 11:

Ut te Deum cólerè	7	C
Et te patrem dilígerè	8	C
Possimus semper síncerè	8	C
Et superna gaudia possíderè.	11	C

The more irregular triplum begins with nine-syllable lines to fit the six-beat phrases of the melody, then proceeds to a mixture of shorter and longer lengths:

Veni, virgo beatíssimà,	9	A
Veni, mater honestíssimà,	9	A
Esto nobis semper próximà,	9	A
Dei genitrix pía,	7 ⎤	B
O María!	4 ⎦	B
Nos claríficà,	5	C
Nos puríficà;	5	C
Ora filium túum	7 ⎤	D
Pro nobis, dóminà,	6 ⎦	E
Ut cuncta fidélìùm	7 ⎤	D
Terat peccáminà,	6 ⎦	E
Conferens superna gáudià	9	B
Per te, celi regína.	7	E

All indications are that, generally speaking, musical phrase length took precedence over poetic style in motet composition. Yet it cannot be proven that a given poem never influenced the composition of a motet, nor even that poet and composer were always separate individuals, although that is the common assumption. In the same way that many motets display a unity of musical construction that belies a strict interpretation of the concept of successive composition, so the frequent good match of poetry and music displays, at the very least, an excellent collaboration between composer and poet.

Practicum

COMPOSITION OF MOTET-STYLE MIDTHIRTEENTH-CENTURY DISCANT

General Procedures

Thirteenth-century discant places a slightly ornamental upper voice (or voices) above a simpler tenor foundation. All the voices are related through adherence to a basic rhythmic pattern (mode). Typical motet structures have already been analyzed. The following rules approach the subject from the point of view of the fledgling composer, wishing to construct a three-voice example.

1. Thirteenth-century discant is constructed additively upon a plainchant foundation. Begin, therefore, by choosing a tenor cantus firmus and arranging it according to a chosen rhythmic pattern (Examples 10-3a and b).

2. Above this, write a second part in simple discant, harmonizing the beats only (two per measure in this transcription system) (Example 10-3c). This will form a fundamental succession of consonances that need not be interesting in itself and that may use much parallel motion. Although fourths are considered consonances throughout the first half of the century, their use was much more variable than the fifth. Accordingly, it is simplest to follow the later thirteenth-century practice and use only the unison, fifth, and octave as discant tones. On-the-beat thirds are rare (normally one or two per composition).

3. Add a simple two-note-per-measure discant in the triplum to complement the melodic outline of the motetus (Example 10-3d). Contrary motion with the motetus is best, but parallel motion is acceptable, especially when contrary motion with tenor results. The interval of the octave is seldom exceeded between the tenor and the highest voice with the result that voice crossing is mandatory and an essential part of the style. Either the unison or the fifth may be doubled (and octave omitted) when it is desirable to keep the voices close.

4. Following the outlined discant structure, ornament the upper voices in a simple first mode pattern, leaving occasional offbeat rests in appropriate places to create an interesting phrase structure. Common melodic procedures include passing tones, neighboring tones, escape tones, anticipations, and skips of a third (Example 10-3e). Notation should always be such as to show the underlying modal structure: thus ♩♪ , not ♫♩ ; ♫♪ , not ♫♩ .

5. Notes between beats may be dissonant, but should be constructed in such a way as to logically resolve into the next consonance with a graceful melodic motion. The motet and clausula examples in the Anthology should be studied in this regard. Common resolutions are a sixth outward to an octave, a seventh inward to a fifth, a third to either a fifth or a unison:

Occasional parallel motion may be used, including parallel perfect intervals.

6. Embellish the first-mode rhythms of the upper voices with faster melodic motion to make an interesting and finished composition (Example 10-3f). These faster rhythms were very stereotyped in the thirteenth century, the only acceptable patterns being:

It is at this final stage of melodic working-out that one may wish to alter some of the basic discant structure to make a more melodically interesting composition. This would illustrate the process of trial and error and of experience on the part of the medieval composer in handling musical material.

Melodic Considerations

The above rules will give an approximation of midthirteenth-century discant style and structure. A more authentic effort will take account of the specific characteristics of thirteenth-century melodic style. These are best learned through study and performance of the music itself, but may be approached through the earlier comments on melodic style, which are only summarized here:

1. Melodic motion is basically stepwise, relieved through the occasional introduction of thirds and fourths. Larger skips are extremely rare, except between phrases.

2. Most melodic motion tends to descend. Rising passages do occur, but tend to be contained and counterbalanced within the phrase. The tendency to descend applies in an even stronger way to semibreve ornamental figures (♪♪♪ , ♪♪ and ♪♪♪), which are overwhelmingly descending in nature.

3. The melodic range of the individual phrase is most often a fifth or a sixth, although it may vary from a second to an eleventh.

4. The melodic phrase, whatever its internal shape, tends to end on the beginning tone or within a second above or below it almost half of the time. Of the remaining instances almost half will end a fourth or more lower.

5. Phrase lengths typically vary within each voice, and the upper-voice phrases generally overlap each other (and the tenor), creating an overall sense of continuity.

6. Voice crossing between the upper voices (and occasionally the tenor) is normal and further serves to nullify the individual melodic characteristic of each voice.

Assignment

Compose an example of three-voice, midthirteenth-century discant in the style of a textless motet. Use one of the tenor melodies of Example 10-4, arranging it in one of the tenor rhythm patterns given. The melodies of chants 3, 4, and 5 should be repeated in order to give the motet proper length.

Rhythms: 1. ♩. ♩ ⁊ | ♩ ♪ ♩ ⁊
           2. ♩ ♪ ♩ ♩ ⁊ | ♩. ♩ ⁊
           3. ♩ ♪ ♩ ⁊ | ♩ ♪ ♩ ⁊

EXAMPLE 10-3. Thirteenth-Century Discant Construction.

Tenors:

1.   Virgo.

2.   Regnat

3.   Eius.

4.   Portare.

5.   Et gaudebit.

EXAMPLE 10-4.   Tenors for Discant Composition.

BIBLIOGRAPHY

Music

A complete edition of all known continental motets prior to *Mo*, in all known versions, is available in Hans Tischler's massive *The Earliest Motets (to Circa 1270): A Complete Comparative Edition*, 3 vol. (New Haven: Yale University Press, 1982). The related analytical material is contained in Tischler, *The Style and Evolution of the Earliest Motets (to Circa 1270)*, Musicological Studies 40, 3 vol. (Henryville, Pa.: Institute of Medieval Music, 1985). Of the earliest group of manuscripts, the motets of only two have been transcribed separately: those of W_2, with translations and commentary, in Gordon A. Anderson, *The Latin Compositions in Fascicles VII and VIII of the Notre Dame Manuscript Wolfenbüttel Helmstadt 1099 (1206)*, Musicological Studies 24, 2 vol. (Brooklyn: Institute of Mediaeval Music, 1968), and *MüA* in Luther Dittmer, *A*

Central Source of Notre Dame Polyphony, PMMM 3 (Brooklyn: Institute of Mediaeval Music, 1959).

Later manuscripts are well represented in transcription: *Cl*: Gordon A. Anderson, *Motets of the Manuscript La Clayette*, CMM 68 (AIM, 1975), with critical commentary in Anderson, "Motets of the Thirteenth Century Manuscript La Clayette," *MD* 27 (1973): 1–40; *Mo*: facsimile, transcription, and commentary in Yvonne Rokseth, *Polyphonies du XIIIe siècle*, 4 vols. (Paris, Éditions de L'Oiseau-Lyre, 1935–39), transcription in Hans Tischler, *The Montpellier Codex*, Recent Researches in the Middle Ages and the Early Renaissance, 4 vol. (Madison, Wis.: A-R Editions, 1978); *Ba*: facsimile, transcriptions, and commentary in Pierre Aubrey, *Cent Motets du XIIIe siècle*, 3 vols. (Paris: A. Rouart, Lerolle & Co., P. Geuthner, 1908; rpt. New York: Broude Bros., 1964), transcription in Gordon A. Anderson, *Compositions of the Bamberg Manuscript*, CMM 75 (AIM, 1977); *Tu*: facsimile, transcriptions and commentary in Antoine Auda, *Les Motets wallons du manuscrit de Turin: Vari 42*, 2 vols. (Brussels: Chez l'Auteur, 1953); *Hu*: facsimile and transcription in Higini Anglès, *El Còdex musical de Las Huelgas*, 3 vols. (Barcelona, Institut d'estudis Catalans, Biblioteca de Catalonya, 1931; rpt. New York: AMS Press, 1977), and transcription in Gordon A. Anderson, *The Las Huelgas Manuscript: Burgos, Monasterios de las Huelgas*, CMM 79, 2 vols. (AIM, 1982).

Theory

For translations of the most important treatises, see Stanley H. Birnbaum, *Johannes de Garlandia, Concerning Measured Music (De mensurabili musica)*, Colorado Springs Music Press Translations 9 (Colorado Springs: Colorado College, 1979); Jeremy Yudkin, *The Music Treatise of Anonymous IV — A New Translation*, MSD 41 (AIM, 1985); and idem., *De musica mensurata: The Anonymous of St. Emmeram* (Bloomington: Indiana University Press, 1990); and Albert Seay, *Johannes de Grocheo, Concerning Music [De Musica]* (Colorado Springs: Colorado Music Press, 1967).

Critical editions of the texts are available in Erich Reimer, *Johannes de Garlandia: De Mensurabili Musica*, 2 vol., supplement to *Archiv fur Musikwissenschaft* 10 and 11 (Weisbaden: Franz Steiner, 1972); Fritz Reckow, *Die Musiktraktat des Anonymus IV*, 2 vol., supplement to *Archiv fur Musikwissenschaft* 4 and 5 (Wiesbaden: Franz Steiner, 1967); and Ernst Rohloff, *Der Musiktraktat des Johannes de Grocheo*, Media Latinitas Musical 2 (Leipzig: Kommissionsverlag Gebrüder Reinecke, 1943).

Readings

The basic catalogue of motets, in addition to the Ludwig *Repertorium* (see Chapter 9), is Friedrich Gennrich, *Bibliographie der ältesten frannzösischen und lateinischen Motetten*, Summa Musica Medii Aevi 2 (Darmstadt: n.p., 1958).

A major summary of the two-hundred years of motet composition is Ernest Sanders, "The Medieval Motet," in *Gattungen der Musik in Einzeldarstellungen: Gedenkschrift Leo Schrade*, ed. Wulf Arlt et al. (Bern: Francke, 1973), 497–573.

Both Gordon A. Anderson and Hans Tischler have written voluminously about the early motet. For Anderson, these studies include "Notre Dame Bilingual Motets—A Study in the History of Music (c. 1215–1245)," *MM* 3 (1968): 50–144; "A Small Collection of Notre Dame Motets ca. 1215–1235," *JAMS* 22 (1969): 157–96; and "Notre Dame Latin Double Motets ca. 1215–1250," *MD* 25 (1971): 35–92. Tischler's articles include "The Evolution of the Harmonic Style in the Notre-Dame Motet," *AM* 28 (1956): 87–95; "The Evolution of Form in the Earliest Motets," *AM* 31 (1959): 86–90; "Some Rhythmic Features in Early 13th-Century Motets," *RBM* 21 (1967): 107–17; "Intellectual Trends in Thirteenth-Century Paris as Reflected in the Texts of Motets," *Music Review* 29 (1968): 1–11; "Latin Texts in the Early Motet Collections: Relationships and Perspectives," *MD* 31 (1977): 31–44.

Studies by other authors include Norman E. Smith, "From Clausula to Motet: Material for Further Studies in the Origin and Early History of the Motet," *MD* 34 (1980): 29–67; Delores Pesce, "A Revised View of the Thirteenth-Century Latin Double Motet," *JAMS* 40 (1987): 405–42; H. Nathan, "The Function of Text in French Thirteenth-Century Motets," *MQ* 28 (1942) 445–62; Dennis Harbinson, "Imitation in the Early Motet," *ML* 45 (1964): 359–68; and idem, "The Hocket Motets in the Old Corpus of the Montpellier Motet Manuscript," *MD* 25 (1971): 99–112.

Poetic theory and its relationship to modal rhythm is taken up in Margot E. Fassler, "Accent, Meter, and Rhythm in Medieval Treatises 'De rithmis,' " *JoM* 5 (1987): 164–90.

Problems and possibilities of performance are discussed in Christopher Page, "The Performance of Ars Antiqua Motets," *EM* (1988): 147–64.

11

The Continental Motet of the Late Thirteenth Century
(ca. 1270–1300)

As we have observed, the development of the motet went through several stages in the first two-thirds of the century, from trope-related to independent, from Latin to French, from clausula-based to newly composed, from two voices to three or four, from single text to double or even triple texts. All of these styles were, however, based on the same fundamental procedure: through-composed upper voices over a usually repetitive tenor, all governed by the rhythmic modes. The final third of the century, however, saw more far-reaching stylistic changes. This involved altered rhythmic procedures as well as moves toward a more unified approach to upper-voice writing and even the use of French chansons in the tenor.

MENSURAL RHYTHM

In the modal rhythm of the first part of the century, the duration of a given note was regulated by its place in a regularly recurring modal pattern. The new *mensural* rhythm of the final third of the century emphasizes instead the duration of the individual note, freeing it from restrictive patterns.

The time of this change seems to have been in the early 1270s or even the 1260s. It is first distinctly noticeable in the treatise of Lambert (ca. 1270–75) and receives its definitive codification in the *Ars musica mensurabilis* of Franco of Cologne (ca. 1280).

New styles did not immediately replace the old, however, for this time, the 1270s and thereabout, was also a time when the final modal documents appear: the last two collections of modal-period motets, *Cl* and the "old corpus" (fascicles 1–6) of *Mo*, and the final major codifications of modal rhythmic procedures, the Anonymous of Saint Emmeram of 1279 (who attacks the new ideas of Lambert) and Anonymous IV in the 1280s. Accordingly we have old and new coexisting side by side, a situation that continues throughout the period, for old and new rhythms are found in manuscripts into the 1310s.

Just the same, the new rhythmic principles strongly demarcate the period and in fact establish the fundamentals of rhythm for all of the later Middle Ages and Renaissance and down to the present. Fourteenth-century writers refer to this period (logically from their vantage point) as the *Ars antiqua* or *Ars vetus* — the older art or older practice. (Regrettably, many modern writers incorrectly apply the term to the earlier thirteenth and even late twelfth century, nullifying its specific medieval meaning.)

The primary musical sources for this period, the real *Ars antiqua*, are the "new corpus" of *Mo* (fascicles 7 and 8) and portions of *Ba* and *Tu*, discussed in the previous chapter. *Mo*, fasc. 7, is a Parisian source with close ties to both *Tu* and *Ba*. *Mo*, fasc. 8, originally a separate manuscript, has an independent repertoire that may be slightly later and of possible French provincial original.

Franconian Rhythm

The new rhythmic principles received their definitive codification by Franco of Cologne around 1280, and his name has been applied to those principles by fourteenth-century as well as modern writers. The new style shifts the level of declamation from the long and breve to the breve and semibreve while simultaneously shifting the level of beat from the ternary long to the individual breve. The modal unit (a ternary long, divisible into three breves, of which only the first need be consonant) remains intact but now slows to the point where the consonant or dissonant quality of each breve is clearly discernible. This development suggests, at least in latent form, a ternary meter in which beats (breves) are differentiated by degrees of consonance and dissonance.

The change can be grasped most readily through the analogy of modern notational equivalents:

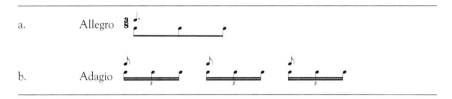

In *a*, the fast tempo places the beat on the dotted quarter, and eighth notes subdivide the beat. In *b*, the slow tempo shifts the beat to the eighth note, and sixteenth notes subdivide the beat. In many motets after 1270, there is a similar shift from long to breve and from breve to semibreve:

Beat	¶ → ∎	
Beat subdivision	∎ → ◆	

In this style the first breve is always consonant and is given a place of importance (and potentiality for stress) not only by the superior resonance of its octave-fifth sonority, but by being the point of resolution of the preceding dissonance. The second and third breves are dissonant or less consonant, the carriers of melodic motion. Thus, by this shift of the beat to the breve, there occurs in Western music the first expression of the potential for accentual meter based on stress and beat differentiation.

To accommodate the new rhythm, with its emphasis on semibreve declamation, Lambert first proposed extending the number of modes to nine to embrace the new fast semibreve motion (his mode 8 consists of paired unequal semibreves, mode 9 of equal triplet semibreves) and then placed the old fifth mode first, stating "it is called the first and correctly precedes all others; to it all the other modes may be reduced and within it is contained the essence of all the other modes." Franco names the new three-beat unit the *perfection* and amplifies Lambert's statement: "And note that all the modes may run together in a single discant, for through perfections all modes are reduced to one. It is not necessary to judge the mode of such a discant, although it may be said to belong to that in which it chiefly or principally remains." Grocheo adds, "To this measure [a *tempus* or time unit] others have added a larger one, which they have called a perfection. A perfection is a measure composed of three *tempora* (time units). This measurement is used by the moderns, and with it they measure all their song in singing and in notation." The three-beat perfection is now a primary unit of measure.

Terminology used to identify the longer note values was simultaneously modified to fit this new concept. The ternary long, formerly considered *ultra mensuram* (beyond normal measure), is now designated *perfect*. The binary long, Garlandia's *recta longa* (true long), is now called *imperfect* (that is, less than perfect). Finally, the breve, which had never been given a precise means of division in modal theory, is now considered uniformly ternary, being divided into three equal or two unequal semibreves, a seeming extension of the ternary subdivision of the long (as shown in modes 1, 2, and 6) into the now ternary breve.

As can be observed in Anthology Example 54, the triplum moves in the equivalent of a $\frac{9}{8}$ rhythm, completely devoid of any reference to the rhythmic modes. The motetus, in rhythmic mode 1, is considerably slower and acts as a foil to the rapid declamation of the triplum. The tenor serves as a rhythmically neutral foundation for the upper voices; other tenors, the majority, retain the rhythmic patterns of the early motet.

Petronian Rhythm

The rhythmic system of the Franconian motet relies on a uniform ternary division of the breve. Beginning about 1290, some motets go beyond this in an exploration of even shorter de facto note values (but without as yet a corresponding change in notation). The original impetus may have come, as is hinted at by Anonymous IV, through the introduction of more rapid ornamentation in instrumental performance. This then may in turn have affected vocal performance: note the alternate modes of ornamentation in Example 11-1.

Whether or not this was the exact cause, near the end of the century occasional fast, parlando passages appear in otherwise Franconian motets, passages that go beyond the normal division of the breve. This new motet style is known as *Petronian*, after Petrus de Cruce (sometimes called Pierre de la Croix by modern writers), who is credited by his medieval contemporaries with the introduction of this style.

As can be seen in *Amours qui—Solem justicia—Solem* (Anthology Example 55), the basic rhythm is Franconian: a fast, nonmodal triplum over a slower modal motetus and tenor. The beat is in the breve, divided normally in ternary fashion. Only occasionally do faster flourishes occur where the breve is divided into four, five, six, or seven semibreves.

The precise manner of performance of these faster flourishes is a matter of conjecture. Late thirteenth-century writers treat the matter with indifference, while early fourteenth-century ones tend to suggest a measured manner of performance, but do not agree on the precise rhythms to be used.

One conclusion suggested by this contradictory testimony is that there were in fact a variety of ways of performing these faster passages and that their exact rhythm was only casually important. It is also possible, moreover, that these flourishes began as relatively free declamatory bursts, with precise rhythmic solutions devised subsequently. These faster flourishes almost always take place over either a rest or a sustained tone on the lower voices, making rhythmic flexibility in the triplum at least possible. A hint that such a rubato may have been used may be seen in the occasional four- and five-breve "perfections" that occur in the triplum of Anthology Example 55 (which is an exact transcription of the original notation) in measures 40, 48, and 60. While these may be scribal

EXAMPLE 11-1.   Alternate Ornamentation in the Motet *J'ai mi toute – Je n'en puis – Puerorum*, triplum, perfections 50-52.

errors, it is also the traditional, and indeed only, thirteenth-century method of notating a ritard, four-breve "perfections" frequently appearing in a single voice in the penultimate measure of a motet, the place where theorists indicate there should always be a ritard (note Anthology Examples 48, 51, and 52, where the original notation is shown above the penultimate measures).

Notation.   The definitive codification of mensural notation was by Franco of Cologne in his *Ars cantus mensurabilis* of around 1280. In his system the length of notes in ligatures is precisely established by the presence or absence of tails at the beginning, end, or both, in a manner that would hold through the Renaissance. Single notes are also more precisely defined. The ternary long, now called the *longa perfecta* or perfect long, could be "imperfected" (reduced to a binary long) by a single breve placed before or after. This imperfecting could be prevented by separating the long and breve with a short vertical stroke or *divisio modi*. The shortest note value, the semibreve, is now precisely valued at one-third of a breve. If only two are written in the time of a breve, they are to be performed in a short-long fashion (like a reduced second mode). Petrus de Cruce added to this the use of a dot or *punctus* to separate groups of semibreves.

This may be seen through a comparison of Facsimile 11-1 with Anthology Example 55. In typical motet manuscript layout, the triplum is notated in the left-hand column, the motetus in the right-hand one, below which, at the ornate capital and the word *Solem*, is the tenor. (In each column, the top line and the *end* of the second line hold the conclusion of the previous motet; the ornate capitals mark the beginning of the new one.)

Notation is on five-line staves with C clefs. The Petronian dots separating groups of semibreves may be seen on the third line of the triplum column, over the words *si me maistrie me fet*. The short vertical lines (as in triplum lines 4 and 6, motetus lines 1, 2, and 3) indicate rests; the longer the line, the longer the rest.

Conservative Rhythmic Style

New did not immediately replace old: fully one-half of the motets attributable to the late thirteenth century are written in a conservative rhythmic style, with old-style long-breve declamation (see, for instance, Anthology Example 53). Formerly considered either English or "peripheral," the fact is that nearly half use French-language texts, a language only used in the central compositional area, and many show such progressive stylistic features as French tenors and isomelic construction (see below). The continuation of this style may have been due to a composite of factors, including a desire for rhythmic variety (modal rhythm results in a de facto $\frac{6}{8}$, mensural in $\frac{9}{8}$), liturgical conservatism in religious motets (only one of the Latin motets in Mo fascicle 7 and 8 is fully Franconian), and peripheral taste, which tended toward simpler, more conservative styles.

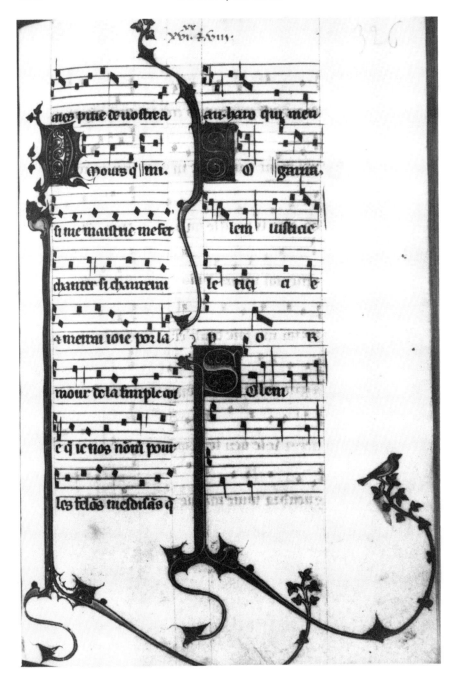

Facsimile 11.1 Motet Notation, Late Thirteenth Century. Montpellier, Faculté de medicine, H 196, fol. 328.

ISOMELIC STRUCTURE

The through-composed upper voices of earlier motet writing gave way in some motets of the late thirteenth century to varying degrees of melodic repetition corresponding to the repetitions of the tenor melody. This technique is termed *isomelism* (or *isomelodicity*). It may be defined as the repetition of significant amounts of upper-voice material over subsequent tenor repetitions. Flourishing in the late thirteenth century both on the continent and England, it could be used as an element in an otherwise through-composed motet or could comprise the entire musical substance.

An excellent example of the latter, a fully isomelic motet, may be seen in Example 11-2. The tenor, which here is printed once on the bottom stave, is performed four times. The motetus and triplum accompanying each of the four tenor statements are printed above one another to show the melodic correspondence. This is greatest in statements 1 and 3, but 2 and 4 also show a high degree of relationship, with an exchange of melodic material between voices. The altered phrase structure of each section creates additional variety.

Isomelism, which may include voice exchange and altered phrasing, can in many ways be considered a sort of medieval variation technique; each stroph or section rearranges the given material and combines it more or less freely with varying amounts of new material. In this motet a remarkable sense of climax is achieved through the alteration of single notes on each repetition: consider the alteration in the triplum of b to b-c-b (measure 6 of sections 1 and 3), the greater strength gained in the final statement of that passage by beginning on low G, the insertion of a high c' in the third bar before the end, and the shaping of that phrase from the octave below.

Isomelism can be found in all types and categories of motet, from conservative to Petronian (for example, Mo 254 has frequent isomelic passages over repeated tenor notes, even though the second tenor statement is altered through the omission of rests).[1] Fully 50 percent of the motets in Mo, fasc. 7 are at least partially isomelic, the range of use varying from the seeming haphazard to the structural (for example, the triplum "refrain" at the end of each tenor statement in Mo 266 and the free application in the ostinato motet Mo 267).

The period represented by the repertoire of Mo, fasc. 7, seems to be the high-water mark of isomelism in the continental motet. Only 30 percent of the motets in the slightly later Mo, fasc. 8 and the added appendix to Mo, fasc. 7, are isomelic, and only 23 percent in the *Roman de Fauvel* of 1316.

SECULAR TENORS

Plainchant tenors continue to make up the great majority of tenors in the period, but evidence of the continuing secularization of the motet can be seen

---

[1]Mo numbers given are those of the published editions of Rokseth and Tischler.

EXAMPLE 11-2. Isomelic Motet: *Plus joliement-Quant li douz-Portare.*
⌐‾‾‾⌐ *Material from the first triplum statement*
⌐– – –⌐ *Material from the first motetus statement*

in the presence of a number of motets based on tenors drawn from the French song repertoire, often in rondeau or virelai form. Unlike a plainchant tenor, which functions to determine the sequence of recurring sonorities, a chanson tenor will usually be equal in range and melodic motion to the other voices, forming with them an intertwining trio of equal voices. It is not a foundational voice, for each of the voices will in turn supply the lowest-sounding note. An example of this is *Tout solas—Bone amour—Ne me blasmes mei* (Anthology Example 53), where the ranges of the three voices are almost identical: F–f for the tenor, F–g for the motetus, and a–a′ for the triplum. The motetus sounds the lowest pitch in thirteen of the thirty-two measures and supplies the final tonic

note. If, as sometimes happens, the French tenors are texted in the manuscript, the resulting form is that of a three-voice triple motet.

The structure of the chanson tenor may be ignored in through-composed upper voices, or be reinforced by a full or partial use of isomelism, occasionally approaching the concept of a motet in rondeau or virelai form. Isomelism may reinforce particular sections (for example, the A sections of the rondeau-based Mo 269 and the B sections of the virelai-based Mo 290) or duplicate the entire chanson structure in upper-voice isomelism as in Anthology Example 53, in the virelai-related form AB bb ab AB. Here the isomelism relates the AB sections, and internal isomelism is used to mark the beginning of the b sections of the verse (Example 11-3).

EXAMPLE 11-3. Isomelic Motet on a Virelai Tenor, *Tout solas — Bone amour – Ne me blasmes mie,* Anthology Example 53.

        ┌────────┐ Material from first triplum section
        ╞════════╡ Material from interior triplum section
        ┌ - - - ┐ Material from first motetus section
        ┌ · · · ┐ Material from interior motetus sections

MUSICAL STYLE

Voice Relationships

Whereas rhythmic layering—such as the placement of a mode 6 triplum over a mode 1 or 2 motetus and a mode 5 tenor (see Anthology Example 48b)—is present in less than 10 percent of the pre-1270 motets, it became predominant in the Franconian motet and exclusive in the Petronian, where a rapid, nonmodal triplum moves over a slower, modally oriented motetus and tenor. Rhythmically equal upper voices are still found, however, both in conservative motets and in a number of motets that in other ways conform to Franconian style.

After 1270, three-voice texture became the norm as two- and four-voice writing disappeared. Only in peripheral areas did the vogue for two-voice motets (many reduced from three-voice originals) continue.

Sonorities

The late thirteenth century marks the demise of the fourth as a stable consonance, and it is now reserved for weak-beat use in the Franconian and Petronian styles and between-the-beat use in conservative-style motets. Strong-beat sonorities are uniformly an octave, a fifth, or both.

Harmonic Rhythm

Motets in the newer styles, with their shift of beat from the long to the breve, operate with a slower, more audible harmonic rhythm than the early motet. A stable sonority on the first part of each perfection leads to a second- or third-beat dissonance that is resolved on the first beat of the next perfection. Typical progressions include a sixth resolving outward to an octave and a seventh resolving inward to a fifth (Example 11-4).

Example 11-5 outlines the governing intervallic progression in a typical Franconian motet. While most motion is from a dissonance or an imperfect consonance to a medium or perfect consonance, parallel motion is still admitted (as in measures 1–2). When a tenor note is repeated (as in measures 5–6 and 7–8), the stable harmony is retained for four or five beats, anticipating a fourteenth-century harmonic technique.

EXAMPLE 11-4.   Typical Intervalic Progressions.

Tonality

Concern about tonal unity appears as casual as earlier in the century. Tonal unity is still dependent on the structure of the tenor melody, and when that melody is tonally ambiguous, the entire motet must remain also.

THE TEXTS

The standard subjects of late thirteenth-century motets continue to be courtly love and the pastourelle in French texts (although a few celebrate the joys of student life in the city) and sacred topics in Latin texts. The new rhythmic style, however, with its emphasis on nonmodal breve-semibreve declamation, demands a shift in poetic technique.

In modal writing the rate of poetic declamation is tied to the rhythmic mode: two syllables to a ternary long in modes 1 and 2, three syllables to a duplex long in mode 3. The rate of declamation is thus steady throughout the voice part. In addition, phrases are short and easily accommodated by single or composite poetic lines.

In breve-semibreve declamation all this changes. Phrases become lengthy and declamation patterns irregular. This may be seen in the Franconian motet *J'ai mis—Je n'en puis—Puerorum* (Anthology Example 54), where the triplum moves in phrases of four to six perfections but encompasses declamation of thirteen to twenty-one syllables:

PERFECTIONS		SYLLABLES
4	J'ai mis toute ma pensee lonc tans En amour loiaument servir,	18
4	Encore veul je bien obeïr A son commant, Ne pour quant Je n'en puis joïr.	21
5	Tant me fait de mal soufrir Cele que j'aim, que je ne sai Que puisses devenir:	21
4	Trambler et fremir Me fait et la coulour palir.	13
4	Souvent plour et souspir, Et si ne me puis de li amer repentir.	16
5	Las! tant la desir Que bien sai K'en la fin pour s'amour me convendra morir,	20
5	S'aucun confort n'ai De li, car trop cruelment M'a fait lonc tans languir.	17
6	Hé! dame au cler vis, Secoures moi, vo loial ami, S'il vous vient a plaisir,	20
5	Car du mal que jesent Et ai senti, Nus fors vous ne m'en puet garir.	18
5	Si vous pri Merci, Car un seul biau samblant, Se de vous le veoie venir,	20
5	M'aroit conforté Et espoir douné De joie recouvrer, Ou je crien fallir;	21
6	Car se pities Ou amours nen veut pour moi ouvrer, Je n'i puis avenir.	19

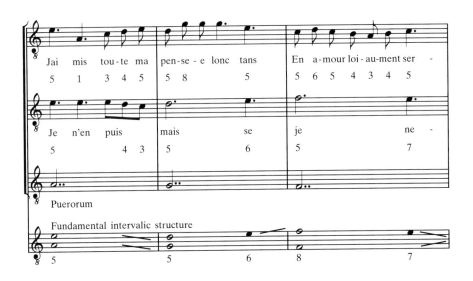

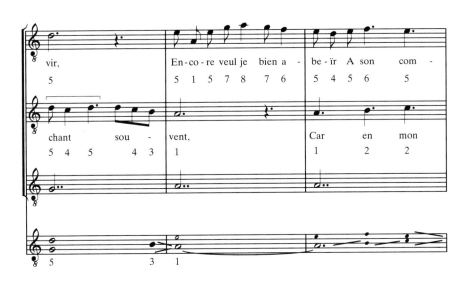

EXAMPLE 11-5. Basic Intervalic Progressions in Franconian Rhythmic Style: *J' ai mis – Je n'en puis – Puerorum* (Anthology Example 54), beginning.

EXAMPLE 11-5 *continued.*

Even greater variance in phrase length and syllable ratio may be seen in the Petronian motet *Amours qui—Solem justicie—Solem* (Anthology Example 55):

PERFECTIONS		SYLLABLES
3	Amours qui si me maistrie, me fet chanter:	11
4	Si chanterai et merrai joie Por l'amour.	12
4	De la simple coie Que je n'os nommer,	11
4	Pour les felons mes disans, (Que Dieus puist grever.)	12
4	Mes en mon chant, Puis que je n'i os aler, Li pri, qu'ele mi daigne ami reclamer:	22
3	Puis porrai ma joie doubler	8
3	Et grant envoiseüre demener.	10
4	Et s'ele ne fet, il m'en convendra toute ma vie plourer	17
7	Sans nul secours Ne sanz nule raen çon C'on puist en tout le siecle trover.	18
5	Ha! bonne amour, par ta franchise, En qui j'ai mon entente mise, Te pri que la vuelles hoster	26
3	Et metre li une estincele De ton	11
3	Feu desous la ma mele Pour embraser;	11
3	Car je n'i sai mellour Avocat en ceste cause trover,	16
4	Ne qui si bien parfaitement i sache proceder;	14
7	Et s'il li plaist, tel guerredon Com li plaira rendre a son gré Sui pres et serai, sanz mesproison Penser.	28

The rate of declamation varies in the number of syllables per perfection, which (omitting from consideration the perfect longs that end each phrase) ranges from three to eight in Anthology Example 54 and from three to ten in Anthology Example 55. It also varies in the number of syllables per phrase, the four-perfection phrases in Anthology Example 54 varying from thirteen to twenty-one syllables, while Anthology Example 55 ranges from eight to sixteen syllables in three-perfection phrases and from eleven to twenty-four syllables in four-perfection ones.

Such long, irregular phrases require a proselike poetry marked by end-of-line rhymes. These long lines may be divided poetically into subphrases of irregular length (indicated in the above examples by capitalization), often, but not always, marked by rhyme. These subphrases have little musical importance, however, as they seldom cadence on strong beats and are often passed over in the midst of semibreve motion (see, for instance, Anthology Example 54, perfections 6–7, 11, 15, and 18, and Anthology Example 55, perfections 6, 16, 17, 31, 33, 46, 48, 59, and 60).

Regardless of the length of the line, the final syllable is placed on a strong beat and is normally held through a perfect or imperfect long followed by a rest. Thus it is longer than the other notes of the phrase, halts the previous rapid motion, and provides musical and poetic articulation, as does rhyme—usually the same rhyme throughout the part, but occasionally a pattern of alternate rhymes.

The contrast between the rapid triplum and the slower motetus is enhanced through their radically different rates of declamation. The motetus of Anthology Example 54 moves in mostly five-perfection phrases in a mode 1 pattern with an extra syllable in the first measure of each phrase. Accordingly it carries a mere 115 syllables to the triplum's 223. In the Petronian Anthology Example 55, with its rhythmically free, mode 3 motetus, the ratio is even greater: 68 to 225. The contrast in length is immediately apparent in viewing the original of Anthology Example 55, Facsimile 11-1, where the first section of the triplum, covering perfections 1–14 in the transcription, takes the best part of seven staves, while the same length of motetus takes only three and a half, and those not crowded.

THE HOCKET

Hockets (see "Hocket" in Chapter 9) occur occasionally in both early and late motets. In the later repertory we also find textless motetlike compositions based entirely on the use of hocket. The tenor carries the cantus firmus in normal motet fashion, while the two upper voices engage in hocket interplay that in effect often reduces the two upper lines to one (a series of seven such hockets occur at the end of the motet section of Ba).

Hocket, already observed in Parisian conductus, may thus occur as an incidental feature in thirteenth- and fourteenth-century motets, or be a form in itself. Evidence also suggests the improvisation of hocket variations on existing motets, and one motet text speaks of imbibing students in a tavern singing hockets "faster than a flute can play."

BIBLIOGRAPHY

Music

Modern publications of the relevant motet manuscripts, *Mo*, *Ba*, and *Tu*, are given in Chapter 10.

Theory

Franco's *Ars cantus mensurabilis* is translated in Strunk, 139–59. The second important treatise of the period, that of Lambert, has not yet been translated, although the important section on the extension of the modal system is translated and discussed in Gordon Anderson, "Magister Lambertus and Nine Rhythmic Modes," AM 45 (1977): 57–73.

The original of the Franco treatise is available in Gilbert Reaney and André Gilles, *Franconis de Colonia Ars Cantus Mensurabilis*, CSM 18 (n.p.: American Institute of Musicology, 1974); Coussemaker 1:117–36; and Simon M. Cserba, *Hieronymous de Moravia O.P.: Tractatus de Musica* (Regensburg: Friedrich Pustat, 1935), 230–59. The treatise of Lambert is in Coussemaker 1:251–81.

Readings

Gordon A. Anderson, "Mannerist Trends in the Music of the Late Thirteenth Century," MM 11 (1980), 105–10. Concerning the conservative motets, see Dolores Pesce, "A Revised View of the Thirteenth-Century Latin Double Motet," JAMS 40 (1987), 405–42; and Ernest Sanders, "Peripheral Polyphony of the 13th Century," JAMS 17 (1964), 261–87.

Text-music relationships are explored in two dissertations: Linda J. Speck, "Relationships between Music and Text in the Late Thirteenth-Century Motet" (Ph.D. diss., UMI no. 77-18124), and Beverly J. Evans, "The Unity of Text and Music in the Late Thirteenth-Century French Motet: A Study of Selected Works from the Montpellier Manuscript, Fascicle VII" (Ph.D. diss., UMI no. 83-26284).

Hocket as a technique and a form is explored in William E. Dalglish, "The Hocket in Medieval Polyphony," MQ 55 (1969): 344–63; and Ernest Sanders, "The Medieval Hocket in Practice and Theory," MQ 60 (1974): 246–56. Other concepts, including isomelism, are discussed in Dalglish, "The Use of Variation in Early Polyphony," MD 26 (1972): 37–51.

12

The English Motet
(ca. 1250–1350)

English music throughout the Middle Ages was related to, and yet distinct from, that of the continent. Although musical activity in the centuries after Charlemagne was concentrated in what is now France and western Germany, England was an important meeting ground for two alien cultures, the French and the Scandinavian.

The earliest trace of English polyphony dates from Anglo-Saxon times, the music of the Winchester Troper of around 1000 (see Chapter 4, "The Sources," and Anthology Example 18). Although incapable of precise transcription, it evidences a use of organum of the Guidonian type, and testifies to a flourishing Anglo-Saxon musical culture before the Norman conquest.

Musical developments in the succeeding centuries are more elusive: a single example of free organum from the late eleventh century (Anthology Example 22), a manuscript of twelfth-century-style melismatic organum of either English or northern French origin (Cambridge Ff. 1. 17)—existing sources from this period are rare.

Although the effects of the Norman conquest of England in 1066 are well known, the Scandinavian influences are more elusive. England was subject, even more than the continent, to repeated Norse raids and invasions from around 800, and to permanent Norse settlements by 850. We know little about their music, but the Norse are believed to have favored the third.[1] At least England seems to have developed a preference for the third well in advance of the continent, and this remains a mark of English music throughout the later Middle Ages.

---

1. A single existing piece of music, possibly originating in the Orkney Islands, north of Scotland, proceeds largely in parallel thirds (*Nobilis, humilis,* HAM, 25c). On the other hand, an Icelandic folk idiom existing into this century, but of seemingly ancient origin, *Tvisongvar* or "Twin-song," moves in parallel fifths.

The early thirteenth century shows a continuation of Britain's position as a cross-cultural musical center. W_1, the major source of Notre Dame polyphony probably copied at Saint Andrew's, Scotland, around 1240, is ample evidence of continental influence. But fascicle 11 of the same manuscript, a complete section of polyphony in a distinctly non-Parisian style, also attests to the presence of a native, insular tradition.[2]

It would have been at about this time that the motet concept spread to England. Although we know from the existence of W_1 that Parisian-style melismatic organum and discant clausula were known in England, there is little trace of native English composition in either style, and no trace of English motets on discant clausulae. Rather, the English predilection, shown in W_1 as well as later in the century, was toward the setting of complete chants in discant style.

THE ENGLISH CONCEPT OF MOTET

The English definition of motet is much more inclusive than that of the continent. It encompasses not only motets in the continental sense (cantus firmus motets), but settings in motet style of complete liturgical plainchants (troped chant settings) and of motets using newly composed tenors (motets on a *pes*).

The Cantus Firmus Motets

Like the familiar continental type, the cantus firmus motet takes its tenor from a plainchant melisma or, exceptionally, a French chanson. The upper voices have individual Latin texts that normally relate to the tenor chant. The texture is three or four voices, two-voice motets being a rarity. The tenor is normally repeated at least once.

Troped Chant Settings

If the English were ever moved toward the composition of melismatic settings of complete liturgical chants in the Parisian organum style known from W_1, there is little evidence of it in the existing manuscripts. What does exist are many settings of complete chants in discant form. Many of these settings are three-voice versions in what could be called a conductus style, with the chant text declaimed simultaneously in all voices. Just as frequent, however, are settings in which the upper voices have independent texts troping the chant of the tenor. These become in effect motets on the entire chant.

---

[2]These English two-voice pieces are in discant style, with the tenors generally set out in fifth-mode rhythm, less often in first or sixth mode. The primary intervals are unisons, fifths, and octaves (79 percent of all on-beat sonorities). The third is more numerous (10 percent) than the fourth (5 percent). Seconds, sixths, and sevenths together account for the remaining 6 percent.

Compositional procedures are analogous to those of the cantus firmus motets, although the overall structure is inevitably affected by the shape of the chant, which generally prohibits the repetition of the tenor melody. The liturgical chants employed represent a much wider spectrum than was the case in Parisian organa and include a variety of texts from the Ordinary as well as the Proper.

Motets on a Pes

A more radical departure from the continental concept are English motets constructed not on a preexisting melody but on one newly invented for the occasion (called a *pes* by the English). A variant of this is certain four-voice single-texted motets in which the two tenors share the tenor function while the upper voices share the same text and engage in textless melismatic preludes, interludes, and codas.

STRUCTURAL TECHNIQUES

Compared to the continent, English rhythm is conservative. Indeed, even the full modal system seems not to have been adopted; mode 2 and the normal form of mode 3 almost never appear. Interest instead seems to lie in richer sonorities, tonal unity, and a more systematic use of isomelism. In the exploitation of isoperiodicity, however, England was ahead of the continent.

Isoperiodicity

The term periodicity is used to denote a regularity of phrase length in a single voice. Isoperiodicity indicates a rational phrase relationship between two or more voices. At its simplest, this regularity of phrase structure can form the kind of corresponding isoperiodicity found at a very early stage in the continental motet (see Anthology Examples 47 and 48a and Chapter 10, "Rhythmic Style"). Whereas regularity of this sort was soon disregarded in France in favor of an overlapping irregular phrase structure, it remained important in England. An example of such a simple corresponding isoperiodicity may be seen in Anthology Example 56, where all sections cadence in conjunction with the tenor phrases.

A more imaginative and artistic use of isoperiodicity occurs at the turn of the fourteenth century. Here, a chosen phrase length permeates most or all of the voice parts, but is offset rhythmically in order to create a structure of overlapping phrases, altering the first and final phrases of each voice.

The four-voice triple motet *Solaris ardor—Gregorius sol—Petre, tua—Mariounette douche* (Anthology Example 60) illustrates this. Notated in Franconian rhythm, it is based on a virelai tenor. After being offset by initial phrase lengths of variously eight, fourteen, and ten perfections, the upper-voice phrases proceed in regular lengths of nine perfections—the triplum and quadruplum throughout, the duplum throughout the first two-thirds. As the virelai tenor moves in twelve- and nine-perfection phrases, the composite design may be charted as:

Quadruplum	10 +9 +9 +9 +9 +8
Triplum	14 +9 + 9 + 9 + 9 + 4
Duplum	8 + 9 + 9 + 9 + 5 + 5 + 9
Tenor	12 + 9 + 9 + 12 + 12

which can also be expressed by the formula:

Quadruplum	10 + 4(9) + 8
Triplum	14 + 4(9) + 4
Duplum	8 + 3(9) + 2(5) + 9
Tenor	12 + 2(9) + 2(12)

A pattern of phrases is established that will create constant overlap—no more than one voice pauses at any given moment. The essential relationship is, however, between the upper voices themselves, and only coincidentally the tenor (unlike the later fourteenth-century continental motet).

The duet motet.   Another idiom in which isoperiodicity becomes especially common in the second quarter of the fourteenth century is the so-called duet motet, in which a pair of texted voices, of equal rhythmic activity and range, although spaced an octave apart, surround a central tenor. *Rosa delectabilis —[Regali ex progenie]—Regalis exoritur* (Anthology Example 62) is typical of the genre. The outside voices move in fast semibreve motion around a patterned tenor in long-breve notation alternating fifth- and first-mode rhythms. All voices move in phrases of four perfections, the outside voices offset by one perfection each:

Triplum	5 + 12(4) + 7
Tenor	15(4)
Duplum	6 + 12(4) + 6

Isomelism

English polyphony uses both simple and highly structured applications of *isomelism*, the repetition of upper-voice melodic material over repetitions of the tenor. In this it goes beyond continental procedures. A simple type of isomelic motet may be seen in Anthology Example 56, a setting of a chant that usually serves as a prose or sequence for the responsory *Gaude Maria*. In typical sequence fashion, the tenor proceeds in double versicles: AABBCCDDE (the similarity of the A sections is disguised by an altered rhythm). The upper-voice settings of lines BB and CC are rigidly and totally isomelic, and the same is probably true for lines DD, although the incompleteness of the manuscript does not give absolute proof.

A far more imaginative use of the technique may be seen in the pes-based motet *O Maria stella maris—Jhesu fili—*[Tenor] (Anthology Example 57). Here, a moderately long, newly composed pes is presented three times. Above each presentation, much of the same melodic material appears, adjusted through the use of voice exchange and combined with a small amount of new material. The repetition of melodic material is frequently varied through the alteration of one or another note or through modified ornamentation (compare the motetus, measures 1–2, with the triplum, measures 9–10). The identity of the melodic fragments is further disguised through the use of varied phrasing within each section: unlike the sectional phrase structure of the previous example, the overlapping, continuous phrase structure here disguises the sense of sectional return.

As with the continental use of isomelism, its appearance in English motets may vary from incidental to nearly complete. In the kind of variation technique used both here and on the continent, voice exchange may be used as an accompanying technique. Only the English, however, go beyond to make voice exchange the basis of a technique in itself.

Voice Exchange

Voice exchange, known since the time of the Aquitanian versus, reached the height of its continental development at the time of Perotin, then became an incidental technique in the continental motet. The English, however, developed it into a major compositional device resulting, by the end of the thirteenth century, in the related musical forms of the *rondellus* and the voice exchange motet.

Rondellus and voice exchange. Although the rondellus is a type of conductus, its relationship in procedure to the voice-exchange motet requires brief discussion here. Rondellus is a technique involving voice exchange between all three voices:

c	b	a	f	e	d	
b	a	c	e	d	f	
a	c	b	d	f	e	etc.

Voice-exchange technique in the motet consists of voice exchange over a repeated tenor:

a	b	c	d	
b	a	d	c	
A	A	B	B	etc.

Both techniques may be seen in the troped *Alleluya Christo iubilemus—Alleluya: Dies sanctificatus* (Anthology Example 58).

Alleluia settings such as this were structured in four sections, the opening alleluia and the verse both being preceded with freely composed introductory tropes. As on the continent, only the soloists' portions are set, resulting in the form (polyphonic sections in italics):

> *Introductory Trope to the Alleluia*
> *Alleluia*
>   Conclusion by the choir
> *Introductory trope to the verse*
> *Verse, possibly with interlinear tropes*
>   Conclusion by the choir
> *Repeat of the introductory trope to the alleluia (or a new one)*
> *Alleluia*
>   Conclusion by the choir

In the *Alleluya Christo iubilemus*, the opening trope is composed as a three-voice rondellus, each voice in turn taking up each melodic phrase. Voice-exchange technique is shown in the second introductory alleluia trope (section 8), preceding the repeat of the alleluia, where the upper voices exchange material above repeated tenor phrases. A similar procedure may be seen at the words "sanctificatus illuxit" in section 4 and "Verus nunc est deus factus caro vere" in section 5, where the composer has taken advantage of short repeated segments in the chant itself to introduce brief passages of voice exchange.

The simple voice-exchange motet.   The voice-exchange motet of the end of the thirteenth century displays a systematic yet simple exploitation of the technique. Typical is the motet *Dulciflua tua—Precipua michi—Tenor de Dulceflua* (Anthology Example 59), constructed on a newly composed pes designed to include the requisite series of tenor repeats. Following the form typical of this type of motet, it includes five repeated segments, appearing here in the pattern AAx BB CC DD EEy, with x and y representing short extensions to the second and last phrases. Above each repeated tenor segment, voice exchange occurs in the duplum and triplum. The first section is textless, as are the concluding measures. The resulting form is typical: a textless introduction, four texted sections, and a short textless coda, all but the last in voice exchange.

The eight-line text alternates between the two upper voices. Equally typical would be a single four-line text, each line repeated along with its music in voice exchange (as in section 8 of the preceding example), or two different texts heard in alternation.

The large-scale voice-exchange motet.   As the fourteenth century progressed, the technique of voice exchange was expanded into two types of large-scale voice-exchange motets, both typically in four voices.

The first type, represented by *Ave miles—Ave rex* (Anthology Example 61), consists of simultaneous voice exchange between triplum and duplum over a pair of tenors also in voice exchange. The motet is sectional (measures 1–15 equal measures 16–30 through voice exchange, and so on), but the overlapping phrase structure disguises the pattern of repetition. Motets of this type typically consist of five sections, each repeated with voice exchange, followed by a short textless coda (measures 92–95). The basic design could be diagrammed thus, with texted passages in bold face:

A	B	**C**	D	**E**	F	**G**	H	**I**	J	**K**	L
B	**A**	D	**C**	F	**E**	H	**G**	J	**I**	L	**K**
M	N	O	P	Q	R	S	T	U	V	W	X
N	M	P	O	R	Q	T	S	V	U	X	W

The second large-scale voice-exchange design consists of four complete sections performed without internal repetition and with the text in one voice, after which the entire structure is repeated with the duplum and triplum material exchanged:

A	**B**	**C**	**D**	E	F	G	H
E	F	G	H	**A**	**B**	**C**	**D**
M	N	O	P	M	N	O	P
Q	R	S	T	Q	R	S	T

TONAL CONCEPTS

Tonal Unity

Unlike the often tonally diffuse music of the continent, English polyphony is tonally unified. This is achieved largely by controlling the tonality of the tenor. When setting whole chants, the entire chant itself provides the unity. When chant melismas are used, they are either already tonally stable in themselves or are adjusted to be so. The freely composed pes is always tonally stable, often more so than the chant segments. A high premium on tonal unity may have led English composers to prefer such tenors.

Sonorities

The third figures prominently in English music, and triadic sonorities are not unusual. The earliest English motet in the Anthology, *O Maria stella maris*

—*Jhesu fili*—[Tenor], (ca. 1240–60), (Anthology Example 57), already contains a number of main-beat triads (for example, measures 4, 5, 6, 7, 8, 10, 14, 15, 16, 18, 22, 24). A sequence of such triads, drawn from Anthology Example 58, is given in example 12-1.

Sixths and tenths are treated as relative consonances in late thirteenth-century English writing, as in Example 12-2, from Anthology Example 59.

All these sonorities become more common as the fourteenth century progresses, appearing more frequently as parallel consonances—see the opening of *Ave miles*—*Ave rex* (Anthology Example 61) and the parallel-sixth passages of measures 4, 8, 12, 16, 20, 24, and so forth of Anthology Example 62. Four-part writing in particular is often rich in triadic sonorities, as their use enables the achieving of a truer four-part texture within a narrow range. (See also Chapter 14, "The English Cantilena.")

THE SOURCES

Because no complete English musical manuscripts between W_1 (ca. 1240) and the Old Hall Manuscript (early fifteenth century) have survived, the study

EXAMPLE 12-1. Sequence of Triads in Modal Style Writing, *Alleluya Christo iubilemus*—*Alleluya: Dies sanctificatus.* Section 5.

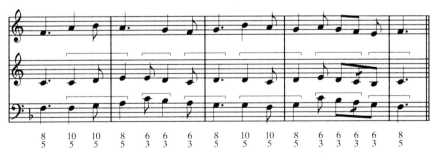

EXAMPLE 12-2. $\frac{6}{3}$ and $\frac{10}{5}$ Sonorities, including Parallel Motion. *Dulciflua tua* – *Precipua michi* – *Tenor.* Measures 45-49.

of English musical style relies on a multitude of scraps and manuscript fragments, many of them having a more or less accidental preservation through their use as fly leaves or binding material in later manuscripts. Recent study (and manuscript rebinding) has revealed many of these oddments, from which it is fortunately possible to draw a relatively conclusive picture of English polyphony.

These small fragments derive from various places and times. The largest collection from one place and a fairly restricted time is the so-called Worcester Fragments, a twentieth-century composite of binding fragments and flyleaves spread among three different libraries. These are probably, if not conclusively, associated with the medieval liturgical center of Worcester. About three-fifths of the fragments may be dated around 1270, a few are earlier, others date from around 1280–1315, and still others from around 1330. They include, in complete or fragmentary form, over one hundred examples of all the forms of English composition then current.

For the fourteenth-century repertoire, the fragments *Onc 362* (Oxford, Bodleian Lib., Bodley 652), *F-TO 925* (Tours, Bib. Municipale, 925), *Cgc 512* (Cambridge, Gonville and Caius College, 512/543), *Ob 7* (Oxford, Bodleian Lib., E.mus.7) and *DRc 20* (Durham, Cathedral Library, C.I.20) are among the more important.

NOTATION

English notational practice is related to that of the continent, but has its own unique features. Its development may be divided into four main phases.[3]

Modal Notation

Midthirteenth-century manuscripts use continental-style modal notation. Declamation is primarily placed on the long, and breves when present are generally bound in ligatures.

English Mensural Notation

English Mensural Notation is in most respects equivalent to the Garlandia stage of continental notation and appears in manuscripts of the 1260s and 1270s. Its special feature is the shape of the breve, which is lozenge- or diamond-shaped (like a continental semibreve), rather than the standard square of the continent. When these *English breves* appear in connection with a long, their duration is clear: ⧈ ◆ = ♩ ♪ . When appearing in pairs they are read in a

---

[3]English notational styles are not included in Apel's *Notation* and in only summary fashion in Parrish. The best current source of information is Peter M. Lefferts, *The Motet in England in the Fourteenth Century* (Ann Arbor, Mich.: UMI Research Press, 1986), 93–154.

long-short mode 1 rhythm: ◆ ◆   = ♩ ♪ . As a result, regular third mode is rare in England, the preference being for the alternate variety: ¶ ◆ ◆ ¶   = ♩· ♩ ♪♩· . English taste is for trochaic rhythms, in distinction to the growing continental taste for iambic ones.

Franconian Notation

Franconian notation did not reach England until the end of the thirteenth century, but became pervasive by the early fourteenth century. Contrary to normal Franconian doctrine, however, the English may have preferred a long-short valuation in groups of paired semibreves, an apparent extension of their similar valuation of paired breves. (For alternate realizations of paired semi-breves, compare Anthology Examples 60 and 61.)

Circle-Stem Notation

This is an English variant of fourteenth-century continental notation, in use by 1330, that uses a dot to set apart breve groups, a downward stem to mark the major or longer semibreve (↑), and a small circle (∘, the *signum rotundum*) or upward tailed minim (↓) to show shorter vlaues. The *signum rotundum* may be seen in Facsimile 12-1, a fragment now in Westminster Abbey. The page represents the triplum of a motet whose first line is transcribed in Example 12-3. The only noteshapes used are diamond-shaped semibreves, a few with downward tails, and the occasional square breve. The duration of the semibreves is determined by whether each group of two or three is separated from the next by a dot or a circle. In the latter case, they become de facto minims.

Breve-Semibreve Notation

Roughly contemporary with circle-stem notation, this notation uses prima-rily breves and semibreves, with few longer or shorter values. In theory, the

EXAMPLE 12-3.   Transcription of First Line of Facsimile 12-1.

Facsimile 12-1. English Circle-Stem Notation. London, Westminster Abbey, W.A.M. 12185, fol. 1, by courtesy of the Dean and Chapter of Westminster.

breve could be perfect or imperfect, but its imperfect form is seldom found. As a result the prevailing rhythm is what the French would call *perfect time* ($\frac{9}{8}$). A double downward tail (✸ , the *cauda hirundini* or "swallow tail") is often used to distinguish major from minor semibreves.

MUSICAL STYLE

Range

Overall range increases as musical style develops. In the late thirteenth-century English repertoire collected in PMFC 14, ranges vary from a ninth to a fourteenth:

9th	10th	11th	12th	13th	14th
19%	9%	22%	25%	12%	12%

The fourteenth-century range is enlarged to vary from a twelfth to a sixteenth (with a single range of a seventeenth and one of a ninth):

12th	13th	14th	15th	16th
9%	22%	30%	26%	11%

This wider overall range permits the stratification apparent in most fourteenth-century motets.

Four-Voice Idioms

Although the norm is three-voice writing, four-voice composition continues throughout the later thirteenth and fourteenth centuries, comprising about 20 percent of the late-thirteenth and 40 percent of the fourteenth-century repertoire. The four-voice writing falls into two distinct categories.

The triple motet.   The first fits the definition of a continental triple motet: that is, three texted voices above a tenor. This type of scoring may be seen in Anthology Example 60, *Solaris ardor—Gregorius sol—Petre, tua—Mariounette douche.*

The double motet with two tenors.   The second may be likened to a double motet with a double tenor, as in Anthology Example 61, *Ave miles—Ave rex.* The two pair of voices are distinctly separated in range. The function of the second tenor part may be simply to fill in harmonically and to serve as bass when the first tenor rests, or it may be of equal importance with the first, exchanging melodic material, as in *Ave miles.* Many times, however, the use of hocket or patterns of alternating rests makes a de facto single voice out of the two, so that a notated four-voice motet is effectively in three-voice texture.

THE TEXTS

The English motet, unlike that of France, but like that of the peripheral areas of Spain and Germany, is almost exclusively in Latin. The troped chant settings are intended for use in the service, and so, apparently, are many of the other motets. The texts, invariably sacred, honor a wide range of saints as well as the Virgin Mary and the Nativity of Christ.

Many motet texts are structured like those of the continent: verses are irregular in length, to fit the irregular musical phrases. Regular verse, however, is associated with isoperiodic motets, such as *Solaris ardor — Gregorius sol — Petre, tua — Mariounette douche* (Anthology Example 60). Here, all three upper voices carry texts in eight-syllable dactylic lines. In the motetus and quadruplum the texts are arranged in uniform four-line stanzas with a regular rhyme scheme (the diagonal slashes indicating musical phrase endings):

QUADRUPLUM			MOTETUS		
Perfections		*Rhyme*	*Perfections*		*Rhyme*
10	Solaris ardor Rómulì	A	8	Petre, tua navícula	A
	Solvit gelu Británnìè/	B		Vacillat alliqúocièns,/	B
9	Mundana corda pópulì	A	9	Resultat set perícula	A
	A scoria resánìè/	B		Post plurima multócièns./	B
9	Cometa cum signíferà	C	9	In insula Británnìè	C
	Dum lucem moderáncìè/	B		Fides olim conváluìt,/	D
9	Dedere dena sídera	C	9	Timore sed vesánìè	C
	Quater in ortu Cáncìè;/	B		Gentilis diu látuìt./	D
9	Que tenebras perfídiè	B	5	Sequacem per Gregóriùm/	E
	Demere flamme fídeì,/	B	5	Tuum pati consúlitùr/	F
8	Quocumque fluctus hódiè	B	9	Per Augustinum mónachùm	E
	Claudent Anglos eqúoreì.	B		Et fidei redúcitùr.	F

The poems' lines of 8 + 8 syllables neatly match the prevailing nine-perfection (eight perfections plus rest) first-mode rhythm, with consistent entrances on the upbeat. Slight adjustments occur at the beginning and end of each voice to achieve the desired isoperiodic structure.

The triplum, which in order to attain the desired periodic structure begins with a fourteen-perfection phrase, requires an adjustment in the stanzaic pattern. This is achieved by arranging the lines in asymmetrical stanzas of five, four, and three lines and by adjusting the rhyme scheme accordingly:

Perfections		Rhyme
14	Gregorius sol séculì	A
	Iovem de cancro Rómulì	A
	Misit in libram Ángliè/	B
9	De medio qui pópulì	A
	Tulit lunam perfídiè./	B
9	Zodiaci per síngulà	C
	Transit sina triphárìè/	B
9	Lucescens sine máculà	C
	De cursoque summárìè/	B
9	Cursu se finxit fírmitèr	D
	Mansurum eternálitèr/	D
4	In gradu Cantuáriè.	B

While each poem uses its own rhyme scheme, certain rhymes are shared: *uli* (rhyme A in both triplum and quadruplum), *ie* (rhyme B in triplum and quadruplum and C in the duplum), and *ula* (rhyme A in the duplum and C in the triplum).

A different and even tighter musical-poetic structure may be found in the isoperiodic duet motet *Rosa delectabilis—[Regali ex progenie]—Regalis exoritur* (Anthology Example 62). Both texted voices have consistent lines of 7 + 8 syllables to fit equally consistent four-perfection phrases, again with adjustments at beginning and end. The isoperiodicity is corresponding rather than offset: the outer voices cadence together, the last note of their phrase corresponding to the first note of the tenor's; the motetus sometimes anticipates the triplum at the beginning of the phrase. The tandem movement of the two voices is made more audible through the refrainlike duet passage in parallel sixths that occur in the third bar of each phrase over the tenor rest.

The triplum maintains a similarity of musical rhythm and a relative identity of declamatory rhythm throughout. The motetus, though less precise, is identical in the second half of each four-perfection phrase. It consistently places a rest within rather than between the text phrases, but varies the placement— sometimes after four, sometimes two, sometimes three syllables.

Rosa delectabilis is as tightly knit a composition as any continental isorhythmic motet, but on distinctly English terms.

BIBLIOGRAPHY

Music

All the relevant complete or virtually complete compositions have been published in PMFC 14 (*English Music of the Thirteenth and Early Fourteenth*

Century, ed. E. Sanders) and PMFC 15 (*Motets of English Provenance*, ed. Frank Ll. Harrison), with a few strays in PMFC 17. The complete Worcester Fragments, including the incomplete compositions, are in Luther Dittmer, ed., *The Worcester Fragments*, MSD 2 (AIM, 1957); through a misunderstanding of English breve notation, some motets are incorrectly transcribed in a simple duple meter.

Facsimiles of the Worcester fragments have been published in Luther Dittmer, ed., *Worcester Add. 68, Westminster Abbey 33327, Madrid, Bibl. Nac. 192* and *Oxford, Latin Liturgical D 20; London, Add. MS 25031; Chicago, MS. 654APP*, PMMM 5 and 6 (Brooklyn: Institute of Mediaeval Music, 1959 and 1960). Facsimiles of many of the fourteenth-century fragments are available in *Manuscripts of Fourteenth Century English Polyphony: Facsimiles*, ed. Frank Harrison and Roger Wibberley, Early English Church Music 26 (London: Stainer and Bell, 1981).

Theory

All English theory of the late thirteenth and fourteenth centuries is based on fundamental French concepts. Notable works are Walter Odington's *Summa de speculatione musicae* (ca. 1300–16), of which the polyphonic portion is translated in Jay A. Huff, *Walter Odington: De speculatione musicae, Part VI*, MSD 31 (AIM, 1973); Robert de Handlo's *Regule* (1326), translated in Luther Dittmer, *Robert de Handlo*, Music Theorists in Translation 2 (Brooklyn: Institute of Mediaeval Music, 1959). Two other important treatises have not yet been translated: the Anonymous *Quatuor principalia* (1351?), Coussemaker 4:200–298; and Johannes Hanboys *Summa* (ca. 1375?), Coussemaker 1:403–48.

Readings

The most complete account of the fourteenth-century English motet, with reference back to thirteenth-century styles, is in Peter M. Lefferts, *The Motet in England in the Fourteenth Century* (Ann Arbor, Mich.: UMI Research Press, 1986). The general repertory has been covered in Ernest H. Sanders, "English Polyphony and Its Significance for the Continent" (Ph.D. diss., UMI no. 65-7472), and idem, "England: From the Beginnings to c. 1540," in *Music from the Middle Ages to the Renaissance*, ed. F. W. Sternfeld (New York: Praeger, 1973), 255–313.

Other articles by Sanders include "Tonal Aspects of Thirteenth-Century English Polyphony," AM 37 (1965): 19–34, and "Duple Rhythm and Alternate Third Mode in the 13th Century," JAMS 15 (1962): 249–91.

Frank Llewellyn Harrison's *Music in Medieval Britain*, 2nd ed. (London: Routledge and Paul, 1963), provides an overview of the entire English contribution to the music of the Middle Ages.

13

The Continental Motet in the Fourteenth Century

The first twenty to thirty years of the fourteenth century were a time of transition on the continent, which saw a realization of the rhythmic potential of shorter note values, a better means of notating them, experiments in binary mensuration, and the exploration of a procedure for musical organization based on isorhythm. Only near the end of that period did a fully-developed fourteenth-century style emerge.

In the deepest sense, this style is a direct outgrowth of thirteenth-century practice. Fourteenth-century writers, whether French, English, or Italian, constantly refer back to Franco as the prime authority in matters of rhythm, and with justification. His valuation of perfect and imperfect longs and perfect and imperfect breves, as well as his means of notating these values, remained standard throughout the Renaissance. Fourteenth-century theorists expanded his procedures in two ways. One was the introduction of the minim to regulate the rhythm and notation of the new, faster motion opened up by Petrus de Cruce's rhythmic expansion. The other was the extension of Franco's concept of the "imperfection" of notes to shorter note values and to "nonadjacent" ones (such as the imperfection of a long by a semibreve). These refinements permitted the notation of all meters and of syncopation.

The second chief feature of fourteenth-century style, musical organization based on *isorhythm*, also developed as a logical extension of normal thirteenth-century tenor patterns. Initially found only in the tenor, the extension of isorhythm into the upper voices came about only gradually; partially isorhythmic upper voices did not become common until the mature motets of Vitry and

Machaut (that is, after 1330), and complete isorhythm became standard only after 1360.

This fourteenth-century style, labeled the *ars nova*, is one that modern writers have tended to set in opposition to the thirteenth-century *ars antiqua*, the former being a revolutionary departure from the latter. The music itself and contemporary theoretical writings, however, do not support that concept. Instead, theorists of the first half of the century discuss an ars antiqua or *ars vetus* (old practice) and an ars nova (new practice) less as opposites than as practical matters that a musician must understand in order to perform two different repertories: that of the ars antiqua based on declamation on the breve and semibreve, that of the ars nova based on declamation on the semibreve and minim.

The propaganda for the new is no more or less than occurs at many generational shifts. Conservative Jacob of Liège of the 1320s, who wishes to preserve the old Franconian System, has his counterpart in the Saint Emmeram Anonymous of 1279, who similarly holds to the old modal rhythms in the face of the then-new Franconian rhythms partially codified by Lambert. In fact, a strong argument could be made that the real revolution in rhythm occurred in the 1270s. The fourteenth century is part of a continuum that had its origins in the rhythmic changes codified by Franco.

It is now apparent that de Vitry's "Ars nova" was not a written treatise of around 1322 but an oral teaching of much less definite dating written down later in a variety of deviating anonymous sources. Nevertheless, other treatises— those of Jean de Muris, Jacob of Liège, and Marchettus of Padua—help set the time of the formulation of the new notational procedures in the early 1320s. The first two report an ongoing debate on the forms of notation and the correct names for the notes: "We have yet to indicate by what figures, signs, or notes the things we have talked about may be properly shown or represented, and by what terms or names these may be called, for at this very time our doctors of music dispute daily with one another about this" (Jean de Muris, *Ars novae musicae*). Indeed, there is evidence that Machaut's earliest compositions may have been notated in Franconian or Petronian notation.

THE SOURCES

There are four main sources for the fourteenth-century continental motet.

1. *Fauv*—the *Roman de Fauvel*, Paris, Bibl. Nat., f.frç. 146; a singular illustrated copy of the satirical story of Fauvel, amplified with 130 musical insertions, including 34 motets. The manuscript, copied in 1316, is clearly illustrative of a time of transition, containing motets of all styles from conservative through Franconian and into what must be called post-Petronian: motets implying a measured style of semibreve-minim declamation, but without as yet a clear notational means of expression.

2. The *Machaut manuscripts,* a group of manuscripts devoted to the complete works, musical and literary, of Machaut. The major ones are:

A	Paris, Bib. Nat., f.frç.	1584
B	"	1585
C	"	1586
E	"	9221
F–G	"	22545–46
M	"	843
Vg	New York, Wildenstein & Co.	no number

These manuscripts are unique among medieval manuscripts in appearing to have been compiled under Machaut's direct supervision and to place the compositions in a generally chronological sequence: they seem to represent the composer's deliberate effort to order and preserve his work.

3. *Iv*—Ivrea, Biblioteca Capitolare, MS without shelfmark. A manuscript of around 1365 containing motets, Mass movements, and chansons. Its thirty-seven motets range in date from the late thirteenth century to the time of copying. Its origin is in Piemonte in northern Italy, at that time ruled by the French-speaking counts of Savoy.

4. *Ch*—Chantilly, Musée Condé 564 (formerly 1047). A manuscript of aristocratic origin, very likely from the court of Foix-Béarn in southwestern France. The repertoire has strong connections with that court and those of Aragon and Navarre in Spain and the papal court in Avignon. The manuscript contains ninety-seven chansons and thirteen motets, two of which also appear in *Iv*. The manuscript was copied around 1393–95 and contains a repertoire dating largely from after 1370.

THE COMPOSERS

Even though many composers and musicians are named in poetry and song texts, most fourteenth-century music remains anonymous. Specific attributions began to become common only at the end of the century. Of those composers whose works we know, two dominant figures stand out.

The first, Philippe de Vitry (1291–1361), played an important part in the early establishment of concepts leading to isorhythm. The anonymous *Les Règles de la Seconde Rhétorique* states: "Philippe de Vitry . . . discovered the manner of motets and of ballades and of lais and of simple rondeaux and, in the area of music, found out the four prolations and red notes and the novelty of proportions." He studied at the University of Paris where he attained a Master of Arts. Although he held various church positions, his primary area of activity was with the French court, where he acted as secretary and adviser to three kings: Charles IV, Philippe VI, and Jean II. He became bishop of Meaux in 1351, ten years before his death. We have no trace of his "ballades, lais, and rondeaux," and only a few motets survive (published in PMFC I, although the authorship of the *Fauvel* motets attributed to him therein is not universally accepted).

The second composer, Guillaume de Machaut (ca. 1300–1377), dominates the middle of the century, excelling as poet and musician in all forms of music. Born in or near Rheims, he became secretary to John of Luxembourg, king of Bohemia, in 1323 and remained in his service, through expeditions to Italy, Poland, and Lithuania, until the king's death in 1346. In the meantime, however, Machaut had been awarded the position of canon at Rheims, and he settled there permanently about 1340, continuing nevertheless to serve some of the highest nobility in France from time to time until his death. In 1361 he was awarded the signal honor of being visited in his own home by the future king Charles V. His bittersweet romance with the nineteen-year-old Peronne when in his sixties led to the autobiographical poem *Voir dit*. Machaut wrote in all of the current styles of the day and was renowned as a poet as well as a musician. His twenty-four motets range in style from that of the late thirteenth century to fully isorhythmic.

NOTATION

The primary advance that made the notation of more intricate rhythms possible was the invention of a note value shorter than the semibreve. Fourteenth century musicians expanded the Franconian relationship of the long, breve, and semibreve by analogy into the shorter note value of the minim (♩).

Expansion of the Franconian doctrine of perfection and imperfection provided the means for showing all varieties of duple and triple meter, syncopation, and crossrhythms. The basic concepts, which underlie Renaissance notation as well, are briefly described below.

1. The relationship of long to breve is termed mood (*modus*) and may be perfect (ternary) or imperfect (binary):

    Perfect mood   ¶ = ■ ■ ■
    Imperfect mood ¶ = ■ ■

2. The relationship of breve to semibreve is called time (*tempus*) and may likewise be perfect or imperfect:

    Perfect time   ■ = ◆ ◆ ◆
    Imperfect time ■ = ◆ ◆

3. The relationship of semibreve to minim is known as prolation (*prolatio*) and may be major (ternary) or minor (binary):

    Major prolation ◆ = ♩ ♩ ♩
    Minor prolation ◆ = ♩ ♩

Through the interrelationship of these different values, several metrical schemes may be shown:

Perfect time, major prolation = $\frac{9}{8}$

Perfect time, minor prolation = $\frac{3}{4}$

Imperfect time, major prolation = $\frac{6}{8}$

Imperfect time, minor prolation = $\frac{2}{4}$

Because the beat lies now in the semibreve, *mood* (the relationship of long and breve) generally applies only to slow-moving motet tenors. In modern notational equivalents, the semibreve may be considered as representing the beat, the breve the measure, and the long a macrorhythm involving groups of measures. In effect, prolation relates to beat subdivision (simple or compound) and time to the number of beats in a measure.

An example of fourteenth-century French notation may be seen in Facsimile 13-1, the opening page of the motet sequence in one of the main Machaut manuscripts. The triplum begins in the right-hand column, directly below the illustration. The motetus takes up the left-hand column and is completed by the bottom of the page. This is not true of the triplum, which takes up over three-quarters of the following page, allowing only four column lines for the tenor. The facsimile should be compared with the transcription in Anthology Example 64.

Red Notation

A special device, used by de Vitry and others, is the use of red or white notes to indicate a temporary shift from perfect to imperfect mensuration or vice versa, often in an individual voice part. This may be seen in de Vitry's motet *Tuba sacre—In arboris-Virgo sum* (Anthology Example 63), in which the tenor is marked, "Black notes are imperfect and red ones are perfect." The effect in this case is a temporary shift from imperfect to perfect mood in the tenor,

Facsimile 13-1. Paris, Bib. Nat. f. frç, 1584 (*Mach A*), fol. 414', reprinted by permission of Phot. Bib. Nat. Paris.

indicated by the brackets below measures 25–30, 49–54, 73–78, 91–93, 103–5 and 115–17.

ISORHYTHM

The fourteenth-century motet is a longer and more complete structure than its thirteenth-century predecessors. Its increasing size demanded large-scale organization. This was found not in isomelism, which was dropped early in the century, but in a large scale rhythmic organization known as *isorhythm*.

The Isorhythmic Tenor

As the end of the thirteenth century approached, the tenor's short, repetitive rhythmic patterns became longer and more complex. By the mid-fourteenth century, they had become elaborate and extremely lengthy (Example 13-1). In the fourteenth century this type of long rhythmic pattern became known as the *talea* ("segment"), the tenor melody being called the *color* (plural *colores*).[1]

In the thirteenth-century motet *Virgo plena gratie*—Go (Anthology Example 47), the tenor melody is presented twice and is divided into twenty statements of the rhythmic pattern, ten per melodic statement. In fourteenth century terminology, this would be described as two *colores* divided into twenty talea or, better, as one color, divided into ten talea, presented twice. This can be shown in abbreviation in the formula 1c = 10t × 2.

With the longer talea of the fourteenth century, each color will necessarily contain fewer statements of the talea (typically two to four). Other, more sophisticated designs are also used. The talea can for instance equal two-thirds of the length of the color, so that the second statement of the talea will overlap the beginning of the repetition of the color:

color	——————————— | ———————————	
talea	————————— | ————————— | —————	

This results in the design 2c = 3t; each color appears in a different rhythm.

A second pervasive technique involves the repetition of the tenor in diminution, making a bipartite structure. The formula 1c = 4t × 2(2:1) indicates that one color, divided into four talea, is repeated in halved note values (a 2:1 ratio); 2c = 3t × 2(2:1) means that a tenor pattern consisting of two colores and three talea is repeated in a 2:1 ratio.

---

[1]Note that thirteenth-century musicians used the term *color* in a different sense, to indicate specific melodic techniques such as motivic repetition, sequence, quotation of a refrain, and so on. See Chapter 10, "Melodic Style."

Analysis of two Machaut motets (Anthology Examples 64 and 65) can clarify this. Taleas are represented by Roman numerals at normal speed and by Arabic numerals in diminution; capital letters are used to represent the colores. In *Quant en moy—Amour et biaute—Amara valde* (Anthology Example 64) the first color (A, measures 1–108) is divided into three talea (I, II, III), while the second color (B, measures 109–end), also divided into three talea, is presented in note values one-third the length of the first section (taleas 1, 2, 3). The result is the form 1c = 3t × 2(3:1). In the motet *De bon espoir—Puis que la douce—Speravi* (Anthology Example 65) the first two colores (measures 1–53 and 54–102, respectively) are divided into three talea (measures 1–34, 35–68, and 69–102). Measures 103–52 present the same tenor arrangement in half values. Thus, 2c = 3t × 2(2:1).

Isoperiodicity

Continental isoperiodicity is distinct from the English in one important respect: the upper-voice phrasing repeats itself not in relation to itself, but over the tenor talea. In the first section of Anthology Example 64, whose tenor structure we have just examined, the triplum's phrases follow a pattern of 13 + 3 + 13 + 3 measures; each phrase is followed by a one-measure rest. This

EXAMPLE 13-1. Typical Tenor Patterns.

pattern repeats over each tenor talea to create the following larger pattern (rests are shown in parentheses, while the plus signs indicate the connection of the phrase to its concluding rest):

Talea I		14 + (1)	3 + (1)	13 + (1)	3 +
Talea II	(1)	13 + (1)	3 + (1)	13 + (1)	3 +
Talea III	(1)	13 + (1)	3 + (1)	13 + (1)	3 +

Patterns of phrases are symmetrical throughout the section, the omission of the rest over the beginning of the first talea being a logical and normal deviation in order that all voices may sing at the beginning of the motet. The diminution section has its own pattern, also repeated over each tenor talea:

Talea 1	(1)	11 +
Talea 2	(1)	11 +
Talea 3	(1)	10

This phrasing and its relation to the tenor is made graphic in Example 13-2, where the three upper-voice sections are laid out one above another. The motetus as well is isoperiodic, but with its own phrase pattern.

The entire motet may be diagrammed as follows, with underlining for the diminution sections:

TRIPLUM

	14 + (1)	3 + (1)	13 + (1)	3 +
(1)	13 + (1)	3 + (1)	13 + (1)	3 +
(1)	13 + (1)	3 + (1)	13 + (1)	3 +
(1)	11 +			
(1)	11 +			
(1)	10			

MOTETUS

	13 + (1)	6 + (1)	10 + (1)	4 +
1 + (1)	11 + (1)	6 + (1)	10 + (1)	4 +
1 + (1)	11 + (1)	6 + (1)	10 + (1)	4 +
1 + (1)	10 +			
1 + (1)	10 +			
1 + (1)	9			

Upper-Voice Isorhythm

Isoperiodicity led to upper-voice isorhythm, the use of identical upper-voice rhythms at the same place in each tenor talea. Sometimes these are clearly

EXAMPLE 13-2.   Guillaume de Machaut, *Quant en moy – Amour et biaute–Amara valde* (Anthology Example 64). Notated with superimposed talea.

(continued)

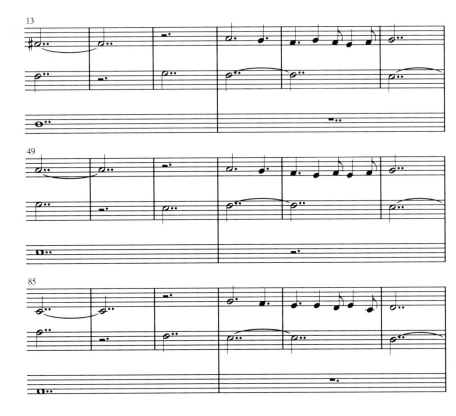

(continued)

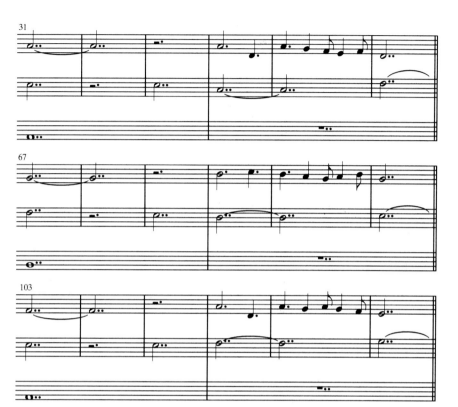

Section II
Talea

audible, as in the hocket sections that occur in measures 22–24 of each talea of the main section and measures 3–4 and 9–10 of each talea in the diminution section in Example 13-2. More often they operate as a less apparent means of rhythmic unification. In Example 13-2 (Anthology Example 64) the triplum is isorhythmic in measures 13–24 and 31–36 of each talea in section 1 and in measures 2–4 and 9–12 of each talea in section 2. Similar isorhythmic passages may be found in the motetus in measures 1, 13–28, and 31–36 of each talea in section 1 and measures 1–5 and 8–12 of each talea in section 2. The upper voices of motets founded on isorhythmic tenors may vary from no passages of isorhythm to complete isorhythm (a *panisorhythmic* motet).

The motet just examined, *Quant en moy—Amour et biaute—Amara valde,* would be described as being built on an isorhythmic tenor, as being isoperiodic throughout, and being partially isorhythmic in the upper voices. Its rhythmic structure is charted in Figure 13-1; phrase lengths are indicated by short, vertical lines, non-isorhythmic passages by dotted lines, isorhythmic ones by solid lines, and hocket passages by x—x.

In Anthology Example 65, Machaut's *De bon espoir—Puis que la douce—Speravi,* the upper voices are isorhythmic throughout (with minor deviations at the beginning of the triplum in section 1—see the schematic diagram given as Example 13-4 below). This is a panisorhythmic motet.

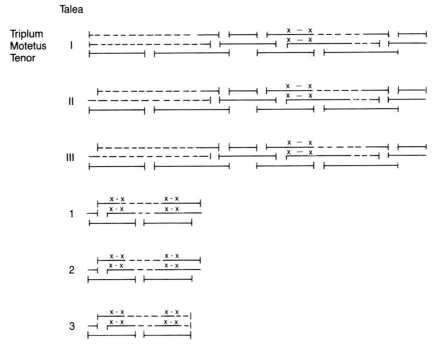

Figure 13-1. Isorhythmic Structure, Machaut *Quant en moy—Amour et biaute—Amara valde,* Anthology Example 64.

The Introitus

A free *introitus*—an introductory section performed alone by one or both upper voices—precedes the entrance of the tenor in some fourteenth-century motets. It may be used as a means of carrying additional text or for purely musical reasons. An example may be seen in de Vitry's *Tuba sacre—In arboris—Virgo sum* (Anthology Example 63). The motet begins with a melismatic solo entrance in the motetus, which is joined by the triplum in measure 7. The isorhythmic structure begins with the entrance of the tenor in measure 13.

MUSICAL STYLE

New concepts of range and of the rhythmic relationship between voices lead in turn to changes in melodic and harmonic style.

Range and Voice Relationships

The composite range of the continental motet, like that of the English motet, expands throughout the fourteenth century. The thirteenth-century motet seldom exceeded a twelfth in range, with the voices constantly crossing one another within that space. Now the musical space widens to approximately two octaves, and a definite stratification of voice ranges occurs, the triplum and motetus lying above the tenor and countertenor.

Similarly, a rhythmic distinction is made between the upper and lower voices. The tenor and countertenor, notated in the traditional note values of thirteenth-century tenors (breves, longs, sometimes duplex longs), now move at a considerably slower pace than the upper voices with their notation and declamation in semibreves and minims. (This is where the concepts of mood and time come into play: the triplum and motetus use only time and prolation, the tenor and countertenor, mood and, occasionally, time.)

Harmonic Rhythm

A slow-moving tenor part changes the harmonic function of the upper voices, for while in thirteenth-century style a new sonority occurs at the beginning of each perfection, now a basic sonority may last six, eight, or even twelve beats. Harmonic rhythm is therefore much slower, and we find the long tenor notes serving, on a smaller scale, the same pedal-point function as in three- or four-voice Notre Dame organa.

Typically, an octave-fifth sonority will be held over most of the sustained tenor note, embellished with numerous neighboring and passing tones, which may result in temporary sonorities including thirds, sixths, or both. Only at the last moment will a dissonance occur that will lead to a resolution on the succeeding tenor note.

Melodic Style

As a result, melodic writing, still basically conjunct, is now controlled by a new imperative, the need to prolong harmonic sonorities over long tenor notes.

Accordingly, the relatively active melodic contours of the thirteenth century are reduced to a far more static profile including much neighboring-tone ornamentation. Real melodic motion is much simpler than the surface rhythmic activity would seem to imply as is seen in Example 13-3.

Fourteenth-century French motet writing is also conditioned by a studied discontinuity in rhythmic movement. While thirteenth-century melody, whether modal or Franconian, maintains a relatively consistent degree of melodic activity throughout a given voice, now melody is typified by a changeable rhythm: passages in quick notes end suddenly in long-held ones, and the voices generally alternate with each other. Upper-voice melodies are controlled simultaneously by the sequence of sonorities dictated by the tenor, the rhythmic phrase relationship established by the isoperiodic structure, and their calculated rhythmic and melodic interrelationship.

Sonorities

Fourteenth-century theory tends to ignore the fourth, now simply classing unison, fifth, and octave together as perfect consonances. The imperfect consonances now include the major sixth as well as the major and minor third. The equivocal treatment of the minor sixth, which was not recognized as an imperfect consonance until the end of the century, bears no ready explanation. Possibly it was because of the major sixth's common function as a sonority resolving into the octave. Odington speaks of thirds and the major sixth as "concordant dissonances" (*concordes discordias*), and fourteenth-century writers continually emphasize the need for resolution.

Practical sources seem to make no distinction between the two types of sixths, however, and treatises of the second half of the century specifically accept progressions of parallel thirds or sixths without specifying the species of sixth. Analysis of the repertoire still shows the fifth and octave as fundamental. Thirds and sixths appear as embellishing sonorities particularly on weak beats, less often on strong.

Four-Voice Writing

Although the standard texture continues to be the three-voice double motet, four-voice writing becomes increasingly common as the century progresses. Invariably it consists of texted triplum and motetus and untexted tenor and countertenor. The pairs of texted and untexted voices are stratified by

EXAMPLE 13-3.   Melody and Skeletal Outline of Triplum, Machaut, *Quant en moy –*
Amour et biaute – Amara valde (Anthology Example 64), measures 1-18.

range and degree of rhythmic activity. Unlike the countertenor of some English
motets, which may occasionally share in the tenor's melodic material (as in the
voice-exchange motets), the additional tenor in the continental motet serves
instead to enrich the sonority, to assume the lower note when the tenor rests,
or sometimes to partake in a composite isorhythmic structure.

The Solus Tenor

A *solus tenor,* occasionally found in continental and English manuscripts, is a substitute tenor derived from the usual tenor-countertenor pair by following whichever is the lower voice at a given moment (see Anthology Example 67). It retains the original pair's function as a tonal substructure for the upper voices, but obscures the rhythmic interplay and, often, isorhythm of the original. Its exact purpose—whether for optional three-voice performance, or as an aid in composition or rehearsal—is unclear.

THE TEXTS

In the late thirteenth century, progressive rhythmic tendencies were associated almost exclusively with the French-language motet. Beginning with the Fauvel manuscript, this is reversed: it is the Latin motet that has ascendancy in the fourteenth century, only Machaut displaying a continued preference for French love texts. French texts drop from 70 percent in *Mo,* fasc. 7 and 8, to 12 percent in *Fauv,* rise to 65 percent with Machaut, then fall to 41 percent in the Ivrea Codex of around 1365 and 23 percent in the end-of-century Chantilly manuscript. (The decline of French love texts in the motet is coincident with, and probably caused by, the rise of a new genre, the French polyphonic chanson, as the vehicle for the expression of the sentiments of courtly love.)

The Latin motet is now, however, no longer exclusively sacred, but has become a medium for expressing political, admonitory, laudatory, and devotional sentiments.

The profound change in motet structure that typifies the fourteenth century brought with it a move away from the asymmetrical versification required in the thirteenth. Somewhat parallel to what has been observed in the English motet, rigid musical structure invites poetic regularity. The isoperiodic and isorhythmic structures of the fourteenth-century motet are accompanied a great extent by texts in regular poetic forms.

One important holdover, however, from the Petronian and Franconian motet is the relative length of triplum and motetus texts. The triplum poem is often two or three times as long as that of the motetus, even though now there is much less rhythmic disparity between the two voices. As a result, triplum declamation tends to be largely syllabic while that of the motetus is neumatic or even melismatic.

The complex relationship of text and music may be observed in Machaut's motet *Quant en moy—Amour et biaute—Amara valde* (Anthology Example 64), which we have already seen to be isoperiodic and partially isorhythmic, including hocket sections.

The triplum sets a lengthy text of three identical eleven-line stanzas followed by three three-line segments or *terzets.* (In this and the following, / is used to indicate end-of-line rests, | to indicate interruptions by hocket.)

TALEA		RHYME
I	Quant en moy vint premierement	A
	Amours, si tres doucettement	A
	Me vost mon cuer enamourer	B
	Que d'un resgart me fist present,/	A
	Et tres amoureus sentement/	A
	Me donna aveuc doulz penser,/	B
	Espoir/	C
	D'avoir/	C
	Merci sans refuser.	B
	Mais onques entout mon vivant/	A
	Hardement ne me vost donner;/	B
II	Et si me fait en desirant	A
	Penser si amoureusement	A
	Que, par force de desirer,	B
	Ma joie convient en tourment/	A
	Muer, se je n'ay hardement./	A
	Las! et je n'en puis recouvrer,/	B
	Qu'amours/	D
	Secours/	D
	Ne me wet nul prester	B
	Qui en ses las si durement/	A
	Me tient que n'en puis eschaper;/	B
III	Ne je ne weil, qu'en attendant	A
	Sa grace je weil humblement	A
	Toutes ces doleurs endurer.	B
	Et s'Amours loyal se consent/	A
	Que ma douce dame au corps gent/	A
	Me weille son ami clamer,/	B
	Je scay/	E
	De vray/	E
	Que aray, sans finer,/	B
	Joie qu'Amours a fin amant/	A
	Doit pour ses maus guerredonner./	B
1	Mais | elle attent trop | longuement	A
	Et j'aimme si follettement/	A
	Que je n'oze | merci rouver,/	B
2	Car | j'aim mieus vivre | en esperant	A
	D'avoir merci | procheinnement/	A
	Que refus me veigne tuer./	B
3	Et | pour ce di en | souspirant:	A
	Grant folie est de tant amer	B
	Que | de son doulz face on | amer./	B

On the surface, the poem coincides with the motet structure. Each eleven-line stanza matches a talea in the main part of the motet; each terzet, a talea in the diminution section. Two-syllable lines in part 1 neatly match the recurring hocket sections, but in part 2 these sections fall in the middle of the poetic lines. Also, the initial six lines of stanzas 2 and 3 make a poor syntactical fit with the 4 + 1 + 1 musical division of the three stanzas. The poem thus loses part of its symmetry and its distinct pattern of rhyme. Note the pattern when the first stanza is printed as sung:

Quant en moy vint premierement Amours, si tres doucettement Me vost mon cuer
    enamourer Que d'un resgart me fist present,/
Et tres amoureus sentement/
Me donna aveuc doulz penser,/
Espoir/
D'avoir/
Merci sans refuser. Mais onques entout mon vivant/
Hardement ne me vost donner;/

In broad terms, the musical and poetic forms reinforce each other, but this is frequently not so in matters of detail, when musical considerations take precedence over poetic ones. This is even more apparent in the construction of the motetus, whose text is strikingly shorter than that of the triplum: 99 syllables against 303:

TALEA		RHYME
I	Amour et biaute parfaite/	A
	Doubter./	B
	Celer/	B
	Me font parfaitement/	C
II	Et vrais desirs, qui m'a faite/	A
	De vous/	D
	Cuer doulz,/	D
	Amer sans finement./	C
III	Et quant j'aim si finement,/	C
	Merci/	E
	Vous pri,/	E
	Car elle me soit faite,/	A
1	Sans | vo- | stre honnour amenrir,/	F
	Car | j'aim mieus einssi languir/	F
2	Et | mo- | rir s'il vous agree,/	G
	Que | par moy fust empiree/	G
3	Vo- | stre | honnour, que tant desir,	F
	Ne de fait ne | de | pensee./	G

The shortness of the poem dictates a melismatic setting for the first part of the motet, with at least a full measure, sometimes two or three, per syllable. Even then, space must be filled up with textless melismatic passages after the first and fourth line of each section, a procedure that is unique to this motet. Hocket sections and the pair of two-syllable lines are neatly synchronized. The section in diminution, which has a greater ratio of syllables to notes, is partly syllabic, partly melismatic, but with the hocket rhythms breaking up not just text lines but words themselves: *vo-|stre, mo-|rir.*

Egidius de Murino is the only contemporary theorist to discuss music-text relationships in the motet. His brief treatise *Tractatus cantus mensurabilis* dates from midcentury (Coussemaker 3:124–28). There his explanation is very general: divide the text and the music into four parts, and apply the corresponding part of the text to the corresponding part of the music. Often dismissed as trivial, his explanation does nevertheless have relevance when considered in terms of applying a distinct segment of the poem to a distinct section of the music as established by the talea structure. This seems to have been the ideal throughout the century, although not always achieved in practice.

It is missing, for instance, in the motetus of de Vitry's *Tuba sacre — In arboris — Virgo sum* (Anthology Example 63). Each talea begins within a phrase, and often within a word. Even though the poem is regular in structure, the number of syllables applied to each talea fluctuates widely:

TALEA		SYLLABLES	RHYME	SYLLABLES
		per line		*per talea*
I	In arboris empiro prospere	10	A	27
	Virginatas sedet puerpere	10	A	
	Mediatrix fides in			
II	medio	10	B	21
	Cum stipite cecata ratio/	10	B	
	In-|-secuta septem soror-			
III	ibus	10	C	17
	Sophismata sua foventibus/	10	C	
	Hec|ut scandat dum			
1	magis nititur|	10	D	8
	Debili-			
2	tas ramorum frangitur|	10	D	13
	Petat ergo fide-			
3	i dexteram	10	E	14
	Vel eternum nitetur perperam./	10	E	

The application of text to music was a variable procedure in the fourteenth-century motet.

THE MOTET IN ITALY

Although the chief thrust of continental motet composition was in France, Italy played a significant role as well, although the evidence indicates that most of the repertoire has been lost. French polyphonic concepts and theory were known in northern Italy and Rome in the thirteenth century, but we have no trace of Italian motet composition until the beginning of the following century. Then the repertoire varies from re-creations of thirteenth-century idioms to pieces in conservative fourteenth-century style.

Of those datable to the first half of the century on the basis of manuscript transmission, four appear in *lauda* manuscripts along with a few motets of late thirteenth-century French origin. These (PMFC 12, nos. 32–34 and 36, and the similar no. 35) are all modally oriented (for example, nos. 33 and 36 in mode 3 and no. 34 in mode 4). Nos. 33 and 34 are in two voices, and no. 35 displays the identical upper-voice texts and primitive isoperiodicity of a single-texted three-voice motet. None are isorhythmic, although some tenors have longer rhythmic patterns: no. 32 sets out the tenor in four patterns of 8 + 7 longs, separated by a long rest; no. 33 uses an 11 + 13 + 8 pattern, presented three times. In all cases the tenor's rhythmic pattern coincides with the color.

Two other early motets, however, nos. 37 and 38 in PMFC 12, make conservative use of tenor isorhythm. The first, by Marchettus of Padua, has a tenor isorhythm of 1c = 3t × 2, plus a short closing section, but without the use of diminution. No. 38, a ceremonial motet in honor of the transference of the bones of Saint Stephen to Venice, precedes each section of the motet with a non-isorhythmic *introitus* divided between the three upper voices, each singing monophonically in turn. Both motets use colorful and surprising harmonies.

A three-voice Sanctus trope in which the triplum and motetus share a troped text over the complete untroped melody and text in the tenor, is reminiscent of similar settings by the English, but partakes of a madrigal style and texture (see Chapter 16, "The Madrigal").

The remaining two motets date from the very end of the century. PMFC 12, nos. 41 and 43 are isorhythmic, no. 41 completely, no. 43 in the upper voices only.

A FIFTEENTH-CENTURY EPILOGUE

The motet style described in this chapter continued, with new refinements, into the early years of the fifteenth century, a time when medieval techniques were merging with those that would form the Renaissance. In this period of opposing styles, the grand ceremonial motet marks the waning of the Middle Ages. Thereafter its techniques become merged with others to form the supreme genre of Renaissance music, the cantus-firmus Mass.

The final group of cantus firmus–based motet manuscripts dates from the early fifteenth century: the Old Hall manuscript of England; the French-Cypriot repertoire of Turin, Bibli. Naz. J. II. 9; the motets of the Flemish-born, Italian-resident Ciconia; and the motets of Dufay and his contemporaries.

Two primary innovations may be noted here. First, the panisorhythmic motet develops ever larger dimensions with longer talea and greater complexity. Bisectionality no longer suffices, and three and four sections, all related by increasingly complex proportionalities, become the norm. Second, other motets abandon isorhythm to exploit structures built on proportionality itself, a technique that had direct influence on the emerging structures of the cantus-firmus mass. Along with this came a return to isomelism, particularly in the motets of Dufay.

Practicum

ISORHYTHMIC MOTET ANALYSIS

The process of recopying an isorhythmic motet, superimposing each tenor talea, reveals the isoperiodic and isorhythmic structure. In Example 13-2 the first six pages represent the main portion of the motet, the final two the section in diminution (see the analysis of this motet under "Isoperiodicity" and "Upper-Voice Isorhythm").

Example 13-4 illustrates a simpler method of charting isorhythmic structure, ignoring the melodic material and notating only the rhythmic structure. The source here is Anthology Example 65.

Assignment

Analyze a fourteenth-century continental motet, drawn from Anthology Examples 63 and 66–67. A complete analysis will include five points:

1. Complete rhythmic analysis of tenor and upper-voice isorhythm

2. Melodic modality, if any, of tenor, motetus, and triplum

3. Intervallic analysis of page 1:
    (a) between tenor and motetus
    (b) between tenor and triplum
    (c) composite three-voice discant sonority
    (d) types of nonharmonic tones

4. Analysis of poetry in terms of:
    (a) line lengths
    (b) rhyme scheme

EXAMPLE 13-4.   Schematic Diagram of Anthology Example 65, Guillaume de Machaut, *De bon espoir – Puis que la douce – Speravi.*

Section II
Talea

5. Musical-poetic relationship:
   (a) the syllabic relationship of words and notes
   (b) the relationship of poetic line length to musical phrase length
   (c) the relationship, if any, of lines of poetry and the basic talea structure of the motet

The talea structure should be indicated on the music, as should be the basic intervallic analysis. All aspects should be summarized in written form.

BIBLIOGRAPHY

Music

The complete fourteenth-century French motet repertoire is published in PMFC 1 (the *Roman de Fauvel* and the Philippe de Vitry motets), 2 and 3 (Machaut), and 5 (motets of *Iv* and *Ch*). The complete Machaut works are also published in Friedrich Ludwig, ed., *Guillaume de Machaut: Musikalische Werke*, 4 vols. (Leipzig: Breitkopf & Härtel, 1926, 1954).

A color facsimile of the *Roman de Fauvel* is published in François Avril, Nancy Regaldo, and Edward Roesner, *Le Roman de Fauvel and Other Works: Facsimile with Introductory Essay* (New York: Broude Bros., 1986).

Theory

Excerpts from the treatises of Jean de Muris and Jacob of Liège are included in Strunk, 172–90. A very useful compendium of later fourteenth-century theory (ca. 1375) is translated in Oliver B. Ellsworth, *The Berkeley Manuscript: A New Critical Text and Translation* (Lincoln: University of Nebraska Press, 1984).

Concerning the existence of Philippe de Vitry's treatise *Ars nova*, see Sarah Fuller, "A Phantom Treatise of the Fourteenth Century? The *Ars Nova*," JoM 4 (1985–86): 23–50. The presumed text of the "Ars nova" had been translated by Leon Plantinga, "Philippe de Vitry's *Ars Nova*: A Translation," JMT 5 (1961): 204–23.

Readings

Ursula Günther, "The 14th-Century Motet and Its Development," MD 12 (1958): 27–47; Willi Apel, "Remarks about the Isorhythmic Motet," in *Les Colloques de Wégimont* (Paris: Société d'édition "Les Belles Lettres," 1959), 2:139–48; Daniel Leech-Wilkinson, "Related Motets from Fourteenth-Century France," PRMA 109 (1982–83): 1–22; and Shelley Davis, "The Solus Tenor in the 14th and 15th Centuries," AM 39 (1967): 44–58, all deal with aspects of motet writing.

For a concise biographical study of Machaut, with stylistic analyses, see Gilbert Reaney, *Guillaume de Machaut,* Oxford Studies of Composers 9 (London: Oxford University Press, 1971). An overview of compositional techniques, notation, and chronology is contained in Elizabeth A. Keitel, "A Chronology of the Compositions of Guillaume de Machaut Based on a Study of Fascicle-Manuscript Structure in the Larger Manuscripts" (Ph.D. diss., UMI no. 76-15885).

14

Fourteenth-Century Polyphonic Mass Movements

From outward appearances, the fourteenth century should not have been a good time for church music. The papacy, always dependent on worldly powers for protection, grew too dependent on the French and, under King Philip the Fair, fell under his sway. When the archbishop of Bordeaux was elected pope in 1305, taking the name Clement V, he took up his residence not in Rome but in Avignon, in what is now southern France. Although technically across the border from the French territory of that time, there is little doubt about the extent of French influence. Of the twenty-eight cardinals (chief officers of the church) created by Clement, twenty-five were French. French popes, with a predominantly French papal court, would live in Avignon for the next seventy-two years. Later popes tried to steer a more independent line of foreign policy, but French influence remained strong.

As a result, the papacy during the fourteenth century was no longer the strong positive spiritual force it had been in the previous century, a situation that was compounded when, in 1378, two different popes, one an Italian, one French, were elected to succeed the deceased Gregory XI. One, Clement VII, took up residence in Avignon, the other, Pope Urban, in Rome. The next forty years saw the presence of two rival popes until, in 1409, a general council of the church elected a third and ordered the other two deposed, an order that was calmly ignored. It was only in 1417 that the schism was brought to an end, and a single pope again led the church.

Even though the fourteenth century was not outwardly favorable for the papacy, it was not an irreligious time. Religious activity continued unabated on the local level and, indeed, the latter part of the century was marked by several outbreaks of popular religious enthusiasm. Worship continued, and with it a resurgence in the composition of sacred music. Indeed, the somewhat cantankerous Pope John XXII issued a proclamation in 1324 condemning the innovations of fourteenth-century sacred music, with its faster note values and hockets—a proclamation that, like many similar attempts to turn back the clock, had little effect.

In fact, the location of the papacy in Avignon may have had beneficial effects on music, for it placed this wealthy center of Christendom adjacent to the progressive tendencies of France, yet not far from the resurgent music of northern Italy. It became a meeting ground for many styles and, by the second half of the century, had reestablished southern France as an active compositional center, one that was for a time more radical than Paris, its northern French counterpart.

Liturgical composition suffered a decline in the late thirteenth century. Organum and conductus had run their course by around 1240, and although they continued to be sung in some churches, little composition occurred after that time. The continental Latin motet of the later part of the century may have had a paraliturgical use, but there is little evidence of the setting of liturgical texts (although we can assume a continued use of improvised polyphony). The only exception is England, where the entire motet repertoire is sacred and troped chant settings are strictly liturgical.

When large-scale sacred composition was resumed in the fourteenth century, the liturgical emphasis had shifted. No longer was the stress on settings of the Proper. Emphasis now was on the chants of the Ordinary and their polyphonic elaboration. This is noticeable in all of the three countries—France, Italy, and England—that would dominate fourteenth-century composition. While there were national stylistic differences, there is also an overall similarity of approach. These we can subsume under the names motet style, song style, and the simultaneous style.

MUSICAL STYLE

Motet Style

Motet style was most prevalent in France, particularly in the early part of the century. Almost two-thirds of the Ordinary settings in *Iv*, copied around 1365, are of this style.

These settings resemble the motet, with two faster upper voices over a slower tenor or tenor-countertenor pair. They differ in that the same text, that of the liturgical chant, is sung in both upper voices, unless a trope is introduced by one. The tenor will often be freely composed, rather than taken from plainchant, and seldom will be isorhythmic. What is taken over from the motet is thus primarily the texture.

Special cases are *Ite missa est* motets (the concluding formula for a Mass) which are often full-fledged multitexted motets (for example, the *Ite missa est* of the Tournai Mass, mentioned below). Sometimes the classification of function is difficult to determine. For instance, the motet given as Anthology Example 67, with its two texts dealing with matters at the end of Mass and concluding with the words *Deo gratias* (the choral response after the words *Ite missa est*), could be classified either as a paraliturgical motet or as a liturgical piece ending Mass.

In England and Italy such motet settings are absent. This is most surprising in England, for motet-style settings of complete chants from the Proper, both troped and untroped, were common in the late thirteenth century (see Chapter 12, "The Troped Chant Settings," and Anthology Examples 56 and 58). The only motet-like English Ordinary settings in the fourteenth century are a few that resemble the duet motet (for example, PMFC 16, nos. 15, 19, 48, 51–55, 61, 65 and 66).

Song Style

Composers in France and Italy in the mid-fourteenth century began to turn to the newly developing polyphonic song forms as models for Mass composition. In France the accepted song style, discussed in more detail in Chapter 15, comprised a highly melodic top voice supported by an untexted tenor-countertenor pair. By the end of the century this was the predominant texture for mass settings.

Italy also turned to its own song-style settings (discussed more fully in Chapter 16). At first, as witnessed by a midcentury Gloria and Agnus Dei by Gherardello (PMFC 12, nos. 3 and 20), the style was that of the then-current madrigal: a florid melody over a slower-moving, supportive tenor, with both voices texted. By the end of the century, however, Italian taste had shifted from the two-voice madrigal to the three-voice ballata, and to the use of untexted lower voices in the French manner. End-of-century song-style settings were little different from those of the French, except for a continued propensity toward Italian melodic idioms (see PMFC 12, nos. 6–8, 13–14, and 17–18).

The use of a liturgical cantus firmus is rare in song-style settings, unlike the liturgical compositions of earlier periods.

The Simultaneous Style

The simplest of the procedures in use is what can be called the simultaneous style, in which all voices declaim the text in essentially homophonic rhythm. It is another reincarnation of the note-against-note textures of parallel, oblique, and free organum and of the twelfth- and thirteenth-century conductus. Though simple, it nonetheless was different in each country.

In Italy, it is evident in two forms. One, in two-voice texture, retains much of the feeling and sound of note-against-note improvisation. The voices are seldom more than a fifth apart, with frequent voice crossing and short passages of parallel thirds or fifths (see PMFC 12, nos. 2, 11a, and 21).

The other form resembles the thirteenth-century conductus, with three voices, simultaneous declamation, modal rhythms, and even long-breve notation (see PMFC 12, nos. 22–25, all *Benedicamus* settings).

French simultaneous style is generally in three voices, but with definitely fourteenth-century rhythms. Simultaneous declamation and rhythm are occasionally relieved by moderate ornamentation in one or two voices.

The English style is also in three voices, which usually move together in homophonic rhythm. In a few instances the top voice is ornamented, creating a superficial resemblance to the song style.

Italian simultaneous style composition is normally based on a plainchant tenor. About half of the English settings likewise make use of a chant cantus firmus, but place it instead in the middle voice.

MASS CYCLES

In the early chant manuscripts it was customary to copy the Ordinary chants in groups of like idioms: Kyries first, then Glorias, and so on. The celebrants would merely pick a suitable chant from each group for a given service. By and large, the same custom was followed in fourteenth-century polyphonic manuscripts. Only occasionally do those manuscripts suggest a more structured approach, one that indicates a sequence of the five Ordinary items (six, if the *Ite missa est* is included) as a unit for consecutive performance.

Four such cycles, each with some seeming association with Avignon, are known in the French repertory. Named after the present location of the manuscript rather than their place of origin, they are the masses of Tournai, Toulouse, Barcelona, and the Sorbonne (also known as the Mass of Besançon). They are all anonymous and show little attempt to unite like styles into a unified cycle.

The Mass of Tournai illustrates the general procedure. It consists of six movements, including the *Ite missa est*. The Kyrie, Sanctus, and Agnus Dei are in simultaneous style, using modal rhythms and a thirteenth-century notation in longs and breves. The Credo maintains the same style, but in fourteenth-century notation. The Gloria is in a distinctly newer style, with freer rhythms and breve-semibreve-minim notation. The *Ite missa est* is a three-voice double motet in fourteenth-century style with a French triplum and a Latin motetus (both with moralistic rather than tropelike texts) placed over an *Ite missa est* tenor.

Like the Mass of Tournai, the other fourteenth-century "cycles" are mere collections of disparate movements gathered together for convenience of performance. An exception is the unique *Messe de nostre dame* by Machaut. The only known setting of the complete Ordinary by a single composer prior to the

Renaissance, it is in four voices, sets all six texts (including the *Ite missa est*), and considerably exceeds in length other fourteenth-century Mass cycles. As with the Mass of Tournai, it encompasses contrasting styles. The Kyrie, Sanctus, Agnus Dei, and *Ite missa est* are set as isorhythmic motets (although using only the liturgical text in all voices), and each is based on an appropriate Ordinary chant. The Gloria and Credo, in contrast, are in simultaneous style and without cantus firmus, but with melismatic *Amens* in motet style, that of the Credo panisorhythmic, that of the Gloria not. There are no obvious means of unification between movements (the descending scale figure often cited being little more than a melodic cliché of the period), and the mass is not tonally unified (movements 1–3 cadence on D, 4–6 on F).

There is no known occasion for the composition of Machaut's Mass, and it is doubtful that it was written as a unit. It remains in many ways an enigma: a masterpiece without direct predecessor or descendent and for which there is no known exterior cause.

THE ENGLISH CANTILENA

Standing apart from these settings of the Ordinary, but sharing many characteristics with the English simultaneous-style Mass settings, are numerous English devotional pieces. They are characterized by a close three-voice texture and frequent use of triadic sonorities, particularly sequences of parallel $\frac{6}{3}$ (or sometimes $\frac{10}{5}$) chords, and are generally freely composed without reference to a cantus firmus. Like all English music, they display a strong tonal focus and, in their rich triadic sonorities and $\frac{6}{3}$ passages, strongly influenced the oncoming Burgundian style. They concentrate the chief melodic interest in the top voice, though not as much as the continental song style.

BIBLIOGRAPHY

Music

Italian Mass movements are found in PMFC 12, English ones in PMFC 16. The French Mass cycles (except for the Sorbonne) are printed in PMFC 1 and the collected Mass movements in H. Stäblein-Harder, *Fourteenth-Century Mass Music in France,* CSM 29 (AIM, 1962), with commentary in MSD 7. The Machaut Mass is available in PMFC 3 and in Friedrich Ludwig, ed., *Guillaume de Machaut: Musikalische Werke,* vol. 4, revised by Heinrich Besseler (Leipzig: Breitkopf und Härtel, 1954).

The English cantilena repertoire is found in PMFC 17, with late thirteenth- and early fourteenth-century antecedents in PMFC 14.

Readings

For the French repertoire, see Leo Schrade, "The Mass of Toulouse," *RBM* 8 (1954): 84–96; idem., "A Fourteenth-Century Parody Mass," AM 27 (1955): 13–39; idem, "The Cycle of the Ordinarium Missae," in *In Memoriam Jacques Handschin*, ed. Anglès et al. (Argentorati: P. H. Heitz, 1962), 87–96; and R. Jackson, "Musical Interrelations between 14th-Century Mass Movements," AM 29 (1957): 54–64.

The most complete coverage of the Italian repertoire is B. J. Lawton, "Italian Music for the Ordinary of the Mass" (Ph.D. diss., Harvard Univ., 1960). Periodical references include Kurt von Fischer, "The Sacred Polyphony of the Italian Trecento," PMRA 100 (1973/74): 143–57, and idem, "The Mass Cycle of the Trecento Manuscript F-Pn 568 (Pit)," in *Essays on Music for Charles Warren Fox*, ed. Jerald C. Grove (Rochester, N.Y.: Eastman School of Music Press, 1979), 1–13.

English styles are taken up in Ernest Sanders, "Cantilena and Discant in 14th-Century England," *MD* 19 (1965): 7–52.

Part IV

THE POLYPHONIC SONG
1330–1400

Introduction

> Near the tower I saw a garden where there were lawns and fountains, ladies, knights and maidens and a great company of other people, very happy and gay, dancing gracefully. There were no instruments or minstrels there, but only pleasing songs, courteous and pure. When I saw them I rejoiced greatly, and all the more when I entered the dance like one who is thinking of his lady. . . . But I had not danced for long when she sweetly said to me that it was time for me to sing. . . . I replied immediately, "My lady, I wish to do as you bid me, but I know but little of singing. Nevertheless, so be it, as you desire it." And without delay I began this *virelai* called a *chanson beladée*.[1]

It was this kind of luxurious, aristocratic environment, artificially removed from pestilence and war, that saw, in the second third of the fourteenth century, the emergence of the polyphonic song in the vernacular as a leading form in both France and Italy. Although this emergence was gradual and relatively unnoticed, its implications in the field of composition were remarkable. All previous polyphonic composition had been built from the bottom up—tenor, duplum, triplum. This was true not only of cantus-firmus settings, but of free musical compositions. Franco wrote, "he who wishes to write a conductus should first compose as beautiful a melody as he can; then he should use it in the way a tenor is used in writing discant."

All this changed in the new polyphonic song. Here, the typical order is text, cantus (the principal melody), tenor, countertenor or triplum, or both. An amalgam of secular monophonic song and discant technique, this new idiom would survive the stylistic changes of the end of the century and remain a productive style throughout the early Renaissance.

Before the fourteenth century, intellectual and artistic leadership from the time of Charlemagne had lain in countries north of the Alps, and above all, in France. Italian energy, in contrast, had gone into more practical matters, most particularly the development of commerce. Much more so than northern Europe, with its greater territory, Italy had become since the eleventh and twelfth centuries an urban civilization, where nobility and wealthy merchants moved in relative equality. Cities such as Bologna and Venice had capitalized on their strategic position as seaports astride the trade routes from the Near East to Europe to become wealthy mercantile cities. At the end of the thirteenth

---

[1] Guillaume de Machaut, *Remede de Fortune* (ca. 1342), in F. Albert Gallo, *Music of the Middle Ages II*, trans. Karen Eales (Cambridge: Cambridge University Press, 1985), 132.

century, however, there appeared in these northern Italian towns the sudden explosion of artistic activity that presages the Italian Renaissance: the poet Dante (1265–1321), the painter Giotto (ca. 1266–1336), the contemporary theorist and musician Marchettus of Padua, to be followed in the fourteenth century by the novelist Boccaccio, the poet Petrarch, and a veritable cornucopia of musicians, culminating in the legendary Francesco Landini. These musicians raised Italy's artistic expression to the high aesthetic level of that of France.

15

Polyphonic Song in Fourteenth-Century France

France, the home of the troubadours and trouvères, possessed a long history of secular song. Its idiom was universally monophonic; polyphony was the special idiom of the church. This began to change in the later thirteenth century when, in Adam de la Hale, composer of trouvère chansons and polyphonic rondeaux and motets, we find an early expression of polyphonic secular song.[1]

Machaut stands astride the two traditions, for in addition to writing motets, he was a prolific composer of both monophonic and polyphonic song: nineteen monophonic lais, twenty-five virelais, and one ballade, and, in polyphony, forty-one ballades, twenty-one rondeax, and eight virelais. He stands both as the culmination of a centuries-long tradition of monophonic song and as a prime architect of a new polyphonic idiom.

It was during the first half of the fourteenth century that Machaut, de Vitry, and possibly other unknown contemporaries established the style of French polyphonic song, which reached a mature stage by midcentury. These songs were not freely composed chansons, but rather settings of poems in one or another of the newly popular *formes fixes*, whose poetic form gave shape to the music.

Although both de Vitry and Machaut are credited by fourteenth-century writers with the composition of polyphonic chansons, only those of Machaut have come down to us. Only a handful of works by other midcentury composers, remain: a ballade and a rondeau by P. de Molins; two ballades by Magister Franciscus; a ballade, three rondeaux, and a virelai by Johannes Vaillant; and a

---

1. The midthirteenth-century two-voice motet was also moving in the direction of accompanied song; see Chapter 10, "Midcentury Styles."

few anonymous works. Because of the relatively overwhelming quantity and quality of Machaut's music and poetry, this chapter focuses on his songs, with the end-of-century *Ars subtilior* reserved for the end of the chapter.

THE SOURCES

The main sources for this chapter are the Machaut manuscripts identified in Chapter 12. (*Iv* carries a few additional works.) The roughly chronological nature of these manuscripts permits an approximate dating of the Anthology Examples: Anthology Example 68 before 1349, Anthology Examples 69 and 72–74 between 1349 and 1363, Anthology Example 70 between 1363 and 1371, and Anthology Example 71, one of his last compositions, around 1371–72.

The late fourteenth-century repertoire (along with a few earlier pieces) may be found in:

Ch—Chantilly, Musée Condé 564 (formerly 1047), a southern French manuscript originating probably at the court of Foix-Béarn;

MOe 5.24 (Mod; Mod A)—Modena, Biblioteca Estense, MS a M. 5.24, a northern Italian manuscript from around 1410 containing a French repertoire from Avignon as well as Italian pieces;

Pn 6771 (PR; Rei; R)—the Riena Codex; Paris, Bibliothèque Nationale, nouv. acq. frç. 6771, a northern Italian manuscript from the Padua-Venice area of which fascicles 1–7 pertain to the fourteenth century, 8–9 to the early fifteenth.

Repertoire

The relative popularity of motet and chanson may be seen through a comparison of manuscripts. The *Roman de Fauvel* manuscript (1316) has one polyphonic song to thirty-four motets, although there are many monophonic chansons; *Iv* (ca. 1365) fifteen polyphonic chansons to thirty-seven motets; *Ch* (end of century) ninety-seven polyphonic chansons and thirteen motets. The chanson form continues to dominate early fifteenth-century manuscripts as well.

Notation

The notation of the Machaut manuscripts varies from Petronian in a small number of pieces to standard fourteenth-century procedures in most (see Chapter 14, "Notation"). The end-of-century manuscripts use more advanced notational techniques discussed later in this chapter.

THE FORMS

The *formes fixes*—virelai, rondeau, ballades, and lai—are poetic forms that received their final shaping in the early fourteenth century. The flowering of the polyphonic chanson is inextricably linked with these poetic forms, with which it was united.

The Virelai

The virelai first appears in France near the end of the thirteenth century. One three-voice example appears among the "rondeaux" of Adam de la Hale. Other, monophonic examples are found among the chanson tenors of *Mo*, fas. 7 and 8 (see Chapter 11, "Secular Tenors," and Anthology Example 53), and in the *Roman de Fauvel*.

The derivation of the form is not particularly clear. It may come from Spain, where songs in this form are fairly common in the late thirteenth-century *Cantigas de Santa Maria*, or, though less likely, from the thirteenth-century Italian *lauda*. On the other hand, two Notre Dame conductus anticipate this form. In thirteenth-century literature the name refers to a dance and also to a song to accompany a dance. It is possibly the type of dance song described by Grocheo under the heading of the vocal *ductia*. Many of Machaut's virelais are dancelike, as is the contemporaneous Italian *ballata*, which uses the same musical form. The textural simplicity of Machaut's settings reflect the virelai's popular character; twenty-five are monophonic, seven are for two voices, and only one is for three voices.

A virelai consists of a poem in three stanzas, with a refrain that appears before, between, and following the verses. The verse is composed in *pedes cum cauda* form, and the refrain uses the same music as the *cauda* portion of the verse (see Anthology Example 69):

	REFRAIN	RHYME
	Se je souspir parfondement	A
	Et tendrement	A
	Pleure en recoy,	B
	C'est, par ma foy,	B
	Pour vous, quant vo faitis corps gent,	A
	Dame, ne voy.	B
	VERSE ONE:	
pedes	Vostre dous maintieng simple et coy,	B
	Vo bel arroy,	B
	Cointe et plaisant,	A
	Et vo maniere sans effroy,	B
	Pris m'ont cil troy	B
	Si doucement	A

cauda	Qu'a vous tres amoureusement	A
	Entierement	A
	Doing et ottroy	B
	Le cuer de moy	B
	Qui loing de vous esbatement	A
	N'a n'esbanoy.	B
	REFRAIN:	
	Se je souspir parfondement	A
	Et tendrement	A
	Pleure en recoy,	B
	C'est par ma foy,	B
	Pour vous, quant vo faitis corps gent,	A
	Dame, ne voy.	B

The remaining two stanzas will use the rhyme scheme of the first. The two sections of the pedes are equal in syllable length and rhyme, and the same is true of the cauda and the refrain. Line lengths are highly variable in the virelai, as are the number of lines per section.

The basic poetic form of a single stanza may be diagrammed: R a a b R. Inasmuch as the cauda section of the verse uses the same music as the refrain, the musical form of a single stanza may be diagrammed: A b b a A (uppercase letters represent repetitions of music and text, lowercase repetition of music with new text), and an entire three-verse virelai: A b b a A b b a A b b a A.

The two *b* phrases may have identical endings or be distinguished from each other through the use of *ouvert* (open or nontonic) and *clos* (closed or tonic) cadences. The A section is most often through-composed, but may be divided into two halves with open and closed endings (compare Anthology Examples 68 and 69). Therefore a single stanza of a virelai of Machaut's time may take any of the following specific forms (the subscripts 1 and 2 referring to first and second endings regardless of their open or closed nature):

$$A \quad b \quad b \quad a \quad A$$
$$A \quad b_1 \quad b_2 \quad a \quad A$$
$$A_o \quad A_c \quad b_1 \quad b_2 \quad a_o \quad a_c \quad A_o \quad A_c$$

In the musical settings, however, A tends to form an equal counterpart to the two *b*s, so that the second *b* cadence marks the midpoint of the form. Musical rhyme (an identity of cadential passages) may occur between the end of *a* and the end of *b*, but its occurrence is much less frequent than in the ballade.

In the eight polyphonic virelais of Machaut, the preferable open cadence is an unusual one, the subtonic with a third (for example, C and E in the D mode). Open cadences in the monophonic virelais reflect modal practice; virelais in D and G (including D transposed to G) use primarily the supertonic, those in F and C the mediant.

The Rondeau

Although in some ways the most intricate of the *formes fixes* in its musical-poetic relationship, the rondeau was the first to assume a distinctive shape. It appears in monophonic form in the early thirteenth-century rondellus/rondeau compositions of F and the *Roman de la Rose* (see Chapter 9, "The Rondellus/Rondeau," and Anthology Example 43) and reappears around 1270–85, in polyphonic form, in the three-voice rondeaux of Adam de la Hale.

Adam's rondeau no longer has the multiple verses of the earlier type and has gained an initial refrain, creating the musical form A B a A a b A B. This became the standard pattern in the fourteenth century, but Adam's poetry is short and popular, with normally one, seldom more than two, short poetic lines per musical section, as in his *Tant con je vivrai*:

A	*Tant con je vivrai*	As long as I live
B	*N'amerai autrui que vous;*	I will not love another;
a	*Ja n'en partirai*	I will never leave you
A	*Tant con je vivrai,*	As long as I live,
a	*Ains vous servirai:*	Rather I will serve you:
b	*Loiaument mis m'i sui tous.*	To this I have loyally dedicated myself.
A	*Tant con je vivrai*	As long as I live
B	*N'amerai autrui que vous.*	I will not love another.

This basic eight-line form was inherited by Machaut and followed in similar concise form in his *Puis qu'en oubli* (Anthology Example 70). Noticeable in Machaut, however, is the tendency toward the establishment of consistent line lengths throughout the poem, a procedure that became standard with later writers.

Expansion of the form came by degree.

First was Machaut's introduction of melismatic writing into the rondeau. By so doing, he was able to greatly enlarge the standard eight-line rondeau; compare Anthology Example 71 with the syllabic Anthology Example 70. (Later composers seldom attempt so large a melismatic extension.)

Another means of expansion was the creation of longer poems, setting two or more poetic lines to each section of music. In three of Machaut's rondeaux (numbers 10, 11, and 13), two poetic lines are set to each A section, resulting in a thirteen-line form:

Poetic lines and rhyme:	AB	B	ab	AB	ab	b	AB	B
Musical form:	A	B	a	A	a	b	A	B

Composers after Machaut continued this expansion by progressively adding lines to each section of the refrain, resulting successively in rondeaux of sixteen, twenty-one, and twenty-four lines. These longer forms were known as *rondeau quatrain* when the refrain comprised four lines, *cinquain* when it comprised five (divided three and two) and *sixain* when it comprised six.

Musically the key element is the refrain, for the entire musical substance is contained in it; one need only the text of the verse to create a complete rondeau. Musically, the rondeau falls into two sections: an A section designed to either go forward or return to the beginning, and a B section that is conclusive. As a result the cadence for A must be an open one, that of B closed. Of the twenty-one Machaut rondeaux with music, all but four use the supertonic as the open cadence.

The Ballade

Although considered by many writers to be the equivalent of the *pedes cum cauda* form of troubadour and trouvère music (see Chapter 7, "Musical Form"), it is probably more a derivative than an equivalent, for the earlier form was a generalized procedure permitting a variety of individual applications. As a *forme fixe*, the ballade has a precise poetic shape of three stanzas, identical in syllable count and rhyme, unified through the use of a one-line refrain at the end of each verse.

Machaut's early ballades are quite flexible in form. By the second half of the fourteenth century the typical ballade stanza consists of seven or eight lines, of which the first four, divided into two pairs, constitute the pedes section. The remaining lines, including the one-line refrain, make up the cauda. (In mid-century style, the refrain is set as part of the verse; by the end of the century it is set separately; see Anthology Example 75.) The poetic lines are of either 7 or 10 syllables, and both the seven- and the eight-line ballade forms have a set rhyme scheme that is followed in all stanzas (see Anthology Examples 75 and 73):

SEVEN-LINE STANZA:	RHYME
Fuions de ci, fuions, povre compaingne,	A
Chascuns s'en voist querir son aventure	B
En Aragon, en France ou en Bretaingne,	A
Car en brief temps on n'ara de nos cure.	B
Fuions querir no vie, no seüre,	B
Ne demorons yci eure ny jour,	C
Puisque perdu avons Alionor.	C

EIGHT-LINE STANZA:	
Une vipere en cuer ma dame meint	A
Qui estoupe de sa queue s'oreille	B
Qu'elle n'oie mon dolereus compleint:	A
A ce, sans plus, toudis gaite et oreille.	B
Et en sa bouche ne dort	C

L'escorpion qui point mon cuer a mort;	C
Un basilique a en son doulz regart.	D
Cil troy m'ont mort et elle que Dieus gart.	D

Like the other *formes fixes*, the ballade's musical structure consists of only two sections. The *a* section forms one *pes* of the pedes section and is accordingly repeated, the repetitions normally distinguished from each other by the use of open and closed cadences (see Anthology Examples 72 and 73). The remaining lines and the refrain are set in the *b* section. Musically, the form may be shown as (subscripts showing open and closed endings): $a_o \, a_c \, b_c$.

A variant of this form, used particularly with twelve-line poems, includes a repeat of the *b* section, again with open and closed endings (see Anthology Example 72). Each section sets three lines of poetry, the refrain being the final line of the second b section: $a_o \, a_c \, b_o \, b_c$. In Egidius de Murino's *Tractatus Cantus Mensurabilis*, this is called a *ballada duplex*,[2] in distinction to the *ballada simplex* described above.

The normal procedure, achieved in the later Machaut ballades, is for both a and b to cadence on the tonic and to have their identity reinforced through *musical rhyme*: the musical identity of the two cadences—and, most often, a substantial amount of precadential material. Compare, for instance, measures 10–18 and 26–34 of Anthology Example 72, 24–31 and 54–59 of Anthology Example 73, and measures 22–32 and 57–65 of Anthology Example 74.

These cadences, at the end of the pedes and the refrain sections of the poem, musically define the middle and the end of each stanza. When musical rhyme is also present, they also act as strong agents of unification.

The Lai

The *lai* is the longest of the medieval monophonic forms, often lasting fifteen minutes or more in performance. In the thirteenth-century trouvère manuscripts it is a flexible form with a varying number of stanzas and stanzaic forms.

As standardized by Machaut, the *lai* consists of twelve stanzas, differing from each other in length of poetic lines. Only the first and last are related, rounding off the form. Each stanza will be divided into either two or four parts, identical to each other in structure.

The musical setting reflects the poetic form. The first and last stanzas are sung to the same music, although more often than not in a transposed key. All the interior stanzas will have their own musical settings; their division into two or four parts is shown musically by alternate *ouvert* and *clos* endings. Individual

---

[2]Coussemaker, 3:128. This should not be confused with the "double ballade," a modern musicological term for a ballade with two independent upper voice texts, such as Machaut's *Quant Theseus—Ne quier veoir*.

stanzas may vary in tonality, and while each individual stanza will lie in the range of an octave or ninth, the composite range may well be almost two octaves (see OAMM, 69, and HAM, 19i). Although typically monophonic, two of Machaut's use three-voice canon, one throughout, the other in alternation with monophony.

The entire fourteenth-century repertoire consists of four in *Fauv* and nineteen by Machaut. After this the form virtually disappears, only one other being known, in a late fourteenth- or early fifteenth-century manuscript from Dijon.

The Chace

Although there are no examples of the form by Machaut, and only four complete examples still exist, the *chace* warrants mention as one of a number of manifestations of canonic writing that appear in various countries in the fourteenth century. The name means "hunt," and the form, a three-voice canon at the unison, resembles a musical chase.

The texts are programmatic: an *alba* (a watcher warning lovers of the approach of dawn), a hunt, a comical adventure, an aspiring singer. The depiction of lively events at times includes nonsense syllables, hocket, and animated rhythms (see AMM, 60).

MELODY

Fourteenth-century writers credited Machaut and de Vitry with establishing the new song forms. Regrettably, de Vitry's music is lost to us, but Machaut's contributions stand out clearly: the stabilizing of the poetic forms, the creation of a new style of melody, and the devising of a contrapuntal framework to support that melody.

Machaut's melody writing evinces a sense of unity and cohesion, a more consciously "compositional" manner than that of thirteenth-century melody. This is true in both his monophonic melodies and the cantus parts of his polyphonic songs, and is largely due to a melody's use and reuse of a limited number of characteristic motives that occasionally spill over into the other parts.

Machaut also makes a distinction between chanson melodies and those of the motet. In the motet, with its relatively slow rate of harmonic change, melody must be designed to move within a series of sustained sonorities, functioning as a means of harmonic prolongation. In the chanson, with its faster harmonic rhythm, dictated by the melody itself, melodic motion moves through frequently changing harmonies, leading the ear from one sonority to the next.

Syllabic and Near-Syllabic Melody

Many of Machaut's melodies set the text concisely—syllabically, neumatically, or with the inclusion of occasional short melismas. This style includes the virelais, some rondeaux, and the lais.

In the monophonic virelai *Dame, vostre doulze viaire* (Anthology Example 68), the first phrase rises scalewise to e, a doubled melisma descends from g to first d then c, a second scale rises from c to e, and, in the ouvert ending, another ornamented descending passage outlines a sixth. The result is a flowing, finely contoured melody in which the descending passages are disguised descending scales, embellished through the manipulation of a four-note turning figure: (Example 15-1).

The verse begins with the same motive and modifies it over the word *greifte* and again in the *ouvert* and *clos* endings. (The remainder of the virelai verse of course repeats the melody of the refrain.) The melody attains cohesion through the combination of two ideas: a rising, unadorned scale passage and an ornamented descent based on permutations of a basic motive.

Similar procedures may be seen in imperfect prolation in the two-voiced virelai *Se je souspir* (Anthology Example 69). The cantus begins with a phrase that rises and falls scalewise. Phrase 2 begins with the four-note turning figure, repeated with shifted rhythm in bar 8. The verse begins with a dramatic change of pitch in the cantus, then gradually descends; the motive appears in measure 23 and in the *ouvert* and *clos* endings. The tenor functions as discant support for the cantus, but nevertheless includes the motive at measures 3 and 14 and, in rhythmically expanded fashion, in the *clos* ending.

Melismatic Melody

The expansive, melismatic idiom of the ballades and most rondeaux demands a less compact technique, illustrated in two melismatic examples in the Anthology, in imperfect and perfect prolation respectively. In the rondeau *Quant je ne voy* (Anthology Example 71), the A section has little of the obvious motivic use found in the syllabic melodies. Rather, its somewhat amorphous melody is organized around three motivic patterns: the cadential figure of the first phrase, our familiar four-note motive, and the three-note ascent and falling

EXAMPLE 15-1.   Underlying Melodic Structure, *Dame, vostre doulze viaire*, Cantus, measures 1-9.

fourth of measures 21–22. Their interrelationship is best seen through a juxta-position of the six melodic phrases of the section (Example 15-2).

Section B is based on the same material. Measures 41–42 relate to a_2, while measures 43–47 are a modification of measures 4–8. Measures 52–53 and 55–60 juxtapose motives *c* and *b*, while measures 56–74 form musical rhyme with the end of A, measures 20–39.

In the ballade *Une vipere en cuer* (Anthology Example 73), a similar process occurs, but with a more distinct use of a single motive. Phrase 1 presents within the first four measures (1) a descent of a seventh, (2) the ornamentation of that descent with a neighboring-note expansion of our familiar four-note motive (b–c–b–c–a), and (3) a distinctive opening rhythm of a semibreve and a rest. The remaining melodic fabric comes from these ideas. Phrases 2, 3, and 4 expand and modify the neighboring-note figure within a descending sequence covering a sixth in all, while the final phrase of the section re-creates, after an introductory statement of the neighboring-note motive, a transposition of the ornamented descent of a seventh found in phrase 1, introduced by the opening rhythmic motive.

Similar procedures govern section 2. The phrase beginning in measure 32 echoes that of measure 9, while measure 39 introduces the series of short de-scending phrases with the opening rhythmic motive. Musical rhyme governs the final six bars of the refrain, simultaneously referring back to the end of the pedes and to the ballade opening.

POLYPHONIC TECHNIQUES

The Two-Voice Framework

The fundamental structure of the chanson style is that of a two-voice discant between the cantus and the tenor. In the process of composition, the cantus, shorn of its ornamentation, would be conceived as a basic melodic progression. To this would be added a tenor, following basic discant rules. The process is that of two-voice discant constructed from the top down and designed to accommodate a preconceived melody. This framework may be seen most clearly in the two-voice works, although even here it may be disguised through ornamentation or syncopation, as in Example 15-3. The intervals used are those common to all fourteenth-century discant: the perfect and imperfect conso-nances. In general, the range of the cantus lies about a fifth above that of the tenor.

Three- and Four-Voice Writing

Again, the tenor is constructed in relationship to the principal melody, the cantus. Once established, however, it becomes the principal foundation on

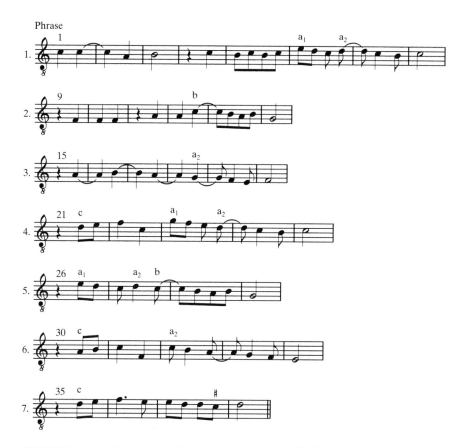

EXAMPLE 15-2. Motivic Analysis, *Quant je ne voy* (Anthology Example 71), Cantus, measures 1-38.

EXAMPLE 15-3. Two-voice Discant Structure, *Se je souspir* (Anthology Example 69), measures 18-24.

which additional voices may be built. This is apparent in analysis. It is also confirmed in the only fourteenth-century theoretical discussion that deals with three-part writing, a short section in the *Ars Discantus* (Coussemaker, 3:92–95) formerly attributed to Johannes de Muris. The third and fourth voices fill in and enrich the sonorities and add melodic and rhythmic interest when required.

Three-voice texture takes two shapes in the works of Machaut. One, harking back to the thirteenth century, adds a textless triplum to the cantus and tenor (see Anthology Example 72). The triplum moves in the same range as the cantus and is melodic in much the same way. Only four of the thirty-one three-voice chansons use this format.

The other, more distinctly fourteenth-century procedure adds a textless countertenor to the cantus-tenor pair (see Anthology Examples 70, 71, and 73). As in the motet repertoire, the countertenor moves in the range of the tenor and often exchanges places with it as lowest-sounding voice (Example 15-4).

A full four-voice texture consists of a texted cantus and a textless triplum, tenor, and countertenor (see Anthology Example 74). The arrangement is that of two pairs of voices operating a fifth apart. Eight ballades and two rondeaux exist in four-voice format, but in a number of cases the triplum and countertenor should be considered alternate rather than complementary voices. This is shown by differing manuscript transmissions. Probably only about half of the works published today in four-voice form were originally intended for four-voice performance.

Displacement Technique

Compositions in major prolation, with their swinging $\frac{6}{8}$ or $\frac{9}{8}$ rhythms, are harmonically straightforward and highly consonant. Those in minor prolation are much more complex rhythmically, making use of the technique of *displacement syncopation* to create a highly dissonant style.

This procedure takes advantage of notational possibilities inherent in minor prolation to displace small segments by one-half of a semibreve (a quarter note in transcription). By dividing the two minims of a semibreve and inserting one or more semibreves between them, composers could easily create interesting syncopated figures by means of a temporary metric shift (Example 15-5).

EXAMPLE 15-4.   Countertenor Function, *Puis qu'en oubli* (Anthology Example 70), measures 1-2.

EXAMPLE 15-5. Displacement Syncopation, *Quant je ne voy* (Anthology Example 71), measures 5-8.

In polyphonic chansons this technique displaces consonance before or after the beat. Excerpts from *Se je souspir* (Anthology Example 69) show the procedure in a two-voice setting. As shown in the discant reduction of Example 15-6a, the initial movement is from a fifth inward to a unison. In this, however, the tenor is delayed a minim (an eighth note in transcription), producing a temporary (dissonant) fourth on the second beat. In Example 15-6b, the delay of the tenor F creates a dissonant fourth on the fourth eighth note. In Example 15-6c, the forward displacement of the tenor G by an eighth note produces a temporary second.

Displacement technique in three-voice writing. A more complex use of displacement technique may be seen in Example 15-7, measures 3–4 of *Puis qu'en oubli.* In measure 3 the delay of an eighth note in the cantus and countertenor produces dissonances of three consecutive sevenths between cantus and tenor and on-beat chordal configurations such as C–D–b flat (fourth quarter note), A–F–G (fifth quarter note), and B–E–a. Other, between-the-beat dissonances are the result of passing and neghboring-note motion.

The displacement technique, although based on discant, bends it in the direction of greater linear independence. In performance, it sounds far less dissonant than the eye (or the piano) would indicate. Instead, coupled with its accompanying rhythmic impulse, it propels the ear onward toward the eventual cadence.

Nonharmonic tones. Normal nonharmonic tones in the fourteenth century include unaccented passing and neighboring tones. The displacement technique may result in anticipations, suspensions, appoggiaturas, and accented passing and neighboring tones. No overall rule governs their placement; the only rule is resolution from lesser to greater consonance. An appoggiatura may be 9–8, 2–1, or 7–8 (that is, a dissonance resolving to a perfect consonance); 7–6 or 4–3 (a dissonance resolving to an imperfect consonance); or 6–5, 3–5, or 3–1 (an imperfect consonance resolving to a perfect one).

TONALITY

In contrast to the continental motet, which is based on a preexisting cantus firmus that often lacks tonal coherence, the chanson operates within a gener-

a. First and second beats delayed: measures 1-3

b. Second beat delayed: measures 8-9

c. Second beat advanced: measures 27-28

EXAMPLE 15-6. Displacement Techniques in Two-Voice Writing, *Se ie souspir* (Anthology Example 69).

EXAMPLE 15-7. Displacement Technique in Three-Voice Texture, Machaut, *Puis qu'en oubli* (Anthology Example 70), measures 3-4.

alized concept of tonal unity. This is in fact an almost inherent attribute of the refrain styles: a repeated refrain means a periodic return to its tonality. Such a concept is implicit in the concept of *ouvert* and *clos* cadences, for an open cadence cannot exist without an awareness of an implied tonic.

Relationship of Ouvert and Clos

The usual position for the open cadence is on the second scale degree, creating a tonic-supertonic relationship pervasive in fourteenth-century writing. The only other tones used with any frequency for open endings are those of the third scale step (about 15 percent, particularly for the tonalities of F and C) and the fifth (about 9 percent, with an occasional example in all modes).

Polyphonic Cadence Structures

Closed cadences consist of perfect sonorities only. In two-voice cadences this will normally be root and octave, although root and fifth are sometimes found. Three-voice cadences are normally root, fifth, and octave, while four-voice cadences include the twelfth as well.

Open cadences usually consist of perfect intervals as well, but may include one or more imperfect intervals: root and third in two-voice writing; root-third-fifth, root-third-sixth, or root-sixth-octave in three-part composition.

Cadential approaches are not yet standardized, but the most frequent is that derived from thirteenth-century practice: cantus and tenor resolving from a sixth to an octave in contrary motion. The countertenor, if present, resolves in parallel motion to the cantus, doubled in four-voice writing by the triplum an octave higher (Example 15-8a).

The progression may be ornamented. Cantus ornamentation normally includes the seventh and eighth scale degrees, but may include the fifth and sixth as well (Example 15-8b–d; Example 15-8d may be compared with the "Landini" cadence of Example 16-6).

TEXT-MUSIC RELATIONSHIPS

Although the poem comes first, the relationship of music and text in the chanson is less close than might be expected. Only in the virelai, where the long text receives a largely syllabic musical setting, is there a close relationship between poetry and musical setting. In the ballade and most rondeaux, melismatic writing and musical concerns take precedence. The use of melisma is spread throughout the composition in a far less structured way than in Italian practice. The close relationship is between poetic line and musical phrase structure, each line being marked by a cadence or at least a cessation of rhythmic movement.

As in all medieval composition, the music does not attempt to "interpret" the text; rather, it is a vehicle for a poetry that is already highly stylized.

Performance Considerations

The presence of from one to as many as three untexted voices accompanying the texted cantus is a hallmark of the French polyphonic chanson. The common assumption of much twentieth-century musicology has been that the untexted voices are instrumental in nature, and that the polyphonic chanson was, in essence, instrumentally accompanied song. While this is one option, recent research has shown an all-vocal performance to have equal validity, one supported by Machaut's pupil Eustache Deschamps in his *Art de Dictier et de Frere Chançons* of 1392 and portrayed in illustrations of chanson performances. In this case, singers of the tenor and countertenor must have either vocalized on a neutral syllable or adapted the cantus text to their parts.

ARS SUBTILIOR

In the generation after Machaut, composers in northern France continued a gradual development of mid-century Machaut style. Much more startling is the exploitation of those procedures by composers associated with the southern courts of Foix-Béarn, Navarre, Aragon, and the papal city of Avignon, reaching a complexity not seen again until the twentieth century.

Sometimes called the *manneristic style*, the medieval term was *ars subtilior*, the "more subtle art." First apparent in the 1370s, this style reached its height in the 1380s and lasted beyond the end of the century, when it began to merge with other styles in the new music of the incipient Renaissance.

EXAMPLE 15-8. Basic Cadential Structures and Cantus Ornamentation.

Important *ars subtilior* composers include the Frenchmen Solege, Trebor, Senleches, Susay, Guido, Matheus de Sancto Johanne, and Magister Egidius and the Italians Philipoctus de Caserta, Matheus de Perugia, and Anthonello da Caserta. Aragon, southern France, and Avignon were areas of international attraction at that time, gathering in composers from both northern and southern France and Italy. Most of the repertoire is found in two end-of-the-century manuscripts, *Ch* from Foix-Béarn and *MOe5.24* from northern Italy.

Musical Style

The *Ars subtilior* leaves behind the balance of parts characteristic of mid-century composition, in favor of one that exploits rhythmic complexity and a much greater independence of voice parts. This can be seen in *Fuions de ci*, Senleches's lament on the death of his patron, Eleanor of Aragon (Anthology Example 75). There the three voices move in almost complete independence of one another, coinciding only on the cadences in measures 7, 13, 24, 31, 35, 38, 46, and 55. Even the tenor, which in many compositions in this style maintains a regular rhythm, is rhythmically complex.[3]

Displacement syncopation.   Used only in short segments and only in minor prolation in the first two-thirds of the century, displacement now becomes a primary technique, being extended to passages of great length and to perfect as well as imperfect prolation. It can be best exemplified in imperfect prolation by renotating the opening cantus passage from *Fuions de ci* (Example 15-9).

The medieval singer, independent of notated or conceptualized bar lines, would simply shift his performance of the passage ahead by half of a semibreve, balance being restored when the second portion of the note value subsequently appears. This displaced rhythm is shown in the small note shapes above the cantus part in Anthology Example 75.

Improved methods of notation now made it possible to extend this displacement syncopation into perfect prolation as well. In Example 15-10 a minim rest

---

[3]The irregularity of the rhythm negates any clear concept of *tempus*, the relationship of the semibreve (a quarter note in this transcription) to the breve. Compare for example the published transcriptions of Apel ($\frac{3}{4}$, as in Anthology Example 75) and Gordon Greene (PMFC 18:28–30), who uses an alternation of $\frac{4}{4}$ and $\frac{3}{4}$.

EXAMPLE 15-9.   Displacement Syncopation, Senleches, *Fuions de ci*, cantus.

EXAMPLE 15-10. Displacement Syncopation in Perfect Prolation, Magister Egidius, *Courtois et sages*, MOe 5.24, fol. 35.

and a minim note in the cantus of measure 2 (equaling two-thirds of a perfect semibreve) are interrupted by a long displaced passage that remains one minim ahead of the more regular tenor and countertenor until the missing minim of the original perfect semibreve appears eight measures later. (The countertenor also has a short displacement in measure 7.)

Proportions.   We have seen a simple use of proportions in the tenors of iso-rhythmic motets, where the tenor is repeated in diminished time values. The *ars subtilior* applied the concept in a much more imaginative and complex manner, involving proportional changes both within a given voice part and between simultaneous voices. The potential for this lay in the perfect and imperfect prolations of the fourteenth century, but most particularly in Italian rhythmic procedures in which the breve, as the basic unit of time, could be variously divided into two to twelve parts (a procedure discussed more fully in Chapter 16). By using proportional signs or special note shapes, proportional shifts and conflicts became a second basic technique of the *ars subtilior* composers.

This can be seen in Example 15-11, an excerpt from Cunelier's *Se Galaas et le puissant Artus*. The tenor maintains the basic perfect prolation throughout, albeit with passages of displacement syncopation. In the excerpt quoted, the cantus and countertenor alternate within themselves and against each other in the proportions of 2:3 and 4:3, creating considerable rhythmic conflict, but one of a different nature from displacement syncopation.

Discant

In spite of rhythmic complexities and the extreme importance given to the independence of voice parts, all voices do in fact relate to a basic discant structure, even if that structure is often severely attenuated. This can be seen by comparing the analysis of the opening of *Fuions de ci* in Example 15-12 with the original (Anthology Example 75).

Partial Signatures

Noticeable in *Fuions de ci* is the difference in key signatures between the cantus and the lower voices. This is a phenomenon that occurs sparingly in the early part of the century, but with increasing frequency thereafter. Difficult to explain completely, it is best thought of as a type of bimodality in which the upper and lower voices move in their own versions of the same mode, one in transposed form, the other not. In most cases the lower voice has one additional flat, indicating a transposition of its mode down a fifth (or up a fourth). Inas-much as the ranges of the cantus and of the tenor and countertenor tend to be a fifth apart, this gives each voice its own character while simultaneously avoid-ing many tritones.

EXAMPLE 15-11. Use of Rhythmic Proportions, Cunelier, *Se Calaas et le puissant Artus,* Ch fol. 38.

Notation

The notation of these complex rhythms demanded a more elaborate system than the relatively simple procedures of the early part of the century (see Chapter 13, "Notation"). For instance, the notation of *Se Galaas et le puissant Artus* (Example 15-11) requires, in addition to black notes, red breves (indicated by the sign ⌐ ⌐ and acting here to change the breve from perfect to imperfect), hollow red minims (indicated by ⌐∙ ∙⌐, four equaling three regular minims), and elsewhere in the piece, hollow white notes (shown by the sign ⌐ ⌐ and doubling the speed of the notes so written). Other note forms, borrowed from Italian notation and involving variously tailed semibreves (e.g., ♪ ♩ ♯), also came into use.[4]

In theory, all these note forms, along with the use of proportional signatures (O C Ɔ ⊙ ℂ), could have left a very precise indication of the rhythms

---

[4]Only the last, the semiminim, would remain a permanent part of the notational vocabulary. For a full discussion of *Ars subtilior* notation, not possible here, see Apel, 403–25 and the discussion of syncopation on 398–402.

EXAMPLE 15-12.   Discant Structure, Jacob Senleches *Fuions de ci* (Anthology Example 75), beginning.

intended. In fact, usage was inconsistent and varied from composer to composer so that correct solutions often require considerable trial and error. Frequently the composer deliberately notated simple rhythms in complex fashion, as if challenging an experienced performer to decipher an abstruse puzzle. Indeed, the whole *ars subtilior* movement seems to have taken place among a group of erudite composers working within a limited geographical area and in a cultural environment that encouraged the avant-garde.

Practicum

COMPOSITION IN FOURTEENTH-CENTURY SONG STYLE

Composition in midfourteenth-century song style involves, to a certain extent, a reversal of the procedures studied in the thirteenth-century discant style of Chapter 10, where construction began with the lowest voice, the tenor, and built upwards. In the polyphonic song of the fourteenth-century the starting point is rather the melody or cantus.

Taking as the focus of study the French style of Machaut, we may begin, by way of illustration, with the opening phrase from Machaut's ballade *Riches d'amour* (Example 15-13).

1. The first step in the compositional procedure is to reduce the melody to its essential structural tones—one, two, or at most three per measure, depending on the meter and rhythm of the melody. In the case of Example 15-13, assuming one structural tone per measure, there is little doubt about measures 1, 3, 5, and 6, but measures 2 and 4 are subject to varying interpretations (Example 15-14). Each of these alternatives will affect the underlying discant structure differently.

2. The second step is to create a two-voice framework by composing a tenor under the cantus, following the rules of discant. It is here that the importance of step 1 becomes apparent, because the discant relates to the structural rather than to the ornamental tones of the melody.

In the choice of tenor notes, the following fourteenth-century procedures apply:

1. The normal distance between the two voices is a fifth to an octave, but may extend to a twelfth, particularly if a third voice is to be added.

2. Voice crossing between cantus and tenor may occur, particularly if the finished composition is to be in two voices.

3. The first and final sonorities may contain only perfect consonances, which in a fourteenth-century sense means unison, fifth, octave, or possibly twelfth; the fourth is generally treated as an unstable interval.

4. The interior discant intervals include thirds, sixths, and tenths, as well as fifths, octaves, and twelfths.

5. Parallel perfect intervals will be avoided, but a limited number of parallel imperfect ones are acceptable.

6. Although the idiom permits thirds and sixths as structural intervals, they should not permeate the texture, which is still based on the use of frequent unisons, fifths, and octaves.

Following these rules, a variety of possible discant structures could be erected under the given melody, six of which, exploiting the alternate structural interpretations of measures 2 and 6, are given in Example 15-15. The cadence is treated as an internal one, thus permitting an imperfect consonance at that spot.

The chosen discant structure establishes both the harmonic color and the tonal sense of the composition. Options, such as 3 and 6, that suggest a modern tonal movement are the farthest from fourteenth-century practice. Machaut's choice is option 1. Example 15-16 shows the six discant structures in connection

EXAMPLE 15-13.   Opening phrase, Machaut, *Riches d'amour.*

EXAMPLE 15-14.   Example 15-13 Reduced to Essential Structural Tones.

EXAMPLE 15-15.   Possible Discant Structures for Example 15-14.

with the original melody. The e of measure 2 is effective as either a consonance or a suspension-type dissonance. The b of measure 4 becomes an appoggiatura in versions 1, 2, and 6; the tritone of version 4 is less effective. The a of measure 5 is effective either as a consonance or as an upward resolving suspension. Version 1 represents Machaut's original.

3. Adding the third voice, the countertenor, depends on the two-voice framework already established. Its function is to fill in the sonorities and to possibly add rhythmic interest (the rhythmic element is purposely kept simple in these sample compositions). It will be consonant with the discant structure of the tenor and the cantus. The use of thirds and sixths may result in triadic

harmonies in both root position and first inversion, but they should not be permitted to permeate the sonority. Two or three triads in a row should be the limit.

Example 15-17 shows possible countertenors for versions 1, 4, and 5 of 15-16. (Machaut's ballade is only in two voices.) A wider two-voice framework would permit other possibilities, and enlivening the tenor and countertenor by introducing passing or other harmonic or nonharmonic tones or rhythmic displacement would add finishing touches.

Assignments

1. Compose settings in two and three voices of one or more of the following short melodies adapted from Machaut (Example 15-18). Each falls into three phrases, which should end in cadences. During the long cantus notes at the ends of phrases, interest should be maintained through the introduction of ornamental movement in the tenor or countertenor. The last cadence should be final. Example *c* requires at least two discant intervals per measure.

2. Using one of the structural frameworks given in Example 15-19, compose an eight-measure melody, incorporating some of the typical melodic motives discussed under "Melody," and develop it into a complete two- or three-voice composition.

EXAMPLE 15-16.   Alternate Discant Accompaniments.

EXAMPLE 15-17.   Possible Countertenors for Versions 1, 4 and 5 of Example 15-16.

BIBLIOGRAPHY

Music

For Machaut, see Chapter 13. The general fourteenth-century repertoire is transcribed in two overlapping series: PMFC 5 (*Iv*), 18–19 (*Ch*), 20 (ballades and canons), and 21 (virelais), and CMM 36 (*R*), 39 (*Tor*), and 53 (French secular compositions). The end-of-century repertoire is also contained in Willi Apel, *French Secular Music of the Late Fourteenth Century* (Cambridge, Mass.: AIM, 1950).

Theory

See Chapter 13.

EXAMPLE 15-18. Melodies for Composition.

Readings

The literature on the French fourteenth century is relatively extensive. The articles by Reaney listed below, although old, are still basic except for the treatment of harmony (for this, see Crocker, "Discant," and Leech-Wilkinson, "Rose, Liz"). Hirshberg, in addition to the subject of its title, also contains an excellent treatment of Machaut's structural procedures.

Gilbert Reaney, "Fourteenth Century Harmony and the Ballades, Rondeaux and Virelais of Guillaume de Machaut," MD 7 (1953): 129–46; "The Ballades, Rondeaux and Virelais of Guillaume de Machaut: Melody, Rhythm and Form," AM 27 (1955): 40–58; "The *Lais* of Guillaume de Machaut and Their Background," PRMA 82 (1955–56): 15–32; "The Poetic Form of Machaut's Musical Works," MD 13 (1959): 25–41; "The Development of the Rondeau, Virelai and Ballade Forms from Adam de la Hale to Guillaume de Machaut," in *Festschrift Karl Gustav Fellerer, zum 60. Geburtstag*, ed. Herbert Drux (Köln: Arno Volk, 1962), 421–27; and "Notes on the Harmonic Tech-

a.

b.

c.

EXAMPLE 15-19.   Basic Structural Frameworks for Compositional Use.

nique of Guillaume de Machaut," in *Essays in Musicology: A Birthday Offering for Willi Apel*, ed. H. Tischler (Bloomington: Indiana Univ. Press, 1968), 63–68.

Richard L. Crocker, "Discant, Counterpoint, Harmony," *JAMS* (1962): 1–21. Daniel Leech-Wilkinson, "Machaut's *Rose*, *Liz* and the Problem of Early Music Analysis," *Musical Analysis* 3 (1984): 9–28. Jehoash Hirshberg, "The Music of the Late Fourteenth Century: A Study in Musical Style" (Ph.D. diss., UMI order no. 71-26031); and idem, "Hexachordal and Modal Structure in Machaut's Polyphonic Chansons," in *Studies in Musicology in Honor of Otto E. Albrecht*, ed. John W. Hill (Kassel: Bärenreiter, 1980), 19–42. Richard Karp, "Compositional Process in Machaut's Ballades," in *Music from the Middle Ages through the Twentieth Century: Essays in Honor of Gwynn McPeek*, ed. Carmelo P. Comberiati and Matthew C. Steel (New York: Gordon and Breach, 1988), 64–78.

Other style studies include Arnold Salop, "The Secular Polyphony of Guillaume de Machaut," in his *Studies on the History of Musical Style* (Detroit: Wayne State University Press, 1971), 39–80; George Perle, "Integrative Devices in the Music of Machaut," *MQ* (1948): 169–76; David Fallows, "Guillaume de Machaut and the Lai," *EM* 5 (1977): 477–83; and Jean Hardon, " 'Musica Ficta' in Machaut," *EM* 5 (1977): 473–76.

For an overview, see Willi Apel, "The Development of French Secular Music During the Fourteenth Century," *MD* 27 (1973): 41–59.

Important discussions of performance practice include Christopher Page, "Machaut's 'Pupil' Dechamps on the Performance of Music: Voices or Instruments in the Fourteenth-Century Chanson?" *EM* 5 (1977): 484–98, and Sarah Jane Williams, "Vocal Scoring in the Chansons of Machaut," *JAMS* 21 (1968): 251–57.

16

Polyphonic Song in Fourteenth-Century Italy

There was at that time in the garden a delightful breeze which refreshed the joyful gathering. After the valiant men had been seated, Francesco [Landini], who was full of joy, requested his small [portative] organ and began so sweetly to play his songs of love that there was no one present who did not feel that his heart wished to escape from his chest for very joy, so sweet was that sweet music. . . .

And soon, to everyone's delight, and especially to the delight of Francesco the musician, two young girls began to sing a *ballata,* while Biago di Sernello provided a bourdon for them. They sang so pleasingly and with such angelic voices that not only the assembled men and women, but even the birds in the cypress trees were seen and heard to draw nearer and sing their songs more sweetly and more abundantly.[1]

Italian literature of the fourteenth century abounds in scenes of daily life in which music plays a part. The sudden blossoming of musical culture in Italy took place primarily within the aristocratic, cultured cities of Verona, Padua, Milan and, above all, Florence—a first presage of the artistic and intellectual surge that would become the Italian Renaissance. Ironically, this musical efflorescence lasted little more than a hundred years, dying out in the early fifteenth century at the very time the other arts were approaching their greatest heights. Italy was to wait until the sixteenth century to see the return of a native musical culture.

The musical heritage of thirteenth-century Italy was based on monophony and improvised polyphony. The dispersion of the troubadours after the Albi-

---

[1]Giovanni Gherardi del Prato, *Il Paradiso degli Alberti,* in F. Alberto Gallo, *Music of the Middle Ages II,* trans. Karen Eales (Cambridge: Cambridge University Press, 1985), 132–33.

gensian Crusade found many taking residence in the courts of Italy and Sicily. Their language and poetry became intertwined with that of the native Italian *trovatores,* who only late in that century abandoned Provençal for Italian as the language of poetry. It was Dante, friend of many troubadours, who made this change decisively.

In addition, the monophonic idiom was also strong among the confraternities of the penitents, lay religious groups that played a prominent part in Italian life at that time. The singing of monophonic *laudi spirituali* (hymns in verse form) was of major importance in this popular religious response to the political and moral stresses of the day.

Liturgical worship involved both chant and polyphony. The lack of written music, however, suggests an improvised practice, a hypothesis reinforced by the handful of written examples that have been found: simple pieces in the style of free organum, using perfect and medium consonances in contrary and parallel motion in note-against-note style, a style within which a well-trained liturgical singer might improvise.

We find traces of Parisian polyphony and conservative continental motets in Italian manuscripts and libraries. The English priest Amerus (Alfred), working in Italy, included a chapter on mensural discant in his *Practica artis musicae* of 1271. The Italians were aware of the polyphony of northern Europe, and its influence begins to show in the Italian motets that first appear in the early fourteenth century (see Chapter 13, "The Motet in Italy"). Nevertheless, the major impetus behind the surge of polyphonic writing, and above all the writing of secular polyphony, derived from native Italian sources.

In Italy, even more than in France, the new style of polyphonic song grew from a mixture of the traditions of monophonic melody and improvised polyphony. The texture of the earliest existing examples of two-voice secular polyphony, for instance, at times approach a heterophonically decorated unison melody (see measures 65–66 of Anthology Example 77). The first trace of secular polyphony appears in two-voice madrigals of the 1330s, and two-voice writing remains the norm into the 1360s, even after three-voice composition became familiar.

The music of the *trecento* (the Italian term for the fourteenth century) was distinct from that of France. Italian musicians were aware of, but not overly influenced by, French style, which they consciously imitated and assimilated only in the latter third of the fourteenth century.

THE SOURCES

Only one of the Italian sources dates from within the century. The remainder, partially or largely retrospective, were copied in the late fourteenth or early fifteenth centuries. The sources are:

Rs—The Rossi Codex: Vatican, MS. Rossi 215;

RsO—The Rossi Codex, additional fragments: Ostiglia, MS. Rossi 215. These fragments contain eighteen of a probable thirty-two folios from the earliest extant trecento manuscript. Copied probably around 1340–50, the repertoire appears to reflect the period a decade earlier. All the compositions are anonymous, although four can be identified as compositions of Giovanni da Firenze and Magister Piero from other manuscripts;

Lo—London, British Library, Add. 29987; forms identified (*madrialle, ballata, chaccia*); last years of the fourteenth century;

Pit—Paris, Bibliothèque Nationale, fonds ital. 568; 163 Italian, 35 French and 9 Latin works; end of the fourteenth century;

Fl—Florence, Biblioteca Nazionale Centrale, Panciatichi 26; 51 Italian and 24 French pieces;

Pn 6771—The Reina Codex (see Chapter 15); 117 French, 104 Italian, and 2 Flemish works;

Sq—The Squarcialupi Codex: Florence, Biblioteca Laurenziana, Palatino 87. The largest of the collections, it once belonged to the Florentine organist Antonio Squarcialupi and appears to be a wealthy aristocrat's lavishly illustrated, retrospective collection; around 1415–20.

NOTATION

The first distinct knowledge we have of Italian *trecento* music comes not from musical manuscripts but from the writings of Marchettus of Padua, who completed two major works on music theory between the years 1315 and 1325: the *Lucidarium*, which deals with plainchant, and the *Pomerium*, which discusses in detail Italian mensural notation and compares Italian rhythmic preferences with those of France. Marchettus stresses the independence and importance of the simple meters ($\frac{2}{4}$ or $\frac{3}{4}$ in our terminology, minor prolation in that of France) and the Italian preference for those meters over the French preference for major prolation ($\frac{6}{8}$ and $\frac{9}{8}$).

As explained by Marchettus and confirmed by other early, fragmentary writings, the notational system of Italy was independently derived from the precepts of Franco and Petrus de Cruce. It retains the Petronian breve as the constant unit of measure, dividing it systematically into two to twelve shorter values in a hierarchical system:

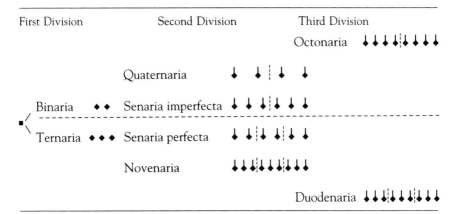

As shown, the division of the breve falls into three levels or *divisions*. The first represents a simple duple or triple division of the breve and is denoted by the semibreve. The second division involves the duple or triple subdivision of the semibreve and uses a note form with an upward tail (equivalent to the French minim). The third level divides the semibreve into four shorter values, but without the use of a distinctive note shape.

In the Italian system all triple and duple meters can be shown, and the intended rhythm of a piece or a passage is identified through the use of the proper initial: q *(quaternaria)* $= \frac{2}{4}$; *si* or *i* *(senario imperfecta)* $= \frac{6}{8}$; *sp* or *p* *(senario perfecta)* $= \frac{3}{4}$; *n* *(novenaria)* $= \frac{9}{8}$; *o* *(octonaria)* $= \frac{4}{8}$; and *d* *(duodenaria)* $= \frac{12}{16}$.[2] In these mensurations, all semibreves are equal. As a result it would be possible to change from *senaria perfecta* to *novenaria* within a voice part or to superimpose them simultaneously in different voices. All *binaria* measures are equal in duration, as are all *ternaria* ones—the semibreve remains constant, the minim values change (the opposite of the French system, where the minim is constant and it is the larger values that change).

For instance, in Anthology Example 76, which is transcribed so that a semibreve is represented by a quarter note, the composition begins in duodenaria (twelve sixteenth notes per "breve" or measure), changes to novenaria at measure 17 (nine eighth notes per measure), to quaternaria at 21 (four eighths per measure), and back to duodenaria at 27. The semibreves remain equal throughout, although their division changes. We have already seen how the *ars subtilior* composers exploited these possibilities in their development of proportions.

In Italian notation, the breve becomes, in effect, equivalent to a modern measure, and the dots of division that separate each breve-length group of notes become the equivalent of bar lines. Specific rhythms can be shown by the use of

---

[2] In modern notation sixteenth notes are used in transcribing the third division, eighth notes in the second.

additional tails. For instance, if three minims appear instead of four in quaternia, the natural manner of rhythmic interpretation (*via natura*) would be to lengthen the last note: ♩♩♩ (♫♩). If the composer wished a different interpretation, the desired longer note could be "artistically" distinguished (*via artis*) by a downward tail: ♩♩♩ (♩♫), ♩♩♩ (♪♩ ♪). Flags on upward stems could indicate triplets: ♩♩♩♩♩ (♫♫).

The system possesses considerable flexibility. All rhythms within a measure are capable of precise notation. The only limitation is a difficulty in showing rhythmic displacement of syncopation over a bar line, but this procedure did not play the great part in Italian music it did in French.

Later in the century, as French influence became more and more prevalent, a type of mixed notation developed, including elements of French and Italian systems. The earliest move in this direction was in the notation of octonaria and duodenaria in which the unit of measure was shifted from the Italian breve to the French long. The equivalent rhythms are the same, but the means of notation changed.

THE COMPOSERS

Contrary to normal medieval custom, many *trecento* composers are clearly identified in the manuscripts. Possibly this is a heritage of the troubadours, whose names were carefully noted, although they were recorded primarily as poets, not composers. More likely, it is because the Italian musicians worked within a close aristocratic environment. In an age that was becoming conscious of individual merit, their music was collected in retrospective "collector's editions."

Often the composer is identified by the name of the town of his birth (for example; Giovanni da Firenze—Giovanni of Florence), but other biographical details, including precise dates of birth and death, are missing. It is best to consider the composers in terms of an early and a late generation, covering approximate years of musical activity: around 1330–70 and around 1360–1400, with an inevitable overlap between generations.

The First Generation

In the first period of active composition there were two major locations of musical activity. In the plains of the north, it centered in the courts of the Visconti in Milan and the Scaligeri in Verona and Padua; in the hill country to the south, in Florence. Those active in the Padua-Verona-Milan area were Giovanni da Firenze (also known as Giovanni da Cascia), Jacopo da Bologna, and Magister Piero. All three emulated each other, composing madrigals honoring the same lady (the "Anna" of Anthology Example 76) or setting versions of the same text (such as the *Chon brachi assai* of Anthology Example 78).[3] Contemporary or slightly later composers working in Florence include Lorenzo Masini da Firenze (Anthology Example 77), Gherardello da Firenze, and Donato da Firenze (or da Cascia).

The Second Generation

By midcentury or slightly after, musical activity in the northern cities began to decline, and almost all late-century composition is centered in Florence. Without question the leading composer of this generation is Francesco Landini (ca. 1325–97). Born in Florence, he became blind in childhood, probably from smallpox. Renowned as a singer and a player of the organ and many other instruments, as an organ builder and tuner, and as a maker of stringed instruments, he became the most esteemed Italian composer of the century, a fitting counterpart to Machaut. He left a large corpus of music. In addition to Landini, other Florentine composers include Nicolò da Perugia, Andrea da Firenze (also known as Andrea dei Servi), Bartolino da Padova, and Paolo Tenorista.

THE FORMS

Like the music of France, Italian music is based on fixed forms, but ones indigenous to Italy.

The Madrigal

The madrigal first comes to attention as a poetic form in the last third of the thirteenth century. A popular type of poetry, its form was still fluid in the early fourteenth century, and Antonio da Tempo's description in his *Trattato delle rime volgari* of 1332 lists many different schemes, with and without ritornello.

The particular form defined in the musical madrigal is bipartite: a first part comprising two or three three-line stanzas (*terzetti*) followed by a two-line *ritornello* in a different meter, which functions as a coda. The terzetti sets a scene or describes an event; the ritornello comments on it. Two of the terzetto's three lines rhyme. The ritornello consists of two rhymed lines. All Italian poetry of the period is regularized into either seven- or eleven-syllable lines.

The poem for Giovanni da Firenze's *Appress' un fiume* (Anthology Example 76) contains two terzetti and a ritornello:

---

[3]The other madrigals for "Anna," a pseudonym for the lady's actual name, were Giovanni's *O perlaro gentil*, Jacopo's *O dolce apres'un bel* and *Un bel perlaro*, and Piero's *A l'ombra d'un perlaro* and *Sovra un fiume regale*, all contained in PMFC 6, as is Piero's *Chon brachi assai*.

		RHYME	SYLLABLES
Terzetti	Appress' un fiume chiaro	A	7
	Donn'e donçelle ballavan d'intorno	B	11
	Ad un perlaro di be' fior adorno.	B	11
	Fra queste una ne vidi	C	7
	Bella e çentil e amorosa tanto	D	11
	Che'l cor mi tolse con soave canto.	D	11
Ritornello	ANNAmorar mi fa tuo vis'umano,	B	11
	El dolcie guardo e la pulita mano.	B	11

The musical form sets the three lines of the terzetto in through-composed fashion (abc), repeating the entire section for the succeeding stanza. The two lines of the ritornello may be set to the same (dd) or different music (de).

In diagram the musical form would be:

TERZETTI	RITORNELLO
abc abc (abc)	dd *or* de

Although some modern writers superficially relate the madrigal to the French ballade, the aab aab aab structure of a complete ballade in reality bears little resemblance to the madrigal, and it should be considered a totally separate form. Furthermore, while the ballade, as we have seen, tends to be strongly tonal and in the same meter throughout, the madrigal has an inconsistent tonality and emphasizes the division of the terzetti from the ritornello with a meter change.

In the madrigal, the essential cadences are those at the ends of the terzetti and the ritornello. Cadences sometimes occur at the end of internal verse-phrases or even within them. As a result the terzetti sections may have as few as one or as many as five cadences. The Italians did not practice tonal unity in these compositions, and it is rare that the cadences relate tonally to one other or to the cadence of the ritornello.

The Caccia

Of all the fixed forms of the fourteenth century, the caccia is the least fixed. The only universal characteristic is the use of canon, although most *caccia* have descriptive, often programmatic texts. The caccia is a counterpart to the French *chace* and the Spanish *caça*: a canonic "chase" of voices.

The texts.   Seventeen of the twenty-six extant cacce describe realistic events, including hunting, fishing, sailing, a fire, market scenes, and rural events. The other nine deal with less literal matters: love, nature, satire, and philosophical questions.

Fifteen of the seventeen realistic texts treat their subjects programmatically, leading from a setting of the scene to excited personal involvement, including dialogue, shouts to the hounds, and so on. These texts mix regular rhymed lines with irregular short lines that portray the excitement of cries, commands, and bargaining, as in the first verse of Giovanni da Firenze's *Chon brachi assai* (Anthology Example 78):

Chon brachi assai e con molti sparveri	With plenty of hounds and many hawks
Uccellavam su per la riva d'Ada	We hunted birds on the banks of the Ada;
E qual diceva,	And one cried,
"Da', da'!"	"Go! Go!"
E qual,	And another,
"Vacià, Varin,	"Over here, Varin,
Torna, Picciolo!"	Come back, Picciolo!"
E qual prende a le quaglie a volo,	Others took the quail on the wing,
Quando con gran tempesta un'aqua venne.	When a great rainstorm came.

Seven of the nine nonrealistic texts use madrigal verse: one or more terzetti followed by a two-line couplet for the ritornello. Some modern writers call this second type a canonic madrigal, reserving the designation caccia for the realistic first type and its freer poetic idiom.

Musical form.   The most prevalent musical form for either type of text resembles the bipartite madrigal: an opening section, which may be repeated for a second stanza, followed by a ritornello with a change of meter. Six of the realistic cacce, on the other hand, omit the ritornello.

The first section is normally set as a two-voice canon at the unison over a slower, nontexted tenor. Exceptions include a three-voice canon, three two-voice canons without a supporting tenor, one case where the canon is between the lower voices and at the fifth, and three cases of texted tenors.

The ritornello shows even greater variety of treatment. Eight are like that of Anthology Example 78, a new two-voice canon over a nontexted tenor. Two others have a three-voice canon (one at the unison, one at the unison and fifth). Seven of the ritornelli are noncanonic (but one includes voice exchange), while two others reduce the number of voices (one from three voices to two, the other from three voices to one). In addition, there are also two cases where a previously untexted tenor becomes texted in the *ritornello*.

This rather confusing variety of procedures is summarized in Table 16-1. Except for the fact that the four two-voiced compositions are by first-generation composers, there is no obvious correlation between procedure and chronology.

The Ballata

An anonymous Venetian tract of around 1315–20 gives the following definition of the *ballata*:

Ballate are texts applied to music, and are called *ballate* because they are danced. And they should have a *reprisa* [refrain], which can be formed of two or three lines. If of two lines, both should have eleven syllables, though if one wishes the first can be of seven syllables, the second of eleven; alternatively, if one wished, the first could be of eleven, the second of seven. They also have two *piedi,* which should be formed of four lines, followed by a *volta* similar in every respect with the refrain.[4]

The ballata is the last of the Italian forms to assume a polyphonic guise. It is first heard of as a dance song in the late thirteenth century and continues as a popular dance idiom at least until the time of Boccaccio's *Decameron* (1353), where daily scenes of dancing to monophonic ballate are described. Indeed, there is evidence suggesting that the monophonic ballata was the prevailing musical form of the first half of the century, existing in a number of guises; it was called a *ballata* when sung for dancing, a *canzone* when sung by itself, and a *lauda* when set to religious poetry.

Although laude are found in late thirteenth-century manuscripts, the earliest preserved ballate come from the Rossi Codex, copied before 1340; all these are monophonic. The polyphonic ballata did not begin to appear until the 1360s, first in two voices, then in three. It rapidly replaced the madrigal in popularity and became the predominant secular form of the last third of the century. A consideration of Landini's compositions amply tells the story: 91 two-voice and 49 three-voice ballate, 11 madrigals, 2 cacce, and 1 virelai.

In form the ballata is the counterpart of the French virelai, although there is no provable cross-relationship except for the appearance of prototypes of the form in both *cantiga* and *lauda.*

The Italian terminology is that given in the quotation above. The refrain is known as the *reprisa.* The verse portion consists of two *piede* and the *volta,* which, as stated above, uses the music of the *reprisa.* Assuming, as seems probable, that the reprisa was repeated between each verse, the composite form would be:

reprisa	*piedi*		*volta*	*reprisa*	*piedi*		*volta*	*reprisa*	*piedi*		*volta*	*reprisa*
A	b	b	a	A	b	b	a	A	b	b	a	A

As with the virelai, open and closed endings (*aperto* and *chiuso* in Italian) may be used at the end of either the A or b sections.

---

[4]In Gallo, *Music of the Middle Ages II,* 120.

Table 16-1. **Fourteenth-Century Caccia by Subject and Style.**

SUBJECT	POETIC STYLE	COMPOSER COMPOSITION	GENERATION	VERSE	RITORNELLO	CANON?
Hunt	R	Lorenzo, A poste messe	1st	C3	a1	
	R	Jacopo, Per sparverare	1st	a3	a2/tt	—
	R	Anon (Rossi Codex), Or qua	1st	a3/2v	—	
	R	Piero, Seghugi a corte	1st	a3	—	
	R	Giovanni, Chom bracchi	1st	a3/2v	a3	a2
	R	Piero, Chon bracchi	1st	a3/2v	a3	a2
	R	Gherardello, Tosto che	1st	a3	a3	a2
	M	Giovanni, Nel boscho	1st	a3	a3/tt	a3
	M	Giovanni, Per larghi	1st	a3/Quat	a3	—
Market	R	Vincentius, In forma	2nd	a3	—	
	R	Vincentius, Nell'acqua	2nd	a3	—	
	R	Zaccara, Cacciando per	2nd	a3/tt	—	
Sailing	R	Piero, Con dolce	1st	a3	—	
Fishing	R	Landini, Cosi pensoso	2nd	a3	a3	a2
Fire	R	Niccolò, Dappoi che	2nd	a3	a3	a2
Rural	R	Niccolò, Passando con	2nd	a3	a3	a2
	R	Niccolò, State su	2nd	a3	a3	a2
Nature	M	Jacopo, Guinge'l bel	1st	a2	a2/V-Ex	—
Love	M	Piero, Chavalcando	1st	a2/2V	a2	—
	M	Piero, Ogni diletto	1st	a2 1t-Fr	a2	—
	M	Anon, Quan voy	?	a3 Fr	a3	—

Satire	M	Jacopo, Oseletto	1st	a3	a3	—
	M	Landini, De' dimmi tu	2nd	a3/1w vc	a3	a3
Philosophic	M	Donato, Facia chi dee	1st	a3/tt	a3	a2
	M	Niccolò, La fiera	2nd	a3/tt It-L	a3	—
	Ballata	Andrea, Dal traditor	1st	a3		

Code:

C3	Three-voiced canon
1v vc	Canon at the fifth in the two lower voices
Fr	French text
It-Fr	Mixed Italian and French text
It-L	Mixed Italian and Latin text
Quat	Quatrains instead of terzetti
V-Ex	Voice exchange

Code:

R	Realistic text
M	Madrigal-style text
a1	Single voice or unison
a2	Two-voice
a3	Three-voice
tt	Texted tenor
2v	Two verses of poetry
C2	Two-voiced canon (over a non-canonic tenor)

MELODY

The *dolce et soave* (sweet and suave) melody of Italy has both an easy melodic appeal and a sense of freshness and grace. While it is more formulaic than French melody in relying on a small stock of motives and a standardized phrase structure, it is also freer in the loose application of these formulas to convey fresh spontaneity.

Typically, Italian phrase structure begins with a sustained note that leads into a lengthy melisma on the first text syllable, followed by a more rapid, usually syllabic or neumatic declamation in the center of the phrase and, on the next-to-last syllable, another long melisma. The melisma flows easily out of the initial long note; its rapid ornamentation comes from a small stock of short motives common to the Italian repertoire. Interruption of the melody by rests may further enhance a sense of casual spontaneity (see Anthology Example 76, measures 6, 9, 15, 17, and so on). Absent is the highly integrated use of motives found in the Machaut style.

This typical Italian construction is apparent in every phrase of the two madrigals in Anthology Examples 76 and 77 (the only exception is the ritornello of Anthology Example 76 with its play on the name *Anna*). The lower voice supports and at times acts as a connective between cantus phrases. The melismas use six common motives found throughout the repertoire (see Example 16-1). Most of these reappear in the caccia of Anthology Example 78 and Landini's *I' priego amor*, Anthology Example 79.

Specific proof that the application of these motives was casual and ornamental may be seen through a comparison of various manuscript transmissions. The flow and contour of the phrase remains intact, but the details of ornamentation vary, as in Example 16-2.

This melodic style, which developed within the madrigal in the first half of the century, carries over into other forms as well. Cacce melodies begin with a madrigal-style phrase, but continue in rapid declamation, as befits their descriptive texts. As can be seen in Anthology Examples 79 and 80, madrigal-style phrasing is still present in the ballata of the second part of the century, although applied less rigorously, with the opening melisma often omitted in interior phrases.

The Italian preference for simple duple and triple meters rather than the French compound meters also affects melodic style. Displacement syncopation has no part in the Italian style, which instead cultivates rhythmic flexibility within the measure.

POLYPHONIC STRUCTURE

Two-Voice Composition

Two-voice writing was the norm during the first half of the century, probably to around 1365. The range of each voice varies from an octave to a tenth,

a.   Turning motive

b.   Neighboring-note

c.   Sequential descending seconds

d.   Four-note descending scales

e.   Neighboring-note / Escape-tone

d.   Escape-note motive

EXAMPLE 16-1.   Standard Italian Ornamentation Motives.

with the cantus lying a fourth or a fifth higher than the tenor. The entire range of both voices will be a twelfth or a thirteenth. Both voices remain in their range with little or no voice crossing, unlike the concurrent French style or the free organum style of the few existing examples of thirteenth-century sacred Italian polyphony. It reinforces the novelty of two-voice madrigal style, deriving from secular song and improvised accompaniment rather than previous polyphonic practice.

Discant structure. Like the French, the Italian song forms are melodically oriented. The cantus, as chief voice, is supported by the tenor in a two-voice discant structure that forms the harmonic framework on which melodic orna-

EXAMPLE 16-2. Alternate Melodic Ornamentation, Magister Piero, *Quando l'aire comenca*, Ritornello, beginning.
a. Fl, fol. 57'-58
b. Rs, fol. 7'

mentation and flow is suspended. This is immediately apparent in the early madrigals, where the discant structure not only is transparent, but often has the structural simplicity of ornamented parallel organum (Example 16-3). The tenor

EXAMPLE 16-3. Melodic Ornamentation of the Discant Structure, Giovanni da Firenze *Sedendo all'ombra,* Ritornello.

is in a supporting role and only at times partakes of important melodic motion.[5] Its movement is normally conjunct, but because of its supportive role may include occasional fourths and fifths.

Sonorities.   The sonorities are those common to the fourteenth century: unison, fifth, and octave as perfect consonances, thirds and sixths as imperfect consonances. The perfect consonances are the basic underpinning of the discant structure in the first half of the century; thirds and sixths become more common as the century develops. In the first half of the century the major sixth often appears prominently within a phrase, leading to resolution on the octave (as in Anthology Example 76, measure 3), while the third is the normal precadential dissonance (see "Cadence structures" below). The sixth, often combined with the third, assumes this function in the latter part of the century.

---

[5]For instance, Lorenzo Masini da Firenze's madrigal *Sovra la riva* (Anthology Example 77) uses imitation (mm. 34–35 tenor = 36–37 cantus); pseudoimitation (m. 62 cantus = 63 tenor = 63b cantus); and two-voice sequence (mm. 57–59a, 59b–60a, and 65–66).

Nonharmonic tones.   Strong beats are normally consonant. The only exception is a lower or upper appoggiatura, most often approached by step (as in Anthology Example 76, measures 13, 15, 17, and 33, and Anthology Example 77, measures 3, 14, 21, and 22). Rhythmic displacement, not common until late in the century, rarely crosses the bar line (that is, the breve in Italian notation). Between-the-beat dissonances are passing tones and neighboring tones.

Cadence structures.   Normal cadence structure in two-voice Italian polyphony is that of a third resolving inward to a unison. In this, the tenor and cantus reverse the positions normal in the French style: the cantus descends 2-1 and the tenor ascends 7-8. Most usually the tenor approaches from a third or fourth below (6-7-8 or 5-6-7-8), while the cantus descends, in simple or ornamented fashion, from the third scale degree (Example 16-4).

Three-Voice Composition Using Canon

The earliest Italian polyphonic secular form seems to have been the two-voice madrigal, appearing possibly by the 1320s or 1330s. The earliest three-voice writing appears in the caccia, a caccia being in fact the only three-voice piece in the Rossi Codex. (The three-voice ballata dates from the 1360s, with its major compositional period after 1365.)

The relationship and influence of the madrigal on the caccia can be seen in the use of madrigal form and phrase idiom. The relationship becomes closer when we realize that six otherwise noncanonic madrigals use two-voice canons as ritornelli and that the madrigal poetic idiom carries over into the nonrealistic canonic madrigals.

Canonic procedures.   With rare exceptions, all Italian canonic writing is at the unison. The first voice begins simultaneously with a slower-moving tenor and this opening, madrigal-style phrase gradually descends in order to sound a fifth or a fourth on the entrance of the second canonic voice. The timing of that entrance is highly variable and may occur anywhere from four to twenty-two

a.   Simple form.

b.   Sample ornamentations.

EXAMPLE 16-4.   Unison Cadence Structure.

measures (breves) after the first entrance. Canons in ritornello sections are more closely spaced due to the relative shortness of those sections.

Melodic writing is in normal fourteenth-century style except where the excitement of cries and dialogue take over in the realistic cacce. Here the melodic flow may be interrupted by animated rhythms and two- or three-part hocket.

The tenor is generally slower than the upper voices and acts as harmonic support. Its range may partially overlap that of the canonic voices, permitting some voice crossing. (Voice crossing is of course constant in the canonic upper voices.)

Three-Voice Composition without Canon

Noncanonic three-voice writing begins to appear only after 1345 and becomes common only after 1365. Melodic techniques and range remain as for two-voice writing. A third voice, uniformly called a countertenor regardless of range, is added to the cantus-tenor frame. Variations in the function and range of the countertenor form three distinct idioms in the existing repertoire, ones that may represent both chronological change and increasing French influence.

Countertenor as second cantus (ca. 1345–75). In this three-voice style the added "countertenor" is equal in range with the cantus and forms one of a pair of voices above the tenor (see Anthology Example 79). The upper voices cross freely among themselves, but voice crossing between tenor and upper voices is avoided. The countertenor sometimes moves in conjunction with the cantus, at other times alternates with it (see the rhythmic alternation of Anthology Example 79, measures 21–23, 29–30, and 34–35; the motivic imitation in measures 41–44; and the answering fast declamation of measure 32).

All three voices are texted, forming a vocal trio. The paired upper voices over a lower tenor has an analogy in the voicing of the caccia, and this earliest type of noncanonic three-voice music may have been a simple extension of that genre.

Countertenor as middle voice (ca. 1365–1405). Some ballate place the countertenor between the tenor and cantus in range (Anthology Example 80). This type of countertenor is on the whole quieter and less active than the cantus, falling somewhere between the style of that voice and the tenor. Limited voice crossing may occur with either cantus or tenor.

Although the practice varies from ballata to ballata, there is a decided tendency to leave either the countertenor or both the tenor and countertenor textless—possibly a result of increasing contact and influence with French music, where such a practice was the norm. About 50 percent of the existing ballate of this type are given with only the cantus texted and another 37 percent with cantus and tenor texted. The remainder have texts in all voices.

Countertenor as countertenor (after ca. 1375). This last category includes compositions that have absorbed French voicing completely: the countertenor moves in the same range as the tenor, with which it crosses frequently, often forming the lowest sounding voice (Example 16-5). The countertenor, no longer primarily melodic, is now complementary to the tenor, with large leaps as necessary.

Ballate in this style resemble the French accompanied solo song; 54 percent have texts only in the cantus, 33 percent in cantus and tenor, and 13 percent in all voices.

Cadence structures. The unison cadence common in two-voice writing is impractical in a three-voice texture. The octave cadence, already established in the early caccia, inverts the procedures of the unison cadence and approximates that of the French, the tenor now proceeding downward to the final, 2-1, while the cantus resolves upward 7-8. The other voice moves in parallel fourths (or fifths) with the first to cadence on the fifth (or twelfth), as shown in Anthology Example 78, measures 64–65.

Although this procedure was standard practice in France, it became so in Italy only when combined with melodic ornamentation in the cantus (Example

EXAMPLE 16-5. Countertenor in Countertenor Range, Francesco Landini, *Gientil aspetto,* beginning of the volte.

16-6). This is the so-called Landini cadence, so named from its frequent use in his works, although it did not originate with him.

Apparently adopted sometime in the 1360s, this cadence accounts for nearly three-quarters of the final cadences in Landini's three-voice ballate and (without the middle voice) in half of those in the two-voice ones. Landini's ballata *I' priego amor* (Anthology Example 79) gives a curious mixture of transitional cadential types: a three-voice unison cadence at the end of the *piedi,* an ornamented 7-8 cadence that touches on both the fifth and sixth scale degrees at the end of the *reprisa,* and an internal Landini cadence in measures 13–14. The use of syncopation in approaching the cadence is standard practice.

TONALITY

The degree of tonal unity varies according to the genre involved. The ballata, with its tight formal structure, is, like the virelai, tonally closed; the *piedi* cadences generally reinforce those of the *reprisa.* In the madrigal, on the other hand, tonal unity is slight. Instead, the music proceeds through a series of short-term goals that need not relate to one another. Often each phrase of the terzetto and ritornello will have its own individually distinct cadence. Phrases may be divided further by internal cadences that may or may not relate to the end-of-phrase cadence. Most importantly, the final cadence of the terzetto may differ from any of the internal ones and, almost always, will be different than the final one of the ritornello.

THE END OF AN ERA

The late fourteenth century was a time of growing Italian accommodation to French procedures, but without a loss of Italy's distinctive native melodic quality. The papal court of Avignon proved a fertile meeting ground for Italy and France, and three Italian composers, Anthonello da Caserta, Matheus da Perugia, and Philipoctus de Caserta, played a major part in the *ars subtilior.* The

EXAMPLE 16-6. Three-Voice Landini Cadence.

late *trecento* style and the *ars subtilior* form the boundary of the Middle Ages and the Renaissance. Gathering currents from Italy, France, and England heralded a new age and a new style, whose birthplace would not be Italy, but the luxuriant, fairy-tale court of Burgundy.

BIBLIOGRAPHY

Music

The complete Italian song repertoire is published in PMFC 4 (Landini), 6 (Magister Piero, Giovanni da Firenze, Jacopo da Bologna), 7 (Vincenzo da Rimini, Rosso de Chollegrana, Donato da Firenze, Gherardello da Firenze), 8 (Niccolò da Perugia, anonymous madrigals and cacce), 9 (Bartolino da Padova, Egidius de Francia, Guilielmus de Francia, Don Paola da Firenze), 10 (miscellaneous composers) and 11 (anonymous ballate). A second series, that of CMM 8, ed. Nino Pirrotta (AIM, 1954–64), devotes five volumes to composers other than Landini: 1 (Bartolomeo da Firenze, Giovanni da Firenze, Gherardellus de Firenze), 2 (Magister Piero, Codex Rossi, anonymous madrigals and cacce), 3 (Lorenzo Masini, Donato da Firenze, Rosso da Collegrano, nine anonymous pieces), 4 (Jacobus da Bologna, Vincentius da Rimini), 5 (Andreas da Firenze, minor composers). The cacce have also been published in W. Thomas Marrocco, *Fourteenth-Century Italian Cacce*, rev. ed. (Cambridge, Mass.: The Medieval Academy of America, 1961).

The Rossi Codex has been published in facsimile, *Il Canzoniere musicale del Codice Vaticano Rossi 215*, ed. Giuseppe Vecchi, Monumenta Lyrica Medi Aevi Italica 2 (Bologna, 1966), as has *The Manuscript London, British Museum, Additional 29987*, ed. Gilbert Reaney, MSD 13 (AIM, 1965) and *Il codice musicale Panciatichi 26*, ed. F. Alberto Gallo (Florence, 1981).

Theory

Although a number of small treatises exist, the two key treatments of Italian theory are those of Marchettus de Padua, whose *Pomerium* was written around 1320, and Prosdocimo de' Beldomandi, whose *Contrapunctus*, written in 1412, reflects Italian fourteenth-century practice. An excerpt of the Marchettus is available in translation in Strunk, 160–71, while the complete Beldomandi treatise is translated in Jan Herlinger, *Prosdocimo de' Beldomandi: Contrapunctus*, (Lincoln: University of Nebraska Press, 1984).

Readings

Much of the literature on the *trecento* is in Italian. The article by Kurt von Fischer, "On the Technique, Origin, and Evolution of Italian Trecento Music,"

MQ 47 (1961): 41–57, is seminal. The single book-length treatment of *trecento* compositional technique is in German: Dorothea Baumann, *Die Dreistimmige Italienische Lied-Statztechnik im Trecento,* Sammlung Musikwissenschaftlicher Abhandlungen (Baden-Baden: Verlag Valentin Koerner, 1979).

Aspects of constructive technique are explored in W. Thomas Marrocco, "Integrative Devices in the Music of the Italian Trecento," in *L'Ars Nova Italiana del Trecento 2* (Certaldo: Centro di studi sull'ars nova italiana del trecento, 1969), 411–29; idem, "The Ballata—A Metamorphic Form," *AM* 31 (1959); 32–37; Michael P. Long, "Landini's Musical Patrimony: A Reassessment of Some Compositional Conventions in Trecento Polyphony," *JAMS* 40 (1987): 31–52; Kurt von Fischer, "A Study on Text Declamation in Francesco Landini's Two Part Madrigals," in *Gordon Athol Anderson: In Memoriam,* Musicological Studies 59 (Henryville, Pa.: Institute of Mediaeval Music, 1984), 119–30; and Eugene C. Fellin, "The Notation Types of Trecento Music," in *L'Ars Nova Italiana del Trecento 4* (Certaldo: Centro di studi sull'ars nova italiana del trecento, 1974), 211–21.

More general considerations are taken up in Nino Pirrotta, "Marchettus de Padua and the Italian Ars Nova," *MD* 9 (1955): 57–71; idem, "Back to Ars Nova Themes," in *Music and Context: Essays for John M. Ward,* ed. Anne Dhu Shapiro (Cambridge: Department of Music, Harvard University, 1985), 166–82; Howard Mayer Brown, "Fantasia on a Theme of Boccaccio," *EM* 5 (1977): 324–39; idem, "Ambivalent Trecento Attitudes toward Music: An Iconographical View," in *Music and Context,* 79–107; Michael P. Long, "Francesco Landini and the Florentine Cultural Elite," *EMH* 3 (1983): 83–100; and Nino Pirrotta, *Music and Culture in Italy from the Middle Ages to the Baroque* (Cambridge: Harvard University Press, 1984), especially "Ars Nova and Stile Novo" and "Novelty and Renewal in Italy: 1300–1600."

17

An Instrumental Postscript

Most preserved medieval music is vocal. Music for the Mass and Office, which accounts for the bulk of surviving music from before 1250, is completely so. Of the secular music recorded after 1100, there is little indication of specific instrumental participation. Yet the literature and art of the Middle Ages, full of references to instruments, imply that instrumental performance was an important part of medieval musical life.

SECULAR MUSIC

The later Middle Ages possessed a wide range of musical instruments (see jacket illustration), with the following distinct families:

Plucked strings:
    Harp
    Psaltery
    Rotta
    Lute
    Citole
Bowed strings:
    Rebec
    Vielle (Fiddle)
    Giga
    Medieval viol
Mechanically bowed strings:
    Hurdy-gurdy (Organistrum, Symphonia)

Flutes:
    Transverse flute
    Recorder
    Three-holed tabor pipe
Reed instruments:
    Shawm
    Bagpipe
Brass:
    Natural trumpet
    Horns of various types
Percussion:
    Drums of various sizes
    Tambourine
    Triangle
    Cymbals
    Small bells
Keyboard
    Portative and positive organ

How were they used? It seems that all were considered instruments of the professional music-making class, the minstrels and jongleurs, the trumpet alone standing apart as a signaling instrument. Certainly, they were also played by amateurs, but no amateur, man or woman, noble or peasant, is spoken of as excelling at instrument playing (except when in stories one impersonates a jongleur).

The art of the noble amateur, lord or lady, was singing. Instrumental skill was a pleasant but unnecessary adjunct. For those nobles who did play, the bowed and plucked strings are most often named. Winds and simpler instruments were for peasants: bagpipe, flute, pipe and tabor, hurdy-gurdy. Important was the division of instruments into the categories *haut* and *bas*, loud and soft, those suitable for indoor playing and those for outdoor.

Instruments in Secular Monophony

The professional musicians—minstrels, jongleurs and jongleuresses—were the expert instrumentalists, and as such were expected to play a variety of instruments, as well as sing, juggle, perform acrobatics, and do anything else that could contribute to popular entertainment. Their most common task must have been to provide dance music, whether for court banquets or village dances.

Dance music has always been an improvised art, of which little is preserved beyond the immediate moment. The earliest notated examples are in a late thirteenth-century trouvère manuscript, the *Chansonnier du Roy*. It contains eleven monophonic dance tunes, most in a form the theorist Grocheo would identify as an *estampie*, a series of four or more repeated sections, each with open and closed endings. Superficially, the form resembles an instrumental lai or sequence, but there are important structural differences. In the estampie, not only the open and closed endings but the body of the phrase itself is identical throughout. Only the beginning of each phrase is different (see *HAM*, no. 40b). The form would accordingly have to be diagrammed (N standing for the recurring part of each phrase, o and c for open and closed endings): AN_o AN_c BN_o BN_c CN_o CN_c DN_o DN_c, etc.

A few other, similarly structured monophonic dances, some of Italian origin (see *HAM*, nos. 59a and b), occur in fourteenth-century manuscripts, suggesting that monophonic performance was still normal, possibly with added drum. Indeed, the favorite one-man band of the Middle Ages was the pipe and tabor player, with the tabor (small drum) strapped to the wrist of the hand that holds and fingers a three-holed pipe, the free hand striking the drum. Skillful overblowing can permit a range of over an octave and a half on the pipe.

Not all dance repertoire was instrumental; dance songs might be sung without instruments, as in Machaut's charming description of the dance in the garden (see the Introduction to Part 4). Refrain songs appear to have been particularly used for dancing, one singer taking the verse, all joining in on the refrain.

The composite early dance repertoire, then, would have consisted of improvised or composed melodies on an instrument, dance songs for voices and, most likely, instrumental versions of vocal dance songs. On at least one occasion an instrumental dance was the inspiration for a vocal song: the troubadour Rambaut de Vaqueiras wrote the words to *Kalanda maya* (*HAM*, no. 18d) for a dance melody he heard played by two minstrels.[1]

Another important use for instruments was for background or entertainment music, dinner music for banquets, or music to while away the tedious hours of travel. For these times, the minstrel would draw on the vocal repertoire, singing songs or playing and improvising on the melodies on fiddle or flute. The little Italian scene that introduces Chapter 16 speaks of Landini entertaining the guests by playing "songs of love"—undoubtedly ballate of Landini's own composition—on the portative organ; medieval literature is full of references to such instrumental renditions of vocal pieces.

A jongleur was also a singer and an accompanist of singers when needed. The use of instruments in accompanying song has been a much-debated topic during this century, and instrumental accompaniment to secular monophony has become commonplace among many modern performers of early music. Recent research establishes more cautionary guidelines.

"High-style" troubadour and trouvère songs—that is, the normal troubadour and trouvère repertory—were normally sung unaccompanied. Less formal

---

[1]For a detailed discussion of medieval dance forms, received too late for incorporation here, see Timothy J. McGee, *Medieval Instrumental Dances* (Bloomington: Indiana University Press, 1989), 1–22.

songs—dance songs and pastourelles—could be accompanied. Whether instruments played interludes between verses, drones, ornamented versions of the vocal line, or a freely improvised accompaniment is unknown.

In general, small groups of performers seem to have been standard. One reads constantly of performances by one or two minstrels or by an unaccompanied singer; simplicity of means seems to be the key to understanding medieval performance. Although colorful descriptions of feasts sometimes list dozens of performers, a careful reading of the vivid banquet scene of the poem *Flamenco* quoted earlier (see Chapter 7) shows that the many performers do not join together, but rather compete, each trying to outdo the others.

Instruments in Secular Polyphony

Instrumental performance. The first distinct hint of polyphonic instrumental performance is in a lengthy late thirteenth-century treatise by Jerome of Moravia. In a section on the *vielle* (five-string fiddle), he gives three different tunings, and then discusses in a very cryptic way a procedure used by "advanced players." It has been suggested that this advanced technique applied to the vielle the vocal improvisatory technique known as *fifthing*. In this process a second singer improvises a discant part by alternating between the octave and the fifth of the notes of the original melody, but including frequent parallel fifths within a word or phrase. Several thirteenth- and fourteenth-century treatises teach this simple improvisatory device, and such techniques could easily have been applied to instrumental performance.

Manuscript evidence of instrumental polyphony dates from the late thirteenth century—two two-voice dances in a British manuscript and possibly the seven textless three-voice hockets that conclude the motet portion of the Bamberg Codex (see Chapter 10, "The Sources").

The earliest music believed to be for keyboard is in the Robertsbridge Codex of around 1330. The small collection there consists of estampies (two complete and one incomplete), two transcriptions of motets from the *Roman de Fauvel*, and one transcription of a sacred piece. Notation consists of regular staff notation for the florid melody line (presumably the right hand) and letter notation for the accompaniment. The vocal arrangements establish a standard keyboard idiom that would be followed into the Renaissance: a highly embellished vocal line over a simple one- or two-part accompaniment. Embellished melodic lines may give a clue to improvised solo instrumental performance, one in which instrumental virtuosity is used to dress up vocal tunes. In fact, Anonymous IV suggests that the faster semibreve movement of the Petronian style came about in imitation of the faster playing of instrumentalists. In truth, the Robertsbridge Codex, although totally playable on keyboard (presumably organ), could also be performed by an ensemble of melody instruments.

A larger collection of similar pieces is contained in the Faenza Codex, an early fifteenth-century Italian manuscript conveying a late fourteenth-century repertoire. These pieces, mostly vocal arrangements, are in a similarly highly embellished melodic style above a simple one-note accompaniment. As with the Robertsbridge fragment, the collection contains a few sacred pieces as well as a majority of secular ones.

Although the Faenza Codex has been published as keyboard music and is frequently discussed on that basis, there is no certainty that this is the case. Voice crossing between the hands seems to demand a two-manual keyboard instrument a century before any is known to have existed. More likely, the music represents duet material for two instruments—perhaps lute, vielle, or rebec on the upper line, lute or harp below.

Instruments and voice.   The use of instruments in accompanying secular polyphony is a much-discussed matter. The simple viewpoint is that anything untexted should be played, not sung. This would include motet tenors and the untexted voices in fourteenth-century polyphonic song. Against this, there is the probability that much vocal music was sung to a neutral vowel or the vowel of the tenor text. Obvious examples are the melismas of organum purum or the caudae of conductus.

The motet tenor, if performed liturgically, would almost certainly have been sung. In a secular situation, either an instrumental or a vocal performance seems warranted, depending on the situation and the particular performers available. Logical instruments would be the harp or vielle. (It must be admitted that in modern performance an instrumental tenor makes a convincing foil to the more melodious upper voices.)

In the nontexted parts of fourteenth-century polyphonic song, the contemporaneous evidence seems to suggest an all-vocal performance. Important in this regard is the testimony of Machaut's pupil Dechamps and poetic and pictorial evidence. Nevertheless, just as all-instrumental performances of polyphonic songs were possible, so would have been the option of instrumentally accompanied song. Indeed, the melodic structures of some tenors and countertenors are more clearly vocal than others (at least by modern standards of vocality).

SACRED MUSIC

Because the words of a chant are liturgically important, medieval church music was traditionally vocal. This was true of polyphony as well as monophony, and except for organ and small tuned bells, instruments played no part in the performance of liturgical music.

What did those instruments play? For the bells we have no information, although we constantly meet illustrations of them happily being played by monk or cleric. Perhaps they doubled melodies in a simplified fashion. Maybe they gave starting pitches. Possibly they were played during certain special occasions, such as during the sequence or during the priest's silent prayers. We do not know.

About the organ we are only slightly better off. We know they were in churches from early times, descending from the Roman *hydraulis* or water organ.

The early ones had keys as broad as a fist and all ranks of pipes were permanently coupled. Soft music and polyphonic music were impossible. Later, key mechanisms improved and it became possible to separate ranks, but by later standards, the organ was still a relatively unwieldy instrument.

Judging from scattered remarks here and there, it would seem that the organ largely functioned as a solo rather than as an accompanying instrument. It appears to have been used in the service at times when the choir was not singing. Its use in playing the long tenor notes of Notre Dame organum purum cannot be ruled out, but it is unsupported by medieval evidence. The one specific use of the organ in the medieval service, established by at least the late fourteenth century if not before, is in *alternatum* performance with the choir.

In this practice, established in the Faenza Codex and current into the seventeenth century, the organ plays polyphonic versions (improvised or composed) of certain portions of the chant, those portions alternating with the other sections in normal sung plainchant. Accordingly an alternatum Kyrie would be performed as follows (italics indicate the organ sections):

Kyrie

Kyrie

Kyrie

Christe

Christe

Christe

Kyrie

Kyrie

Kyrie

BIBLIOGRAPHY

Music

The Faenza Codex is available in keyboard format in *Keyboard of the Late Middle Ages*, ed. Dragon Plamenac, CMM 57 (AIM, 1972), and *Transcriptions from the Faenza Codex*, ed. R. Huestis (Westwood, Cal.: R. Huestis, 1971). A facsimile is available in MSD 10 (AIM, 1961). The Robertsbridge pieces are transcribed in Willi Apel, ed., *Keyboard Music of the Fourteenth and Fifteenth Centuries*, Corpus of Early Keyboard Music 1 (AIM, 1963).

The dance repertoire is available in Timothy J. McGee, ed., *Medieval Instrumental Dances* (Bloomington: Indiana University Press, 1989). The monophonic dance tunes of the *Chansonnier du Roy* were first published in Pierre Aubrey, *Estampies et danses royales* (Paris: Fischbacher, 1906), and appear in a practical edition by Ralph Harriman, *Monophonic Dances of the 13th Century* (Berkeley, Cal.: Musica Sacra et Profana, 1963).

Readings

The most comprehensive discussion of the use of instruments before 1300 is in Christopher Page, *Voices and Instruments of the Middle Ages: Instrumental Practice and Songs in France 1100–1300* (Berkeley and Los Angeles: University of California Press, 1986). An overview of vocal and instrumental performance situations is given in Maria Vedder Fowler, "Musical Interpolations in Thirteenth- and Fourteenth-Century French Narratives" (Ph.D. diss., UMI no. 79-27625), and M. V. Coldwell, "*Guillaume de Dole* and Medieval Romances with Musical Interpolations," *MD* 35 (1981): 55–86.

The theory of fifthing on which Page bases his concept of advanced fiddle playing is expounded in Sarah Fuller, "Discant and the Theory of Fifthing," *AM* 50 (1978): 241–75. Questions concerning the performance medium of the Faenza Codex are addressed in Timothy J. McGee, "Instruments and the Faenza Codex," *EM* 14 (1986): 480–90, and contemporary descriptions of dance forms in his "Medieval Dances: Matching the Repertory with Grocheio's Descriptions," *JoM* 7 (1989), 498–517.

Performance-related articles are included in Stanley Boorman, ed., *Studies in the Performance of Late Medieval Music* (Cambridge: Cambridge University Press, 1984); see also Frederick Crane, "On Performing the *Lo estampies*," *EM* 7 (1979): 25–33. Timothy J. McGee, *Medieval and Renaissance Music: A Performer's Guide* (Toronto: University of Toronto Press, 1985), treats many problems from a performer's point of view. On the question of voices or instruments on untexted lines, see Christopher Page, "Machaut's 'Pupil' Dechamps on the Performance of Music: Voices or Instruments in the Fourteenth-Century Chanson?" *EM* 5 (1977): 484–98.

Concerning medieval instruments, see Crane, *Extant Medieval Musical Instruments: A Provisional Catalogue by Types* (Iowa City: University of Iowa Press, 1972); Jeremy Montague, *The World of Medieval and Renaissance Musical Instruments* (Woodstock, N.Y.: Overlook Press, 1976); Werner Bachman, *The Origins of Bowing*, trans. N. Deane (London: Oxford University Press, 1969); Mary Remnant, *English Bowed Instruments from Anglo-Saxon to Tudor Times* (London: Oxford University Press, 1986); and L. Perrot, *The Organ: From Its Invention in Hellenistic Times to the End of the Thirteenth Century*, trans. N. Deane (Oxford: Oxford University Press, 1970).

David Munrow, *Instruments of the Middle Ages and Renaissance* (London: Oxford University Press, 1976), records the sounds of most medieval instruments, and Jerome and Elizabeth Roche's *Dictionary of Early Music* (London: Faber & Faber, 1981) includes line drawings of the instruments.

INDEXES

General Index

A

Abgesang, 176
Adam de la Hale, 173, 174, 329, 331, 333
Adam of St. Victor, 77, 191
Additive composition, 154, 241
Admonitio, 206, 208
Ad organum faciendum, 119, 121–26, 129
Affinal, 84–85
Agnus Dei, 40–41, 56–57
Alba, 170–71, 336
Alcuin, 10
Alfonso the Wise, 177
Alia musica, 78, 80, 82
Alleluia, 40–41, 48–51, 60, 75–76, 120, 183–84, 200
Alternatum, 384
Amalarus of Metz, 12–13
Amerus (Alfred), 358
Andrea da Firenze (Andrea dei Servi), 363
Anonymous dictus St. Martial, 200, 220
Anonymous IV, 185–86, 191, 192, 196, 197, 198, 200, 202, 220, 256, 258, 382
Anonymous of St. Emmeram, 256, 290
Anthonello da Caserta, 346, 375
Antiphon
    Marian, 54
    Office, 38, 46, 47, 60, 78
    processional, 55–56
Antiphonal chants, 45–47
Antiphonale monasticum, 28
Antonio da Tempo, 362
Aperto, 365
Aquitania, 116, 135–37, 189, 228–29
Aquitanian sacred monophony, 138–47
Aquitanian sacred polyphony, 147–56, 200, 277
Arnaut Daniel, 170
Ars antiqua, 256, 290
Ars discantus (Pseudo Jean de Muris), 340

Ars metrica. See Poetry
Ars nova, 290
Ars ritmica. See Poetry
Ars subtilior, 330, 344–50, 360, 375–76
Ars vetus, 256, 290
Assonance, 77, 235
Aufgesang, 176
Aurelian of Reóme, 14–15, 20, 41, 51
Authentic modes, 16. *See also* Modes, liturgical
Avignon, 319–20, 322, 344, 375

B

Balada, 171
Ballade, 174, 334–35, 363
Ballata, 178, 321, 331, 357, 364–65
Bar form, 176, 208
Bartolino da Padova, 362
Bas, 380
Beauvais circumcision Office, 187
Benedicamus Domino, 39, 40, 60, 138, 155–56
Benedict of Aniane, 10
Berlin B, 128–29
Bernart de Ventadorn, 167
Berno, 79, 82, 143
Bertran de Born, 170
Bilingual motet, 232
Binaria, 360
Black Death, 229
Boccaccio, 328, 365
Boethius, 4–5, 78
Breve (*brevis*), 234, 257
Breve, English, 281
Burgundy, 229, 376
Byzantine Empire, 7–9, 11, 116
Byzantine modal system, 14–16, 25, 78

C

Caça, 363
Caccia, 363–64

Index of Compositions

Compositions are listed by title and by composer. Those contained in the Anthology are identified by the abbreviation A., those on the accompanying Recording by an asterisk—e.g. [A. 1˙]. Compositions contained as complete examples herein have the abbreviation Ex.—e.g. [Ex. 2-8]. Those contained in easily accessible anthologies or other common publications use the appropriate abbreviations.

BY TITLE

BY COMPOSER